THE WRITINGS OF

WILL ROGERS

I - 3

SPONSORED BY

The Will Rogers Memorial Commission
and Oklahoma State University

THE WRITINGS OF WILL ROGERS

OTHER VOLUMES TO BE ANNOUNCED

The Illiterate Digest

BY

WILL ROGERS

Edited with an Introduction by
Joseph A. Stout, Jr.

OKLAHOMA STATE UNIVERSITY PRESS
Stillwater, Oklahoma
1974

HOUSTON PUBLIC LIBRARY

© 1974 Oklahoma State University Press

International Standard Book Number 0-914956-04-3

Library of Congress Catalog Number 74-82796

Printed in the United States of America

CONTENTS

ILLUSTRATIONS

INTRODUCTION

Between 1922 and 1935 Will Rogers wrote approximately 700 weekly articles which the McNaught syndicate distributed to newspapers throughout the United States. He began writing these weekly articles after giving a speech supporting Ogden Mills, who was seeking reelection to Congress from New York City. Rogers made the speech and gave an elaborated follies routine tailored for the occasion at the request of Theodore Roosevelt, Jr. The result was published in the *New York Times* of October 27, 1922. V. V. McNitt, who with Charles V. McAdam founded the McNaught Syndicate, read the article and realized Rogers' potential. Although Rogers at the time was seeking distribution of his work with another company, McNitt and McAdam remained interested. Rogers' negotiations subsequently fell through, and shortly thereafter he agreed to write for the McNaught Syndicate. During his writing career Rogers authored weekly articles and later telegrams. The first weekly article appeared on December 30, 1922, and weekly thereafter until Rogers' death. The Oklahoman continued his relationship with the McNaught Syndicate, and after 1922 his business was conducted solely with Charles Vincent McAdam, who became first vice president of the company in 1922 and president in 1930.

Rogers' weekly articles covered various subjects, including politics, international diplomacy, personal friends, business, and other items. Usually, although there were exceptions, these insightful and humorous offerings were about one thousand words. Rogers' first weekly article, "Settling the Affairs of the World as They Should Be," was included in *The Illiterate Digest* under the title, "Breaking into the Writing Game."

Will Rogers first used the title "Illiterate Digest" to refer to a series of short films he made for movie houses in 1919 and 1920. These were inspired by "The Literary Digest Topics of the Day," which also were short film flashes. Early in December of 1920 Rogers learned that his humorous film quips had affronted the prestigious *Literary Digest,* which was producing the series of film short subjects using its name as part of the title. The *Digest* was an old and responsible periodical which had begun publication on March 1, 1890. Founded by Isaac K. Funk and Adam W. Wagnalls, the *Digest* became very popular during the first two decades of the twentieth century. According to the founders, the magazine was to be "a repository of contemporaneous thought and research as presented in the periodical literature of the world." After 1905 the publication expanded to include comment on daily news. Funk died in 1912, and the magazine became largely the creation of Robert J. Cuddihy. For ten years after World War I the periodical achieved its greatest circulation and influence. In 1920 the *Digest* initiated the first of the nationwide public opinion polls which were very successful until 1936, when the periodical incorrectly predicted that Alfred M. Landon would win the Presidential election of that year. From a circulation of 1,200,000 in 1924, the *Digest* slowly lost subscribers and influence after 1930. By 1937, with the profits from the 1920s used to maintain publication, the stockholders sold the publication to the *Review of Reviews*. Four months later the periodical again was sold, but it discontinued publication in February of 1938. Thus Rogers indeed had chosen a well respected journal as a pattern for his quips.

The lawyer for the *Digest*, William Beverly Winslow, advised Rogers that his client believed the use of the similar title was damaging to the prestige of the magazine. Winslow told Rogers that the publishers legally could start proceedings through the Federal Trade Commission charging the humorist with "unfair competition." However, before seeking an injunction to stop him, Winslow wished to allow Rogers an opportunity to avoid a lawsuit by his agreeing to discontinue using the title.

Rogers immediately and humorously answered the attorney. He claimed that he was "swelled up," for he did not realize he was sufficiently important to deserve the attention of the prestigious *Digest*. Rogers replied that he no longer was writing "gags" for the film industry, but he enclosed the movie company's address if the firm wished to begin court proceedings. And Rogers informed Winslow that he had no lawyer and suggested the attorney represent him also. Rogers offered to split the settlement at "the usual lawyer rates of 80-20, the client of course getting the 20." He received no answer and was never involved in litigation over the matter, but about six months later, after returning to the Ziegfeld Follies, he met William Winslow. Backstage after a performance, the two talked for some time. Winslow had enjoyed thoroughly Rogers' answer. In fact, the attorney had made copies of the letter and had sent them to all his friends. Thus after the exchange of letters and the personal meeting with Winslow, Rogers decided to dedicate *The Illiterate Digest* to his newfound friend.

The Illiterate Digest, illustrated by Nathan Leo (Nate) Collier, a cartoonist for national magazines and newspapers, contained thirty-three of Rogers' weekly articles on such varied subjects as corsets and chewing gum. One of the more humorous articles concerned a total eclipse of the sun. Allegedly the eclipse could be seen more clearly from Mexico, and therefore many people decided to travel there and combine "scientific" studies with a vacation. Rogers was not at all convinced that any of the "scientists" traveling to Mexico were really going for the eclipse. He caustically remarked that, "a great many Scientists, I had read in the papers, were bringing Cameras to Photograph this remarkable phenomenon. But most of the Scientists that I saw had Jugs and Flasks." And, as usual, Rogers commented about politics during the different administrations. On one occasion when Rogers entertained, President Woodrow Wilson was in the audience. The humorist joked about the President and his administration, but was apprehensive, for he did not know just what to expect from the usually austere Wilson. When the President laughed at the jokes, the audience followed suit and all enjoyed the evening.

The Illiterate Digest was well received by critics throughout the country. John Crawford of the *New York Times* wrote a detailed review of the book and complimented Rogers' mannerisms both written and on stage. Crawford insisted Rogers knew a lot more than he admitted about politics and other worldly matters, and that he read more about the politics of the country than anyone except copy editors and political reporters: "He reads it all, and turns out nifties about it without raising his voice or pointing to himself with pride." Crawford added that *The Illiterate Digest* was "goods off the same bolt." He said Rogers gives the impression of being a country talker, "but the fact of the matter is that he knows just what he wants to do, just how he wants to do it, and he does it. He is an expert satirist masquerading as a helpless, inoffensive, ineffectual zany." Those who read the following pages will agree with this assessment.

In editing this volume of *The Writings of Will Rogers* several difficult decisions were made. As this volume is comprised of weekly articles, rather than a single manuscript, and as Rogers often mentioned items or people that can be located in general encyclopedic reference sources, we have had to choose carefully those items to be annotated. Contemporories of Rogers, most of them obscured by time, have been annotated. And, except where absolutely necessary, we have identified individuals the first time they were named, a practice usually followed in this type of editing. At times we have chosen to give some information about presidents or others involved in national politics in order that these individuals might be placed in historical perspective or to explain the text. No attempt has been made to annotate every letter or word change between the various texts. Only those changes which show Rogers' style or change the meaning of the text are explained. Where possible the original manuscript has been used for textual analysis, but in the very few cases where the original has been lost, we have referred to the *New York Times.*

Joseph A. Stout, Jr.
EDITOR

PREFACE

To write an introduction for this Will Rogers book is quite an honor and distinction. I am 80 years old and supposed to be one of the few people who really knew him. Although I was acquainted with him before he worked for my McNaught newspaper syndicate it was not until then that we got to be real friends. Our office was in the old Times building in New York at 42d Street. It was right across the street from the Ziegfeld Follies show. He was the star and at the same time was writing his daily telegram for McNaught. Many a day he would come into my office and chat. He had a habit of asking the office girls to come in and listen to what he would say that same evening in his show—it was a sort of rehearsal. The public relations man at the theatre would tell him what important person was going to be in the audience and he would do a little researching and really give him the works humorously that evening. If the girls thought he was funny so much the better.

He had a number of characteristics that amazed me. He did not smoke so when he came in the office he would be twirling a silver dollar between his fingers just like a magician. Then people thought he chewed gum. I never saw him. Instead he would take a rubber band or a string from my desk and chew on them. When I met him on the street one day he wanted to talk with me about some things and sat on a fire hydrant at the corner of 41st Street and before we knew it we had at least 50 people gathered around us and he would make them all laugh. He really was a character. In business we had plenty of fun with him. Our editor asked him not to use the word "aint" in his articles and his answer was that he knew people that "never said aint that aint eatin'." Now aint is in the dictionary. A very important moment came in my relations with him and that was when his writings became so important that my competitors were after him. So one day he came in and asked me to close my door as he wanted to tell me about the offer of $800 a week that competitors were willing to give him. My reply was that I would make the weekly salary $1000 a week whereupon he said "you're nuts but I love you and I will never leave your outfit." Incidentally, at the time, I was paying him $500 a week. His column was so popular that we got him up to $2500 a week and when one competitor offered him $3500 a week he told me that he would never leave us and told them the same. The strange thing about our business dealings was that we never had a written contract. It was always a handshake. What a guy!

It was a sad day to the United States and the world when he

passed on. I remember distinctly going to the Waldorf-Astoria hotel where Betty (his wife) was staying. We all knew he was going to take the flight and I had an idea that I could persuade his wife to stop him. I told her how hazardous it was and that I would never fly in a plane with one pilot. Wiley Post as everyone knows had one eye. I always insisted that there be two pilots. Betty said: "Everybody has their hobbies. People like to collect stamps, some play bridge and you, Charlie, like to play golf. Will loves to fly. I cannot stop him." He was too young to die, and the world really cried. His philosophy was terrific and how this country needed him to continue entertaining them. What more can I say about one of the GREATS of our time.

Charles V. McAdam

THE ILLITERATE DIGEST

I-3

TWO LETTERS AND A DEDICATION

Most Books have to have an Excuse by some one for the Author, but this is the only Book ever written that has to have an Alibi for the Title, too. About 4 years ago, out in California, I was writing sayings for the Screen and I called it the Illiterate Digest. Well one day up bobs the following letter from this N. Y. Lawyer. It and the answer are absolutely just as they were exchanged at that time.

WILLIAM BEVERLY WINSLOW
LAWYER
55 Liberty Street,
New York, N.Y.

Nov. 5th, 1920.

Will Rogers, Esq.,
   c/o Goldwyn Studios,
     Culver City, Calif.
Dear Sir:—

My client, the Funk & Wagnalls Company, publishers of the "Literary Digest" have requested me to write to you in regard to your use of the phrase, "The Illiterate Digest," as a title to a moving picture subject gotten up by you, the consequence of which may have escaped your consideration.

For more than two years past it (my client) has placed upon the moving picture screen a short reel subject carrying the title "Topics of the Day," selected from the Press of the World by "The Literary Digest." This subject has achieved a wide popularity both because of the character and renown of "The Literary Digest" and through the expenditure of much time, effort and money by its owners in presenting the subject to the public. "The Literary Digest" is a publication nearly thirty years old, and from a small beginning has become probably the most influential weekly publication in the world. Its name and the phrase "Topics of the Day" are fully covered by usage as trademarks as well as by registration as such in the United States Patent Office.

During several months past your "title," "The Illiterate Digest" has been repeatedly called to our attention and we are told that the prestige of "The Literary Digest" is being lowered by the subject matter of your film as well as by the title of your film because the public naturally confuse the two subjects. We are also told that exhibitors are being misled by the similarity of titles and that some of them install your subject in the expectation that they are securing "The Literary Digest Topics of the Day."

1

It seems to me self-evident that your title would scarcely have been thought of or adopted had it not been for our magazine and for our film. If this were not the case the title which you use would be without significance to the general public.

I have advised the publishers that they may proceed against you through the Federal Trade Commission in Washington calling upon you to there defend yourself against the charge of "unfair competition," because of your simulation of their title, or that they can proceed against you, the producers of your film, its distributors and exhibitors in court for an injunction restraining you from use of the title, "The Illiterate Digest."

Before, however, instituting any proceedings in either direction they have suggested that I write directly to you to see if your sense of fairness will not cause you to voluntarily withdraw the use of the objectionable title.

Unless I hear favorably from you on or before the first of December, I shall conclude that you are not willing to accede to this suggestion and will take such steps as I may deem advisable.

Yours truly,

WBW/als

(signed) William Beverly Winslow.

Los Angeles, Cal.,
Nov. 15, 1920.

Mr Wm Beverly Winslow,

Dear Sir,

Your letter in regard to my competition with the Literary Digest received and I never felt as swelled up in my life, And am glad you wrote directly to me instead of communicating with my Lawyers, As I have not yet reached that stage of prominence where I was committing unlawful acts and requireing a Lawyer, Now if the Literary Digest feels that the competition is to keen for them—to show you my good sportsmanship I will withdraw, In fact I had already quit as the gentleman who put it out were behind in their payments and my humor kinder waned, in fact after a few weeks of no payments I couldent think of a single joke. And now I want to inform you truly that this is the first that I knew my Title of the Illiterate Digest was an infringement on yours as they mean the direct opposite, If a magazine was published called Yes and another Bird put one out called No I suppose he would be infringeing. But you are a Lawyer and its your business to change the meaning of words, so I lose before I start,

Now I have not written for these people in months and they

2

havent put any gags out unless it is some of the old ones still playing.
If they are using gags that I wrote on topical things 6 months ago then
I must admit that they would be in competition with the ones the
Literary Digest Screen uses now. I will gladly furnish you with their
address, in case you want to enter suit, And as I have no Lawyer you
can take my case too and whatever we get out of them we will split
at the usual Lawyer rates of 80-20, the client of course getting the 20,

Now you inform your Editors at once that their most dangerous
rival has withdrawn, and that they can go ahead and resume publi-
cation, But you inform Your clients that if they ever take up Rope
Throwing or chewing gum that I will consider it a direct infringement
of my rights and will protect it with one of the best Kosher Lawyers
in Oklahoma,

Your letter to me telling me I was in competition with the Digest
would be just like Harding writing to Cox and telling him he took
some of his votes,

So long Beverly if you ever come to California, come out to
Beverly where I live and see me

Illiterately yours

WILL ROGERS.

When I sent him my answer I read it to some of the Movie Company I was working with at the time and they kept asking me afterwards if I had received an answer. I did not, and I just thought, oh
well, there I go and waste a letter on some High Brow Lawyer with
no sense of humor. I was sore at myself for writing it. About 6 months
later I came back to join the Follies and who should come to call on
me but the nicest old Gentleman I had ever met, especially in the law
profession. He was the one I had written the letter to, and he had
had Photographic Copies made of my letter and had given them
around to all his Lawyer friends.

So it is to him and his sense of humor, that I dedicate this Volume
of deep thought. I might also state that the Literary Digest was broad-
minded enough to realize that there was room for both, and I want
to thank them for allowing me to announce my Illiteracy publicly.

INTRODUCTION

This book should have been long before now on the Bookshelves of every reader of worth while Literature in the English speaking World, in addition to being well worn in our best reference Libraries, and should have been already translated into every known and unknown tongue. What you will immediately ask delayed such an important event? Well the principal reason is it had not been written, and the next is We had no introduction for it. You let a Book go out without an Alibi by some other writer, and it is practically a commercial suicide. When the Publishers were all clamoring for a Book from me, and were practically annihilating (Boy there is a word I never used before in my life and I hope it fits in, I read it in some War Novel) each other for the Publishing rights and assured profits, they of course felt that through my wide Literary acquaintance, gained during years of association at the Democratic National Convention, and the late World Series with some of the best contemporary Writers of modern times, I should through my Literary standing and personal friendship, allow some of them to have the honor of penning the introduction to this Time Table of National Catastrophes.

William Emporia Allen White[1] was my first thought, on account of his having a middle name, which always sounds Literary, even if its owner is not. Then I had heard he himself had written a Book once, and by now should know what Introductions should not be. Then he went home and announced himself as a Candidate for Governor. So that eliminated him from my thoughts. To have a big broad-minded book have any narrow Political endorsement would mean certain calamity among people who think. To run for Governor is bad enough, But to run for Governor of Kansas and then write an Introduction of my worthy efforts, would simply make the book a laughing stock.

Then my thoughts turned to Arthur Brisbane,[2] I don't know what I could have been eating that my thoughts should have done such a mental somersault. But I guess it was because I had known Arthur for years, — I knew him before William Randolph Hearst[3] started working for him. I approached him on it, and he said, Sorry Will but what I write must point a moral, there must be a lesson in every paragraph; mine must not only be news but it must be instructive news. For instance, I read China will not go to war on rainy days. What does that bit of news mean to the individual that dont think? Nothing! What does it mean to me? It means that a Chinaman would rather get shot

5

than wet. It points a moral to peace: Have all so-called civilized Nations stop wars on rainy days. Then hold all wars in Portland, Oregon where it rains every day, and you will eliminate Wars and have universal Peace.

So he could see no particular Moral in writing an Introduction to my book, unless it was that Books should not depend entirely on their introductions as they do now. So I next thought of my friend Irvin Cobb.[4] I had set next to him at so many Speakers Tables, at banquets, and had always given him any little extras that I might not want. Ice Cream and Sweets and things like that he just loves and ruins them at a Banquet. Well he was going Duck shooting down in Louisiana and said he wouldnt miss one Duck for the pleasure of writing the Introduction to the Encyclopedia Brittanica. So you just let the old fat thing try to get my Ice Cream at another Banquet.

Of course Ring Lardner[5] was one of my very first thoughts, because I knew he could add the little touch of comedy that the book really needed. I went to him and told him that I only wanted something light and airy, maybe just one good joke would do the trick and take away from the serious nature of the Book. He is not only a Humorist but has got plenty money to show that he is. He said before he shook hands with me, What is there in it? I said well this is just a kind of an honorary thing, a kind of courtesy from one Author to another. He then asked me why should he give me a joke for nothing? He could put the joke into his Sunday Newspaper Article; then he could put the joke into his weekly Newspaper Cartoon; then he could sell it to a Musical Comedy and they would tell it so bad it would sound new. Then the Movies would buy it and make a drama out of it; then he would still hold the Phonograph, and broadcasting rights, and after it got well enough known write a Song around it. So he said I would be a fine egg to give you a joke for nothing.

I wish that Spaniard Ibanez,[6] that wrote the 4 Horsemen was over here, I knew him well, I had read 5 or 6 of his Books and I was to a big reception given to him in Los Angeles, and during our conversations through an Interpreter he learned I had read so many of his Books. No one else he met there even among the Literary ones had ever read any but the 4 Horsemen, So when he went home he sent me an Autographed Copy which read "To an American Cowboy, the only person in America I found who had read all my Books." The funny thing about it is that he is the only Author I ever read. Now if he was here he would write me an Introduction, But of course it would be in Spanish and nobody could read it, so I would be just as bad off as I am now.

6

I also know Elinor Glyn,[7] I met her when she was out in California looking around for some one to cast as Paul in "Three Weeks." She sent for me but I had just started on another new Picture. She could have cooked me up a hot Introduction. She would have draped the first few paragraphs with Tiger skins, and described me in such a way that I would have really looked like something. So I just says to myself, why monkey with these writers, why not write my own Introduction? So here goes.

I have known Mr. Rogers for years and have long been familiar with his Literary masterpieces, both in Novels, and in Books of technical knowledge. I think there are few writers of Poetry or prose today who equal him, and I am certain he is surpassed by none.

I say this because I have lived and known the life he has pictured so well in this Book; I spent my late youth in these shaded oak lands where so many of his scenes are so pictorially laid, and he has made me live over again the scenes of my freshman manhood. No writer since the days of Remington[8] can give you such a word picture of the west. That's because he is a westerner himself, and has only an eye for the beautiful things as he and nature alone can describe them. He alone of all our modern writers knows the people of which they write. When he describes a Corset you can feel it pinch. If it's a Sunrise he describes, you reach for an Umbrella. His jugglery of correct words and perfect English sentences is magical, and his spelling is almost uncanny.

The words, *Illiterate Digest,* which appear upon the title page of this book, has been generally compared to Don Quixote and to the Pickwick Papers while E. M. Vogue places its author somewhere between Cervantes and LeSage.[9] However, considerable the influence of Cervantes and Dickens may have been, the first in the matter of structure, the other in background, humor, and detail of characterization, the predominating and distinguishing quality of this Author's work is undeniably foreign to both and quite peculiar to itself. Something that for want of a better term might be called the quality of American Soul, any reader familiar as I know you all to be with the works of Dostoiefsky, Turgenev, or even Tolstoi,[10] will grasp the deeper meaning of a work like this. Some consider the Author a realist, who has drawn with meticulous detail a picture of contemporary life, others more observing see in him a great symbolist.

He always remembers that it is dangerous to jest with laughter. This man in writing this has done a service to all thinking mankind. It is a revelation, as an omen of a freer future. Belinsky, the great Russian Critic to whom Mr. Rogers had read the manuscript, said "it looked like another Ben Hur to him."[11]

So now Mr. Cobb, and Mr. Lardner, and all you introduction

writers, what do I want with you? There is not a one of you could have said the things of me that I have said, because you Guys dont know what books to look in to get all that big league stuff out of,

Yours for Arts sake,

WILLIAM PENN ADAIR ROGERS

(boy that is my real name, let some Literary Guy top that)

P. S. I got enough Introduction left over to write another Introduction if I had anything to write another book about.

BREAKING INTO THE WRITING GAME

YOU ARE GOING TO GET THE LOW-DOWN ON SOME OF THOSE BIRDS WHO ARE
SENDING HOME THE RADISH-SEED.

BREAKING INTO THE WRITING GAME

EVERYBODY is writing something nowadays. It used to be just the Literary or Newspaper men who were supposed to know what they were writing about that did all the writing. But nowadays all a man goes into office for is so he can try to find out something and then write it when he comes out.

Now being in Ziegfeld Follies[1] for almost a solid year in New York has given me an inside track on some of our biggest men in this country who I meet nightly at the stage door.

So I am breaking out in a rash[2] here. I will cite an example to prove to you what you are going to get. Not long ago[3] there was a mess of Governors here from various Provinces. And a good friend of mine brought back to the stage and dressing room Governor Allen[4] of Kansas.[5] Well, I stood him in the wings and he was supposed to be looking at my act, but he wasn't. He was watching what really is the Backbone of our Show. He anyway heard some of my Gags about our Government and all who are elected to help missrun it.

So at the finish of my act I dragged him out on the stage and introduced him to the audience. He made a mighty pretty little speech and said he enjoyed Will's Impertinences, and got a big laugh on that. Said I was the only man in America who was able to tell the truth about our Men and Affairs.

When he finished I explained to the audience why I was able to tell the truth. It is because I have never mixed up in Politics. So you all are going from time to time to get the real Low Down on some of those Birds who are sending home the Radish Seed.

You know the more you read and observe about this Politics thing, you got to admit that each party is worse than the other. The one that's out always looks the best. My only solution would be to keep 'em both out one term and hire my good friend Henry Ford[6] to run the whole thing and give him a commission on what he saves us. Put his factory in with the government and instead of Seeds every spring mail out those Things of his.

Mail Newberry[7] one every morning Special Delivery.

Speaking of Henry Ford, I see where Uncle Henry has a new Rule in force out in his Factory where they paste those Knick Knacks together. Every man working there has to have his breath smelled every morning. That, of course, seems like a pretty strict Rule to put in force in a So called Free Country, and it has come in for a lot of criticism in the papers, but the way I look at it, it is absolutely necessary.

11

Should a man go to work in there who had had a few strong shots of some of our National Drinks of today, he would blow his breath on one of those FOB'S, and blow all the bolts right out of it.

Now Mr. Ford is a very smart man and in passing these rigid rules I bet you he knows where to stop. I bet you that he won't instruct his Salesmen to be so strict with a Purchaser. In fact his salesmen smell of your breath when you come in to buy one and if it shows no signs of drink they don't try to sell you. He is smart enough to know a sober man would never buy one. Mind you, all this smelling of breath is done, not on the Company's time, but on the time of the Workers. Some men have to get up at 4 o'clock in the Morning to get their breath examined so they can get to work at 8. Imagine a line of 50 thousand all waiting to blow at a single individual TESTER! Think what he must be with all those Italian workmen passing by him. He is just 180 pounds of Garlic by night.

The University of Michigan is putting in a Chair in their Faculty devoted to the Art of Breath Detecting. But there is always a way to defeat any reform. Drinkers will learn to hold their breath like a Diver.[8]

I tell you Folks, all Politics is Apple Sauce.

The President gave a Luncheon for the visiting Governors, where they discussed but didn't TRY Prohibition.

It was the consensus of opinion of all their speeches that there was a lot of drinking going on and that if it wasn't stopped by January that they would hold another meeting and try and get rid of some of the stuff.

Senator Curtis[9] proposed a bill this week to stop Bootlegging in the Senate, making it unlawful for any member to be caught selling to another member while on Government property. While the bill was being read a Government employe fell just outside the Senate door and broke a Bottle of Pre-War stuff (made just before last week's Turkish War).[10] Now they are carpeting all the halls with a heavy material so in case of a fall there will be no serious loss.

Well, New Years is coming[11] and I suppose we will have to hear and read all those big men's New Year greetings, such men as Schwab and Gary and Rockefeller[12] and all of them. Saying the same old Apple Sauce. That they are Optimistic of the coming year and everybody must put their shoulder to the wheel, and produce more and they predict a great year. Say, if we had those Birds' Dough we could all be just as optimistic as they are. But it's a good Joke and it's got in the papers every year and I suppose always will.

Now the Ku Klux is coming into New York and kinder got it in for the Jewish People. Now they are wrong; I am against that. If the Jewish People here in New York hadn't jumped in and made them-

12

THEY ARE CARPETING ALL THE HALLS OF THE SENATE SO IN CASE OF A FALL
THERE WILL BE NO SERIOUS LOSS.

selves good fellows and helped us celebrate our Christmas, the thing would have fell flat. They sold us every Present.

The Ku Klux couldn't get much of a footing here in New York. If there was some man they wanted to take out and Tar and Feather they wouldn't know where he lived. People move so often here their own folks don't know where they live.

And even if they found out the Elevator man in the Apartment wouldn't let 'em up.

See where there is bills up in Congress now to change the Constitution all around, elect the President in a different way and have Congress meet at a different time. It seems the men who drew up this thing years ago didn't know much and we are just now getting a bunch of real fellows who can take that old Parchment and fix it up like it should have been all these years.[13] It seems it's just been luck that's got us by so far. Now when they get the Constitution all fixed up they are going to start in on the 10 Commandments, just as soon as they find somebody in Washington who has read them.

See where they are talking about another Conference over here. The Social Season in Washington must be lagging.

Well, I think they ought to have it. These Conferences don't really do any harm and they give certain Delegates pleasure. Of course nothing they ever pass on is ever carried out. (Except in Greece, where they are all carried out.) But each Nation gets a certain amount of Publicity out of it, and us masses that read of it get a certain amount of amusement out of it.

Borah[14] himself admits he don't know what it's for or what they should do. But it looks like a good Conference season and there is no reason why we shouldn't get in on one.

BESIDES, DID YOU EVER REALIZE THIS COUNTRY IS 4 CONFERENCES BEHIND NOW?[15]

I want to apologize and set my many readers straight as to why I am blossoming out as an infliction on you all.

It seems a prominent newspaper syndicate had Lloyd George[16] signed up for a pack of his Memoirs. Well, after the late election Lloyd couldn't seem to remember anything, so they sent for me to fill in the space where he would have had his junk.

You see, they wanted me in the first place, but George came along and offered to work cheaper, and also to give his to charity. That benevolence on his part was of course before England gave him his two weeks' notice.

Now I am also not to be outdone by an ex-Prime Minister donating my receipts from my Prolific Tongue to a needy charity. The total share of this goes to the civilization of three young heathens, Rogers by name, and part Cherokee Indians by breeding.[17]

Now, by wasting seven minutes, if you are a good reader—and ten to twelve if you read slow—on me, you are really doing a charitable act yourself by preventing these three miniature bandits from growing up in ignorance. So please help a man with not only one little Megan, but three little Megans.

A great many people may think that this is the first venture of such a conservative paper as the Illiterate Digest in using something of a semi-humorous nature, but that is by no means the case. I am following the Kaiser,[18] who rewrote his life after it was too late. I realize what a tough job I have, succeeding a man who to be funny only had to relate the facts.

Please don't consider these as my memoirs. I am not passing out of the picture, as men generally are who write those things.

SETTLING THE CORSET PROBLEM OF THIS COUNTRY

(An After Dinner speech made at a Banquet of the Corset Manufacturers of America at the Waldorf-Astoria, New York.)

SETTLING THE CORSET PROBLEM
OF THIS COUNTRY

SINCE I last wrote you all[1] there has been an awful lot of fashion Shows and all their By Products held here in New York. All the out of Town buyers from all over have been here. So, on behalf of New York City, I had to help welcome them at their various Banquets. There was the retail Milliners' big fashion show at the Astor Ball Room where they showed 500 Hats and me. Some of the hats were just as funny looking as I was.

Well, I settled the Hat and Dress business to the satisfaction of everybody but the Milliners. So the next night at the Commodore Hotel I mingled with those Princes of Brigands, the Leather and Shoe men, and later[2] I want to tell all you people just how they operate. For we never paid more for our Shoes and were nearer barefooted than we are today, so don't think that I am bought off this week by those Pasteboard Highbinders: it's only that I want to talk to the Ladies today.

During this reign of Indigestion I was called on to speak at a big Banquet at the Waldorf to the Corset Manufacturers. Now that only shows you what a degrading thing this after Dinner speaking is. I want to get out of it in a few weeks and back to the Movies.

This speaking calls on a fellow to learn something about articles that a self-respecting man has no business knowing about. So that's why I am going to get away. If a Man is called on to tell in a Public Banquet room what he knows about Corsets, there is no telling what other Ladies' wearing apparel he might be called on to discuss. So me back to the Morals of Hollywood before it's too late.

I was, at that, mighty glad to appear at a dinner given by an essential Industry. Just imagine, if you can, if the flesh of this Country were allowed to wander around promiscuously! Why, there ain't no telling where it would wind up. There has got to be a gathering or a get-together place for everything in this world, so, when our human Bodies get beyond our control, why we have to call on some mechanical force to help assemble them and bring back what might be called the semblance of a human frame.

These Corset Builders, while they might not do a whole lot to help civilization, are a tremendous aid to the Eyesight. They have got what you would call a Herculean task as they really have to improve on nature. The same problem confronts them that does the people that run the Subways in New York City. They both have to get so many pounds of human flesh into a given radius. The subway does it by having strong men to push and shove until they can just close the door with only the last man's foot out. But the Corset Carpenters arrive at the same thing by a series of strings.

They have what is known as the Back Lace. This is known as a One Man Corset.

Now the Front Lace can be operated without a confederate. By judiciously holding your breath and with a conservative intake on the Diaphragm you arrange yourself inside this. Then you tie the strings to the door knob and slowly back away. When your speedometer says you have arrived at exactly 36, why, haul in your lines and tie off.

We have also the Side Lace that is made in case you are very fleshy, and need two accomplices to help you congregate yourself. You stand in the middle and they pull from both sides. This acts something in the nature of a vise. This style has been known to operate so successful that the victims' buttons have popped off their shoes.

Of course, the fear of every fleshy Lady is the broken Corset String. I sat next to a catastrophe of this nature once. We didn't know it at first, the deluge seemed so gradual, till finally the Gentleman on the opposite side of her and myself were gradually pushed off our Chairs. To show you what a wonderful thing this Corseting is, that Lady had come to the Dinner before the broken string episode in a small Roadster. She was delivered home in a Bus.

They have also worked out a second line of control, or a place to park an extra string on the back. You can change a string now while you wait, and they have demountable strings.

Now, of course, not as many women wear Corsets as used to but what they have lost in women they have made up with men. When corsets were a dollar a pair they used to be as alike as two Fords. A clerk just looked you over, decided on your circumference and wheel base and handed you out one. They came in long Boxes and you were in doubt at first if it was a Corset or a Casket.

Nowadays with the Wraparound and the Diaphragm-Control, and all those things a Corset Manufacturer uses more rubber than a Tire Co.

Imagine me being asked to talk at a Corset Dinner, anyway; Me, who has been six years with Ziegfeld Follies and not a Corset in the Show.

Men have gone down in History for shaping the destinies of Nations, but I tell you this set of Corset Architects shape the Destinies of Women and that is a lot more important than some of the shaping that has been done on a lot of Nations that I can name off hand.

Another thing makes me so strong for them, if it wasn't for the Corset Ads in Magazines men would never look at a Magazine.[3]

HOW TO TELL A BUTLER AND OTHER ETIQUETTE

AS I OPENED THE DOOR TO LET HER IN 2 OF OUR DOGS AND 4 CATS CAME IN.

HOW TO TELL A BUTLER,
AND OTHER ETIQUETTE

SOMEBODY must have seen me out in Public; I think it was Emily Post,[1] for she sent me a book on ETIQUETTE that she had written herself.

It has 700 pages in it. You wouldn't think there was that much Etiquette, would you! Well, I hadn't read far when I found that I was wrong on most every line of the whole Book.

Now, you wouldn't think a Person could live under fairly civilized conditions (as I imagined I was doing) and be so dumb as to not have at least one of these forms of Etiquette right. Well, when I got through reading it, I felt like I had been a heathen all my life. But after I got to noticing other people I met I didn't feel so bad. Some of them didn't know much more about it than I did.

So I predict that her Book and all the other things you read now on Etiquette are going to fall on fertile soil. Now take, for instance, being introduced, or introducing someone; that is the first thing in the Book. I didn't know up to then that inflection of the voice was such a big factor in introductions.

She says that the prominence of the party being introduced determines the sound of the voice, as she says for instance, "Are you there?" and then on finding out you are there she says, "Is it raining?"

Now the inflection that you use on asking any one if they are there, is the same inflection that you are to use on introducing Mr. Gothis, if he is the more prominent of the two. Then for the other person, who Mr. Gothis probably got his from, why, you use the "Is it raining?" inflection.

You see, a fellow has to know a whole lot more than you think he does before he can properly introduce people to each other. First he has to be up on his Dunn and Bradstreet to tell which of the two is the more prominent. Second, he has to be an Elocutionist so he will know just where to bestow the inflection.

Well, I studied on the introduction Chapter till I thought I had it down pat. So I finally got a chance to try it out. My wife had invited a few friends for Dinner, and as she hadn't finished cooking it before they come, I had to meet them and introduce them to each other.

Well, I studied for half an hour before they come, trying to figure out which one was the most prominent so I could give her the "Are you there?" inflection. It was hard to figure out because any one of them couldn't be very prominent and be coming to our House for Dinner. So I thought, well, I will just give them both the "Is it raining?" inflection.

Then I happened to remember that the Husband of one of them had just bought a Drug Store, so I figured that I better give her the benefit of the "Are you there?" inflection, for if Prohibition stays in effect it's only a matter of days till her Husband will be prominent.

So, when they arrived I was remembering my opening Chapter of my Etiquette on Introductions. When the first one come I was all right; I didn't have to introduce her to anyone. I just opened our front door in answer to the Bell which didn't work. But I was peeping through the Curtains, and as I opened the door to let her in 2 of our Dogs and 4 Cats come in.

Well, while I was shooing them out, apologizing, and trying to make her believe it was unusual for them to do such a thing, now there I was! This Emily Post wrote 700 pages on Etiquette, but not a line on what to do in an emergency to remove Dogs and Cats and still be Nonchalant.[2]

The second Lady arrived just as the Dog and Cat Pound of ours was emptying. She was the new Prescription Store Owner's Wife and was to get the "Are you there?" inflection. Her name was (I will call her Smith, but that was not her name). She don't want it to get out that she knows us.

Well, I had studied that Book thoroughly but those animals entering our Parlor had kinder upset me. So I said, "Mrs. Smith, Are you there? I want you to meet Mrs. Jones. Is it raining?"

Well, these Women looked at me like I was crazy. It was a silly thing to say. Mrs. Smith was there of course, or I couldn't have introduced her, and asking Mrs. Jones if it was raining was most uncalled for, because I had just looked out myself and, besides, any one that ever lived in California knows it won't rain again till next year.

But that didn't discourage me. I kept right on learning and from now on I am just mangy with Etiquette.

Why, just the other day, I heard what I had always considered up to then a well behaved Woman, introduce one Gentleman friend to another and she said, "Allow me to present."

Now anybody that's ever read the first 5 lines in the book knows that the word Present is never used only on formal occasions. You should always say "May I introduce" on all informal occasions. There was a Woman who, to look at her, you would never have thought she could possibly be so rude and uncultured as to have made a mistake like that.

26

It just spoiled her for me. I don't care how many nice things she may do in the future, she just don't belong.

Rule 2, Chapter 5—: "No Gentleman under any circumstances chews Gum in Public." Now that kinder knocked me for a Goal, for I had been Chewing Gum before some of the best families in this country. But from now on it is out. I am going to live according to the Book.

Chapter 6—: "Gentleman should not walk along the Street with their Cane or Stick striking the picket fence. Such habits should be curbed in the nursery."

Now that rule didn't hit me so hard for I am not lame and I don't carry a Cane yet, and furthermore, there is no Picket fences in California. If they had enough pickets to make a fence they would take them and build another Bungalow and rent it.

Outside of eating with a sharp knife, there is no rule in the Book that lays you liable to as much criticism as the following: "Whether in a private Car, a Taxi, or a carriage, a lady must never sit on a Gentleman's left, because according to European Etiquette a Lady 'on the left' is no lady."

I thought at first when I read that it was a misprint, and meant a Lady should never sit on a Gentleman's Lap, instead of Left. But now I find that it really was Left. So I guess you can go ahead and sit on the lap. It don't say not to. But don't sit on his Left, or you can never hope to enter smart society.

Then it says "the Owner of the car should always occupy the right hand side of the rear seat." No matter how many payments he has to make on it, that is considered his seat.

Chapter 7 is given over entirely to The Opera. What to wear, when to applaud—it tells everything but how to enjoy the thing. The fellow that figures out how to enjoy the Opera in a foreign tongue, without kidding himself or fourflushing, has a fortune in store for him.

Chapter 12 tells how the Butler should dress. You don't know what a relief it was to me to find that news. I never had one, but if I do I will know what to costume him in.

The Book says: "At six o'clock the Butler puts on his dress Suit. The Butler's suit differs from that of a Gentleman by having no braid on his trousers."

Now all you Birds that never could tell the Servants from the Guests, except somebody called one of them a Butler and the other a Gentleman, you can't tell them that way. More than likely the Butler is the Gentleman of the two.

BIRDS THAT NEVER CAN TELL THE SERVANTS FROM THE GUESTS.

But I can tell the Butler. He has no braid on his trousers.

Now, all I got to do is find out how to tell the Gentleman.

If you see people walking around looking down at your trousers, in the future, you will know they are looking to see if the braid is left off.

DEFENDING MY SOUP PLATE POSITION

I WOULD INVENT A TRIANGLE SHAPE SLIDE THAT COULD BE PUSHED UNDER
THE PLATE.

DEFENDING MY SOUP PLATE POSITION

A COUPLE of weeks ago in my weekly Hamburger, I had the following, "If Mrs. J. W. Davis[1] ever gets into the White House we will have a mistress to preside whom no titled European visitor can embarrass by doing the right thing first. She will never tip her Soup plate even if she can't get it all."

Now comes along an old friend of mine, Percy Hammond,[2] a Theatrical Critic on a New York Paper (Pardon me, Percy, for having to tell them whom you are, but my readers are mostly provincial). He takes up a couple of columns, part of which follows:

"For years I have been tipping my Soup plate, but never until Mr. Rogers instructed me, did I know that I was performing a Social error. Consultation with the polished and urbane head waiters of the Middle West, where I spent my boyhood, taught me, I believed, to eat Soup. One wonders if Mr. Rogers has given as much thought to soup as he has to the Lariat. Perhaps he does not know, being recently from Oklahoma, that in many prominent eastern Dining rooms one may tip one's Soup plate, without losing his social standing. I regard Mr. Rogers' interference as prairie, impudent and unofficial. The Stewards of the Dutch Treat Club[3] assure me that it is proper to tip one's plate, provided (and here is the subtlety that escapes Mr. Rogers), provided that one tips one's Soup plate from and not toward.

"Mr. Rogers might well observe the modesty in such matters that adorns Mr. Tom Mix[4] his fellow ex-cowman. Mr. Mix, telling of a dinner given in his honor at the Hotel Astor, said, 'I et for two hours and didn't recognize a thing I et except an olive.'"

Them are Percy's very words. Now Percy (you notice I call you Percy, because if I kept saying, "Mr. Hammond, Mr. Hammond," all through my Article it might possibly appear too formal), Percy, I thought you were a Theatrical Critic. Now I find you are only a Soup Critic. Instead of going, as is customary, from soup to nuts, you have gone from Nuts to soup. Now, Percy, I have just read your Article on "my ignorance of Etiquette" (I don't know if that Etiquette thing is spelled right, or not; if it is not it will give you a chance for another Article on my bad spelling). Now you do not have to write Articles on my lack of Etiquette, my ignorance, my bad English, or a thousand and one other defects. All the people that I ever met or any one who ever read one of my articles know that. That would be just like saying W. J. Bryan[5] was in Politics just for Chatauqua Purposes. It's too well known to even comment on. Besides, I admit it.

Percy, I am just an old country boy in a big town trying to get

33

along. I have been eating Pretty regular, and the reason I have been is because I have stayed an old country boy. Now I wrote that Article, and technically I admit I may have been wrong, but the Newspapers paid me a lot of money for it, and I never had a complaint. And by the way, I will get the same this week for writing about you that I did about Soup. Now both Articles may be wrong, But if you can show me how I can get any more money by writing them right, why I will split with you.

Now you took my soup article apart to see what made it float. I will see if we can't find some SMALL technicalities in your Literary Masterpiece. You say I came recently from Oklahoma, while You come from the Middle West and "by consultation with the Head Waiters have learned the proper way to eat soup." I thought Oklahoma was in the Middle West. Your knowledge of Geography is worse than my Etiquette. You say you learned to eat Soup from a Head Waiter in the Middle West. Well, I admit my ignorance again; I never saw a head waiter eat Soup. Down in Oklahoma (probably near Siberia) where I come from, we wouldn't let a head waiter eat at our Table, even if we had a head waiter, which we haven't. If I remember right I think it was my Mother taught me what little she knew of how I should eat, because if we had had to wait until we sent and got a head waiter to show us, we would have all starved to death. If a head waiter taught you to eat soup, Percy, I suppose you were sent to Bordens to learn how to drink Milk.

Then you state, "The Stewards of the Dutch Treat Club assure me that it is proper to tip one's plate." Now if you had learned properly from the great social Head Waiters of the urbane Middle West, why did you have to consult the Stewards of the Dutch Treat Club? Could it be that after arriving in N.Y. you couldn't rely on the information of the polished Head waiters of your phantom Middle West? Now I was in the Dutch Treat Club once, but just as a Guest of Honor at a Luncheon, and of course had no chance to get into any intimate conversations with the Stewards. At that time, the place did not impress me as being where one might learn the last word in Etiquette.

And as for your saying that "anything of subtlety would escape me," that I also admit. I attribute it to my Dumbness. But as for me being too Dumb to get the idea of "the Soup plate being tipped away and not toward one," that's not Etiquette; that's just Self Protection. As bad as you plate tippers want all you can get, you don't want it in your lap. Custom makes manners, and while I know that it is permissible to tip plates, I still say that it is not a universal custom. Manners are nothing more than common sense, and a person has no more right to try and get every drop of soup out of his plate than he has to take a piece of bread and try and harvest all the Gravy in his plate. If you are that hungry, they ought to feed you out of a Nose Bag. So, "prairie impudence" or no "prairie impudence," I claim there are lots of them that don't do it, even if it is permissible (Head Waiters and Dutch Stewards to the contrary). It's permissible to get drunk but we still have a few that don't.

Now, Percy, suppose they all did as is permitted. Picture a big dinner with everybody with their soup plates all balanced up on edge, with one hand holding them up and the other hand with the spoon rounding up what little soup was left. They would resemble a lot of plate jugglers instead of Dinner Guests. Why if that was the universal custom, I would invent a triangle shape slide that could be pushed under the plate, so it would permit you to have one hand free, in case you were sitting next to your own wife, or if by chance you might want to use your napkin. According to your hungry plan, every Guest practically handcuffs himself during the latter end of the soup course. He is absolutely helpless. So don't ask head waiters and stewards what to do, Percy, look around yourself. You will find hundreds of them that are satisfied with just what Soup they can get on the level. Why I bet you are a fellow Percy, if you took Castor Oil, you would want to lick the spoon.

You know, Percy, I might know more about Etiquette than you think I do. I wrote a review on Emily Post's Book on Etiquette, and it was recopied in the Literary Digest[6] (and by the way it did not mention the Digest's name, and it is unusual for them to re-copy anything unless they are mentioned in the article). Now have you or any of your Mid-Western head waiters, or retinue of Stewards, ever been asked to write a criticism on such an authoritative work as that? So you see I am somewhat of a Critic myself. I am the Hammond of the etiquette Book business.

Another thing, Percy, I spoke of a particular case; I mentioned Mrs. Davis. Well, I happened to see the Lady in question eat soup, and she did not try and corral the whole output. She perhaps knew it was permissible, still, she did not seem eager to take advantage of it.

Now, you speak of my friend, Tom Mix, where he says, "he et two hours and did not recognize anything he et but an olive." Now, that is bad Grammer, even I will admit, but it's mighty good eating. Don't you kinder envy him, that he has lived his life physically so that now he can eat for two hours. I bet you that you would trade your knowledge of the English language now for his constitution. Tipping that soup plate at all your meals for years is what put that front on you, Perc. Leave some, that's why I am trying to prove to you it's permissible to tip the plate, but it's bad physically. The fact that Tom has done something to be given a dinner for, should make him immune from attacks from the Press Table.

Vice Dawes, the profanity end of Coolidge's Campaign, just went through New York last week cussing everything, and everybody, a Hell'n Maria'ing all over the place.[7] But he has other qualities to offset his cussing, so personally I don't think this word, "et" on Mix's part will seriously affect the drawing power of his pictures. You see, Percy, Tom said, "et," but you know better than him what to say. Still, if a Western Picture was to be made to amuse the entire World, I would trust Tom's judgment to yours. You know, Percy, everybody is ignorant, only on different subjects.

So, Perc, you string with the High Brows, but I am going to stick to the Low Brows, because I know I am at home with them. For remember, if it was not for us Low Brows, you high brows would have no one to discuss. But God love you, Percy, and if you ever want to leave them and come back to us where you started, we will all be glad to welcome you, even if you do feel like you are slumming. You must remember, Perc, that the question of the World today is, not how to *eat* soup, but how to *get* soup to eat.

HELPING THE GIRLS WITH THEIR
INCOME TAXES

HELPING THE GIRLS WITH THEIR INCOME TAXES

WELL, I haven't had much time lately to dope out many new jokes. I have been helping the Girls in the Follies make out their Income Tax.[1] A vital question come up, do Presents come under the heading of Salary? You know that's a mighty big item with us. When I say Us, I don't mean Me, as no one has given me anything yet, but I stick around in case a few crumbs drop.

I have been looking for a bribe from some of our prominent men to keep their name out of my act, but the only ones who even speak to me are the ones I mention. So I guess about the only way you can get a Man sore nowadays is to ignore him.

One Girl wanted to charge off Taxi Cab fares to and from the Theatre. I told her she couldn't do that. She said, "Well, how am I to get there?" I said "Well, as far as the Government is concerned, you can come on the Subway." She said, "Oh! What is the Subway?"

Another Girl who has been with the various Follies for ten years wanted to know what She could charge off for Depreciation. And she was absolutely right because if, after being with them for that long, and you haven't married at least one Millionaire, you certainly have a legitimate claim for Depreciation.

I reminded one of the Girls that she had neglected to include two of her Alimony allowances. She said, "Do I have to put them all in?" I said, "Why, certainly you do." The Girl said, "Well, how did the Government keep track of them? I couldn't."

One Girl charged off a non-providing Husband under the heading of Bad Debts. We charged off all Cigarettes smoked in Public under the heading, Advertising.

One Sweetheart who paid for a Girl's Dinner every night, went thoroughly broke in Wall Street by trying to corner Canned Tomatoes in the late Piggledy-Wiggledy[2] uprising. We figured up what the dinners would be for the rest of the year and charged him off as a Total Loss.

And right here I want to say what an honest bunch these Girls are. They don't want to beat the Government out of a thing. One Girl who had been away for a few weeks last winter to Palm Beach left a Husband in the good hands of her Girl Chum. When she returned the Girl Chum gave her a Two Thousand Dollar Bracelet. Now she wanted to include this Item in her Tax and we couldn't figure out where to put it. Finally we decided it was Rents, so we put it in, "For Rent, of One Husband, two Thousand Dollars."

Of course while the girls had these tremendous salaries I was able to help on account of my technical knowledge of them (as I dress with their Chauffeurs), and on account of my equal knowledge of making out an Income Tax, with any man in the World. As none of us know a thing about it.

Look what I saved them on Bathing Suits! I had them all claim they bought various Suits. And I defy even a Congressional Investigating Committee (and you certainly can't pick any more useless Body of men than they are), I defy them to say that a Bathing Suit on a Beautiful Girl don't come under the heading of Legitimate Advertising.

Now, as I say, these Girls all wanted to do what was right as they could afford to but this Income Tax has not acted that way with the Men. The Income Tax has made more Liars out of the American people than Golf has.

Even when you make one out on the level, you don't know when it's through if you are a Crook or a Martyr.

Of course, people are getting smarter nowadays; they are letting Lawyers, instead of their conscience, be their Guide.

There is some talk of lowering it, and they will have to. People are not making enough to pay it.

And, by the way, the only way they will ever stop Bootlegging, too, is to make them pay an Income Tax. (At present it is a Tax exempt Industry.) Income Tax has stopped every other Industry, so there is no reason why it won't stop Bootlegging.

Of course, some of our more thrifty Girls have followed the example of their Male Tax Dodging friends and Incorporated (as the rate is lower on Corporations). Wall Street attended to that little matter when they were drawing the Tax Bill up in Washington.

These Girls had to do that, the same as men, to protect their Salaries. Of course, the big Gamble in buying into these Individual Corporations is the Lucky chance that she might make one or more wealthy marriages during the year. When of course, her being Incorporated, all she gets comes under the heading of Income, and you, as a Stockholder, get your Pro Rata Share. If she lands a big one you have struck Oil. Then, on the other hand, she may marry for love. In that case you have brought in a Duster.

For example, down on the Exchange you will find the Anastasia Reed, incorporated,[3] along with General Motors and Blue Jay Corn Plasters. At the end of the year, the Stockholders, after adding up the Salary along with the accumulated Alimony, can either declare a dividend, or vote a Dinner and put the Undivided profits back into the growing Concern.

Now, I can't tell you the name but I was lucky enough to land 5 shares just before a Blond Corporation married a Multi-Millionaire who was over 70 years of age. Us Stockholders have figured out at our last meeting that if he dies when we think he will (and we have no reason to believe otherwise, unless the Poison acts as a Monkey Gland) why, just those 5 shares will make me independent for life.

I don't want to use this space as an ad, but I have been able for a small monetary fee to tip off my friends just what stock to buy. You see I am in a position to judge as I watch who is in the front row every night and I can just tell when Mendelssohn's Spring Song[4] will start percolating for some particular Corporation. Now, at the present time, there is every night in the front row a Millionaire Oklahoma Oil Magnate and a Bootlegger, both angling for the same Corporation. If this Bootlegging person lands her, why her Stockholders are made for life, but if the Oil Magnate comes through (for sometimes these female Corporations are swayed by sentiment), why the stock won't be worth within a thousand Percent of what it will be if the Bootheel Party lands.

Now take me personally; this Income Tax thing don't bother me at all. You are allowed 200 dollars for each Child, and my Children and my Income are just coming out even now.[5]

THE GREATEST DOCUMENT IN
AMERICAN LITERATURE

SONG WRITERS SHOULD BE SEGREGATED AND MADE TO SING THEIR SONGS
TO EACH OTHER.

THE GREATEST DOCUMENT
IN AMERICAN LITERATURE

THE subject for this[1] brainy Editorial is resolved that, "Is the Song Yes We Have no Bananas[2] the greatest or the worst Song that America ever had?"

I have read quite a lot in the papers about the degeneration of America by falling for a thing like it. Some lay it to the effects of Prohibition, some say it is the after-effects of War, that it is liable to follow every big war. I see where some have written editorials on the Song claiming that things are always in an unsettled state the year before a Presidential Election. I claim it's due to none of these causes at all; neither is it due to the French occupation of the Ruhr. I claim that it is the greatest document that has been penned in the entire History of American Literature.

And there is only one way to account for its popularity, and that is how you account for anything's popularity, and that is because it has Merit. Real down to earth merit, more than anything written in the last decade. The World was just hungry for something good and when this Genius come along and got right down and wrote on a subject that every Human being is familiar with, and that was Vegetables, Bologna, Eggs and Bananas, why he simply hit us where we live. You know a War Song will only appeal to people that are interested in war, a Love Song to those who are in love, A Mammy Song to nobody at all, but when you get down and write of Cabbages, Potatoes, and Tomatoes, you just about hit on a Universal subject.

You see, we had been eating these things all our lives but no one had ever thought of paying homage to them in Words and Harmony. It opens up a new field for Song Writers. I look for an epidemic of Corned Beef, Liver and Bacon, Soup and Hash Songs to flood the Market. So more power to an originator. Did you ever stop to realize that that Song has attracted more attention than anything that has taken place in this Country since Valentino[3] gave up the screen for a mud Face preparation?

Magnus Johnson[4] of Wisconsin or Minnesota (they ought to put those States together; nobody can ever remember which one anything even happens in, generally the same thing happens in both of them); well as I say, Magnus was unfortunate enough to be elected to the United States Senate at a time when Bananas was at its height. Ten thousand people can sing the song that dont know that Magnus can milk a Cow with one hand and broadcast a Political speech with the

45

other. Millions can hum the Song that cant tell you what Lloyd George is sore at England about.

Hiram Johnson[5] arrived from Europe a Presidential possibility, and spoke to 2 thousand people. The creator of Bananas to Music, penned one Gem of constructive thought, and spoke not to two thousand but to one hundred and ten million.

Then some Editorial Newspaper writer has the nerve to sneer at this marvelous Song, when perhaps his writings never cross the County line. Why, Italy has already made arrangements on account of his honoring their National Diet to place his name alongside of Michael Angelo, Garibaldi, and Louis Firpo.[6] It is already bringing on International complications. England is sore because he didn't say something about Tea and Cake.

If we had had a Man like that to write our National Anthem somebody could learn it. It wouldn't take three wars to learn the words.

Mother has been done to death in Songs and not enough consideration shown her in real life. We thought when we sang about her we had paid her all the respect there was. I tell you, conditions were Just Ripe for a good fruit Song.

Geo. M. Cohan[7] wore out more Flags than a war waving them to music. He transferred the Flag from Cloth to Paper, he made it a two verse and Chorus affair. Now George was original. He saw an idea; he knew that a big percentage of the American people had seen the flag, so that would give him a subject to write on that people knew about. But look what a Universal subject this Bird hit on. There are thousands of Foreigners landing here daily that know Spin-ISH and HON-ions, that dont know an American Flag from a Navajo Blanket.

Did you ever just dissect the Words to some of our so-called Popular Songs? One has the words "Its not raining Rain, its raining Violets," Now can you imagine any more of a Cuckoo idea than that? You cant hardly raise the things, much less Rain em. Now which do we owe the most to, the Violet or the Banana? Even such a Genius as Geo. M. Cohan himself has a Song, "You remind me of my Mother when Mother was A Girl like you." How can any man remember his Mother when she was a girl? Its a Physical impossibility. You would have had to be born almost simultaneously with your Mother.

Now on the other hand take the Banana Classic. "We just killed a Pony so try our Bologna, It's flavored with Oats and Hay." Now that's not only good Poetry but his honesty should be rewarded. He is on the level, he is telling you just what you get. Then those History-making lines, "Our Hen Fruit have you tried em, real live Chickens inside em." Now I think in the rhyming line that is a positive Gem, and will live when Gungha Din has lost his Hot Water Bottle. That shows originality. He is not just simply going along rhyming Girl and Pearl, Beauty and Cutey, Bees and Knees.

This Boy has got the stuff. Get this one and then read all through Shakespeare and see if he ever scrambled up a mess of words like these, "Try our Walnuts and Co- CO- Nuts, there aint many nuts like They." Now just off-hand you would think that it is purely a commercial Song with no tinge of Sentiment, but dont you believe it. Read this: "And you can take home for the WIM-mens, nice juicy per-Sim-mons." Now that shows thoughtfulness for the fair sex and also excellent judgment in the choice of a Delicacy. Then there is rhythm and harmony that would do credit to a Walt Whitman,[8] so I defy you to show me a single song with so much downright merit to it as this has.

You know, it dont take much to rank a man away up if he is just lucky in coining the right words. Now take for instance Horace Greeley I think it was, or was it W.G. McAdoo,[9] who said "go West, young man." Now that took no original thought at the time it was uttered. There was no other place for a man to go, still it has lived. Now you mean to tell me that a commonplace remark like that has the real backbone of this one: "Our Grapefruit I'll bet you, Is not going to wet you, we drain them out every day." Now which do you think it would take you the longest to think of, that or "Go West, Young Man."

Some other fellow made himself by saying "War is Hell." Now what was original about that? Anyone who had been in one could have told you that, and today he has one of the biggest Statues in New York.[10] According to that, what should the Banana man get? He should be voted the Poet Lariet of America.

Now mind you, I am not upholding this man because I hold any briefs for the Songwriters. I think they are in a class with the After Dinner speakers. They should be like Vice used to be in some towns. *They should be segregated off to themselves* and not allowed to associate with people at all, *and should be made to sing these songs to each other.* That is the only way you will ever do away with the Song writing business.

Another thing that has made it bad is these People that used to send Scenarios to Moving Picture Studios, after getting them back have turned them into Songs. Its been a Godsend to the Picture business but a blow to the Music business. And those Mammy Songs — those writers should have all been banished to Siberia, and as they went through on their way to Siberia dont let them stop in Russia to see their Mammy. But when one does come along and display real talent as this one has proven, I think he should be encouraged. Some

47

man said years ago that he "cared not who fought their Countries' Wars as long as he could write their Songs." But of the two our Songs have been the most devastating.

I understand this Boy was a Drummer in a Jazz Band before this World renown hit him. Now I personally have always considered the Drummer the best part of the Jazz Band. I think if all the members of a Jazz band played the Drums it would make better music. I would rather have been the Author of that Banana Masterpiece than the Author of the Constitution of the United States. No one has offered any amendments to it. Its the only thing ever written in America that we haven't changed, most of them for the worst.

PROSPECTUS FOR "THE REMODELED
CHEWING GUM CORPORATION"

WHY CAN'T I DO SOMETHING WITH SECOND-HAND GUM?

PROSPECTUS FOR
"THE REMODELED
CHEWING GUM CORPORATION"

LAST week I made, on account of my Movie work, a trip to Catalina Island and along with the Glass bottom Boat I had pointed out to me the home of Mr. William Wrigley[1] on the top of the highest mountain. He also owns the Island. We were not allowed to go nearer than the gate as the Guide said some other Tourist had carried away a Grand Piano, and he had gotten discouraged at having them around. Another tourist was caught right on the Lawn Chewing an opposition Brand of Gum. That is really the thing that gummed up the Tourist Parade.

Then I remembered having seen his wonderful building in Chicago, all, mind you, accumulated on Chewing Gum at a Cent a Chew. Now I felt rather hurt at not being allowed to at least walk through maybe the Kitchen, or the Cellar, because I know that I have contributed more to the Building of that Home than any one living. I have not only made Chewing Gum a pastime but I have made it an Art. I have brought it right out in Public and Chewed before some of the oldest Political Families of Massachusetts.

I have had Senator Lodge[2] (who can take the poorest arguments in the World and dress them up in perfect English and sell them) after hearing my Act on the Stage, say: "William" (that's English for Will), "William, I could not comprehend a word of the Language you speak, but you do Masticate uncompromisingly excellent."

This reception which I received at the Wrigley Home was so in contrast to the one which I received at Mr. Adolphus Busch's[3] in St. Louis. When he heard that one of his best Customers was at the outer Gate, Mr. Busch not only welcomed me, but sent me a fine German Police Dog to California, the stock of which had come direct from the Kaiser's Kennels in Pottsdam. The Dog did wonderful until some one here by mistake gave him a drink of Half of One Percent Beer. He would have been six years old next May.

After looking on Mr. Wrigley's home with much admiration and no little envy, the thought struck me: A man to succeed nowadays must have an Idea. Here I am, struggling along and wasting my time on trying to find something nice to say of our Public Men, when I should be doing Something with Dividends connected with it. So then the thought struck me: WHAT BECOMES OF ALL THE CHEWING GUM THAT IS USED IN THIS COUNTRY?

I just thought to myself, if Bill Wrigley can amass this colossal fortune, and pay the Manufacturing charges, why can't I do something with Second Hand Gum. I will have no expense, only the accumulation of the Gum after it is thoroughly masticated. Who would be the most beneficial to mankind, the man who invented Chewing Gum, or me who can find a use for it? Why, say, if I can take a wad of old Gum and graft it onto some other substance. I will be the modern Burbank. (With the ideas I have got for used Gum I may be honored by my Native State of Oklahoma by being made Governor, with the impeachment clause scratched out of the Contract.)[4]

All Wrigley had was an Idea. He was the first man to discover that the American Jaws must wag. So why not give them something to wag against? That is, put in a kind of Shock Absorber.

If it wasn't for Chewing Gum, Americans would wear their teeth off just hitting them against each other. Every Scientist has been figuring out who the different races descend from. I don't know about the other Tribes, but I do know that the American Race descended from the Cow. And Wrigley was smart enough to furnish the Cud. He has made the whole World chew for Democracy.

That's why this subject touches me so deeply. I have chewed more Gum than any living Man. My Act on the Stage depended on the grade of Gum I chewed. Lots of my readers have seen me and perhaps noted the poor quality of my jokes on that particular night. Now I was not personally responsible for that. I just happened to hit on a poor piece of Gum. One can't always go by the brand. There just may be a poor stick of Gum in what otherwise may be a perfect package. It may look like the others on the outside but after you get warmed up on it, why, you will find that it has a flaw in it. And hence my act would suffer. I have always maintained that big Manufacturers of America's greatest necessity should have a Taster—a man who personally tries every Piece of Gum put out.

Now lots of People don't figure the lasting quality of Gum. Why, I have had Gum that wouldn't last you over half a day, while there are others which are like Wine—they improve with Age.

I hit on a certain piece of Gum once, which I used to park on the Mirror of my dressing room after each show. Why, you don't know what a pleasure it was to chew that Gum. It had a kick, or spring to it, that you don't find once in a thousand Packages. I have always thought it must have been made for Wrigley himself.

And say, what jokes I thought of while chewing that Gum! Ziegfeld himself couldn't understand what had put such life and Humor into my Work.

Then one night it was stolen, and another piece was substituted in its place, but the minute I started in to work on this other Piece I knew that someone had made a switch. I knew this was a Fake. I hadn't been out on the Stage 3 minutes until half of the audience were asleep and the other half were hissing me. So I just want to say you can't exercise too much care and judgment in the selection of your Gum, because if it acts that way with me in my work, it must do the same with others, only they have not made the study of it that I have.

Now you take Bryan. I lay his downfall to Gum. You put that man on good Gum and he will be parking it right under the White House Dinner Table.

Now, some Gum won't stick easy. It's hard to transfer from your hand to the Chair. Other kinds are heavy and pull hard. It's almost impossible to remove them from Wood or Varnish without losing a certain amount of the Body of the Gum.

There is lots to be said for Gum. This pet Piece of mine I afterwards learned had been stolen by a Follies Show Girl, who two weeks later married an Oil Millionaire.

Gum is the only ingredient of our National Life of which no one knows how or of what it is made. We know that Sawdust makes our Breakfast food. We know that Tomato Cans constitute Ford Bodies. We know that old Second-hand Newspapers make our 15 dollar Shoes. We know that Cotton makes our All-Wool Suits. But no one knows yet what constitutes a mouthful of Chewing Gum.

But I claim if you can make it out of old Rubber Boots and Tires and every form of old junk, why can't I, after reassembling it, put it back into these same Commodities? No one has found a substitute for Concrete. Why not Gum? Harden the surface so the Pedestrians would not vacate with your street. What could be better for a Dam for a River than old Chewing Gum? Put one Female College on the banks of the Grand Canyon, and they will Dam it up in 2 years, provided they use discretion in their parking.

Now, as for my plans of accumulation, put a Man at every Gum selling place. The minute a Customer buys, he follows him. He don't have to watch where he throws it when through; all he has to do is to follow. He will step on it sooner or later no matter where they throw it.

When he feels it, he immediately cuts off the part of the shoe where it is stuck on, so he can save the entire piece. Then he goes back and awaits another buyer.

I have gone into the matter so thoroughly that I made a week's test at a friend of mine's Theatre. At one of Mr. Sid Grauman's[5] Movie Theatres here, I gathered gum for one week and kept account of the intake every day. My statistics have proven that every Seat in every movie Theatre will yield a half Pint of Gum every 2 days, some only just slightly used.

Now that gives us an average of a Pint and a Half every six days, not counting Sunday where the Pro Rata really increases. Now figure the seating capacity of the Theatre and you arrive at just what our Proposition will yield in a good solid commodity.

Of course, this thing is too big for me to handle personally. I can, myself, disrobe, after every Show, one Theatre and perhaps a Church on Sunday. But to make it National I have to form it into a Trust. We will call it the "Remodeled Chewing Gum Corporation."

Don't call it Second Hand; there is no Dignity in that name. If we say "remodeled" why every Bird in America falls for that.

Of course, it is my idea ultimately after we have assembled more than we can use for Concrete and Tires and Rubber Boots to get a Press of some kind and mash it up in different and odd shapes.

(You know there is nothing that takes at a Dinner like some[6] Popular Juice Flavor to our Remodeled and overhauled Product. I would suggest Wood Alcohol. That would combine two Industries into one.)

I want to put flavors in there where we can take some of this colossal trade away from these Plutocratic Top Booted Gentlemen. If we can get just enough of this Wood Alcohol into our reassembled Gum to make them feel it and still not totally destroy our Customer we will have improved on the Modern Bootlegger as he can only sell to the same man once.

Now, Gentlemen and Ladies, you have my proposition. Get in early on, "Old Gum made as good as New." Think of the different brands that would be popular, "Peruna Flavor Gum," "Jamaica Ginger Gum," "Glover's Mange Gum," "Lysol Gum."

It looks like a great proposition to me. It will be the only Industry in the World where all we have to do is to just pick it up, already made, and flavor it.

I am going to put this thing up to my friend, Henry Ford. Think, with no overhead, how he could keep the Cost down. It's a better proposition than being President.

INSIDE STUFF ON THE TOTAL ECLIPSE

THE MORE GLASSES YOU USED THE MORE ECLIPSE YOU COULD SEE.

INSIDE STUFF ON THE TOTAL ECLIPSE

WELL, I have just this minute returned from Tia Juana, Mexico, where I along with some thousands of other Scientists went to observe the Total Eclipse.[1] That is that was their excuse for going. You know it don't take much excuse to get a man, or Woman either, to go to Mexico nowadays. So when the Scientists said that Los Angeles was only to get a 99 percent Eclipse, (That is about the only thing I ever knew Los Angeles to fall down on. They are generally 100 percent) it kinder hurt their pride. It was the first time that Nature had ever handed them a mere 99.

I don't really think they would have ever gotten over it but San Francisco only received some 85 or 90 percent so that kinder salved things over.

But the Chamber of Commerce has held a meeting and voted Resolutions to apply for the next Eclipse in its entirety. They claim that it was due to the Club not giving the matter more thought that they lost the One Percent on this one.

Well, the Scientist Road Map showed that Catilina Island and San Diego and Tia Juana, were right in the path of total blackness. Everybody that could get out of a Cafeteria line in time to make the trip started for one of these places. Catilina Island offered wonderful possibilities. You could get two rounds of Seasickness, see the Eclipse and get your Chewing Gum at cost—all in one day's pleasure.

San Diego is a Town built in the most South Westerly part of the United States where Americans who are coming out of Mexico sober up, before being able to go to their various homes, and it is really remarkable what a thriving Town it is. You would be surprised at the business they do.

There are nice Hotels there with Ice Water in every room, and even Banks where you can draw Drafts on your Home Bank after a Day in Mexico at the Tables (as they say in Monte Carlo books). San Diego catches very few going down into Mexico, (only the Punctures) as most People are in a great hurry to get there, once you begin to reach this oasis.

So you see it didn't take much decision on my part to decide that if I, along with the other Scientists who were to write on this Traffic accident in the Skies, wanted to pick out an observatory there was no particular reason why we should select a Dry one.

Well, my friend Mr. Henry Ford may or may not ever be President, but I want to publicly say this to him, that the people he sells his Cars to are of a very high type of intelligence. I never saw so many owners of one make of car so interested in Astronomy in my life. There were not only Autos of every make but people of every make, jammed two rows deep for 150 miles struggling to reach Tia Juana, Mexico FOR THE ECLIPSE.

You would see people going to Mexico to see this eclipse, who, if you looked at them, you wouldn't think they knew when Sunday passed between Monday and Saturday, much less when the Moon passed between the Sun and Earth.

Now, as I say, we passed through some 70 miles of United States Territory that was to be blotted out totally, but there wasn't an observatory in the entire region. Being my first year as a Journalist and this being my first assignment to cover a total Eclipse for the various papers who crave my Scientific knowledge, I am really ashamed to admit it, but, outside of not even knowing what an Eclipse was or when one was to happen, I had never even entered one of their Observatories where they watch these Eclipses; so it was with the greatest anxiety and enthusiasm that I dashed up to the Mexico line.

The Country to the south of us we have lately recognized. (The receipt for any other Nation that wants us to recognize them, is to strike Oil, or some other commodity that our Capitalists want.) But this editorial is not on our Foreign Relations. That I will take up in due time as we have some Foreign Relations. This is to be on the Planets, their various Routes, mode and speed of travel.

A great many Scientists, I had read in the papers, were bringing Cameras to Photograph this remarkable phenomenon. But most of the Scientists that I saw had Jugs and Flasks. Well, not being up on Science, I didn't know what to bring. You know these Scientists are such a queer lot I wouldn't be surprised at anything they do.

Well, I asked the Custom Inspector where the Observatory was. He said, "Which one?" I said, "Lick." (That was the only one I had ever heard of.) He said, "Right over there is one, if it ain't all Licked up."

You never saw such an accommodating Country in the World. Just think the preparations they had gone through for the visiting Scientists' Pleasure. They had built these Observatories all over the place right up to the line where you would lose no time. You could start observing the minute you got into the Country.

Now, there is apt to be among my readers some who are as ignorant as I was about the inside of an Observatory, so for their benefit I will explain just what it is like. On the left, as you enter, is a long Table affair, that runs the length of the room. It's really higher than a Table, and back of it is a long Mirror where you get the reflections of any local Eclipses that might happen. Then on the bottom, outside this high counter, is a little low railing that Singers' Midgets[2] could look over if they wanted to see an Eclipse.

Now, up here in Los Angeles, they talked about smoked Glasses, but down there they just filled them and looked through them, and the more Glasses you used, and the more different kinds of glasses, why, the more Eclipse you could see. Some men would have to get the man to let them try a dozen different Glasses before they could get the right Focus.

Then, on the other side of the room, if you didn't want to look through glasses upside down, why they had various other instruments of knowledge. One was a Table with little Cubes cut square (or apparently square) with Dots on them and the Scientist would shake them in his hand and lay down some Money, and then let them empty out his hand. Then another Scientist, even more of a Scientist, would pick up the money in one hand and the little squares in the other and hand the squares to another Scientist and put the money in his Pocket. Then the same operation would be gone through, till each Scientist, except the good one, would be Gone Through.

I asked a visiting Astronomy Professor what the idea was. He said, "You can see if you are right." I says, "What has that got to do with the eclipse?" He says, "Why you bet on the passing." So I bet him I would pass but I didn't, so now I want the Scientist to figure out in what year I am going to pass.

By that time it was 12.50 p.m. so I come out of the Observatory as that was the time it was supposed to be Total, but there wasn't a Soul on the Streets or outside any place. Everybody was on the inside looking at the Eclipse. It was pretty dark on the Street and a Mexican who lived in the edge of the Town started milking his Cow, and raising the mischief with his wife because she didn't have his supper ready.

One fellow staggered out of an Observatory and I asked him if he had seen the Eclipse and he said, "Which one?" But it certainly was a success from a Scientific point of view, for away along in the evening after it had gotten light, I saw Astronomers piled up in every Observatory just overcome by what the Scientists call the Corona, or after effects of an Eclipse.

Oh yes, the Mexicans also put on for the visiting Astrologers a Bull Fight. It was held at the lower end of the Town. You had to pass every Observatory in town before you reached the Bull Ring.

Well, I went down and there was lots of Natives but very few Americans. As I say, it was held at the wrong end of the Town for them to reach it. I guess it was the only Fight ever held during an Eclipse.

59

Can you imagine getting in a Pen with a Bull in the dark. I wouldn't even get in with one in the light. Well, the Bulls turned out to be Steers. I guess on account of the Eclipse and the Condition the Americans would be in, the Mexicans figured they wouldn't know the difference. They didn't kill the Bulls, and the Bulls wasn't lucky enough to do any damage themselves. As a strict Humane man I could see nothing to kick about, only from an audience's standpoint.

So I left Tia Juana and come back to this side where everybody had looked at the Eclipse from out of doors, and they all seemed to be kinder disappointed. It didn't do anything. You see from the amount of Press stuff written about it most people kinder thought it would do some tricks, maybe juggle or shimmy or something like that. It just passed—that's all. I, personally, along with all the others couldn't see anything so wonderful about it's doing that. If the two planets hadn't passed but had hit, that would have been something to see.

Of course, I will admit in this day of congested Traffic, for any two given objects to meet and pass without hitting is considered wonderful.

Everybody I talked with seemed to be unanimous that they would rather have seen the Dempsey and Firpo fight.[3] So I guess that is why they only have Eclipses every 100 years so they won't have to draw from the same crowd twice.

But no one who saw it from Mexico had any fault to find with it at all. If there is any great thing happening and you are not right sure you will enjoy it, why, go to Mexico and see it.

I tell you a thing looks different from a foreign country. I wish[4] I could have seen the Democratic and Republican Conventions from Tia Juana.

The Eclipse was kinder overrated but I tell you Mexico ain't.

IT'S TIME SOMEBODY SAID A WORD FOR CALIFORNIA

(A speech delivered impromptu at a Dinner to the Old Settlers of California. Mr. Rogers had another speech prepared but when he found everybody boosting California he changed his speech.)

I JUST HAPPENED TO REMEMBER THAT NO ONE HAD SAID A WORD FOR
CALIFORNIA.

IT'S TIME SOMEBODY SAID A WORD FOR CALIFORNIA

I ATTENDED a dinner the other morning given for the Old Settlers of California. No one was allowed to attend unless he had been in the State 2 and one-half years.

I was the last speaker on the Menu. They put me last, figuring everybody would either be asleep or gone by the time I began.

Well sir, do you know, by the time it got to me there was nothing left to talk on! But I just happened to notice that in all the other speeches no one had mentioned California, so as that was all I had left I just had to go ahead and do the best I could with California.

Now, it ain't much of a speech but it is at least a novelty, because in all my time out here I had never heard the subject used before at any Dinners or Luncheons.

Mr. Toastmaster, Ladies and Gentlemen, and Members of the Old California Settlers Association: Your previous speakers have taken up so much time boosting and praising other States and their People that it is now most daylight, and I am at a loss to pick a subject, but at the last minute I just happened to remember that no one had said a word for California. So I will take up this very remote subject and see if I can't do something to drag it out of the obscurity in which it has been placed here tonight.

Being one of your old Timers (I have been a resident of this State now for nearly 4 years; there is only one other older member in the organization) I want to say right here that you often hear it said, "What is the matter with California?"[1] Well, I will tell you what is the matter —it's MODESTY, that's what it is, too much MODESTY.

If we got out and blew our own Horns and Advertised and boosted our State like Delaware, and Rhode Island have, we wouldn't be so little heard of. So, whether you like it or not fellow Statesmen, I for one am going to throw Modesty to the winds and just tell the World off-hand a few of the things that we have got out here.

Now, just picking subjects at random, what do you suppose we could do if we wanted to say something about CLIMATE? Why, that item alone would draw people here. But what do we do? We just set here and say nothing. We go out of the State and we are so darn generous that all we do is brag on the place where we are. We never think of handing our own State a little free advertising.

But you take, as I say, a fellow from Delaware, and he is preaching Delaware and all its advantages from the time you meet him till

63

you leave him, and by golly, it pays to do that. Look at Delaware today! So never mind this old good fellow spirit of giving the other fellow the best of it. I believe in throwing in a little boost for the old Native Heath.

Now I know you other members don't agree with me and think that we should think of our proud traditions and not stoop so low as to have to advertise but I tell you that this day and time is a commercial Age, and we have got to throw our Pride away and let the World know just what we have here.

There is no reason why other People from neighboring States shouldn't know of our Climate. Why keep it hid? It's here. We got it. They can't take it away with them.

Of course, I will admit that we have done a little good in a small way with Picture Post Cards. Five years ago Iowa was a prosperous and satisfied State. They had no idea of leaving. They had shoveled snow for 5 months every year and figured they would always shovel snow 5 months every year. But finally one day a Twenty Dollar Bill come into the State and a Farmer wanted to get change for it, so he started out trying to get it changed and wound up in Long Beach, California.

A fellow selling Roses in January changed it for him, and when the Farmer pulled off his Mittens to count the change he found that it was warm and he didn't have to put the mittens back on again. That made quite a hit with him and he decided to stay awhile. So he sent a Picture Post Card back with the Picture of a Man Picking Oranges off the trees in January, and told them how fine it was and everybody that read the Post Card, including the Postmaster come on out.

So when they came they sent back Picture Post Cards to all their Friends who liked Oranges, and in time they came too, and so on, each newcomer bringing out just as many more as he could afford Post Cards. Now in the short space of 5 years look what has happened. The whole of the State of Iowa is here. The only ones left back there are the ones who can't read the Post Cards, or People who don't care for Oranges, and now I see where they have put in Schools to teach those others to read so that means we will eventually have them all, with the exception of the ones who don't like Oranges.

Now, as I say, if all of that can be done with just Picture Post Cards, what do you suppose could have been done if the Newspapers of our State had thought to have said something in praise of our Climate? So, Fellow Old Timers, if we can get the grand State of Iowa out here on a Picture Post Card of an Orange Tree, what could we do with some of these other States if we really devoted a little of our time to it!

Why, Oranges are a small time commodity with us. We raise more Beans on one farm here without Irrigating than we do Oranges in the whole State. If we had Picture Post Cards of Bean Fields instead of Orange Fields we could get the whole of Boston here the same as we did with Iowa. You will do even better with Boston than you did with Iowa because everybody there likes Beans. So let's get busy and let them know what we are doing in the Bean line.

Take the case of Oil. You all know we struck oil here in Southern California. But did you let anybody else know it? No, you didn't say a word about it, and as a consequence, a man can't even find a place to buy an Oil Stock. Now there are lots of People would buy shares and Units, but no, you are so darn MODEST you won't let the World know what we have.

I would like to have seen what Delaware would have done if they had found this much Oil. They would have sold so much Stock that if the Pacific Ocean had been Oil it wouldn't have paid back the Buyers.

Look at Real Estate. Here we have the greatest Land and Lots that ever laid out of doors, but do we do anything with them? No! We just set here. We never advertise them; we never boost them. I wish you could see what the State of Delaware would do if they had the same class of lots that we have here. Why they would have Sub-Divisions all over the place. They would have Barbecues, and Drawings, and Screen Stars personally appearing, and men under umbrellas selling each lot. But no, we are too conservative; we like to sit here and let the stuff speak for itself. But I tell you, Fellow Old Timers, you can't do that nowadays. It's all right for a State to build up a Reputation for Modesty and be known as always having a good word to say for the other place, but I tell you we have carried it too far for our own good.

Of course I can appreciate you other old Timers' feelings in the matter. You have been here and helped build it to what it even is today, and you resent these Johnny Newcomers coming in and spoiling all of our old customs and Traditions. I know it is hard to change with the Times. We old Timers who have seen this place grow from what it was 2 and a half years ago to what it is today, must realize these stacks of young fellows coming in here the last two weeks must have the right idea, and we must begin to realize that after all it is the general welfare of the entire community we are after.

So, Fellow Members, if my little speech has been the means of changing just one of you from your Iron Clad rule of Modesty in regard to your Home state, why I will feel that my little efforts will not have been in vain.

So from now on I am for letting the World know of California, even if the rest of the State does disapprove of it, and I sit down amid HISSES from the MODEST Oldtimers.

PROMOTING THE OCEANLESS ONE PIECE SUIT

I WANT TO DO SOMETHING FOR THE HOME TOWN GIRL SO SHE CAN STAY AT HOME AND SHOW HOW AND WHAT SHE IS MADE OF.

PROMOTING THE OCEANLESS ONE PIECE SUIT

EVERYBODY at some time in life feels a call within Him or Her, as the gender may be, to try and Promote something or other, that is to form a Company and sell Stock. We have all bought so much and been stung so often that we want to try the side where the Money comes in, instead of going out.

One-third of the people in the United States promote, while the other two-thirds Provide. There are more commissions paid out to Stock Salesmen than are ever collected by Stock Buyers. So, after living honest for years, the thing naturally becomes monotonous and we feel a hankering to Promote.

Now, I had reached that stage in life where I had thought maybe I would get by clear to the end without Promoting something and sticking my Friends. But the old Bug has bit me; the old Make-it-easy-without-working has got me. So I am now branching out as a Promotor, Throwing the Rope, Chewing Gum, Acting a Fool in the Movies, Robbing Ziegfeld, and Writing for a Living. All these are side lines from now on. I am now a Promotor. A Promotor is a man who would rather stick a Friend than to sell Henry Ford a Synagogue.

Of course my proposition is different. (Did you ever hear one of them pull that Gag before?)

My proposition is of Interest to every Town of any size in America. I am forming Clubs, called Swimming or Bathing Clubs, or any Aquatic name. A great many Towns have been denied the privilege of having these Clubs, heretofore, as they were not situated near any Body of Water. Now I have been to all the prominent Beaches in the East, and this summer have had a chance to study the various Water Resorts of California.

I have paid particular attention to the Habits and procedure of Club Members and their Guests and I think I can do the same for the Non-irrigated Portion of this Country as is being enjoyed by the Tidal Wave region.

I come into your Town and start promoting (we will call it a swimming or Beach Club). I sell memberships for, we will say, the nominal sum of 500 dollars a piece. That makes it high enough to keep out the substantial people who really after all are rather old-fashioned, and allows us to take into our Club some of our most prominent Bootleggers, Oil Magnates, who have worked their way up from the bottom in the last year, and just the people of the Town who do things—in other words, the ones who belong.

We build the Club House (a rather long rambling affair) on some ground which we can get at a nominal figure (as I will explain the value of Citizens like we will have being located in their midst, and what our Club will do for the surrounding Land). Now, the great advantage that my Clubs will have over the present ones in our Beach Cities is that we will build ours right in the heart of the Town, so the Tired Business Man can reach it even for Lunch, whereas in other places they have to go miles to reach a Beach Club. We will have a Uniformed man at the door to meet the Cars, as nothing impresses the newly rich so much as Gold Braid.

Our Cafe prices will be high enough so that if a Member takes a friend any other place he will be considered rather a short Sport. Each member will have his Private Locker (including a Corkscrew), where he can change to his bathing Suit. There will be a wide Veranda under awnings where Members may dine in their Suits, and other Tables which are not protected from the Rays of the Sun, where the more Hardy Members may sit and acquire a Tan.

Of course one item of expense in connection with these Clubs which will require me to expend quite a tidy sum is having Ocean Sand transported to these Towns and then by Truck to the center of the City.

This sand must be spread very, very thick, as the principal pastime of the Members and Guests will be to lay right down in it and try and cover each other entirely up. Oh, it's a ripping experience that you in the inland Cities have missed, if you have never tried it.

Mind you, this 500 dollars which I receive per each will not all be profit as I will be called upon to purchase a Medicine Ball or so. That is a Beach Sport that only the most Athletic and reckless of our Membership would dare enter into—tossing this ferocious Ball from one to the other. I have seen a Game of it last, if there were Female Spectators, as long as three or four minutes.

Then, for the more skilled, there is Baseball on the Beach which is played with a Rubber Tennis Ball. I have seen men graduate from that right into some of our best Tea and Cake Hounds.

We will have beautifully striped Umbrellas placed at intervals over the Beach for those who become fatigued in parading. When there is a big crowd and you have to walk by everybody in your Bathing Suit it tires one more than the uninitiated would think. And we'll have a Life Guard (perhaps a Native of Honolulu if we can procure one). At any rate, we will get the most sunburned one we can, for the less fortunate ones to compare their Tan with. He will be provided with Smelling Salts, and other restoratives in case a Wife should unexpectedly discover her own Husband with some other One Piece Suit Female Companion.

70

There will be Life Lines across the sands, so the more fore-sighted of the members can find their way during the afternoon back and forth to their Lockers.

Now, I think I have enumerated all that is required to successfully operate one of these Beach Clubs. Of course, most of them heretofore have had Water but in all my experience (which runs over a term of years) I have never seen a Member willfully enter this Water. Years ago at one of the Eastern Beaches they claim a man went into the water, but this has never been verified, and so far as the ladies go, there hasn't been a swell Bathing Suit wet since Kellerman[1] retired.

Now you see my scheme. I have laid it before you. Nobody ever thought of it because they were not a close observer like I have been. They just naturally thought Water was required, but it is the most unnecessary thing connected with a Beach Club. Of course, Showers are provided for those who do not care to sleep with sand in their bed.

Just think of a Club right at your door where you can run down and change Clothes and display your figure without having to go to Palm Beach or Del Monte! Besides, I am showing you how you can display it to the People who you want to see it—not to a lot of strangers. Show it right where it will do you the most good.

If I have thought of this sooner and we had had one in my home of Claremore, Oklahoma (home of best Radium Water[2] in the World) and I could have paraded up and down with my shape, I would have been able to settle down a lot earlier.

I tell you my scheme is a boost for home Talent. Many a Girl, if she could have shown off properly at home, would have never had to leave there. Now, if you think my scheme is crazy, you go to the Ocean where there is a Beach to parade on and see how many ever go in swimming where there is nothing but Swimming Water.

No sir, the Sand and the Clothes are the thing—not the Water. So I will put my scheme over, not only for the selfish motive of making money, but because I want to do something for the home Town Girl who hasn't the money to go to Narragansett Pier to be properly appreciated, but can stay at home and show how and what she is made of.

WARNING TO JOKERS: LAY OFF THE PRINCE

SO I GOT ME SOME OF THOSE LONG-HANDLED WOODEN HAMMERS AND
STARTED IN AT POLO.

WARNING TO JOKERS: LAY OFF THE PRINCE

I WANT hereby, and hereon, to publicly issue a protest[1] to my fellow Writers, and Comedians, against the use of Cartoons, Editorials, Paragraphs, Free Verse, or any form of Public Notice, Jibing, or Poking Fun or attempting to be Funny, at the Expense of the Prince of Wales,[2] falling off his Horse.

My reasons are two fold, first on account of it being passé, and secondly on account of the happenings of the past week to my own Immediate Person. Now everything is funny as long as it is happening to somebody Else, but when it happens to you, why it seems to lose some of its Humor, and if it keeps on happening, why the entire laughter kinder Fades out of it.

Last year in New York it was one of my sure fire subjects to remark about the Prince of Wales staking himself out a six foot Claim in some part of England. And I remember one choice morsel of Gossip I had was that I was going to get appointed as Ambassador to England so I could go riding with the Prince and be able to rope his Horse and bring him Back to him. And another was, "I see where the Prince of Wales fell off his Horse again today. But that ain't News any more. If he stayed on That Would Be News." Well that always knocked the audience right back on their Flasks.

Now in those days, which was a Year ago, that was very Komical both to me and the audience. But of course now it has finally reached the Comic Strip Cartoons, really earlier than a joke generally does, and even the Editorial Writers are commenting on it, in what they term a lighter vein. Now an Editorial Writer is the last man in the World to find anything out, so you will see how old and out of date it must be to refer to now.

But all this has nothing to do with my real Reason. I always have a few old Ponies for me and the Children to play around with, so somebody said, "Will, why don't you play Polo? Anybody that can ride can play Polo." And me, like a Fool, believed him. Why, that is as absurd as saying anybody that can walk would make a good Golf Player, or anybody that looks good in a Bathing Suit will make a good swimmer.

Now I want it distinctly understood that I did not take up Polo for any Social Prestige, or to make myself pointed out as a Man about Town. If I was the Champion Polo Player of the World, I still couldn't drink a Cup of Tea without using the saucer. And another reason I always hesitated on taking up the Game was account of the White

Breeches. I had always been reared to believe that White Breeches should be concealed beneath Black or Gray ones—at least in Public.

The people that think riding a Horse is all there is to Polo, are the same people that think Curls are all there is to Mary Pickford.[3] I can also walk, but I can't sweep a Golf Ball into one of those Holes with a Broom.

So I got me some of those long handled wooden Hammers and started in at Polo. You know some men like to have their Fields harrowed and plowed, and I had not played Polo two days until I was offered a job to come over and Play on their Ground as they wanted it dug up. Finally I got so every once in a while I would hit the Ball. But it seemed like every time I hit the Ball it would get mad and go off in an opposite direction.

Well, finally I got to playing in Practice Games, more for the Comedy I would cause than through any good I might do my side. If the Purple and Whites had a Game I might wear a Purple Jersey, but in reality I would be playing with the Whites.

Then come a Polo Tournament held at Coronado Beach. So as I was scheduled to play in one of the Minor League, or Small Time events, I go down and one day we are having a Friendly practice Game with a few looking on. Three of us beginners all bump together, Mind you, we are all three on the same side. We knock our Horses down, I fall on my head and of course, am not hurt.

The Referee called an Unusual Foul. He said I had fouled by running over two of my own side. Well, the next day was the Big game; we were to play the 11th Cavalry from Monterey. They sure were a fine bunch of Boys, and hard Riders. Things were going along Pretty Good until along about the 3rd Act, I was on a new Pony who suddenly reared up and Fell Back on Me. There he was, a laying right across my Intermission. My Head was out on one side and my Feet on the other; that was all you could see. When he got up I knew for the first time how the Prince must have felt.

Well, everything goes K.O. for two more periods. I am on a Friend's Horse and coming lickerty split down the field, when for no Reason at all the horse crosses his front legs and starts turning Somersaults. They picked me up just south of Santa Barbara.

The crowd all said, "Oh that's Will Rogers the Comedian. He just does that for laughs." The Papers next day all said, "Comedian Spills off Horse Twice at Polo Game."

Now I will admit there was not quite the same Publicity given to all my various Falls as to those of the Prince. But the hurt was just as bad. Everybody that reads about it had been kidding me about being the Local Prince of Wales of America. But what I want to know from some of these Newspaper Riders is what I am supposed to do in case the Horse falls.

Are the Prince and I supposed to fall With the Horse, or are we supposed to stay up there in the air until he gets Up, and comes back up under us? Every fall that the Prince has had has been caused by a falling Horse, not by being thrown From one. In the future the Prince and I will personally pay in the papers for the extra two lines that will announce that "the Horse going down had something to do with our going off."

England is all worked up over his numerous Falls, but up to now no one has manifested much interest in any of mine, only for laughing purposes. At least none of the prominent Washington Politicians have asked me to cease my Riding. I want some concern paid to my welfare. In my falls I am not fortunate enough to spill any Royal Blood, but it's my Blood, and it's all I got. It's kinder funny but no matter how common our blood is, we hate to Lose any of it.

I saw a Picture in the Paper last summer where the Prince was on one of his Horses and its name was Will Rogers. Now I got all swelled Up when I saw he had a Horse named for me, but maybe that was the one that had been doing all this high and lofty Tumbling. As a suggestion, if our respective Countries want to do something to protect our Welfare, the best thing I can suggest would be to get us some Horses that can stand up, for the Prince and I both have to take every Precaution to protect our Looks. It would be terrible if his face was marred. And I certainly don't want anything to happen to Mine and make it look Better. My living depends on it, just as it Is.

The only thing that makes me sore is that I haven't got the nerve to do some of the riding stunts that the Prince goes after. He goes over Jumps that I wouldn't have the nerve to climb over on foot. Then if he gets a fall a lot of us alleged Humorists (who would be afraid to lead one of his horses to water with a 20 foot Halter rope) start in rewriting original Jokes about the Prince's Horsemanship.

I saw a Picture of one of his Falls, where the Horse had fallen trying for a Water Jump. Why that Jump was so wide, that I bet we haven't got a Joke Writer in this country could swim across it, and not over two could row over it.

I am not overly strong for Royalty, but if I had to have one of Them over me I don't know of one that I would rather have than this same Bird, and most of this Admiration has been won by his Horsemanship, not by the Lack of it.

Lots of women have it in for him because he has not married, But with all of them making a silly play for him, I admire his Judgment as much as his Horsemanship. So here is an appeal to my fellow

Jokesters: If you want to kid somebody on their Riding go to Central Park, don't go to England unless, as I say, you have some Solution for a man staying up while the Horse is going Down.

P. S. I only had one thing to be thankful for in my falls. I practically Ruined the only Pair of White Breeches I had, of course, it's all right with the Prince—he can wear his Daddy's. But from now on I will get to play in Chaps.

SPRING IS HERE, WITH POEMS AND
BATH TUBS

THE FAMILY WASH-TUB WAS DRAGGED UP BY THE FIRE.

SPRING IS HERE, WITH POEMS AND BATH TUBS

WELL, there has been quite a bit happened since I last communed with you. Spring is coming; I can tell by the Poetry and the Real Estate ads. A Poet exists all year just to get his Poem published in the Spring. Then when he sees it in print he starts getting next Spring's verse all ready. These early Spring Real Estate ads read, "This House is located on the shady banks of a Beautiful stream." Say, if there is a beautiful stream anywhere now the Rail Road runs along it and all you have to do is to get run over by a freight train to reach this beautiful stream.

A favorite ad is, "Beautiful Home in heart of the most exclusive Residential District, 5 Master Bedrooms and 9 baths; Owner going to Europe." Now let's just take that ad out and dissect it and see what it is.

In a Real Estate man's eye, the most exclusive part of the City is wherever he has a House to sell. The Dog Pound may be on one side and the City Incinerator on the other but it's still exclusive. And it is, too, for it will be the only house in the world so situated.

Five Master Bedrooms! Now, they get the Master junk from English ads where the man may be the master. Still, I don't know why they call all the rooms his. Over here they call them Master Bedrooms but the Wife will pick out the Poorest one for him, and keep the other 4 Good ones for Company.

Now, to the ordinary man on reading that Ad of 9 Baths, that would be an insult to his cleanliness. A Man would have to be awful Busy to support that many Baths, unless, of course, he neglected some of them. The ad might better have read, "Buy our home and live in a Bath Tub." The biggest part of City homes nowadays have more Baths than Beds. So, while they can't always ask their Company to stay all night as they have no place to put them, they can at least ask them to Bathe. So, when you are invited out now, you can always be assured of your private Bath, but you must leave before Bed-time.

When you visit a friend's newly finished Home you will be shown through all the Bath rooms, but when you leave you couldn't, to save your soul, tell where the dining room was. They seem to kinder want to camouflage or hide that nowadays. There is such little eating being done in the Homes now that a dining room is almost a lost art. Breakfast is being served in bed, Dinner at the Cabaret with dancing attached, and Lunch—no up-to-date Man would think of going anywhere but to his Clubs for lunch. Besides, didn't he hear a funny one and must get to the Club to bore his alleged friends with it? He will talk every-body's left ear off all day and come home and bite his Wife's off if she asks him to tell her the news.

And then they have such an enlightening custom nowadays. Every body of men who can think of a name have a Club. And is not Con-gressman Blindbridle, who has just returned from a free Government trip to Bermuda, going to deliver a Message at today's Luncheon on "Americanism, Or what we owe to the Flag?"

Now, as the dining room space has been eliminated to make room for an additional Bath, most of the eating, if one happens to be enter-taining at home, is done Off The Lap. This custom of slow starvation has shown vast improvement of late. Instead of the Napkins being of Paper, why, they have been supplanted by almost-linen ones with beautiful hemstitching. That's to try and get your mind off the lack of nourishment. As I say, the Napkin is hand sewn but the Lettuce Sand-wiches still come from the Delicatessen.

Why, in the good old days, they couldn't have fed you on your lap 'cause you couldn't have held all they would give you. Now you have to feel for it to find it.

But the Husband does come home some time during the Day or Night, for is not the overhead on his outlay of Baths going on all the time, and shouldn't he be getting home to get some good out of some of them?

It's not the high cost of Living that is driving us to the Poor House,—It's the high Cost of bathing. The big question today is not what are you going to pay for your plot of ground, but what kind of fixtures are you going to put in your legion of Bath Rooms. Manu-facturers of Porcelain and Tile have Supplanted the Pocket Flask as our principal commodity.

The interest on unpaid-for Bath Rooms would pay our National Debt.

Now, mind you, I am not against this modern accomplishment, or extravagance, of ours. I realize that these Manufacturers of Fixtures have advanced their Art to the point where they are practically mod-ern Michael Angelos. Where, in the old days, an Elephant Hook was almost necessary for a Wife to drag her Husband toward anything that looked like Water, today those Interior Bath Decorators can almost make one of those things inviting enough to get in without flinching.

But, in doing so, they have destroyed an American Institution, and ruined the only Calendar that a Child ever had. That was the Saturday Night Bath. Nowadays a Child just grows up in ignorance. From the Cradle to the Altar he don't know what day of the week it is. In those good old days he knew that the next morning after that weekly Ear washing he was going to Sunday School. Now he has not only eliminated the Bath on Saturday but has practically eliminated the Sunday School, for neither he nor his Parents know when Sunday comes.

But, in those days, that old Kitchen Stove was kept hot after supper. And not only the Tea Kettle was filled but other Pots and Pans, and the Family Wash Tub was dragged up by the Fire, and you went out to the Well and helped your Pa draw some Water to mix with that hot. While you was doing that, your Ma, if you stayed Lucky and had a Ma up to then,[1] was a getting out all the clean Clothes and a fixing the Buttons, and a laying out the schedule of who was to be first. And She was the only one could tell just how much hot Water to put in to make it right. And if anybody had to feel of the hot water and get burned it was always her, not you, and she found dirt behind, and in, your Ears that all the highfaluting Fixtures in the World can't find today.

Now that was an event. It meant something. It brought you closer together. But now bathing is so common there's No Kick To It. It's just *Bla!!*[2]

The Romans started this Bath Gag; now look what become of them. They used to have the most beautiful Baths, kind of a Municipal Bath, where they all met and strolled around and draped themselves on Marble Slabs. It was a kinder Society event. It compared to our modern Receptions. I have seen some beautiful Paintings of them, but I have yet to see a Scene where a Roman was in the Water. But they did look, oh, just too cunning, sunning themselves out on the Concrete Banks of those Pools. It must have been like visiting our modern Beaches, where no one can swim but the Life Guard, and they don't know that he can as he has never been called on to go in. But, like the Romans, our Girls can arrange themselves in the most bewitching shapes out on the sand, which, after all, must be much more comfortable than the Asphalt that those little Caesars had to spread themselves over.

I tell you if Baths keep on multiplying in the modern Home as they have lately it won't be 5 Years till a Bath Tub will be as necessary in a home as a Cocktail Shaker.

If two members of the same household have to use the same Bath, it is referred to now as a Community Tub.

Statistics have proven that there are 25 Bath Tubs sold to every Bible.

And fifty to every Dictionary, and 389 to every Encyclopedia.

Proving that, while we may be neglecting the Interior, we are looking after the exterior.

If the Father of our Country, George Washington, was Tutank-hamened[3] tomorrow, and, after being aroused from his Tomb, was told that the American People today spend two Billion Dollars yearly on Bathing Material, he would say, "WHAT GOT 'EM SO DIRTY?"

MR. FORD AND OTHER POLITICAL SELF-STARTERS

MR. FORD AND OTHER POLITICAL
SELF-STARTERS

WELL, there has been quite a stir in the Political News. The big news[1] was the Ford for President talk, made more important by Mr. Hearst announcing that he would back him if he run on an independent Ticket. It only shows you what both of the old line Parties are degenerating into. Nobody wants to associate with either one of them.

I think that it will be the biggest boost Mr. Ford will have that he don't belong to either Party. It's getting so if a man wants to stand well socially he can't afford to be seen with either the Democrats or the Republicans.

I expect, if it was left to a vote right now by all the people, Mr. Ford would be voted for by more people than any other man. But, if it come to a question of counting those votes, I doubt if he even run third. For, with all the mechanical improvements they have in the way of adding machines, and counting machines, they can't seem to invent anything to take the place of the old Political mode of counting —two for me and one for you.

More men have been elected between Sundown and Sunup, than ever were elected between Sunup and Sundown.[2]

Our public men are speaking every day on something, but they ain't saying anything. But when Mr. Harding[3] said that, in case of another war that capital would be drafted the same as men, he put over a thought that, if carried out, would do more to stop Wars than all the International Courts and Leagues of Nations in the World.

Of the three things to prevent wars, League of Nations, International Court, and this Drafting of Capital, this last one is so far ahead of the others there is no comparison. When that Wall Street Millionaire knows that you are not only going to come into his office and take his Secretary and Clerks but that you come in to get his Dough, say Boy, there wouldn't be any war. You will hear the question: "Yes, but how could you do it?"

Say, you take a Boy's life, don't you? When you take Boys away you take everything they have in the World, that is, their life. You send them to war and part of that life you don't use you let him come back with it. Perhaps you may use all of it. Well, that's the way to do with wealth. Take all he has, give him a bare living the same as you do the Soldier. Give him the same allowance as the Soldier—all of us that stay home. The Government should own everything we have, use what it needs to conduct the whole expenses of the war and give back what is left, if there is any, the same as you give back to the Boy what he has left.

There can be no Profiteering. The Government owns everything till the war is over. Every Man, Woman and Child, from Henry Ford and John D. down, get their Dollar and a Quarter a day the same as the Soldier. The only way a man could profiteer in war like that would be to raise more Children.

If any man[4] went before the People on a platform of that kind and put it over, he could remain President till his Whiskers got so long he could make a fortune just picking the lost Golf Balls out of them. But, no, it will never get anywhere. The rich will say it ain't practical, and the poor will never get a chance to find out if it is or not.

Lincoln made a wonderful speech under similar conditions one time: "That this Nation under God, shall have a new Birth of Freedom, and that Government of the people, by the People, for the People, shall not perish from this earth."

Now, every time a Politician gets in a speech, he digs up this Gettysburg quotation. He recites it every Decoration day and practices the opposite the other 364 days.

If our Government is by the people, how is it the Candidate with the most votes by the people, going into a Presidential Convention never got nominated?

Now, Lincoln meant well, but he only succeeded in supplying an applause line for every Political Speaker who was stuck for a finish.

And that's the way with Mr. Harding; he certainly meant well, for I can imagine his feelings after having to mingle for the last 2 years with some of our War Millionaires who are hanging around Washington, just laying off between Wars.

And, in after Years, so will this speech of Mr. Harding's be quoted, but the minute the fellow gets through quoting it he will go sign a War Contract for Cost Plus 10 percent.

In our Decoration day speechmaking Mr. Taft[5] spoke at some unveiling of a Monument in Cincinnati. He made an Alibi for the Supreme Court. I don't know what prompted him to tell the dead what the Court was doing, unless it was some man who had died of old age waiting for a decision from that August Body.

We can always depend on Judge Gary for a weekly laugh in his speeches. But lately[6] he had the prize wheeze of his career. He had his accomplices make an investigation of the Steel Industry, and they turned in a report that it was much more beneficial to man to work 12 hours a day than 8. They made this report so alluring that it is apt to make people who read it decide to stay the extra 4 hours on their jobs, just through the Health and enjoyment they get out of it. I never knew Steel work was so easy till I read that report. Why, the advantages they enumerated in this report would almost make a Bootlegger trade jobs with a Steel Worker. But here is the kick. Judge Gary got up to read this report before the stock holders who had made it out. He read for one hour in favor of a 12 hour day. Then he was so exhausted they had to carry him out, and Charley Schwab had to go on reading the sheet.

Now, if the Judge couldn't work an hour, how did he expect his workers to do 12 every day?

After Schwab read for 2 hours the audience was carried out.

It was the greatest boost for the 12 hour day I ever heard of. I am thinking of going out there and working for them, but, if it is such a pleasure to work 12 hours, I am going to try and get them to let me work 18, at least, for I don't believe I would get enough pleasure out of just 12.

So if you don't hear of me next week, you will know I just enjoyed myself to death in Judge Gary's Steel Mills in Pittsburgh.

WILSON COULD LAUGH AT A JOKE ON
HIMSELF

FINALLY A WARDEN KNOCKED AT MY DRESSING ROOM AND SAID: "YOU DIE IN 5 MORE MINUTES FOR KIDDING YOUR COUNTRY."

WILSON COULD LAUGH AT A JOKE ON HIMSELF

SOME of the most glowing and deserved tributes ever paid to the memory of an American have been paid[1] to our past President Woodrow Wilson.[2] They have been paid by learned men of this and all Nations, who knew what to say and how to express their feelings. They spoke of their close association and personal contact with him. Now I want to add my little mite even though it be of no importance.

I want to speak and tell of him as I knew him for he was my friend. We of the stage know that our audiences are our best friends, and he was the greatest Audience of any Public Man we ever had. I want to tell of him as I knew him across the footlights. A great many Actors and Professional people have appeared before him, on various occasions in wonderful high class endeavors. But I don't think that any person met him across the footlights in exactly the personal way that I did on five different occasions.

Every other Performer or Actor did before him exactly what they had done before other audiences on the night previous, but I gave a great deal of time and thought to an Act for him, most of which would never be used again and had never been used before. Owing to the style of Act I used, my stuff depended a great deal on what had happened that particular day or week. It just seemed by an odd chance for me every time I played before President Wilson that on that particular day there had been something of great importance that he had just been dealing with. For you must remember that each day was a day of great stress with him. He had no easy days. So when I could go into a Theatre and get laughs out of our President by poking fun at some turn in our National affairs, I don't mind telling you it was the happiest moments of my entire career on the stage.

The first time I shall never forget, for it was the most impressive and for me the most nervous one of them all. The Friars Club of New York one of the biggest Theatrical Social Clubs in New York had decided to make a whirlwind Tour of the principal Cities of the East all in one week. We played a different City every night. We made a one night stand out of Chicago and New York. We were billed for Baltimore but not for Washington. President Wilson came over from Washington to see the performance. It was the first time in Theatrical History that the President of the United States came over[3] to Baltimore just to see a Comedy.

It was just at the time we were having our little Set Too, with Mexico, and when we were at the height of our Note Exchanging career with Germany and Austria. The house was packed with the Elite of Baltimore.

The Show was going great. It was a collection of clever Skits, written mostly by our stage's greatest Man, George M. Cohan, and even down to the minor bits was played by Stars with big Reputations. I was the least known member of the entire Aggregation, doing my little specialty with a Rope and telling Jokes on National affairs, just a very ordinary little Vaudeville act by chance sandwiched in among this great array.

I was on late, and as the show went along I would walk out of the Stage door and out on the Street and try to kill the time and nervousness until it was time to dress and go on. I had never told Jokes even to a President, much less about one, especially to his face. Well, I am not kidding you when I tell you that I was scared to death. I am always nervous. I never saw an Audience that I ever faced with any confidence. For no man can ever tell how a given Audience will ever take anything.

But here I was, nothing but a very ordinary Oklahoma Cowpuncher who had learned to[4] read the Daily Papers a little, going out before the Aristocracy of Baltimore, and the President of the United States, and kid about some of the Policies with which he was shaping the Destinies of Nations.

How was I to know but what the audience would rise up in mass and resent it? I had never heard, and I don't think any one else had ever heard of a President being joked personally in a Public Theatre about the Policies of his administration.

The nearer the time come the worse scared I got, George Cohan, and Willie Collier,[5] and others, knowing how I felt, would pat me on the back and tell me, "Why he is just a Human Being; go on out and do your stuff." Well if somebody had come through the dressing room and hollered "Train for Claremore Oklahoma leaving at once," I would have been on it. This may sound strange but any who have had the experience know, that a Presidential appearance in a Theatre, especially outside Washington, D.C. is a very Rare and unique feeling even to the Audience. They are keyed up almost as much as the Actors.

At the time of his entrance into the House, everybody stood up, and there were Plain Clothes men all over the place, back stage and behind his Box. How was I to know but what one of them might not take a shot at me if I said anything about him personally?

Finally a Warden knocked at my dressing room door and said, "You die in 5 more minutes for kidding your Country". They just literally shoved me out on the Stage.

Now, by a stroke of what I call good fortune, (for I will keep

94

them always) I have a copy of the entire Acts that I did for President Wilson on the Five times I worked for him. My first remark in Baltimore was, "I am kinder nervous here tonight." Now that is not an especially bright remark, and I don't hope to go down in History on the strength of it, but it was so apparent to the audience that I was speaking the truth that they laughed heartily at it. After all, we all love honesty.

Then I said, "I shouldn't be nervous, for this is really my second Presidential appearance. The first time was when Bryan spoke in our town once, and I was to follow his speech and do my little Roping Act." Well, I heard them laughing, so I took a sly glance at the President's Box and sure enough he was laughing just as big as any one. So I went on, "As I say, I was to follow him, but he spoke so long that it was so dark when he finished, they couldn't see my Roping." That went over great, so I said "I wonder what ever become of him." That was all right, it got over, but still I had made no direct reference to the President.

Now Pershing[6] was in Mexico at the time, and there was a lot in the Papers for and against the invasion. I said "I see where they have captured Villa.[7] Yes, they got him in the morning Editions and the Afternoon ones let him get away." Now everybody in the house before they would laugh looked at the President, to see how he was going to take it. Well, he started laughing and they all followed suit.

"Villa raided Columbus New Mexico. We had a man on guard that night at the Post. But to show you how crooked this Villa is, he sneaked up on the opposite side." "We chased him over the line 5 miles, but run into a lot of Government Red Tape and had to come back." "There is some talk of getting a Machine Gun if we can borrow one. The one we have now they are using to train our Army with in Plattsburg. If we go to war we will just have to go to the trouble of getting another Gun."

Now, mind you, he was being criticized[8] on all sides for lack of preparedness, yet he sat there and led that entire audience in laughing at the ones on himself.

At that time there was talk of forming an Army of 2 hundred thousand men, so I said, "we are going to have an Army of 2 hundred thousand men. Mr. Ford makes 3 hundred thousand Cars every year. I think, Mr. President, we ought to at least have a Man to every Car." "See where they got Villa hemmed in between the Atlantic and Pacific. Now all we got to do is to stop up both ends." "Pershing located him at a Town called, Los Quas Ka Jasbo. Now all we have to do is to locate Los Quas Ka Jasbo." "I see by a headline that Villa escapes Net and Flees. We will never catch him then. Any Mexican that can escape Fleas is beyond catching." "But we are doing better toward preparedness now, as one of my Senators from Oklahoma has sent home a double portion of Garden Seed."

After various other ones on Mexico I started in on European affairs which at that time was long before we entered the war. "We are facing another Crisis tonight, but our President here has had so many of them lately that he can just lay right down and sleep beside one of those things."

Then I first pulled the one which I am proud to say he afterwards repeated to various friends as the best one told on him during the War. I said, "President Wilson is getting along fine now to what he was a few months ago. Do you realize, People, that at one time in our negotiations with Germany that he was 5 Notes behind?"

How he did laugh at that! Well, due to him being a good fellow and setting a real example, I had the proudest and most successful night I ever had on the stage. I had lots of Gags on other subjects but the ones on him were the heartiest laughs with him, and so it was on all the other occasions I played for him. He come back Stage at intermission and chatted and shook hands with all.

Some time I would like to tell of things he laughed at during the most serious stages of the Great War. Just think there were hundreds of millions of Human Beings interested directly in that terrible War, and yet out of all of them he stands, 5 years after it's over, as the greatest man connected with it. What he stood for and died for, will be strived after for years.

But it will take time for with all our advancement and boasted Civilization, it's hard to stamp out selfishness and Greed. For after all, Nations are nothing but Individuals, and you can't stop even Brothers from fighting sometimes. But he helped it along a lot. And what a wonderful cause to have laid down your life for! The World lost a Friend. The Theatre lost its greatest supporter. And I lost the most distinguished Person who ever laughed at my little nonsensical jokes. I looked forward to it every year. Now I have only to look back on it as my greatest memory.

A JOB WITH THE JAMES FAMILY

I COULD JUST SORTER NONCHALANTLY STEP ON THE BRIDE'S TRAIN.

A JOB WITH THE JAMES FAMILY[1]

Mr. Warren Gamaliel Harding.
 President of these United States and
  Viceroy of the District of Columbia.
  Chevy Chase Golf Club, Washington, D. C.

My dear Mr. President,

I see where Mr. Harvey (I mean Col. or, rather, Ambassador) Harvey[2] is coming back here again. Now I don't know if it's a slumming trip or just what it is, as he was here a few days ago. Maybe he forgot something in one of his Speeches and is coming back for an Encore. But in a later Paper I see where he is talking of resigning and not going back. Now, if that is the case, I hereby make this an open letter to you, Mr. President, as an application to take said Mr. Harvey (I mean Editor) Harvey's place.

I can tell by observation that it does not come under the Civil Service or competitive examination. Neither, on the other hand, is it a purely Political appointment, as Mr. Harvey adapted his Politics to fit the occasion. Now that would not be even necessary in my case as I have no Politics. I am for the Party that is out of Power, no matter which one it is. But I will give you my word that, in case of my appointment, I will not be a Republican; I will do my best to pull with you, and not embarrass you. In fact, my views on European affairs are so in accord with You, Mr. President, that I might almost be suspected of being a Democrat.

Now I want to enumerate a few of my qualifications for the position of Ambassador to the Court of James (I don't know whether it's St. or Jesse). But, anyway, it's some of the James Family.

My principal qualification would be my experience in Speechmaking. That, as statistics have proven, is 90 percent of the duties of a Diplomat. Now I can't make as many speeches as my predecessor, unless, of course, I trained for it. But I would figure on making up in quality any shortcomings I might have in endurance. For you know, Mr. President, there is no Race or People in the world who appreciate quality as the English do.

Now, the way I figure it out, what one has to do is to make his speeches so that they will sound one way to the English, and the direct opposite to the Hearst readers back over here. Now George (I don't mean King; I mean Col.) was rather unfortunate in that respect; he made them so they would sound two ways, but both Nations took the wrong way.

Now, for instance, if I wanted Mr. Balfour[3] to take something

99

back, I would just kid him into it; make him believe I didn't care whether he took it back or not. You know how it is, just like the Democrat Senators do with Lodge.

Another qualification that must not by any means be understimated is my Moving Picture experience. You see, for an official position nowadays, we must pay more attention to how our public men screen if we are to have to look at them every day in the news films. We must not only get men with screen personality, but we must get men who know Camera angles and know when they are getting the worst of it in a picture and not be caught in the background during the taking of some big event.

Europeans are far ahead of us in this line of Diplomacy, and, if you don't watch them, you are liable to be found photographed with the Mob instead of the Principals. The thing is to do some little thing during the taking of the picture that will draw the audience's attention to you. For instance, during some Court ceremony, I could just playfully kick the King. Now you don't know how a little thing like that would get over with the public. Or, at one of the big weddings in the Abbey, I could just sorter nonchalantly step on the bride's train, as they passed by, perhaps ripping it off, or any little Diplomatic move like that. You don't realize how just little bits like that would make our Ambassador stand out over all the other Countries.

We have had an example of screen training right here at home. Take Josephus Daniels[4] when he was working. We spent 4 years sitting in Picture Houses watching him launch Ships, and at every launching he could place himself at such an angle that you not only could not see the Democratic Governor's Daughter who was to break the Ginger Ale, but you couldn't even see the Ship. Now that was not accidental; that was Art.

And did you ever notice in the weekly News pictures how some Senators can take a chew of Tobacco right in the scene and you catch yourself watching them and no one else? Now those are just a few of the little things that we have to look after if we want to hold our own as the greatest Credit Nation north of Mexico.

Now, another thing, I ride horseback, so the Prince of Wales and I could ride together and, on account of my experience with the rope, I could catch his horse for him.

Then I play a little Polo, just enough to get hit in the mouth, but the English would enjoy that. When they heard the American Ambassador had got hit in the mouth and would have to cancel his speech at the Pilgrims Club, why, that would of course be good news to everybody. You see you have to give as well as receive in the Diplomatic Circles.

Now, to offset the above mentioned qualifications, I may lack a few Social ones, but what I lacked in knowledge I could make up in tact. I would not at any dinner pick up a single weapon until I saw what the Hostess was going to operate with first. When in doubt, tell a funny story till you see what the other fellow is going to do.

Then, of course, any glaring error on my part would be laid onto the customs of my Country and not on me personally.

Then I have an economy measure to recommend me. The Government is putting into commission the Leviathan, our biggest Ship, and I could, by entertaining on the Boat going over, save passage fee. I could arrange a Monologue on, "The Benefits and Accomplishments of Prohibition," and, as we pass the three mile limit, I could start in delivering it and perhaps relieve, or rather add to, the dryness of the trip. We would have to explain this to the Farmers of the country so they would not think the ship was getting this feature for nothing. It could not be considered as Ship Subsidy.

Now the feature that I feel rather modest about referring to, but which is really my principal asset, is my being able to wear Silk Knee Breeches—not only wear them, but what I mean, look like something in them.

It seems that the Lord instead of distributing my very few good points around as he does on most homely men, why, he just placed all of mine from the knee down. Now that this thing has come over there, it almost seems like I was inspired for the part. Say, I can put on those silk Rompers and clean up. Now I don't like to grab off a Guy's job by knocking him, but you know we haven't had a decent looking leg over there in years. Now Harvey's! Oh, but what's the use of arguing? You know you can't stay in the Follies 7 years on nothing. Well, it wasn't my good looks. So what was it but my Shape?

That brings us down to Golf. Now I will have to admit that my political education has been sadly neglected as I have never walked over many green pastures. Horses are too cheap for a man to spend half his life walking over the country looking for holes in the ground. But as I understand this lack of Golf will not handicap me in England as it would never here, as Mr. Volstead[5] has not percolated into that land and the game is still fought out at the 19th hole. And, if I do say it myself, I do talk a corking Game of Golf. Then another thing, in looking over the results of the last two International Golf Tournaments I don't think they play the game there at all.

Now, Mr. President, if this suggestion receives the consideration that I think it deserves, I should like to get the appointment at once, as I want to get over there before all the king's Children are married. If one can't attend a royal marriage, why, their ambassadorship has been a failure as far as publicity is concerned for that event is the World's Series of England.

Now, if you can't send me there, don't, just because I have criticized some of the feminine members of official life in Washington, don't, for the Lord's sake, send me to Chile or Honduras or some of the outlandish places. I will even promise to hush rather than that.

Now, as to Salary, I will do just the same as the rest of the Politicians— accept a small salary as pin Money, AND TAKE A CHANCE ON WHAT I CAN GET.

Awaiting an early reply, I remain

Yours faithfully,

WILL ROGERS.

P.S. If you don't want me, Turkey wants me to represent them in Washington. So where would you rather have me—in England or Washington?

LET'S TREAT OUR PRESIDENTS LIKE
HUMAN BEINGS

LET'S TREAT OUR PRESIDENTS LIKE
HUMAN BEINGS

AS I am writing this away out here in California days before you read it, it's Sunday and everybody's thoughts and sympathies are with a train rushing clear across our Country, passing sorrowfully through little Towns with Just Folks standing bareheaded paying their respects to Just Folks going back to Marion to stay with Just Folks.[1]

He goes to his resting place a Martyr, a martyr to the Boneheadedness of Reception Committees. You wouldn't ask your hired man to do in one week the amount of real physical work that each Committee asked him to do on one day Imagine three long Speeches in one day in Seattle at different places, and Parade for two hours in the hot Sun with his hat off most of the time, besides a thousand other things he was asked to do.

Just suppose for instance you had a Guest coming to visit you. Would you start in having him entertain the Neighbors the minute he got in the House, and then keep every minute of his time occupied till train time, and then turn him over to the next bunch? Why, no, you wouldn't think of such a thing. The first thing you think of when a friend comes from a long Journey is to have him rest, but because it is your President he don't need any. So when the next Congress meets they should pass a law to shoot all Reception Committees, or teach them consideration for other People.

If Jack Dempsey had left Washington and undertaken this same strain, when he got back Uncle Joe Cannon[2] could have licked him.

Any of you who have slept, or tried to, on a Train at Night and got into a Town early in the morning, you know you don't feel like speaking or Parading. You want to go to a Hotel and go to bed. Now can you imagine the President's case? Every morning at 6 A. M. to be awakened by a Band (it wouldn't be so bad if it was a good Band) and you look out and there is the Town's best Citizens in Antique Hats, ready to show you the Fire House, the new Aqueduct, the High School, and City Hall. The smell of the Moth Balls from the long tail Coats of the Committee morning after morning, would give a man some kind of disease.

Now, every man on that Committee was nearly tired out at night and took a vacation the next day, but the President must go right on the same thing the next day, only worse, for every Town was trying to outdo the other. It's not only a hardship on the People you are entertaining but hard on everybody participating.

One Town will have a Flag composed of 5 thousand children,

assembled and standing in the Hot sun for hours, not only spoiling their whole day but subjecting them to every known contagious disease. The next Town to be original will get 10 thousand Children to make up their Flag, and Make Their Parade 10 Miles as the Last One Only Paraded 5, even if they have to exhaust their Guest to do it.

Then, of course, he is always asked to speak out in the open. They have 60 acre Fields and put seats around them and call 'em Stadiums, and expect a man to talk in them. Anyone who has ever spoken outdoors knows what outdoor speaking does to your voice The Town with the cheapest land and most Concrete can have the largest Stadium.

I have always claimed that parades should be classed as a Nuisance and participants should be subject to a term in prison. They stop more work, inconvenience more People, stop more traffic, cause more accidents, entail more expense, and commit and cause I don't remember the other hundred misdemeanors. And what good are they? Half of them going along you don't know who they are, or what they are for. Even the People in them hate 'em. The most popular joke I had after the War in New York when the Boys were coming back and parading every day was, "If we really wanted to honor our Boys, why didn't we let them sit on the reviewing stands and make the people march those 15 miles?" They didn't want to parade, they wanted to go home and rest. But they wouldn't discharge a Soldier as long as they could find a new Street in a Town that he hadn't marched down, yet.

Of course, keep Circus Parades, for they really give enjoyment not only to kids but us old ones, too. As a remedy for this parading I would suggest that each Town set aside one Street, away out where there is nothing to interfere and give them that as Parade Street; then when some fellow or gang wants to try out a new Uniform or honor somebody, why let them parade up and down there just as long as they want to. If you think Parading is popular just see how many would go over there to see it. Parades nowadays think they are drawing a crowd when it's only people trying to get across the street to their business, not to see you Parade at all. So just set them aside a Street—that will stop it. The minute a Parader sees that no one is watching him he will stop and in that way you will eliminate all Parades.

I was on the Reception Committee of the Movie Industry that was to have met the President here in Los Angeles. Well, just as an example of what I said about the others, they decided that it might be showing partiality if they took him to any one Studio, so they decided to take him to all of them. In that way they could take up his entire time. Now, no one knew whether he wanted to go to any of them or

106

not; we were deciding for him. Can you imagine being a Guest of the City of Carnegie, Pa., and the Committee showing you through all the Steel mills in Town?

Now, President Harding was quite an admirer of the Movies so I imagine he liked sausage, too. But Chicago didn't rush him off to the Packing Houses the minute he got there, to see it made.

According to his itinerary here, he was allowed 15 minutes to call on an Aunt whom he hadn't seen in years that lived here. That was to be his only relaxation while here. We were waiting to see how long Frisco's Parade would run so we could run ours longer.

Now, as just an example of the trip, he loved Golf (and as the later sad events have proven) it was good for him; it was the very Recreation needed. But do you think these Committees let him do it? No Sir, he only got out three times on the entire trip. I offered a suggestion here when they were making the arrangements, but like everything coming from a Comedian it was considered not practical. I wanted to let the Reception Committee go ahead and rent the Suits and be at the Station looking Funny just like these others he was used to day after day, but instead of dragging him off where he didn't know where he was going, why just say, "Mr. President, we have engaged a room at the Central Hotel. Here's a Ford Car at your disposal. Here's a Card to any Golf Course in our Town. Now we know you are tired, so you just make yourself at home these few days; do just as you please, we have no plans for you at all."

Well, my plan wasn't adopted; it was too late. But if it had been even partly tried in all the Towns on this trip we would have all been happy and had him with us today. The first Town that ever does do that with their visiting Guests and treat them as if Human, they will soon be wondering where all their popularity comes from.

You may have read in the Papers last year that the Diplomatic Relations were strained between President Harding and some of my Jokes on the Administration. Now, I want to say that nothing was farther from the truth. That was simply newspaper stuff. It was reported that he couldn't stand Jokes about the Administration. Why, he had a great sense of Humor and could stand all the jokes ever told about him or his Policies. The first time I met him Will Hays[3] introduced me to him in the White House and he repeated to me a lot of jokes that I had told away before.

And I told him then: "Now Mr. Harding, I don't want you to think I am hard on you—all. You know I told some pretty hard ones on the Democrats when they were in; in fact I think I told funnier ones on the Democrats, as they were doing funnier things." I explained to him that it would not be fair to the Democrats to kid them

107

while they were down, but the minute they get their head above Water again I will take a whack at them.[4]

I met Will Hays just before I left New York in June and he said, "Will, I had lunch with the President last week and he had me tell him all your new stuff on the Administration."

No, I don't think I ever hurt any man's feelings by my little gags. I know I never wilfully did it. When I have to do that to make a living I will quit. I may not have always said just what they would have liked me to say but they knew it was meant in good nature.

I never go to Detroit that I don't spend an entire day out with Henry Ford and I don't suppose there is a man living (barring the owners) that have told any more jokes on him than I have.

I liked President Harding. You see I had met him, and I don't believe any man could meet him and talk to him and not like him. Why, I said after first meeting him, "I thought I would be scared when they took me in but he made me feel just like talking to some good old prosperous Ranchman out home." That's why I can understand him wanting to meet as many people personally as possible, for to meet him meant another friend.

I only hope our Future Presidents can be gifted with his Sense of Humor and Justice.

He was a mighty good friend to us Theatrical People; he was a good friend to ALL kinds of People.

For he had the right dope after all. Everybody is JUST FOLKS. HE WAS A REAL HONEST-TO-GOD-MAN.

WHAT WITH FRUIT JUICE AND CON-
SOMME, IT WAS A WILD PARTY

IF MR. FORD HAD BEEN ELECTED WE WOULD HAVE BEEN THE MOUTHPIECE
OF THE ADMINISTRATION.

WHAT WITH FRUIT JUICE AND CONSOMME,
IT WAS A WILD PARTY

The Illiterate Digest[1] is a weekly publication, devoted to straight reading matter. We have no picture section and I doubt if we will appeal to over 1%, of the Public as the success of a Publication is based nowadays on the amount of Pictures and Advertising that they have in them. Of course, all our news comes by Radio. But The Digest is a tried and operating Paper. In fact we are old timers in the field. This is our 4th issue and we have just bought out and combined The Weekly Blowout, a paper that was sponsoring Mr. Ford's Detour to the White House. After his famous announcement that 90 per cent of the People in this Country were satisfied, why, The Blowout[2] would have become the mouthpiece of the Administration. So, while not crowing over the misfortune of a Competitor, we were able to procure the Title of said Paper as soon as it had lost the chances of getting our Government run as Mr. Ford would have run it on a "Tighten a Bolt as it Goes By" system. Now the Digest and Blowout combined, is looking for some other likely Candidate to boost. We have even got down to such sore straits that a Populist would not be overlooked.

The Digest has some real inside Hollywood dirt to dish up to you.[3] For fear some competitor will get in and publish it first I will tell just what happened at a Wild Party that was given tonight at the home of the Editor of this very Gem of Truth. And what makes it worse the head of our Industry that was hired and supposed to keep the Scandal from our doorsteps, was the main Guest, Will Hays (the only man in the history of Industry that was ever hired for a job without him or the People that hired him knowing what he was hired for, yet still made so good they couldn't replace him). Will Hays, the man who made Harding President, and the Movies (partly) behave.

Well my Wife and I, aided and encouraged by Daughter Mary decided to put on a Wild Party. Hollywood had been getting all the Publicity and selling all the Real Estate through their Scandal, and here was Beverly Hills who could put it on just as Wild as they could, and we couldn't seem to get anywhere. So we looked around to find some Guest that would be well enough known, so that when we carried him home he would be recognized.

We thought of Will Hays. So about 6:30 P.M. who should come staggering in from across the street from the Hotel but our Guest. His brother was to have come with him, but the Brother is a Lawyer from Sullivan, Indiana, and not having had the experience and capacity of

Will he had gone completely[4] out earlier in the evening while being entertained by The Womans' Federation of Churches.

Well, Will was so loaded that he had on a dress suit. It was the first one that had ever been in our House, so Bill Jr. and Jim, who had just come in from Public School and refilled their Flasks[5] commenced to laugh at the Suit, and we put a sheet over the Chairs so that he wouldn't get it dirty.

But by this time he was feeling so good he didn't care anyway, for the Industry had bought it for him—and about this time another Guest who lives right near fell into the door before we knew it. That was Miss Pauline Frederick.[6]

She was all primed for a real old prolonged Rough House. She had brought the stuff along with her. She had under her arm a big bag of knitting. She was knitting a Blanket for one of my Polo Ponies. So we all staggered around there till one of the children thought of introducing Miss Frederick and Will.

Then, to make the Party real devilish I was to go and get another man's wife while he was away at work. She lived next door, so I sneaked out while my Wife wasn't looking and dashed right into the home of the young Mrs. Cornelius Vanderbilt Jrs.[7] She slipped on something and we both complimented each other on account of her Husband having to be at the office getting out his Newspaper. She asked if the Party was to be so wild that she should take her Gun. I said, "Sure, let's do it right." So we blew back just as they are ready to get real wild and start eating.

By this time Jim and Bill are becoming reconciled to Hays' suit and start playing Baseball in the House. Hollywood can't put on anything wilder than that. Hays by this time is feeling so good he is telling a story complimenting a Democrat.

We all start off with a Fruit Cocktail and everybody commenced to loosen up and tell their right Salaries. Then comes some Consomme and I can tell you this old mixing of drinks is getting in its work. Daughter Mary started doing a Wild dance in the Living Room until Jim laid her out with a Baseball Bat. Then Hays got to telling what his Boy could do, and the party just went from one Debauch into another.[8]

Will told us of his trip to England with Ambassador Harvey. He said he went for pleasure, and I tried to get him to really tell what he went for. I think it was to get the Prince of Wales to come out for Coolidge.

Between drinks of Broiled Chicken I tried to find out if he was going to be the Campaign Manager for Mr. Coolidge. But he seemed to think it was such a sure fire thing, that they would waste some less expensive man. I kinder sobered up for a minute and asked him what he thought they would do in this investigation into the Tea Pot Dome Oil Lease. He said he didn't think they could show where Sinclair[9] ever gave Sectry Fall[10] anything. He knew Sinclair was too smooth a giver for that.

I asked him what he thinks of us sending Warships to Mexico. So he tells me what a hard time they had getting down there. Washington wired to the nearest one to go down and it runs on the rocks before they got through reading the telegram. You know our Navigators now depend on Radio to tell them where they are.

The Navy hasn't had a Compass in three years. They start on a trip and the radio operator tunes in and gets Paul Whiteman's[11] Orchestra playing somewhere, and when he comes to he is in a lifeboat. Bedtime stories have put 9 ships to sleep.

Then I asked him who we were going to protect down there, he said, why the Oil Men. I asked him who protects the Mexican Sheep Herder in this Country if somebody interferes with his Industry, and if Mexico had a Navy could she send it up here to protect him. He said No. So the moral of this is, Be an Oil Man not a Sheep Herder, and be sure to be born in a Country that has a Navy.

By this time we are so full we have to leave the table, and the noise of moving chairs is something deafening.

It's now eight thirty and the neighbors can see the light in our house and begin to phone in about it to the Police. Miss Fredericks' Yarn runs out, and she begins to yawn. Jim, Mary and Bill being younger and less unaccustomed to the revelry, had to be literally carried to their beds. Scandal was running rampant, while my wife was getting them off. That left Bill and I with the two Women. I says, "What will we do, Bill," and he says, "Oh, I am in for anything." So I just up and said, "Let's go down to the barn and look at the Horses." So out we staggered at 9 o'clock in the night in the heart of Beverly Hills. Bill Hays, a man that is a leader in the Presbyterian Church—but it only shows you when this old Movie Spirit gets in you, you will do anything.

I lasso four or five horses and bring them out and show them to Bill, but he is all excited talking to the Ladies. They wanted to take a ride, but I didn't want to carry this thing too far. So we go back to the house and I finally get them into their Coats and Hats and walk them home.

My Wife and I we figure the walk will do them good. So when we come back and get in the house why it's actually 9:15.

So I hope by the aid of Bill to put old Beverley Hills on the map. as a Wild Town. Bill says to me, "Will, if the Woman's Club ever find this out they will stop your pictures". I says "That's a good joke on the Woman's Club, my Pictures have never started."

I know all the papers will have this so I just want to beat them to it.

WHAT WE NEED IS MORE FRED STONES

HE STARTED AT FOUR OR FIVE YEARS OF AGE AND HAS WORKED ON NEW
STUNTS EVERY DAY OF HIS LIFE.

WHAT WE NEED IS MORE FRED STONES[1]

NOW I am not going to tell you any jokes today as jokes are not good for you to read every day. You will have to look to the Washington dispatches from Congress for your humor.[2]

A Comedian is not supposed to be serious nor to know much. As long as he is silly enough to get laughs, why, people let it go at that. But I claim you have to have a serious streak in you or you can't see the funny side in the other fellow. Last Sunday night a Young Girl who had made a big hit in the Salvation Army preaching on the Street in New York, decided to go out and give religious Lectures of her own. So on her first appearance I was asked by her to introduce her. She said she would rather have me than a Preacher, or a Politician, or any one else. Well, I could understand being picked in preference to a Politician, as that is one Class us Comedians have it on for public respect, but to be chosen in preference to a Preacher was something new and novel.

The meeting was held in a Theatre, as you have to fool some New Yorkers to get them in to hear a Sermon. Well, it took no great stretch of imagination to say something good for the Salvation Army, which, by the way, lots of People think was made by the late war. Why, the Salvation Army was just as great 10 years ago as it is today—not so big, but just as great. Ask any down-and-out fellow and he will tell you he knew of the good of the Salvation Army long before he ever heard there was a Kaiser.

Well, it seems like a Coincidence that, as I was trying to say something in a serious way for the first time before a New York Audience, why, away out in Butte, Montana, the best friend I have was going up to a Minister with a Bible in his hand and asking him if he didn't think "the Lord would recognize a Comedian."

So that is why you will get this Story and no jokes today.

Now a great many people, knowing my regard and friendship for Fred Stone, asked me if I was surprised. No, I was not. It was the shortest jump, from his life to a religious one, that any man ever made.

But it was a BIG thing to do, and I am certainly pleased that he did it, for it will have a tremendous influence for good, not only on the people of our profession but on every one who reads about it. When you consider that the biggest and highest salaried and busiest Man we have in our profession can stop and give some of his time to religion, it is a lesson·to the rest of us. Now, it has been my good fortune to have been very close friends with Fred for years. I have lived

117

in his home and spend all my spare time there while playing in New York. We Rope and Ride and play together all the time. He has two wonderful homes on Long Island, one all fixed up like a Western Ranch with lots of Horses and a Polo field of his own on his place.

Then I am asked why he did this do I suppose. He did it because from childhood he had been raised up by the Dearest old Mother and Father you ever saw. That Christian teaching which she put into his head as a little Kid, when he started out doing a Tight Rope walking act in a little Circus, is just coming out. He was brought up to do right and never knew anything else. Just to watch him with his Mother and Father today you will understand he didn't have to go far to see a Preacher.

Then he has the most ideal home life. His every thought is for his Family. His Wife is of the profession, and I have often heard my Wife say that Mrs. Stone is the most wonderful and devoted Mother she ever saw (and Women have a way of knowing those things).

And three lovely Daughters, the oldest, Dorothy,[3] 18,[4] who is with him in his show and is as talented as her Father and Mother. And so are the others. All are being trained for a Stage career. So you see he don't think so bad of the Stage.

He is the best loved Actor on the Stage today. He plays to the highest type audience of any Musical Show. He is the only Musical comedy comedian that has Matinees packed with Children, for none of our other Musical Comedy Comedians has ever been able to please the Children and the grown ups too. He is as great a Pantomimist on the stage as Chaplin[5] is on the screen.

Now, people must not get the idea that this is a remote case in our Business. It is, of course, on account of the prominence of the man that we have heard so much of it, and if he had known that it would be broadcasted in this way it would have been the only thing to make him hesitate. No one can say that Fred Stone was ever a publicity seeker. He is too sincere in all he does for that. I think if all Churches in communities where Theatrical people live were canvassed you would find there are as many of them in attendance as any other line of people. And when you come to Charity and trying to help some one who is in need, you will find them, not only holding their own, but far in the lead of any other class.

This could not have come at a more opportune time as Preachers all over are telling us that there is a gradual weaning away from the Church. If this will only make people think for a little it will have done worlds of good.

I have sometimes wondered if the Preachers themselves have not something to do with this. You hear or read a sermon nowadays and the biggest part of it is taken up by knocking or trying to prove the falseness of some other denomination. They say that the Catholics are Damned, that the Jews' religion is all wrong, or that the Christian Scientists are a fake, or that the Protestants are all out of step.

Now just suppose, for a change, they preached to you about the Lord and not about the other fellow's Church, for every man's religion is good. There is none of it bad. We are all trying to arrive at the same place according to our own conscience and teachings. It don't matter which Road you take.

Suppose you heard a Preacher say, "I don't care if you join my Church or the other fellow's across the street. I don't claim mine to be better or worse than any other. But get with somebody and try and do better." Hunt out and talk about the good that is in the other fellow's Church, not the bad, and you will do away with all this religious hatred you hear so much of nowadays. Then you will not only have one Fred Stone but Millions of them.

Besides, it's not that we need more people just to join Churches. It's that we need more Fred Stones, either in or out of a Church. For this Man's life is an object lesson to every Young Man or Boy starting out on a career in any line of business. Sincerity put him where he is. He never faked. No man his age in America has worked harder and been more conscientious.

Another coincidence that happened[6] applies directly to this case. I was called on to testify in Court if I thought a certain Team of Popular performers were UNIQUE AND EXTRAORDINARY.[7] The whole case was based on those two words. Now those two words mean a terrible lot. They mean you must do something that no one else can do. So, regardless of the popularity of the two performers and with all due regard for all that others can do, I said they were not.

And I claim that the only one I know of in our entire profession who I could rightly claim was unique and Extraordinary is this man that went into a store and asked for a Bible. Went out and studied it according to his best knowledge. (Which, by the way, is not so much as Book learning goes. As Fred and I have figured up once. He got as far as the fourth reader while I only reached the third. So that is why I think we always hit it off together so well, neither was liable to use a word which the other couldn't understand.)

Fred Stone can do more things and do them well than any man in or out of the Show Business or the Movies.

Why can he?

He is 49 years old and has spent 45 years practicing. Now, we have not another man in America that has done that. He started at 4 or 5 years of age and has worked on new stunts every day of his life and still does. He always wanted to have something new for people every year. We have performers that have specialized on one thing that are great, but not a one that can do the variety of things that he can. And the wonderful part is it is clean wholesome entertainment that you are glad to have your children see. So the clean does pay after all in any line of business.

He was the originator of the present style of eccentric Dancing on the Stage. In his dances he dances not only with his feet but also his Body and face show you what he is trying to convey. The greatest compliment I ever heard paid a dancer was said about him by another great dancer. "Why Fred Stone can dance in a Barrel where you can't see his feet and still be a greater dancer to look at than the rest of them out of one."

A corking good all-around Acrobat. He practiced for years just to get a perfect One Hand Stand and never used it—just wanted to learn it. He is one of the best Actor Ball Players. Boxed for years with Corbett,[8] who has always said that Fred could have been Champion at his weight.

Here's a little tip for you, too. He can lick more men single handed, if they start something with him, than can any Hero in the Movies where they are trained to fall.

He took up Fancy Rope throwing after he was 37 years old and today there are not a half dozen Boys in this Country that can do more tricks than he can. He learned in 12 years what it's taken me 40 to learn. Hired Rinks to stay open after their seasons closed and paid Instructors for three years to perfect him in fancy Ice Skating. He learned Bareback Riding for a Circus Act, and every kind of Wild West trick riding. Bucking Horses he learned to ride after he was 43, just when at that age most Riders are quitting. He Bull Dogged a Steer at Cheyenne and had never done it before in his life. Now that takes nerve. I wouldn't jump off a horse on a steer even if he promised to lay down. He is a good Polo Player; we had a team composed of the late Vernon Castle,[9] who, by the way was a good Horseman and a nervy fellow, Leo Corrello,[10] Fred and Myself. Well, in our Clown games we all took it as a joke, but Fred took it serious. He wanted to know the thing from every angle.

Now to me I didn't care whether I hit the Ball or not. I knew it would be laying there when I come back. But not so with Fred. Well, there was a lot of falls and spills. The audience who watched us play every Sunday got to learn that in a spill if the falling Rider hit on his feet it was Fred Stone. If he hit on his head it was me. We would both be equally safe.

He is one of the best shots in the Country, has practiced for years

120

IF A RIDER HIT ON HIS HEAD, IT WAS ME.

with Annie Oakley,[11] the Greatest shot this Country ever saw. He hunted big Game with his Brother-in-Law, Rex Beach,[12] in Alaska. Went to Greenland to Lassoo not shoot, Polar Bears, hunted Mountain Lions in Arizona, and Bears wherever he could hear of one.

Now that he has taken up religion and the Bible, he wont have to ask a Preacher to advise him long. Preachers will be coming to him, for he don't half do anything. So when he comes back, and Sunday comes, and I go down to Rope and Ride and play, if he wants to knock off and go to Church I don't think I will mind, and if they will let ME in, I may go too.

ONE OIL LAWYER PER BARREL

IT'S A BIGGER THING FOR WASHINGTON THAN THE SHRINER'S CONVENTION.

ONE OIL LAWYER PER BARREL

THE *Illiterate Digest*[1] has devoted its life work to ferreting out the Persons and things in our National affairs which are not just exactly up to snuff. Now I see where the Senate Investigating Committee has called a recess for 10 days. Scandals were unfolding themselves so fast that the Committee couldn't get one Bribe straight in their minds before another one would bob up. So they retired to kinder see where they were at.

Now, while that committee may be resting, the *Illiterate Digest*[2] never rests; we are on the heels of the evildoer 24 hours of every bribing day. I hope by the time this reaches an eager waiting Public that they will have found two Lawyers to conduct this Oil investigation. Just think, America has one hundred and ten million Population, 90 percent of which are Lawyers, yet we can't find two of them who have not worked at some time or another for an Oil company. There has been at least one lawyer engaged for every barrel of Oil that ever come out of the ground.

You might wonder if they pay so much to Lawyers how do they ever make anything out of the Oil? Foolish question. They don't make anything out of the Oil. They only make money out of the stock they sell. You buy a share of oil stock and for every dollar you pay, 60 percent goes for Lawyer's fees, 30 percent to over Capitalization, and 10 percent goes to the boring of a Dry Hole.

If a Company just put down Wells for Oil, and then sold the oil legitimately, they would have no use at all for Lawyers. But Oil Men engage their Lawyers nowadays even before they have leased the land or know where they are going to prospect. For the lawyer has to make the lease. It's not like any other business where the owner and the man who is going to lease can meet and do business. Oh no, Lawyers must do that. Then, if they happen to be leasing from the Government, why they not only have to be Lawyers but have to be Political Lawyers.

Now, I bet a lot of you thought after the Company had got the land leased, that the next thing to do was to hire a Driller to put the Well down. But you are wrong again. You go out and get another Lawyer. You have to have another Lawyer to draw up the contract with the driller.

Then I bet that you think the next step is to wait until you see whether you have Oil or not. Say, don't make me laugh out loud again. You don't wait for anything of the kind: you engage another Lawyer to draw up some pretty Oil Stock Paper with nice flowered edges. Looks like a marriage license—only worse. Then you start selling the stock, claiming that the BoHunk Oil Company are putting down a Well on Smith 29, North East 40 of South West 80. Then if they do strike something, they shut it up and claim it was a Duster.

Then they get another Local Lawyer who knows everybody around that neck of the Woods, to go out and buy up or lease all the adjoining land. Then, when they get it all leased, they go back and pick the stopper out of this. Well, double the Capitalization of Stock under the direction of still another Lawyer, and then they are in a position to hire more Lawyers to investigate getting a Lease from Persia, or Jugo-Slavia. This just kinder gives you a rough idea of what all these Lawyers do and why we can't get any to help prosecute this Oil Scream.

The *Illiterate Digest* will have to take Editorial attention of the resignation of Sectry Denby.[3] Mr. Denby was requested by the Senate to resign. Now that in itself is a mighty good Omen that he is an unusually able man. Of course, where I think he got in bad was in saying, if he had the same thing to do over again he would do it. It is always bad for any one on trial to say he would do the same thing over again. American People like to have you repent; then they are generous.

But you see lots of times a man gets in wrong just by an ill timed remark. Look at Mr. Doheny's[4] reported remark that he would "make 100 million out of the Elk Hills lease." That will go down in History as the highest priced Gag ever pulled. That's why Mr. Coolidge never gets in bad. If a man will just stay hushed he is hard to find out.

Personally and Editorially, I don't think Mr. Denby is guilty at all of any wrong-doing that he knew of. But somebody has got to go in this thing, and before it's all over you are mighty apt to find a few innocent along with all the guilty strewn along by the Pipe Line.

By the way, sometime this Country, just by accident, is going to get some man Sectry of the Navy who has at least received a Picture Post Card of Annapolis, sometime during his career. Josephus Daniels had never been in anything bigger than a Row Boat up to the time he was made Sectry of the Navy. The first Battleship he got on he kept looking for the Paddle Wheels on the side that made it go. He found the Officers in those days had Cocktail and Cordial Glasses with their Table wear. He made them throw them all overboard. He thought they would sink the Ship. What he lacked in seamanship, he made up in morality.

Then came Mr. Denby who had received his Maritime Education by looking at the Detroit River (which is so thick with Booze Boats that you can't see the Water) naturally his Aquatic viewpoint is rather warped.

126

THEY NOT ONLY HAVE TO BE LAWYERS, BUT POLITICAL LAWYERS.

I guess Young Theodore Roosevelt[5] comes nearer being an Old Salt than anyone connected with our Ex Oil Owners (The Navy). He did live in Oyster Bay overlooking Long Island Sound, and had to look at the Joy Line cruising, 1$ daily, to Providence. Then he had to Subway under the East River to get to New York. So I guess he is the only Sectry we have that knows just by looking at one, which end of a Battleship is the front.[6]

Judging by the previous experience of some of our sectrys, of various things in our Cabinets, it has always been a source of great anxiety to me just why a Vetenerian has never been appointed either Sectry of War or PostMaster General.

Now by the time this reaches our Scandal loving Public I don't know who will be left in Washington. The chances are, when I visit the old stamping ground again,[7] I will have to make entirely new acquaintances. But I will always have the feeling, "Well the old Boys were not so bad. They were just unfortunate in getting caught."

It certainly looks like a tough year.[8] Politicians are so busy trying to hold down their own Jobs that they won't have any time to look out for anyone else. They will be voting a Bonus to men who lost their livelihood in the great morality Panic of 1924.

Children in future years will ask their Parents, "Father how much did you get in the great Year 1924?"

It's been a fine thing for Washington. The Hotels are crowded. Every time a Guest registers the Clerk asks him, "I suppose you will be here until you testify." It's a bigger thing for Washington than the Shriners' Convention, because it has all of them, besides a lot more.

If they would all tell the truth the first time they testify they wouldn't have to testify again like they are doing now, and they would get the thing over a lot quicker. They ought to pass a rule in this Country that in any investigations, if a Man couldn't tell the truth the first time he shouldn't be allowed to try again.

Now we have another Scandal in the Veterans' Bureau. But we are just in such shape that we can't take care of but one Scandal at a time. If any other small affairs come up during the coming season that look like they might develop into a Scandal I will try to let you know.

ANOTHER HOT CONFESSION IN THE OIL SCANDAL

THEY ARE FROM TULSA. I WILL BE RIGHT OUT.

ANOTHER HOT CONFESSION IN
THE OIL SCANDAL

I WISH this Oil Scandal would hurry up and be settled as it is very hard for one writing on affairs of our Country to tell, in writing of our Officials, whether to speak of them as Secretary So and So, or Ex-Secretary So and So. Up to now I claim a very unique distinction. I am the only Person I know of that has not been mentioned as receiving something in the nature of a Fee from some Big Corporation. But I am going to get in early and tell just what I received so when my name comes up later on people will say: "Well there is a Man who has accepted Fees but he was honest about them and come to the front and told it." As I can't get to Washington to testify I want to tell through the Digest,[1] for which I am Scandal Correspondent, just what happened to me. If I was in Washington I probably couldn't get to testify as there is so many ahead of me that it will take years for just the People who work for the Government to tell who gave them something.

I know a Man that went to Washington to testify as to money he had received and there was 29 Cabinet and Ex Cabinet Members in line ahead of him so he had to just write it and send it in. Now this whole thing was a strictly Republican affair until Mr. Doheny (who never lets Politics interfere with his Business) appeared before the Commission, and when it looked like he was the only Oil be-spattered sheep in the Democratic Fold, he just kicked over an Oil Can and hiding behind it were a flock of Democrats that reached almost as far back as Jefferson's Administration.

Personally I am glad that he did unearth members of both Parties for if this thing had gone through showing no one but Republicans, it would have cast a reflection on the shrewdness of the Democratic Party. In other words they would have looked rather dumb to be standing around with all these Oily Shekels falling all around them and not opening their Pockets to catch a few. For the American people are a very generous people and will forgive almost any weakness, with the possible exception of stupidity.

But to get back to my confession for I want to be set right before the people by the time we meet in Madison Square Garden in June to select the worst man. Mine starts out like a Fairy Story.

Once upon a time, I had just gone to work for Florenz Ziegfeld, Jr., and was playing in what was called Ziegfeld's Midnight Frolic, on the Roof of the Amsterdam Theatre, New York. Prohibition and my Jokes were equally responsible in closing the place up. Now my home is (as I think I mentioned before) Claremore, Oklahoma, (The home of the best Curative Waters in the World) and, by the way, one of the best towns in the World to live in if any of you are thinking about making a change.

Well, after I had finished my little 15 minutes of annoyance in the Frolic one night, one of the Waiters (for instead of having Ushers to hand you a Programme, they had Waiters to hand you a drink, and I tell you, you can't beat some of the old customs). Well this well tipped Waiter comes to my dressing room, which I used to hang my ropes in, and said, "There is a Party of folks out front at one of the Tables from Oklahoma, and they want you to come out and see them." I asked what place in Oklahoma did they come from, and he said, "I don't know but they certainly got the Dough; they have ordered everything in the place but the Kitchen Stove." I said, "They are from Tulsa. I will be right out."

Well I hid what few dollars I had down in my Sock, and went out to see them. It was Mr. Harry Sinclair. I had never heard of him before, for he hadn't bought Zev or the Teapot Dome up to then.[2] But we soon felt like we knew each other, on account of him being from Tulsa (a Residential Suburb of Claremore where we park our millionaires to keep them from getting under our feet). He knew my Father who had been a member of the Constitutional Convention, which drafted the Charter of Oklahoma.

Well, this Mr. Sinclair was an awful nice fellow. We hit it off pretty good. We kinder consoled each other, on account of being so far from home, and trying to eke out an existence from these shrewd New Yorkers. He took a fatherly interest in me, and asked, "Now, Will, you are working here but what are you doing with your money?" So I told him just what I was doing with it, that the last three months' wages had gone to paying a Doctor and a Nurse, for assisting us in accumulating another Baby, and that the three months previous to that my wages had gone to making the first payment on a second hand Overland car, and that the year still previous to that I had bought a Baby Buggy and a Victrola.

Well, he seemed mighty pleased that I was putting my money into such staple commodities. So I asked him what he was doing with his. He said, "I struck Oil, but Oil is no good unless its Capitalized."

Well, that was news to me. I thought you could just sell the Oil itself. But I learned that you can get twice as much for the Capital as you can for the Oil.

So then he asked me the names of my Private Herd. I told him I had gone to a great deal of trouble and thought in naming them and after months of research among pretty and odd names of Novels and

Poems, I had decided to name the Children, Bill, Mary and Jim.

Well, he had never heard of anything more original. The names I thought struck him very odd, as he wrote all three of them down on the back of an Envelope. So I left the Table as I didn't want to be there when the Waiter presented his check. For I had seen several Casualties from this same cause.

I never thought much more about it. I went home and told my Wife about meeting him, and what do you think happened! In a couple of days here comes three official letters addressed to Bill, Mary and Jim, and they had enclosed a Share each of Sinclair Oil Stock *free*. Well we thought that was a mighty fine thing for him to do to be so thoughtful of our little Tribe. I accepted it in as good faith as McAdoo did his Fee.[3]

I don't know if the Senate investigating Committee will get around to them soon or not. Of course they will have to get through before Election for the whole thing will be a total loss after election. All I have to say is that the Children were Private Citizens and did not promise to use any influence in any way. Of course, I , as the Father and Guardian of the Children, will be apt to come in for considerable criticism, and I may go so far as to lose any chance I may have as being named as a Presidential possibility.

Now I hate this for the Children's sake that all this must come out for it is liable to put a stigma on their names that they will be two Campaigns living down. One thing, of course, will be in their favor when it all does come out and that is that it was sent openly through the mails. It was not delivered in a Suit Case.

They have had these shares for years and have also received at various times a Dollar or so Interest on said Stock. When this Expose came out Bill and Mary were for resigning and sending in their Stock, so they could show that they were not connected with the Corporation, but Jim, the youngest, who has a touch of Republicanism in him, why, he said, "No, let's stick until they throw us out. Let them prove we took these Stocks for some other reason than Charity!"

What makes it look bad is, that my Wife wrote a note and thanked him. But the children did not sign the Note. So when he is called upon to testify he will have her Note but it won't have the Children's Signature on it. Of course he can say it was tore off, or that his Wife has that part of it, or some other equally good reason. But I want the Public to be lenient with both him and the Children, for as past events have proven they haven't done a thing for him to warrant them getting those Stocks. So I honestly believe he meant no harm when he gave them.

133

As for Mr. Doheny giving me or mine anything, we live right near him here in Beverly Hills. His son did promise me a key, so I wouldn't have to ride clear around his Estate when out Horseback riding, but I never got it yet.

THE WHOLE TRUTH AND NOTHING
BUT THE TRUTH

I OBJECT TO THE SENATOR FROM MASSACHUSETTS' SLURRING REMARKS.

Comedy Drama

Entitled

THE WHOLE TRUTH AND NOTHING BUT THE TRUTH

PLACE—Washington, D. C.
TIME—From 1924 to 1930.
SCENE—One of the 40 Investigating Rooms of the U.S. Senate.
CAST OF CHARACTERS—Everybody that ever worked for, or just
    Worked the United States.
HERO—Senator Walsh,[1] assisted by Lenroot[2] and accomplices.
VILLAINS—Entire list of Who's Who in America.
    The Scene opens on a greasy Monday morning with JOHN F.
MAJOR[3] *being quizzed by* SENATOR WALSH.
SENATOR WALSH[4]

Do you work for a Man that runs a Newspaper?
MR. MAJOR

I draw a salary from him.
SENATOR WALSH

What right have you to send Telegrams to a Man in Palm Beach
if you are only working for him?
MR. MAJOR

I couldn't get him on the Telephone.
SENATOR WALSH

What did you tell him in your Telegrams?
MR MAJOR

What was going on in Washington.
SENATOR WALSH

What did he tell you in his Telegram to you?
MR. MAJOR

What was going on in Palm Beach.
SENATOR WALSH

What was going on at the time in Washington?
MR. MAJOR

Why the Senate Committee was investigating somebody.
SENATOR WALSH

Who were they investigating?
MR. MAJOR

They didn't know themselves.

137

SENATOR WALSH

What did he say was going on in Palm Beach?

MR. MAJOR

I am ashamed to tell you.

SENATOR WALSH

Who were these Telegrams from in Palm Beach?

MR. MAJOR

I can't remember.

SENATOR WALSH

Did you lease a Wire from Palm Beach to Washington?

MR. MAJOR

I can't remember.

SENATOR WALSH

Why did you lease the Wire?

MR. MAJOR

So we could say we had a Wire to Palm Beach. It was good advertising.

SENATOR WALSH

Who operated this wire?

MR. MAJOR

A Telegraph Operator.

SENATOR WALSH

What was his name?

MR. MAJOR

I think it was Jones, or Smith; maybe it was Brown.

SENATOR WALSH

Who operated the wire from Palm Beach?

MR. MAJOR

Johnny.

SENATOR WALSH

Johnny who?

MR. MAJOR

Johnny Johnnnny.

SENATOR WALSH

Did the operator on this end work at the White House also?

MR. MAJOR

Yes he was the Waiter there.

SENATOR WALSH

Did he work there during the Republican or Democratic Administration?

SENATOR LODGE

Mr. Committee, I object to that question. This is not a Partisan affair; I refuse to have the honor and the glory of the Great Republican Party dragged into a thing where up to now their fair name has never been.

SENATOR CARAWAY[5]

Mr. Committee, I object to the Senator from Massachusetts' slurring remarks of the Democratic Party; a Party which has housed such illustrious names as Jefferson, Cleveland, Akron, Youngstown, Bryan, McAdoo, and sometimes Jim Reed.[6]

MR. MAJOR

Senator Walsh have you got a Cigarette on you?

SENATOR WALSH

No I just got some cubebs here.

MR. MAJOR

Never mind I will go across the Street and get some. See you next time I am called.

SENATOR WALSH

Gentlemen, I think the Committee should retire for a week to consider the Testimony of the Gentleman who has just testified.

SENATOR LENROOT

But Mr. Chairman, Mr. Doheny's Yacht is waiting to take him on a Cruise of the Mediterranean, and I don't think it's fair to keep him waiting.

SENATOR WHEELER[7]

Mr. Chairman, I make a motion, that the Committee make a motion, that Attorney General Daugherty[8] resign.

SENATOR LODGE

Mr. Chairman, I object. His motion is out of order. I had a motion before the Committee asking the Committee asking the Committee to make a motion, to ask him to stay. Now, by all the rules of Parliamentary motion making, mine anti-dates his. And I will stake a reputation on it that goes back to the first class Passengers that landed from that Mother Ship of mine the Mayflower, who have so gloriously populated the fair state of Massachusetts.

SENATOR ROBINSON[9]

Mr. Chairman, I object. The fair state of Arkansas houses one direct descendant of that Plymouth Rock Expedition. And I protest when the Gentleman from Massachusetts claims the entire Cargo of that ill-fated Voyage. Never as long as I represent the majority constituency of my Glorious state will I stand by and hear the ozone swept Ozarks spoken of disparagingly, especially by that Moron State of Massachusetts.

SENATOR WILLIS[10]

Gentlemen, I don't think that Mr. Daugherty should be let out without a trial.

SENATOR WHEELER

Why, he has had three year's trial already. His trial is what's letting him out.

SENATOR WALSH

Who will we call next?

DOORTENDER

Why just get a Census return, and call anybody's name on it; they are waiting outside.

SENATOR LA FOLLETTE[11]

Why don't you call somebody unexpectedly, and maybe in their confusion they will tell the truth accidentally.

SENATOR LENROOT

Who said anything about wanting the truth?

SENATOR HEFLIN[12]

I want to ask the Committee why they called on Mr. Fall at his hotel in private.

SENATOR WALSH

We wanted to see where he got the hundred thousand. We may retire ourselves some day.[13]

SENATOR HEFLIN

Why didn't you tell at the time that you went to see him?

SENATOR WALSH

Wait a minute, who is running this investigation? Am I supposed to ask the questions, or to answer them?

SENATOR LENROOT

Where is Sinclair?

MR. ZEVERLY [14]

(whose running name is Zev.)

My Client, Mr. Sinclair has gone to the races and it will be impossible for him to appear until after the season is over.

SENATOR WALSH

Well how about McLane?[15] Can we get him?

SENATOR CARAWAY

You can get him by Telegraph, I guess. Everybody else has.

SENATOR WALSH

Well, where is Detective William J. Burns?[16] He was supposed to testify here today.

DOORTENDER

Mr. Chairman, I met him on the Street and he couldn't find the Capitol Building.

SENATOR MOSES[17]

I make a motion that we examine the Income Tax and see what Mr. Doheny contributed to the Democratic Campaign Fund.

SENATOR JIM REED

I object. Senator Moses is a Republican and he is only throwing a smoke Screen to try and hide his Party behind it. This is not a Partisan question and I object to politics being dragged into it in any way. Let's handle this thing in a dignified way, and don't let Politics play any part. As it was the Republicans that did it, I am in favor of justice being served.

DOORTENDER

Mr. Forbes[18] is here and wants to testify.

ENTIRE SENATE

"My Lord, Is he in this, too?"

P.S.—This play to be continued[19] until somebody tells the truth.

WELL, WHO IS PRUNES?

"THERE'S A BELLBOY AT MY HOTEL AND HE JUST GOT IT FROM THE
CHAUFFEUR OF A PROMINENT OIL-MAN."

WELL, WHO IS PRUNES?

2nd Episode of the great Dramatic Serial,

THE TRUTH, NOTHING BUT THE TRUTH, SO HELP ME GOD.

Same scene as the first Episode—the Third Degree Room of the Grand Jury of the United States Senate. MR. SENATOR WALSH leading question asker of a body of men noted for their inquisitiveness.

DOORTENDER OF THIS TORTURE CHAMBER
Who will we call first today?
SENATOR WALSH[1]
Call the Editorial Writer of that newspaper.
DOORMAN
But, Mr. Walsh, we just called him yesterday.
SENATOR WALSH
I know we did but call him again. A whole lot is happening in this country between yesterday and today. Now Mr. Bennett[2] who was it that you referred to as the Principal in those wires to Palm Beach?
MR. BENNETT
Why, Senator Curtis.
SENATOR HEFLIN
Curses on the Luck. I thought it was Coolidge.
SENATOR HARRISON[3]
Wish it had of been Coolidge. It's no novelty to get a Senator in Wrong.
SENATOR WALSH
What did you confer with Curtis about?
MR. BENNETT
About the Editorial Policy of our Paper.
SENATOR WALSH
Well what does the Editorial Policy of any Paper amount to? You don't suppose anybody reads those things do you? Why one Ad is worth more to a paper than 40 Editorials. That will be all for you Mr. Bennett.
SENATOR CARAWAY
Just a minute before you go. Who was Peaches in those Telegrams?
MR. BENNETT
I don't remember.
SENATOR ROBINSON
Yes, and who was Prunes? I hope it referred to no Democrat.

145

SENATOR WALSH

Call Mr. Curtis.

SENATOR WALSH

Senator Curtis, will you tell the Grand Jury in your own way just what happened between you and this Editorial Writer of the Washington *Post*.

MR. CURTIS

Yes Sir.

SENATOR WALSH

What was it?

MR. CURTIS

Nothing.

SENATOR WALSH

You mean you didn't confer with this Gentleman?

MR. CURTIS

I did not.

SENATOR WALSH

But you know him?

MR. CURTIS

Never saw him in my life.

SENATOR WALSH

But you have heard of him?

MR. CURTIS

Never in my life.

SENATOR WALSH

But you know of the Washington *Post?*

MR. CURTIS

Yes sir, I have heard it.

SENATOR WALSH

Heard it? What do you mean you heard it?

MR. CURTIS

I have heard Sousa's Band play it many a time.

SENATOR WALSH

Play what?

MR. CURTIS

Washington's Post.

SENATOR WALSH

It's not a tune; it's a Newspaper. You talk like a Congressman. Where are you from.

MR. CURTIS

Kansas.

SENATOR WALSH

That will be all.

146

SENATOR CARAWAY

Just a minute, Mr. Curtis, Who is Peaches?

MR. CURTIS

I don't know unless it's Jim Reed.

SENATOR HEFLIN

Just a minute. I object to the Republican Senator's slur on the fair name of the Democratic Party. This Investigation is supposed to be Non Sectarian, and I object to having Politics dragged in, just to make a Republican Holiday.

SENATOR ROBINSON

And I want to know who Prunes was.

MR. CURTIS

You mean you want to know who Prunes IS.

SENATOR LENROOT

Mr. Walsh, and Gentlemen of the Vigilance Committee there is a Bell Boy over at my Hotel and he just got it from the chauffer of a Prominent Oil Man, that Major Leonard Wood's[4] Son had just heard that his Father was offered the Nomination for the Presidency 3 and a Half years ago, if he would appoint Mr. Jake Hamon[5] Secretary of the Interior. Now that is a very serious charge, and one that I think this Committee should look into at once. Public affairs have come to a fine Climax when a Man in this Country offers to make another one President. I tell you it is undermining the confidence of the Great American People and when you do that you shake the very Bulwarks of the American Constitution. I think a Subpoena should be issued for Mr. Wood's Son at once and if this is so I am for a swift and speedy trial for the Culprits.

SENATOR WALSH

I am for calling Mr. Wood himself. There's one thing that this Committee has proven that it won't take, and that is Hear Say Evidence. So call Mr. Wood himself.

MR. MOSES

(The Senator one, Not the Apostle One)
But, Mr. Walsh, Mr. Wood is in the Phillippines.

SENATOR WALSH

I thought he was home. Haven't they got their Independence yet?

MR. MOSES

No, Mr. Coolidge wouldn't give it to them.

SENATOR WALSH

What's the matter? Have they struck oil, too?

MR. MOSES

No, Mr. Coolidge told them that a Nation that would not support

147

Wood's Administration certainly would not be able to support one of their own.

SENATOR HEFLIN

Well, how did America get Independence? They didn't support Wood.

SENATOR REED

Who said we had any independence?

SENATOR LODGE
(The Confucius of Nahant)

I object to having the President of these United States' name dragged into this thing. I think when a Man occupies the exalted position that he does that his name should not be degraded by having it mentioned in The Senate. Now I know that he is doing the best he can. I have known him ever since he got prominent enough for me to know. In the eight months that I have known him, I have found him to be patient, honest, and a Man who would not knowingly rob a single Filipino of his Liberty. This is simply a Political trick to drag his name into this Philippine muddle.

SENATOR HEFLIN

Yes but he sent the Filipinos the Wire didn't he! And it's wires that we are here to investigate ain't it?

SENATOR HARRISON

Does the exalted Senator from Massachusetts recall that during the late Democratic Administration, he himself during the talk on European Affairs mentioned not only once, but twice, the name of the then President, Mr. Wilson? Now he don't want us to mention his President.

SENATOR HEFLIN

Well it's funny to me that a Country can't get their Liberty, when they have advanced far enough to have the Champion Bantamweight Prize Fighter of the World. I know Countries that have their Liberty, when they can't even produce a good Golf Player and that's the lowest form of Civilization.

SENATOR CARAWAY

I would like to ask Mr. Lodge if he knows who Peaches is.

SENATOR LODGE

I do not. It's the only subject I ever admitted being ignorant on.

SENATOR ROBINSON

Well, I want to know who Prunes IS.

SENATOR LODGE

You mean who Prunes AM, don't you.

SENATOR ROBINSON

Darn it; that man is a bear on Grammar.

SENATOR WALSH

I think the committee should adjourn until we can get Mr. Wood himself.

DOORMAN

Excuse me, Mr. Walsh, but there is a Gentleman out here who wants to testify in regard to the Doheny and Sinclair leases. What can I tell him?

SENATOR WALSH

Oh, yes, I had forgotten about those. Tell him as soon as we get this Wood for President affair settled, and Jack Dempsey's mysterious sickness, and Babe Ruth's[6] collapse, that we will be able to get to that Oil Lease thing again.

SENATOR COPELAND[7]

Mr. Walsh, I was in New York last night and I heard Mr. Vanderlip[8] make a Speech to the Rotary Club of Coney Island, and he said, "I have it on absolutely reliable authority that George Washington never crossed the Delaware. That fellow you see in the middle of the Boat was a fellow doubling for him, and if I am called I will be glad to give this information I possess to the Senate Investigating Committee."

SENATOR WALSH

Mr. Secretary, call Mr. Vanderlip at once.

MR. LENROOT

Let's not call him until tomorrow, Mr. Walsh, as he will make another speech tonight perhaps on what he discovered about Lincoln. So we can quiz him on both men at once.

MR. CARAWAY

Well, before we adjourn, I want to know who Peaches is.

MR. ROBINSON

Well, I want to know who Prunes WERE.[9]

POLITICS GETTING READY TO JELL

POLITICS GETTING READY TO JELL

The Illiterate Digest,[1] after reviewing the news,[2] finds that Politics is sure at the point when it is about to jell. My old friend Jim Reed from the smelly banks of the Kaw River has broke out again. If you have done anything against the welfare or conventions of the United States, and everybody has passed their various opinions on you, and you think you have been roasted to a dark bay, why, until Jim Reed breaks out on you, you haven't been called anything.

Well, it was kinder funny Jim was to make a Washington Day speech. Naturally everyone supposed it to be on George Washington, but it was the only speech ever made on Washington's Birthday that didn't have a word about Washington. He didn't even mention his name. I don't know that McAdoo, Denby, Daugherty, Doheny, and others will consider it much Flattery, but it will go down in History as being the only time they ever replaced Washington.

Reed wouldn't have been any good making a speech on Washington, anyway. He would have been expected to compliment him and I doubt if he could think of anything George had even done that really was worth while.

Vanderlip[3] made a speech at the Rotary Club of Ossining, New York, that astonished the United States. Now that speech didn't astonish me near as much as the knowledge that Ossining *had* a Rotary Club. For the sake of the unfingerprinted ones, I will state that Ossining is the Town where Sing Sing is permanently located. Now if Ossining has a Rotary Club they certainly had to take in some lay members from this Musically named Institution.

But when you come to think of it, just think what a Distinguished Rotary Club they could have at that. Rotary is composed of one of the best of each line of work or business. Just think what a competitive thing it would be trying to find in Ossining the leading Burglar sojourning with them at the time, or the most representative Pickpocket to represent them in the Club. And Bankers! Mr. Vanderlip must have felt right at home up there.[4] There are more Bankers in Ossining than any Town of its size in the United States.

A two year residence is necessary to be able to join the Rotary. Can you imagine them questioning members of Sing Sing, "Have you been a resident of this Town for two years?" and the answer would be, "Yes Sir, constantly."

So, as I say, it was not the things Mr. Vanderlip said that attracted the unusual attention. It was the distinguished audience that he delivered it to. Just to show you the difference: Appearing before the

Rotary Club of Sing Sing he caused a commotion by his Speech. He took the same Act down to Washington and nobody would listen to him. It shows you have to have an intelligent audience. Up in Sing Sing they got what he was talking about but down in Washington it went right over their heads.

I know, for last winter while playing in New York I was asked to go over to a big Charity affair given by the 400 of 5th Avenue. I thought I had a pretty good line of Gags, as there was quite a lot happening every day of Public interest. So I go over and start in telling them what I had read in the Papers and nobody even cracked a smile, much less laughed. So I just kept on trying remarks on every subject that had been in the papers since Bryan last got a Hair cut. But it was about one of the worst Flops I ever encountered, and I have had some beauts in my time.

Well, of course, I felt terrible about it, so just by a coincidence on the very next night I had promised to go up to Ossining and do an act for (at that time it wasn't called the Rotary Club). I think then they called it Inmates. There was no show—just me alone went up to add to the hardships of Prison Life. Well I never knew I had as many friends in the World. I knew everybody up there. I was twice as much at home as I had been on 5th Avenue the night before. So now I know why Vanderlip picked out Ossining for his Annual February Oration.

I started in on those same Jokes on up-to-date things that had flopped so completely at the Millionaire's Charity affair. Why, say, they just started right in dying laughing at them. I was sorry Ziegfeld wasn't there, as I would have got in a raise in salary if he had heard how my act went.[5] I don't care what I talked about they knew all about it.

Ordinarily, I only do about 15 or 20 minutes but up there I did an Hour and a Quarter. I was so tickled I offered to take all the whole audience of 12 hundred down to the Follies and pay their way in to see our Show. Now you know I must feel pretty good with myself, when I offer to spend my Dough like that. A lot of people would be kinder sore at the 400 because they didn't laugh like these 12 hundred did, but I am not. I don't blame them. If I had their money I wouldn't read either. So I can understand very readily why Vanderlip's act didn't go so big in Washington as it did in Ossining.

Of course Van and I use just the opposite methods in our Stage performances. Every Gag I tell must be based on truth. No matter how much I may exaggerate it, it must have a certain amount of Truth. Vanderlip bases his Gags on Rumor.

Now Rumor travels Faster, but it don't stay put as long as Truth.

154

I will, however, give him credit for one thing. While here lately everybody is telling what he has heard, and all about this and that rumor, why, he thought of by far the best ones I have heard up to now.

That's no small accomplishment I tell you, in this year of Rumors, to be able to say at the end of it: "Well, I told the best ones."

His were so good that before his audience got through applauding at Sing Sing (or rather Ossining) why, they had him on the stand at Washington. That's the first time a Theatrical troup ever jumped from Ossining to Washington.

They even put him on ahead of Fall, Sinclair, and all the Headliners.[6]

TWO LONG LOST FRIENDS FOUND AT LAST

THEY REHEARSED THEIR OLD ACT HERE YESTERDAY.

TWO LONG LOST FRIENDS FOUND AT LAST

WELL, sir, I have a real Message for my readers.[1] It looked like it would be just the ordinary Article with no flavor or Backbone or Truth, and with no real underlying news or wisdom, that is, nothing that the people would be glad to know and read. As I say, that is the kind of Article I thought it would be. But as I picked up the morning Papers, why, I read who was in our midst out here in Sunny California. Well, sir, it struck me like a thunderbolt here was news which my public had been longing for for years and here I had found it out!

Well, I says to myself, this is too good to keep, for here people had been wondering all this time for just what I knew now. I kinder hated to leave the East on account of thinking I would be out of touch with some of our National Characters but I find that sooner or later they all arrive out here and start in fighting off Real Estate men the same as shooing away Mosquitoes on Long Island.

Well, who should blow in but two of our old long-lost friends, and I know that even 'Frisco (who is jealous of any one being here) will be glad to hear they are here well and hearty, and rehearsed their old Act here yesterday and people enjoyed them just as much as they did in the old days.

Both of these Boys were on the big time and were well known all around the Circuit, and any time they took the Platform standing by the side of a Pitcher of ice water and a glass, why, it just meant 6 columns starting on the front page and ending among the want ads. I bet you hadn't heard of them in years and will thank me for resurrecting this information for you.

I can't keep it any longer. I did want to keep it till the finish of this to tell you but I must tell you now who they are—William J. Bryan and Billy Sunday![2]

Neither did I, but *they are,* and looking fine.

You know, if you have lost any one, look out here, because sooner or later they will come here to visit relatives, for anybody that has relatives comes here so he can write back to other relatives.

They are both just resting here (so is everybody else). Mr. Bryan is waiting till he finds out where the next Democratic Convention will be held, and then be there ready to knock any aspiring Presidential Candidate on the head the minute it shows above the mob.

The only way they will ever fool W. J. is some presidential year decide not to run any one. Then it will be a good joke on him; he will have no one to object to.

Of course, now we don't hear much of Democratic Candidates, as both sides are busy watching to see what Cal. will do. When he first become President there seemed to be quite a Sentiment to nominate him again for Vice President.[3]

Everybody was wondering how he would come out of the Coal strike situation, and figured his political life or death depended on how he decided, so he just fools everybody by appointing some other man to settle it. Now, no other President had ever been smart enough to think of a thing like that; they tried to do it themselves, so I think he will go a long ways. He figured, why should I get in wrong when I can get some man to do it for me, so he just looked around until he found some other fellow who had a political future.

He said, "Gifford,[4] you go get in wrong with which ever side you decide against." Now, the minute a Crisis comes up, all he has to do is to remember some Republican name and appoint him to settle it for him.

Now the only Crisis that Mr. Coolidge can possibly get into, himself, is running out of Republicans to appoint. In that case he would have to appoint a Democrat which would bring on a worse Crisis than the one he appointed him to settle.

But I am not here to talk about Cal. and what he is doing. I am here to tell you of these two long lost Prodigals that I discovered in the wilds of this Village. They were preaching in a Pulpit. I guess that's why no one had seen them for so long. Both these Boys, in the good old days used to talk in a Tent. Now you can always attract a crowd in a Tent, for they figure that it might be a Circus. Come to think of it, their Acts were similar; either one of them could take a Dictionary and sink an enemy with words at 40 paces.

Bryan's speeches have been the only thing to look forward to at a Democratic Convention for years. He has sent more Presidential Candidates home without a Reception Committee meeting them than any Monologist living. He can take a batch of words and scramble them together and leaven them properly with a hunk of Oratory and knock the White House door knob right out of a Candidate's hand.

Bryan has made more Political speeches than Germany has Marks. He kissed, when they were Babies, every man and woman in the United States who is now up to the age of 45. He has juggled the destinies of America more than any two Presidents because he has the choosing or rejecting of them.

His career has varied from Non-intoxication to Evolution; his hobbies have jumped from Grape juice to Monkeys. He tries to prove that we did not descend from the Monkey, but he unfortunately picked a time when the actions of our people prove that we did. He,

160

undoubtedly, is one of our greatest minds and in most of his Theories he has been just too far ahead of the mob.

He preached Prohibition at a time when it meant Political Suicide for himself. I bet the next Democratic Candidate for President, no matter how strong he may think he is, would rather have the support of W. J. Bryan than any doubtful State in the Union.

Now that brings to us his accomplice, Willie Sunday, who I discovered staggering from one of our Local Pulpits last Sunday. To some of you who can't or don't wish to remember, Billy passed out just as Andy Volstead made his entrance. Now Barnum[5] invented the Tent, but Billy Sunday filled it. He can get more people into a tent than an Iowa Picnic at Long Beach, California.

He is the only man in Ecclesiastical or Biblical history that ever had to train physically, for a sermon. He brought more converts to Prohibition before the 18th Amendment come in, than the 18 Amendment has converted to Prohibition since it went in.

He is the first preacher to specialize on Liquor. While Bryan's oratorical wrath in the later years has been hurled at Darwin,[6] Billy Sunday picks his opponent with a carelessness that is almost reckless.

I suppose that he has had more mortal worldly combats with the Devil himself than any man living. He has challenged the Devil publicly more times than Wills,[7] the Negro, has Jack Dempsey. People have been going for years to hear Billy, just figuring that if they didn't go that night it might be the very night the Devil would hear what Billy was calling him and come up, and they might miss what would happen.

I don't know this Devil myself but if he heard Billy say these things and didn't come up and call him for it, I think less of him than Billy does. Of course, the Devil may be just good natured, and figure, well, he can't hurt *ME,* and if he can get anything out of it why let him go ahead.

Now, of course, you can get a fellow wrong. Billy used to lay all the drinking on to this Devil, and claimed that if we had Prohibition we could lick this Devil. Now we got Prohibition, I don't think he can legitimately lay the present drinking onto the Devil.

Course, from this I don't want you to think I am taking sides in this thing. I don't know either one personally. But, as I say, there is a chance that they both may have each other wrong. As I say, Billy must have something on the Devil or he wouldn't dare to call him what he does, especially if the Devil can hear him, and I tell you the Devil must be pretty low if he don't answer him, that is, if he hears him.

I have always figured that the reason that the Devil didn't arise and respond was Billy's slang was too much for him. But Billy sure did do a lot of good in the old days, and no matter if you didn't like his style of sermon, you sure didn't get a chance to do any sleeping.

So I hope we can keep them both out here with us, and help to get some of our population's mind on the Church on Sunday instead of being continually looking for lots.

THEY NOMINATED EVERYBODY BUT
THE FOUR HORSEMEN

"YOU WASN'T HERE AND YOU KNOW THEM AS WELL AS I DO"

THEY NOMINATED EVERYBODY BUT
THE FOUR HORSEMEN

AS I pen you these few lines, the Democratic National Convention is still going on; going on to where, nobody knows. But it has to end some time for even a Delegate can only stand just so much Oratory.[1]

All the first week was taken up with seconding the nomination of McAdoo and Al Smith.[2]

It looked like they were going to run out of people to do it, and they would have to second each other.

I wish you could have been there and heard what great men we have in this Country. We started out with 16 men for President. Here is what each one of them was.—"The only Man who can carry the Democratic Party to a Glorious Victory in November. Whose every act has been an inspiration to his fellow men. Not only loved in his Home State but in every State." Well, there was six continuous days of that.

Then the Ku Klux Klan argument come along, and really it was welcome even in New York. Just to get people's mind off that continuous, " The Man I am about to name to you."

One day and up to two thirty in the Night they fought and argued the Klan. It was the most exciting and Dramatic night I ever saw in my life.

After 11 hundred Delegates voted and recounted and voted the thing stood only about one vote apart, in fact a fraction of a vote, due to North Carolina, instead of having an election and naming 24 Delegates, just letting the whole State come as Delegates and giving each one the usual Volstead Ratio, Half of one percent of a Vote.

Alaska voted one Klu Klux away up there. Can you imagine a man in all that Snow and Cold with nothing on but a thin white Sheet and Pillow Slip?

My old Friend W. J. Bryan made one of his characteristic speeches. He said that if they split the Democratic party with this Klan issue that another great Party would arise to take its place. Some guy up in the Gallery started Booing him. He just stopped and waited a minute until the heckler quit, then he said: "But no great leader of any Party has ever come from the Gallery." After that they laid off him.

Ex-Secretary of War Baker made a Speech on the League of Nations and spoke of the 4 Horsemen of the Apocalypse, meaning I suppose, Borah, La Follette, Johnson and Brookhart.[3]

I arrived late one morning, well only about 15 minutes late, and they had nominated five men for president already. I asked a Man in the Press stand who they were and he said, "You wasn't here and you know them as well as I do."

I had a friend who wanted to be nominated but all the nominating speakers were so given out that he had to let it go until next Election, that is in case they ever have another one.

If the one who is nominated can only swing the votes of the ones who were defeated he will give Mr. Coolidge a tight race.

Talk about Presidential Timber. Why, man, they had whole Lumber yards of it here.

There was so many being Nominated that some of the Men making the nominating Speeches had never even met the man they were nominating.

I know they had not from the way they talked about them.

Every time the speaker nominated somebody, why the Band would strike up what they thought was an appropriate tune. The bird nominated Gov. Brown[4] of New Hampshire kept talking and referring to "The Old Granite State. That Glorious old Granite State." When he finished the Band played "Rock of Ages". There was granite for you.

They nominated from a list of all Democrats. They drew them out the night before the convention.

Some Man named Stuart from Illinois got up to nominate somebody, and we knew we would hear something about Lincoln being born in Illinois, and sure enough we did. He kept quoting Lincoln's famous remark about, "God must have loved the common people because he made so many of them." Well this Bird kept talking about his man being for the common people, and he flopped terribly. You are not going to get people's votes nowadays by calling them common. Lincoln might have said it but I bet you it was not until after he was elected.

The fellow that nominated Charley Bryan[5] from Nebraska was the only truthful one. He said, "I am going to nominate a Politician." You know nobody at these things dare mention Politician. Matchless leader or successor to Jefferson are about as low as they even mention. This fellow told how Bryan had lowered the price of Gasoline in Nebraska. And a crowd of people was seen to leave the hall. I think it was John D. Rockefeller and his Bible Class.

In the Charley Bryan demonstration staged by Nebraska, Florida joined in out of brotherly love.

When Bryan was presented the Band played "Way down Yonder in the Corn Field."

When Jimmy Cox[6] was Nominated the band played, "Should Old Acquaintance Be Forgot." Jimmy Cox is a mighty fine man, But I

166

don't know of any quicker way in the World to be forgotten in this Country than to be defeated for President. A Man can leave the Country and people will always remember that he went some place. But if he is defeated for President they can't remember that he ever did anything.

Smith's Demonstration lasted one hour and a Half. McAdoo's almost as long. But most of them just managed to last through a verse and one chorus by the Band.

Matthews of New Jersey nominated Gov. Silzer[7] also of New Jersey. He made a plea for him on the ground that he came from the same state that President Wilson did. That don't mean anything. Look I come from the same state that Harry Sinclair did. Yet I couldn't find an Oil Well without a search warrant.

His principal plea for Silzer was on the Highways of New Jersey. So if people west of the Mississippi and down south want a President who will keep the Roads of New Jersey up in good shape you can't do better than have him.

A guy from Utah talked so long and loud that all of us couldn't see how it could be anybody in the world he was nominating but Brigham Young[8] that Matchless Father. But at the finish he crossed by saying he was seconding McAdoo's nomination.

You could never tell until one got through who he was going to name. They would pull the name last. That would be the only surprise they had.

Quinn of Minnesota throwed the biggest scare into the Convention. He praised his man so high that everybody in the hall knew it couldn't be anybody but La Follette but he fooled us all by seconding Smith. In his talk he never spoke of anything east of St. Paul and in Smith's travels he has never been west of Syracuse. So you see for yourself how hard it was to follow who they were going to name.[9]

167

IN THE MIDST OF A 7 YEAR HITCH

WELL, I GUESS YOU HEARD ABOUT MY PRESIDENTIAL BOOM.

IN THE MIDST OF A 7 YEAR HITCH

WELL, I guess you heard about my Presidential Boom. You know every calamity in the World befell the Democrats while they were here in session the last couple of years.[1] First they started in nominating. The entire first week was taken up with that. They nominated so many Democrats that if it had kept up another day they would have had to go over into the Republican Column. They talked their Delegates and audience to death the first week. No wonder they couldn't agree there was no two Delegates that could remember the same Candidate.

Well, it ran along week after week and the longer it ran the more confused the Delegates got. They began to get this Convention mixed up with the San Francisco one, because it had been so long since they left home, why, both Conventions seemed about the same distance off. One Delegation got to voting for Cox thinking it was 'Frisco. The Chairman had no more than got that straightened out and explained to them that this was an entirely different year when what does my Native State of Oklahoma do! They woke up the Chairman of their Delegation right quick one day to answer Roll Call and he blurts out, "Oklahoma votes 20 for Robert L. Owen."[2] Well, the chairman had to explain to them that this was not 1920, and that Mr. Owen was not a Candidate, he was only a Delegate. The Missouri Delegation, when they could not get any two to agree, voted for two days for Champ Clark[3], until Telegrams commenced to pour in telling them of his demise.

Nebraska voted for Bryan, and got sore when the rest of the Convention thought it was W. J. They said it was a Son or a Brother or something of his. Mississippi and Louisiana started voting for my old friend Pat Harrison and Pat's Bottle run out, and they found an old Hoffman House Hotel Register,[4] and from that on they just voted for the names on it.

Alabama was the only State that you could absolutely depend on. It seems that years ago Alabama sent a Delegation to some Convention instructed for a Candidate and that when they got there they sold out and voted for another. So they have passed a Law that any time they send a troup away again that they were going to vote for the man they told them to until the Candidate's body had been duly pronounced dead by the Home Coroner. Well, that knocked any chance of profit out of this trip as far as Alabama was concerned.

La Follette, out in Cleveland, wrote a Platform, held a Convention, nominated himself, and went home. All this happened during the time they were polling the Illinois Delegation here at this Convention.

Women Delegates started in with Bobbed Hair and wound up by being able to sit on it. One Woman sent back home for her washing machine. The Arkansas Delegation started in whittling up the Board floor and whittled their way from the Back of the Hall up to the Speaker's Platform. There was so many shavings under their Chairs that if a fire had ever broken out in the building, between these shavings and the long Whiskers, why, there would never in the World have been a way to stop it. There was one old long bearded Man from Utah, that when the voting on the Klan got close shook 4 Delegates with half a vote each out from under his Whiskers and decided the issue right there.

All the members of the National Committees had Gold Badges to start in with. The thing had only gone along a few weeks when they commenced to turn green and finally you couldn't tell whether it was a Badge or a Shamrock.

It's too bad because all the Delegates here will lose their votes when they go home this Fall. The law plainly states that you must have been a resident of the State for the last 6 months. If they were not thoughtful to register when they come to New York, they will lose their votes entirely.

Lots of the Delegates also had Wives who were Delegates, and this has been the longest time they ever spent together in their lives. I bet you will never see another Man go on a Delegation to a Democratic Convention when his Wife is on one. South Carolina has no Divorces, so of course this Convention gave all their members a chance to get out of the State, claim a residence of 6 months, and be divorced before they got home.

Now, mind you, as I pen these lines[5] this thing is still going on. It's Monday morning of the third week. I don't know now who they will nominate. In fact people have lost interest. If they ever do nominate somebody some of the Papers may carry it and you may know it by the time you read this, but I doubt if he will even be nominated by then. If he is, it will be too late to get his name on the Ballot by November, as the racing Forms have already gone to press for the November Classic. I am certainly glad that La Follette entered. That will give Coolidge somebody to run against, anyway.

If they don't hurry up they will be the only Party in the World that ever nominated a Candidate and got him defeated on the same day.

In number of Population the Convention is holding its own. The deaths from old age among the Delegates is about offset by the Birthrate. Personally I think that the Candidates who will finally be nominated will be born in this Convention.

172

THE DEATHS FROM OLD AGE AMONG THE DELEGATES IS ABOUT OFFSET BY
THE BIRTHRATE.

I have been writing a daily account for the Papers for this seven years' Hitch. I took it for so much for the job. If I had signed by the word I would be able now to walk by and hiss Rockefeller.

In 1860, the Almanac says, a Democratic Convention was moved from Charleston to Baltimore. There is nobody here in this Convention to verify it, so I doubt if it ever happened. But, anyway, they talked for two Days about moving this one, on account of it being held here in New York where one of the Candidates lives. Well, they got to figuring and there was no Town they could take it to that didn't have a Candidate who lived there.

Of course their thoughts naturally turned to Claremore, Oklahoma, the best Town between Foyil and Catoosa in Oklahoma. Then when Arizona showed such splendid judgment in putting me in nomination, why of course we couldn't go there on account of the Galleries there being biased in favor of my nomination.[6] Then they figured they might just as well stay here. Everybody had got used to the place, and if they moved them they would just have to get used to sleeping in strange chairs again, and maybe by a different seating arrangement they might be sleeping next to some one they didn't even know. It meant really a lot of trouble, anyway, opening up new credit accounts and getting used to a different Climate.

I want the Democrats to just pass this election by without getting beat and then center all their forces on 1928. Cal. will be ineligible then, unless they may pass a Constitutional amendment to elect a President for life—and he is so lucky they are just liable to do it. But if he is out, the Republicans will have to get a new man too. Then it will be an even break.

But go ahead with this Convention and pick him now. In fact I would pick out three or four to run in rotation in 1928, '32, '36, and so on, because you will never get Democratic Delegates to give up the best part of their lives by attending another one of these things. If they are wise today down there they will pick Jackie Coogan,[7] for President and Baby Peggy[8] for Vice President.

"WILL ROGERS JR." REPORTS THE CONVENTION FOR HIS FATHER, WORN OUT BY LONG SERVICE

*(Mr. Rogers' articles on the Convention attracted more attention than perhaps any other humorous political articles. This one, in particular, brought him comments from all over the country.—*THE PUBLISHERS.*)*

"WILL ROGERS JR." REPORTS THE CONVENTION FOR HIS FATHER,[1] WORN OUT BY LONG SERVICE

WILL ROGERS JR. attended the convention to take up the duties of reporter to replace his venerable old father.

By WILL ROGERS JR.

Papa called us all in last night and made his last will and testament, he called it. He said he had carried his work on just as long as he could and he realized that he was unable, on account of his old age, to go further with it. He put in the will that I being the oldest was to take up his life's work, that of reporting the Democratic National Convention.

He herded us all and told us of how he had given all the best years of his life to this and out of respect to his name and memory that we children should carry on. And that our children were to do likewise and that we should raise them to always know that their mission through life would be to keep reporting the progress of the Democratic National Convention at New York. And it was in the will that if we didn't we would forfeit any claim to any royalties that might still be coming due from books that he had written on the early life of the convention.

Mama wants to send him to the Old Men and Old Women's Home for Survivors of this Convention, but he won't go. Poor Mama is worried about him. He won't talk rational. He just keeps saying, "Alabama" and "for what purpose does the gentleman arise," and "if we can't elect our candidate we will see that you don't get yours" and "unfit" and "release." We don't know what it all means.

Now, Mr. Editor, I am only a little boy and I am not much of a reporter, but Papa told us we didn't have to be very good; that all we must practice was endurance. But you will, Mr. Editor, please take my story, won't you for Mama's sake, for she knew how poor Papa hated to give up and how proud he will be if I can only keep his life's work going?

Mama got our Dad's old press badge and patched it up so it would stick together and I went down today. The hall was full of all those feeble people and it looked kinder like a church; everybody was sleeping. All but one man, who was standing and reading aloud out of a geography the names of States that are situated in the Western Hemisphere and that don't belong to Canada.

Papa had given me an old worn and torn paper with a list on it that he had used to mark off the numbers on when this convention

177

started. He told me to always keep it for comparisons. Also that a museum had tried to buy it from him. I go to school and our teacher had told us what a wonderful country this is we live in, and how it had stuck so well together and, sure enough, when this man kept reading these names and figures, why, on Dad's old paper were a lot of the same ones.

I kept waiting for him to call out the name "Wisconsin" that Dad had, but this fellow didn't have it on his, and according to Dad's old paper we at that time had California and anybody knows that Japan has owned California for years. On Dad's old paper they still had the Philippine Islands, which is now Japan's Naval Base. But as for the candidates, the names were just the same. None of them had dropped out. Their sons were carrying on their father's life work too, trying to hold what votes they had. Saulsbury Jr.[2] had six. Underwood Jr.[3] had a few more than what was on Dad's paper, as the State of Alabama had more population and had naturally increased its number of delegates.

An old man sat by me and I got to talking to him and he seemed to want to be friendly and talk of his early life. He said his name was Coogan. "Jackie Coogan," I think he said, and that he used to be in some old fashioned things called moving pictures, and that he could remember as a child when this started that men used to be wakened up and have to call out the numbers when their States were called. But now they have little phonographs and every time a State is called, why the phonograph says "Two and nine-eighths for Smith Jr. and one and sixty-five fifths for McAdoo Jr." and so on.

A man has a hammer and he couldn't keep them awake with it any longer so they adjourned, and the attendants wheeled them all out. It was only about three o'clock in the afternoon and they were to be back again at nine. I went home to tell Pop what had happened and to write my story. He said, "It's looking better, son; they are adjourning earlier and starting later. Maybe the miracle will happen," and his old eyes began to gleam as he seemed to vision the end of his glorious dream.

Then I told him very enthusiastically, "Oh, yes, Pop, it looks great because a man with a family name of Brennan got up, and one named Cramer,[4] and said they would adjourn and hold a conference of leaders and would have something to report by tonight."

Well, I wish you could have seen my poor old Dad. He went into spasms. He pulled his hair. He raved. None of us could do anything with him. He had been all right before I had mentioned this leader and conference business. He then said:

"Son, those same men's fathers started holding those conferences forty years ago. Going to report something to the convention tonight? That is exactly what is the matter with this convention now, it's those conferences. If they had let the delegates confer instead of the leaders, why, your poor old father could have spent a life of usefulness instead of one listening to a man read off numbers, which we all knew better than he did.

"Son, if it's the Taggarts and Rockwells and Macks and Cramers and all of them that are conferring, you will die, like your poor old father, right at your post, listening for something to happen."[5]

So, please, Mr. Editor, take this story, and tomorrow, when I come home to dear old Dad, I will make him feel good. I won't tell him they are going to hold another conference.

ROPING A CRITIC

ROPING A CRITIC[1]

PROLOGUE—These critics have been interviewing Actors (and us other people that appear on the stage) for years. And none of the interviews have ever been right, cause they never told the truth. Course they couldn't tell the truth about a lot of us, if they had he would have put us out of business. But they tried to be so kind to us and tell all the noble deeds that at the finish we had lost more friends than we had gained by the interview.

Now there is nothing interesting in an Actor but his act and you can get it at the box office price. This season you won't even have to form in line. If you can get a party of three to go with you you can get a rate.

But I figured there was something interesting about a Critic. Why, there are scientists that spend a life time studying a Toad.

Now, I might not find out as much as these Toad experts but I am going to look one of these Critics over at short range for about an hour—as Actors have got plenty of time—we are not bowing much nowadays.

So I picked out the Male of the Species as they are not as venomous as the females. I picked out Ashton Stevens,[2] principally on account of him being frail of statue and because I had seen his name one time on an Ash Can for endorsing a Wintergarden Show.

Act I. DRESSING ROOM COLONIAL THEATER.—Enter Stevens made up as Critic. Gray suit, leather buttons, Black Felt Hat on upside down (same one Dick Little[3] used to wear), middle finger of each hand calloused from knocking Actors. Smoking Pipe which is against all Theater rules, but on account of being critic managers can't say anything. The smoking really wasn't as bad as the Tobacco.

I started in to interview him and he started in like an Actor by lying. So I stopped him right there and said: "Say, this is not a theatrical interview. I am representing the Public and I want the real dope on Critics."

Q—Where were you born? Even a Critic has to be born.

A—I was born in San Francisco in 18—.

Q—Never mind when you were born—the reading public can tell by your jokes how old you are. Why were you born?

A—No answer.

Q—Well, if you can't think of a reason neither can I, so we will let that question go. Did Frisco ever find out that you were born there?

A—Yes.

Q—Is that why you left there?

A—No answer.

Q—When did you first show symptoms of becoming a Critic?

A—When I had lost my job at everything else.

Q—Didn't you tell your folks and didn't they have anything done for you to cure this?

A—I was afraid to tell them.

Q—Who gave you your first job Criticing?

A—William Randolph Hearst.

O—Why did he give it to you?

A—He heard me play the Banjo.

Q—He heard you play the Banjo and gave you a job as Critic. I suppose if he saw me throw a rope he would make me a Society Editor?

A—Oh, but it is not for my Banjoing that he keeps me now, its for my writings.

Q—Oh, he has forgot that you taught him to play the Banjo—that's why you still work for him?

A—No, its my writings. You see he took me from Frisco to New York and put me on the New York Journal.

Q—Now you say he took you there as Critic. Don't you really think he might have been getting a little rusty on the Banjo and needed it tuned?

A—No, I stayed there 4 years.

Q—What happened at the end of 4 years, did you all run out of Tunes, or did you break the Banjo or what?

A—No, then he promoted me to Chicago.

Q—You felt that you had taught him all you knew. Did you bring the Banjo out here with you?

A—Oh, yes I have it; I will bring it over now and show you how I play.

Q—Never mind bringing it over now or any other time. We will drop the Banjo until some time you feel you want a change of jobs. You can take it over to Medill McCormicks[4] and teach him. He could at least amuse the other Senators with it and perhaps make you Editor of the Tribune. Now to get back to Criticing. What makes a Dramatic Critic?

A—Two Free Seats a Night on the Isle.

Q—Is it true that it is the only business in the World with absolutely no qualifications?

A—Yes; next to being a comedian with a Ziegfeld Show its the only thing that requires no training.

Q—Is it true that Dyspepsia is necessary to being a Critic?

A—Yes; its more prevalent now since the Movies come in.

184

Q—Don't you think that Prohibition has lowered the Standard of Dramatic Criticism?

A—Yes; among those that didn't look ahead and supply, I think that to be true.

Q—They still train on Scotch, don't they?

A—Well, they are not as well trained as they used to be.

Q—Don't you find a great many people that think they are Critics?

A—Yes, but I find very few that get paid for it.

Q—Do you believe in constructive Criticism?

A—No; I believe in entertaining Criticism.

Q—Do you get many letters kicking on your opinion?

A—Oh, yes; quite a few.

Q—In that way you can tell just how many read it, can't you? I read where three out of four of every newspaper started failed. What percentage of dramatic Criticisms do you think is responsible for this failure?

A—I don't know; I was never on a failing paper.

Q—That's pretty good; that's a Nifty. Now you Critics having never tried it, you don't realize just how hard it is to be an Actor?

A—Yes, the more plays we see the more we realize it.

Q—Now, you say you have worked for Mr. Hearst twenty-five years for teaching him the Banjo. What instrument did Brisbane teach him and do you think I could interest him in a Base Drum? I hammer a mean Blues on one of those things.

A—You might snare him with that. It takes two heads to make a drum.

Now, Dear Readers—both of you—if this little interview has made you feel more kindly toward the Dramatic Critics, and has brought their overworked profession to the high standards to which I have tried to honestly picture them, my work will not have been in vain.

"THE WORLD TOMORROW," AFTER THE
MANNER OF GREAT JOURNALISTS

"THE WORLD TOMORROW," AFTER THE MANNER OF GREAT JOURNALISTS*[1]

NOW for the last few months I have been writing and I have become ambitious and want to do "Bigger and Better things." I realize that my writings up to now have only appealed to the Morons. (That's not Mormon misspelled. It's *Morons,* just as it's spelled.) So I have been a close Student and admirer of some of our great editorial writers and I have tried to study their style and, beginning with this article, I am changing my entire method of Literature and I hereby bid Adieu to my Half-Wit Audience. (As a writer's Writings never appeal to a higher grade of intelligence than the Writer himself.) So, from now on, I am going to give these learned and heavy thinkers a run for their Laurels. I am out to make the front Page. My Column will be called The World Tomorrow, not only commenting on the news of Today but predicting what the morrow will bring forth.

A Race Horse, In Memorandum, beats the great Zev,[2] the International Favorite and My Own thrown in for good measure. That news will perhaps interest 40 million Human Beings, and 2,000 Bookmakers, while the news of the unearthing of a Prehistoric Skull at Santa Barbara, California, linking us up with the Neanderthal age will only be appreciated by a small Majority of us thinking People. Some anthropologists, however, consider the extinct Neanderthal Man as a separate Species (Homo Neanderthalenis) intermediate between the Java Man (or Pithecanthropus). According to Linneaus, Humanity comprises four races: the Whites, having a light colored skin, belonging to the Caucasian race; the Blacks, the completest possible negation of White; the Republicans, form of genus Homo ape in his earliest Prehistoric State; and, last of the four Races the Democrat. The Democrat doubtless originated in the eastern Hemisphere. The main structural characters distinguishing him are his gait, the modification of the feet for walking instead of prehension, and the great Toe being non-opposable, and, most of all, the enormous development of the brain, and smooth rounded Skull.

But what cares the man of today for the Neanderthal Age! He is of the Speculative Age. If he can get 10 Dollars down on the Nose of a winner at about 15 to one, he don't care if we descend from Goat or Ape.

As Demosthenes, the Great William Jennings Bryan of his time,

*With apologies to Arthur Brisbane.

189

so aptly put it when he causally met Confucius, the originator of Mah-Jong on Epsom Downs:[3] "Good Afternoon, countryman, art thee risking a few Shekels on thy favorite Crow Bait in this Race? And Confucius pulled the following Nifty which has been handed down through the Ages, and made him the Philosopher of Shanghai;

"No, Demosthenes, Betting is a form of unintelligence. So long as we have betting, we will know we have the ignorant with us."

That little remark of Confucius was well said, and the fact that we had 40 million interested in the Race, and only a handful interested in the Neanderthal Man, proves we have a long way to go yet until Civilization is thoroughly reached.

The Crown Prince of Germany[4] is to be allowed to return, proving that War don't pay. You only have to go back into History a short way to the Trojan Wars. What happened to Priam the King of Troy when Prince Paris his Heir and Son was born? Eros, Goddess of Discord, threw out a Golden Apple to the most beautiful, and Juno, Minerva and Venus all claimed it. Paris was to decide. He gave the Apple to Venus. Helen of Troy, the most beautiful Woman in Sparta, got jealous of Paris and that culminated in the War of Troy. Troy was besieged for 9 years. This Trojan War alone should prove to the greedy Interests that War don't pay. And Sons born of Kings don't pay. A law should be passed that all offspring of Royal Birth should be of the feminine Gender.

An American army airman flies at the rate of 258 miles an hour. What does this astounding feat mean to the World? What did Napoleon say at Austerlitz in 1805, just after the battle of Ulm, and after the Old Corsican had rushed his troops from Cologne? He said, "An army travels on its Stomach."

Look at the progress that has been made in the mode of Transportation from the Napoleon days to this! I don't know exactly how far a man could travel in a day on his Stomach. If he had a good Stomach and was an Apt Traveler he might make pretty good headway. There was no way in reckoning speed in those days as there was no way of fixing a speedometer on a Soldier's Stomach, but if you take a Soldier going away from the Enemy, and if his Stomach held out, he certainly ought to have had the abdominal record of his time.

But has Congress heeded what the Airship is doing? No, they go ahead building Battleships which will be as useless as a shipping board. Transportation advances but our Lawmakers are still traveling on their Stomach.[5]

Lloyd George goes home to England after inviting us to join in the Salvation of Europe. You have only to turn to Hugo's Oration on

Voltaire to find out if we should meddle in the selfish affairs of European Turmoil. Hugo said: "Before going further, let us come to an understanding, Gentlemen, upon the word Abyss. There are good abysses: such are the abysses in which evil is engulfed. Rabelais warned royalty in Gargantua. Moliere warned the people at Tartuffe." That proves right there to any thinking person that we should not meddle in the affairs of these envious Nations. The more Trouble you get them out of, the more they get into. No, the time has come when this Country has got to bank up our own fires for a cold morning. Just remember Cicero's words speaking at Glasgow in regard to America's participation in the World's War: "La premiere femme du monde la tete montee en se couchant." Those who want to adjust Europe's Carburetor should remember Horace Greeleys' immortal Gag: "Go west, young man, *Not* east."

A Lady in Chicago is arrested for killing a casual acquaintance. That's news. If she had killed her Husband or Lover that would be commonplace. But friends are seldom killed. What does the 8th chapter, second verse, of the first Book of Matthew teach us? That verse should be enough to teach us that friendship should be trusted. We will never have true civilization until we have learned to recognize the rights of others.

Judge Gary, the head of the great Steel Corporation, eats only the white of a soft boiled egg for breakfast. Which should be a lesson to some of you who think you have to eat the whole egg to subsist. We should look and learn from our Men who have Done Things. Read Einstein's[6] Theory on what constitutes over-gorging. He says: "Light rays, if obstructed, have an observed constant velocity irrespective of the relative velocity between the observer." That should show even the ignorant when they have enough.

A little Girl in Brooklyn started to school and forgot her books and had to go home for them. There you have a bit of news that is valuable. We are at that age when we are rushing headlong and paying no attention to small details. It's only the big things of life that interest us. For instance, the little Girl was only interested in getting to the School, not in what she had when she got there. If we only stopped to realize that it is really after all the little things that count, why, we would be a wiser and more contented race. People that can't remember should remember what Socrates said to Plato on the subject of forgetfulness. He said: "Where then I wonder shall we find Justice and Injustice in it? With which have we contemplated? Has it simultaneously made its entrance?"

A Professor of Columbia University won a prize by writing a Book in 15 hours. That's a good thing. The quicker the Authors write them the quicker they can get to some useful work. But if Pascal were on earth today and heard of that feat he would say: "That's fine, Professor, but what did you do with the other 10 Hours?"

It takes two and a half Tons of Marks to buy a Stein of Beer in Berlin. Before the War you could have bought two and a half Tons of Beer for a Mark. What does Wall Street think of that? It shows you that selfish Interests can't rule the People, when they make up their mind to rebel.

P. S. You see I have an Encyclopedia, too.

SETTLING THE AFFAIRS OF THE WORLD
IN MY OWN WAY

"IF THEY HAVEN'T GOT ENOUGH WATER IN THERE TO FILL THE HARBOR, WE
WILL HAVE TO ASK THE NEIGHBORS TO DRAIN THEIR CORN LIQUOR."

SETTLING THE AFFAIRS OF THE WORLD
IN MY OWN WAY

WELL, they brought our Soldiers back from Germany. Would have brought them back sooner but we didn't have anybody in Washington who knew where they were. We had to leave 'em over there so they could get the Mail that was sent to them during the war. Had to leave 'em over there anyway; two of them hadn't married yet.[1]

Since I wrote you last,[2] an awful lot has happened at the Studio in Washington, D.C. You know out where they make the Movies, the place we make them is called the Studio. We are a great deal alike in lots of respects. We make what we think will be two kinds of Pictures, Comedy and Drama, or sad ones. Now you take the Capitol at Washington, that's the biggest Studio in the World. We call ours, Pictures, when they are turned out. They call theirs Laws, or Bills. It's all the same thing. We often make what we think is Drama, but when it is shown it is received by the audience as Comedy. So the uncertainty is about equal both places.

The way to judge a good Comedy is by how long it will last and have people talk about it. Now Congress has turned out some that have lived for years and people are still laughing about them, and as for Sad productions, they have turned out some that for sadness make "Over the Hills" look like a roaring farce.

Girls win a little State Popularity Contest that is conducted by some Newspaper; then they are put into the Movies to entertain 110 million people who they never saw or know anything about. Now that's the same way with the Capitol Comedy Company of Washington. They win a State Popularity Contest backed by a Newspaper and are sent to Washington to turn out Laws for 110 million people they never saw.

They have what they call Congress, or the Lower House. That compares to what we call the Scenario Department. That's where somebody gets the idea of what he thinks will make a good Comedy Bill or Law, and they argue around and put it into shape.

Then it is passed along, printed, or shot, or Photographed, as we call it; then it reaches the Senate or the Cutting and Titling Department. Now, in our Movie Studios we have what we call Gag Men whose sole business is to just furnish some little Gag, or Amendment as they call it, which will get a laugh or perhaps change the whole thing around.

Now the Senate has what is considered the best and highest priced Gag Men that can be collected anywhere. Why, they put in so many little gags or amendments that the poor Author of the thing don't know his own story.

They consider if a man can sit there in the Studio in Washington and just put in one funny amendment in each Bill, or production, that will change it from what it originally meant, why, he is considered to have earned his pay. Take for Instance the Prohibition Production that was introduced in the Congress or Scenario Department as a Comedy.

Well, when it came up in the Senate, one of the Gag or Title Men says, "I got an Idea; instead of this just being a joke, and doing away with the Saloons and Bar Rooms, why I will put in a Title here that will do away with everything." So they sent around to all the Bars in Washington and got a Quorum and released what was to be a harmless little Comedy—made over into a Tragedy.

Then they put out a Production called the Non-Taxable Bond, or "Let the Little Fellow Pay." Well it had a certain Vogue for a while with the Rich. But it flopped terribly in the cheaper priced Houses.

Another one they put out a lot of you will remember was called the Income or Sur-Tax. It was released under the Title of, "Inherit your money and your Sur-Tax is Lighter."

The main Character in this one was a working man on salary, with no Capital Investment to fall back on, paying more on his income than the fellow who has his original Capital and draws his money just from interest. That Production has been hissed in some of the best houses.

They started to put on a Big one that everybody in America was looking forward to and wanted them to produce called, "The Birth of the Bonus," or "How Could You Forget so Soon!" But on account of Finances they couldn't produce that and the "Non-Taxable Bond Production" both, so they let the Bonus one go.

They have been working on two dandies. One is called, "Refund, Refund, I am always refunding You." It's principally for British Trade.

Then they got a Dandy Comedy; well, it's really a serial as they put it on every year. Everybody in the whole Studio is interested in it and get a share of it. It's really their yearly Bonus in addition to their Salary. It's called, "Rivers and Harbors," or, "I'LL GET MINE."

They got some of the funniest Scenes in there where they take 56 million Dollars of the People's money and they promise to make a lot of Streams wide enough to fish in. Now I saw a Pre-Release of it and here are some of the Real Titles. In Virginia, their Gag Senator has thought of a River called the MATTIPONI. In North Carolina, their Title writer, Overman,[3] thought of a name, the CONTENTNEA

196

CREEK. But the funniest Title in the whole Production is the CA-LOOSEHATCHIE, in Florida. It's located right in the fairway of a Golf Course and Congress must move it or in two years it will be filled up with Golf Balls.

Then they have a scene applying for funds to dredge TOM-BIGBEE CREEK and the BIG SUNFLOWER, in Mississippi. Well, that's money well spent to do that, as they may find some of the missing population.

And there's the CLATSKANIE in Oregon. Now what I am wondering is how our Navy is to make the Jump from the Harbor of Tombigbee to the Docks in Oregon on the Clatskanie. Of course, that's a different appropriation or production, and will be arranged later.

Now I am off my Senators from Oklahoma, especially Robert Owen, who is a part Cherokee Indian like myself (and as proud of it as I am). Now I got names right there on my farm where I was born that are funny, too, and Owen don't do a thing to get me a Harbor on the VERDIGRIS river[4] at OOLAGAH in what used to be the District of COOWEESCOOWEE (before we spoiled the best Territory in the World to make a State).

Right across the river from me lives JIM TICKEATER. Now suppose a foreign fleet should come up there. We can't ask those Turtles and Water Moccasins to move out without Government sanction. If they haven't got enough water in there to fill the harbor (we are only 18 miles from NOWATER, Oklahoma), why, we will have to ask all the Neighbors to drain their Corn Liquor from their stills in there for a couple of days. Then we could float the Leviathan.

Of course I don't get anything done for my Harbor because my River really *exists*.

Now, Folks, why patronise California-made Productions? The Capitol Comedy Co. of Washington, D.C., have never had a failure. They are every one, 100 percent funny, or 100 percent Sad.

They are making some changes in their cast down there and later I will tell you about that. Also something about the Director.

So long, Folks, I will meet you at the Naval Manoeuvers on CONTENTNEA CREEK next year.

197

A SKINNY DAKOTA KID WHO MADE GOOD

A SKINNY DAKOTA KID WHO MADE GOOD

OUT of the west came a little skinny runt kid,[1] born out in the hills of South Dakota. On Sundays the Cowpunchers and Ranchers would meet to have Cow Pony races. On account of his being small he was lifted up and a surcingle was strapped around over his legs and around the horse. He was taken to the starting line on a straightaway and was "lapped and tapped" off. He had the nerve and he seemed to have the head. So they cut the surcingle and he got so he could sit up there on one of those postage stamp things they call a Jockey's saddle. He kept riding around these little Country Shooting Gallery meets, and Merry-Go-Round Gatherings, until he finally got good enough to go to a real race track at New Orleans. There he saw more Horses in one race than he had even seen at one track before.

His first race he ran 2nd. Then he said to himself, "Why run second? Why not run first?" And he did. They began to notice that this kid really *savied* a Horse. He spoke their language. Horses seemed to know when the kid was up. He carried a Bat (Jockey's term for a whip) but he never seemed to use it. Other Jocks would come down the stretch whipping a Horse out when the best he could finish would be 4th or 5th. But not this kid. When he couldn't get in the money he never punished them. He hand rode them. He could get more out of a Horse with his hands than another Jock could get with the old Battery up both sleeves.

He got to be recognized as one of the best, and he passed from one Stable to another until he landed with the biggest, a real Trainer and a Real Sportsman-Owner. How many thousands of People in every line come to New York every year that want to make good, get ahead and be recognized! They come by the millions. How many, if anything happened to them, would get even a passing Notice in the busy and overcrowded New York Press. If some Millionaire died, the best he could get would be a column. Then perhaps it wouldn't be read through by a dozen. But what blazoned across the front pages of every Metropolitan daily a few days ago, in bigger headlines than a Presidential Nomination, bigger than the Prince of Wales will get on his arrival? In a race at Saratoga Springs, N.Y., a Horse had fallen and carried down with him a little skinny Kid (that had slept in his youth not in a 5th Avenue Mansion but in Box Stalls all over the Country with Horses, the Horses he knew how to ride and the Horses that loved to run their best for him).

Here was the Headline: "SANDE[2] IS HURT. He may never ride again." They don't have to give even his first name; few know it. They

201

don't have to explain who he is. They don't have to tell which Rockefeller or Morgan[3] it was. It was just Sande. There is only one. Our Sande! The boy who had carried America's colors to Victory over England's great Papyrus and their Premier Jockey Steve Donohue.[4]

The Ambulance rushes on the track and picks him up; it is followed by hundreds afoot, running. The entire grand stands of people rush to the temporary Track Hospital to see how Sande is, and hoping and praying that it's not serious. He revives long enough to tell his Wife he is all right. Game kid that. Then he faints again. Mrs. Vanderbilt[5] and the elite of Society are assisting and doing all they can to help. A personal Physician to a President of the United States is working over him.[6] He could not have shown any more anxiety over the President than he did over this kid. When the thousands of pleasure seekers and excitement hunters rushed from the stands and saw them lifting that frail lifeless looking form from the track Ambulance there was not one that wouldn't have given an Arm off their body if they had thought it would save his Life, and that goes for Touts, and Grooms, and Swipes, as well as the Public.

Some western people who don't know are always saying Easterners have no Heart, everything is for themselves and the Dough. Say, don't tell me that! Geography don't change Human Nature. If you are Right, people are for you whether it's in Africa or Siberia. A wire was sent by Mr. Widener,[7] a millionaire Racing Official, to Dr. Russell[8] the great Specialist of Roosevelt Hospital, New York, "Come at once. Spare no expense. SANDE is Hurt!" That's all Secretary Slemp[9] could do if President Coolidge was hurt.

Mr. Sinclair withdrew all Horses from the remaining Races. He would withdraw them for Life if he knew it would restore this Kid who worked for him, back to normal again.

Now what made this One Hundred and Ten Pounds (half portion of physical manhood) beloved by not only the racing Public but by the masses who never bet a cent on a Horse race in their lives? The same thing that will make a man great in any line—his absolute HONESTY. The racing public are very fickle and when they lose they are apt to lay blame on almost any quarter. But win or lose, they knew it was not Sande. To have insinuated to one of them that he ever pulled a Horse, would have been taking your Life in your hands. What do you suppose he could have gotten out of some bunch of betting Crooks to have pulled Zev in the big International Race? Why, enough to retire on and never have to take another chance with his Life by riding. He could have done it on the back stretch and no one would have ever known.

Ability is all right but if it is not backed up by Honesty and

202

Public confidence you will never be a Sande. A man that don't love a Horse, there is something the matter with him. If he has no sympathy for the man that does love Horses then there is something worse the matter with him. The best a Man can do is to arrive at the top of his chosen profession. I have always maintained that one Profession is deserving of as much honor as another provided it is honorable.

Through some unknown process of reasoning we have certain things that are called Arts, and to be connected with them raises you above your fellow Man. Say, how do they get that way? If a Man happens to take up Painting and becomes only a mediocre painter, why should he be classed above the Bricklayer who has excelled every other Bricklayer? The Bricklayer is a true Artist in his line or he could not have reached the top. The Painter has not been acclaimed the best in his line hence the Bricklayer is superior. Competition is just as keen in either line. In fact there are more good bricklayers than Painters. If you are the best Taxi Driver you are as much an Artist as Kreisler.[10] You save lives by your skilful driving. That's a meritorious profession, is it not?

A Writer calls himself a Literary Man or an Artist. There are thousands of them, and all, simply because they write, are termed Artists. Is there a Sande among them? Caruso[11] was great, but he had only to show ability. He didn't have to demonstrate any honesty. Nobody tried to keep him from singing his best by bribery.

Now if you think the Racing Public and millions of well wishers are hoping for this Kid's recovery, what about the Horses? They knew him better than the Humans did. Why, that Horse would have broke his own neck rather than hurt Sande. Who is going to ride him in the next race and make him win and not whip him?—not Sande. Who is going to sit on him just where he will be the easiest to carry? Not Sande. Who is going to lean over and whisper in his ear and tell him when to go his best? Not Sande. Who is going to carry a Bat and not use it? Not Sande. Who is going to watch the hand on that starting Barrier and have him headed the right way just when the starter springs it? Not Sande. No, the Horses are the ones who are going to miss him.

If we could speak their language like he can, here are a few conversations that you will hear through the cracks in the Box Stalls: "Gee, I can't run; I don't seem to get any help. I wish Sande were back."

A three year old replies, "I wish there was something we could do. If they would just let us go up to the Hospital and talk to him he would savy," "I wish we had him here in a Box Stall, I would stand up the rest of my life and give him my bed. I would fix him some Clean

Hay to lay on. He don't want those White Caps and Aprons running around. He wants to lay on a Horse Blanket, and have his busted Leg wrapped up with Bandages like he knows how to use on ours. I bet they ain't even got Absorbine up there. That Kid would rather have a Bran Mash than all that Goo they will feed him with up there."

The Old Stake Horse 4 stalls down the line overhears and replies. "Sure, I bet they have one of them Bone Specialists. What that Kid needs is a good Vet."

The old Selling Plater butts in: "Sure, we could cheer him up if he was here. Them Foreigners up there don't speak his Tongue. That kid is part Horse. Remember how he used to kid wid us when he would be working us out at daylight when the rest of the Star Jocks was in feathers. One morning I told him if he didn't quit waking me up so early in the morning I was going to buck him off. He got right back at me; he said, 'If you do I will get you left at the Post your next race.' Gee, he sure did throw a scare into me. And, say, you couldn't loaf on that Bird either. He knew when you was loafing and when you was trying. I throwed up my tail one hot day to make him think I was all through. He give me one cut with the Bat and I dropped that tail and left there so fast I could have run over Man of War. Gee, those were great days; Do youse reckon Zev knows anything about it? I hope they don't tell him; it would break his heart. He sure did love that kid."

Patient readers, Lincoln went down in History as "HONEST Abe," BUT HE NEVER WAS A JOCKEY. If he had been a Jockey he might have gone down as just "Abe."

TAKING THE CURE, BY THE SHORES OF
CAT CREEK

"IF YOU DON'T GET WELL AND THROW AWAY YOUR CRUTCHES I GET NOTHING
OUT OF IT."

TAKING THE CURE, BY THE SHORES OF
CAT CREEK

NOW, in my more or less checkered career before the more or less checkered Public, I have been asked to publicly indorse everything from Chewing Gum, Face Beautifiers, Patent Cocktail Shakers, Ma Junk Sets, even Corsets, Cigarettes, and Chewing Tobacco, all of which I didn't use or know anything about. But I always refused.

You never heard me boosting for anything, for I never saw anything made that the fellow across the street didn't make something just as good.

But, at last, I have found something that I absolutely know no one else has something just as good as, for an all-seeing Nature put this where it is and it's the only one he had, and by a coincidence it is located in the Town near the ranch where I was born and raised.

So I hereby and hereon come out unequivocally (I think that's the way you spell it) in favor of a place that has the water that I *know* will cure you. You might ask, cure me of what? Why, cure you of anything—just name your disease and dive in.

Claremore, Oklahoma, is the birthplace of this Aladdin of health waters. Some misguided Soul named it RADIUM WATER, but Radium will never see the day that it is worth mentioning in the same breath as this Magic Water. Why, to the afflicted and to all suffering Humanity, a Jug of this Water is worth a wheelbarrow full of Radium. Still, even under the handicap of a cheap name, this liquid Godsend has really cured thousands.

Now you may say, "Oh you boost it because you live there," but I don't want you to think so little of me that you would think I would misguide a sick person, just for monetary gain to my Home Town. We don't need you that bad. The city is on a self supporting basis without Patients, just by shipping the Water to Hot Springs, Ark., Hot Springs, Va., West Baden, Ind., and Saratoga, N.Y.

Now, as to a few of the Ignorant who might still be in the dark as to where the Home of this Fountain of Youth is located, I will tell you. I shouldn't waste my time on such Low Brows, but unfortunately they get sick and need assistance the same as the 95 Million others who already know where Claremore is located.

It is located, this Mecca of the ill, about 17 hundred miles west of New York, (either City or State, depends on which ever one you happen to be in). You bear a little south of west, after leaving New York, till you reach Sol McClellan's place, which is just on the outskirts of

Claremore. Before you get into the City proper, if you remember about 500 miles back, you passed another Town. Well, that was St. Louis, most of which is in Illinois.

Now, if you are in the North, and happen to get something the matter with you, we are 847 and a half miles South by West from Gary, Indiana. We have cured hundreds of people from Chicago, Ill. from Gun shot wounds inflicted in attempted murders and robberies. There is only one way to avoid being robbed of anything in Chicago and that is not to have anything.

If you are from Minneapolis, our Radium Water guarantees to cure you of everything but your Swedish accent. If you are from St. Paul, we can cure you of everything but your ingrown hatred for Minneapolis.

I will admit that these waters have quite a peculiar odor as they have a proportion of Sulphur and other unknown ingredients, but visitors from Kansas City, who are used to a Stock Yard breeze, take this wonderful water home as a Perfume.

Approaching this City from the North, don't get it confused with Oolagah, Oklahoma, my original Birthplace, which is 12 miles to the north, as both towns have Post Offices.

From the west, if you are afflicted and you are sure to be or you wouldn't have gone out there, why Claremore is just 1900 miles due east of Mojarve, California, one of the few Towns which Los Angeles has not voted into their Cafeteria. You come east till you reach an Oil Station at a road crossing. This oil station is run by a man named St. Clair. You will see a lot of men pitching Horseshoes. Well, that is the Post Office of Tulsa, Oklahoma, and the men are Millionaires pitching Horseshoes for Oil Wells or for each other's wives.

You should, by this description, have the place pretty well located in your minds. Now, if you are living in the South and are afflicted with a Cotton Crop under a Republican Administration, or with the Klu Klux, or with the Hook Worm, we guarantee to rid you of either or all of these in a course of 24 Baths.

Claremore is located just 905 miles north of Senator Pat Harrison's Mint Bed in Mississippi. In coming from the Gulf Country some have got off the road and had to pass through Dallas, Texas, but have found out their mistake and got back on the main road at Ft. Worth before losing all they had. You easily can tell Ft. Worth. A fellow will be standing down in front of the Drug Store making a speech.

Now, before reaching Claremore, you will pass, even though it's in the middle of the day, a place where you think it's night and you won't know what is the matter. Well, that's Muskogee, Oklahoma, and this darkness is caused by the Color scheme of the population, so put on your headlights and go on in. This Muskogee is really a parking space for cars entering Claremore. Of course, if you want to drive on into the Town of Claremore proper, its only 60 miles through the suburbs from here.

The City is located on Cat Creek, and instead of having a lot of Streets like most Towns and Cities, we have combined on one street. In that way no Street is overlooked.

You might wonder how we discovered this Blarney Stone of Waters. In the early days, us old timers there, always considered these Wells more as an Odor than as a Cure. But one day a man come in there who had been raised in Kansas and he had heard in a round-about way of people bathing, although he had never taken one. So, by mistake, he got into this Radium Water.

He was a one armed man—he had lost an Arm in a rush to get into a Chautauqua Tent in Kansas to hear Bryan speak on Man Vs. Monkey. Well he tried this Bath and it didn't kill him and he noticed that he was beginning to sprout a new arm where he had lost the old one, so he kept on with the Baths and it's to him that we owe the discovery of this wonderful curative Water. Also he was the Pioneer of Bathers of Kansas, as now they tell me it's no uncommon thing to have a Tub in most of their larger towns.

Now, it has been discovered that you can carry a thing too far and overdo it, so we don't want you there too long. A man come there once entirely Legless and stayed a week too long and went away a Centipede.

I want to offer here my personal Testimonial of what it did to me. You see, after this Kansas Guy started it, why, us old Timers moved our bathing from the River into a Tub. Now, at that time, I was practically Tongue tied and couldn't speak out in private much less in Public. Well, after 12 baths, I was able to go to New York and make after dinner speeches. I stopped in Washington on the way and saw how our Government was run and that gave me something funny to speak about.

So, in thanking the Water, I also want to thank the Government for making the whole thing possible. Now, had I taken 24 baths I would have been a Politician, so you see I stopped just in time.

The only thing I get out of this is I have the "Throw Away Crutch Privilege." If you don't get well and throw away your Invalid Chair or crutches I get nothing out of it, so that is why we give you a square deal. If you are not cured, I don't get your Crutches. There is no other resort in the World that works on that small a margin.

W. J. Bryan drank one drink of this Water and turned against Liquor. Senator La Follette drank two drinks of it and turned against everything. So remember Claremore, The Carlsbad of America, where the 'Frisco Railroad crosses the Iron Mountain Railroad, not often, but every few days.

THE END

NOTES

INTRODUCTION

1   William Allen White (1868-1944.) Owner and editor of the *Emporia* (Kansas) *Daily and Weekly Gazette.* Nationally known as social and political analyst and winner of the Pulitzer Prize in 1923. His autobiography, published posthumously in 1946, also won a Pulitzer Prize. He ran unsuccessfully for governor of Kansas on an independent ticket in 1924.

2   Arthur Brisbane (1864-1936). Newspaper editor who worked for both Pulitzer and Hearst owned papers. He was one of the principal perpetrators of sensationalist journalism that helped lead the United States into the Spanish-American War. In 1917 he began his editorial column, "Today," which was eventually syndicated to 200 daily and 1200 weekly newspapers. Built the Ritz Tower building, and with Hearst, the Ziegfeld Theater.

3   William Randolph Hearst (1863-1951). American editor, publisher, and political figure, who owned a huge newspaper empire and at times resorted to sensational journalism. His newspaper career spanned 60 years, and for most of these years he was one of the dominant figures in American journalism. U. S. representative from New York (1903-1907); unsuccessful candidate for mayor of New York City (1905, 1909); unsuccessful candidate for governor of New York (1906).

4   Irvin S. Cobb (1876-1944). Writer, friend, and fellow humorist. Cobb wrote the basic story from which *Judge Priest* was taken. He co-starred with Rogers in *Steamboat Round the Bend.*

5   Ringgold W. Lardner (1885-1933). Journalist best known for his sports in the *Chicago Tribune* and his "Jack Keefe" letters in the *Saturday Evening Post.* On occasion he wrote lyrics for the Ziegfeld Follies.

6   Vicente Blasco-Ibanez (1867-1928). Spanish novelist whose most famous works include *Blood and Sand* (1908) and *The Four Horsemen of the Apocalypse* (1916).

7   Elinor Glyn (1864-1943). Novelist and script writer who wrote *Three Weeks* (1907). This novel was the story of an extra-marital interlude between a Balkan queen and an Englishman. Acquaintances presented her with a tiger skin, for the animal hide was a much publicized feature of the story.

8   Frederick Remington (1861-1909). Artist and author born in New York who traveled in the West and even worked a short while as a cowboy. Although he painted and made sculptures from drawings and sketches, his work was very realistic.

9   Miguel de Cervantes Saavedra (1547-1616). Spanish author whose most famous work, *Don Quixote de la Mancha* was published in two parts, 1605-1615.

Charles Dickens (1812-1870). English novelist who wrote *Pickwick Papers* (1836-1837), and other novels.

Rogers probably referred here to Eugene Melchior Vogue (1848-1910). French writer and diplomat who, during his career, was a staff member of *Revue des Deux Mondes* and the *Journal des Debats.*

Alain Rene Lesage (1668-1747). French novelist and playwright whose best known work is *L'Histoire de Gil Blas de Santillane* (4 vols.) (1715-1735). Rogers mentions these authors because of their reputations.

10   Fedor M. Dostoevski (1821-1881). Russian novelist convicted for conspiracy against the government. He wrote *Crime and Punishment* (1866), *The Brothers Karamazov* (1880), and many others.

Ivan S. Turgenev (1818-1883). Russian novelist whose best known work was *Fathers and Sons* (1862).

Lev Nikolaevich Tolstoi (1828-1910). Russian novelist, moral philosopher, and religious mystic. His best known novels were *War and Peace (1866),* and *Anna Karenina* (1875-1877).

11   Vissarion G. Belinski (1811-1848). Russian literary critic who edited *Moscow Observer (1838-1839).*

211

Ben Hur (1880). Highly successful novel by Lew(is) Wallace (1827-1905). Diplomat, author, and politician.

BREAKING INTO THE WRITING GAME

1 The Ziegfeld Follies was organized by Florenz Ziegfeld who began his career as a promoter of musical features for the Chicago World's Fair, 1893. His musical revue, the "Follies," noted for lavish settings and attractive chorus girls, was introduced to the United States in 1907 and was highly successful for the next twenty years. Will Rogers, with W. C. Fields, Eddie Cantor and hundreds of other entertainers, performed for Ziegfeld for several years. Rogers actually worked for Ziegfeld from 1915-1925.

2 Original Manuscript (hereafter cited OM): *...right here in this paper every Sunday.*

3 OM: *Last Week. . .*

4 Henry Justin Allen (1868-1950). Governor of Kansas (1919-1923); special commissioner of Near East Relief (1923-1924); U. S. senator (April 1, 1929-November 30, 1930); newspaperman at Topeka, Kansas.

5 OM: *(hurry up and print this story or he wont be Governor.)*

6 Henry Ford (1863-1947). Founder of Ford Motor Company. Rogers often commented about Ford and the ubiquitous "flivvers" or model T automobile manufactured by the company. Rogers often remarked about Ford's eccentricity.

7 Truman Handy Newberry (1864-1945). Railway, steel and banking magnate. Assistant secretary of the Navy (1905-1908); secretary of the Navy (1908-1909); U. S. senator from Michigan (1919-1922). Convicted in Michigan courts for corruption in obtaining nomination to Senate; case dismissed in United States Supreme Court.

8 OM: Omitted three paragraphs beginning with *"Speaking of Henry Ford. . . . ,"* through *"I tell you Folks, all Politics is Apple Sauce."*

9 Charles Curtis (1860-1936). U. S. representative from Kansas (1893-1907); U. S. senator (1907-1913, 1914-1929); vice-president under Herbert Hoover (1929-1933). Part Osage, his fractional Indian blood was often referred to by his supporters.

10 During 1922-1923 Greece and Turkey were still fighting over territorial claims.

11 OM: *. . . here now . . .*

12 Charles Michael Schwab (1862-1939). President of Carnegie Steel Company Ltd. (1897-1901); first president of United States Steel Corporation (1901-1903); founder of Bethlehem Steel Corporation (1904).

Elbert Henry Gary (1853-1927). Chairman of the executive committee, United States Steel Corporation (1901-1903). Chairman of the board (1903-1927).

John D. Rockefeller (1839-1937). Founder of Standard Oil Company of Ohio (1870) and various other enterprises.

13 Attempts were being made in Congress to provide for direct election of the president and vice-president thus abolishing the electoral college. Also there were those in Congress who wished to change the date that elected officials assumed office from March 4 to an earlier date in January.

14 William E. Borah (1865-1940). U. S. senator from Idaho (1907-1940). Chairman of Senate committee on foreign relations (1924-1940). He successfully fought against the entrance of the United States into the League of Nations and participated in and supported the Naval Disarmament Conference in Washington (1921-1922).

15 Insert: *"Next Sunday I will tell you about Ambassador Harvey. I am going down to HEAR him land, and see if he has on his Knee Breeches."* (Original article ended with this sentence.)

16 David Lloyd George (1863-1945). Prime Minister of Great Britain, lawyer, orator, and world traveler. Resigned in October 1922 when his opponents feared he was eventually leading the country into war involving Turkey and Greece. Visited United States in September 1923, and was popularly received. Asked American help in stabilizing European conditions created as result of war in Europe.

17 Rogers refers to his three children: William Vann Rogers (1911-   ); Mary Amelia Rogers (1913-   ); James Blake Rogers (1915-   ).

[18] Friedrich Wilhelm Viktor Albert (Kaiser Wilhelm II) (1859-1941). Ruler of Germany (1888-1918). After Germany's defeat in World War I he was exiled and lived the remainder of his life in retirement in the village of Doorn, Holland. Rogers refers to *The Kaiser's Memoirs* (1922).

SETTLING THE CORSET PROBLEM OF THIS COUNTRY

1 OM: *"Since I wrote you all last week . . . "*
2 OM: *. . .in a later Article . . .*
3 OM: Insert: *Now, to jump from Corsets to the U. S. Senate is quite a leap, for, since Ham Lewis left, there has not been a Corset seated there with the doubtful exception of Mr. Lodge. You see we jump directly from a necessity to a Luxury.*

The reason I want to touch on the Senate today is that, as I am writing this, they are having what is called a Filibuster. The name is just as silly as the thing is itself. It means that a Man can get up and talk for 15 to 20 hours at a time, then be relieved by another, just to keep some Bill from coming to a Vote, no matter about the merit of this particular bill, whether its good or bad.

The whole foundation of our Government is based on the majority rule, so they have done their duty when they merely vote against it or for it, which ever they like. There is no other Body of Law-makers in the World that have a thing like that. Why, if a distinguished foreigner was to be taken around to see our Institutions and was taken into the Senate and not told what institution it was, and heard a man ramble on, talking that had been going for 10 or 12 hours, he would probably say, "You have lovely quarters here for your insane but have you no Warden to look after their health to see that they don't talk themselves to death?"

Why, if an inmate did that in an Asylum they would put him in solitary confinement. And, mind you, if any demented person spoke that long there would be something in his speech you could remember, for he, at least, had to be smart or he would never have gone crazy. These just mumble away on any subject.

Imagine a ball player standing at bat and not letting the other side play to keep from having the game called against him. Why, they would murder him; or an Actor, the first one on in a Show, talking all night to keep the rest from going on. You know how long he would last. It's against all the laws of American Sportsmanship, never mind the Parliamentary part of it.

One Senator threatened to read the Bible into the record as part of his Speech. And I guess he would have done it if somebody in the Capitol had had a Bible. Now that would have been a good thing for it would have given a lot of them a chance to hear what it says. But, of course, that was even too sensible to go through.

Instead they just did their own act for 10 or 12 hours each which they thought would be better than anything they could find in the Bible. To imagine how horrible this thing is, did you ever attend a Dinner and hear a Senator speak for 50 minutes or an Hour? If you have, you remember what that did to you! Well, just imagine the same thing only 12 times worse.

HOW TO TELL A BUTLER, AND OTHER ETIQUETTE

1 Emily Post (1873-1960). Writer of books and columns on good manners. Her first widely known book, *Etiquette,* was published in 1922. This article is typical of Rogers' wit as he talks about current fads, rhetoric, and false rhetoric.
2 OM: *. . . remain Non challant.*

DEFENDING MY SOUP PLATE POSITION

1 Mrs. John W. Davis (1869-1943) (Ellen Bassell). Wife of the unsuccessfulful Democratic presidential candidate (1924), John Davis.

² Percy Hunter Hammond (1873-1936). Drama critic for the *Chicago Tribune* and *New York Tribune*. Superb and effortless prose characterized his reviews. He had a light and irreverent style unlike the older pontifical school of play reviewing.

³ Dutch Treat Club. Organized in 1907 by a group of writers and illustrators who lunched together every Tuesday.

⁴ Thomas Edwin Mix (1880?-1940). Famous cowboy motion picture star. Born in Pennsylvania, Mix later moved to Oklahoma. He was one of the greatest box office attractions in the history of the screen.

⁵ William Jennings Bryan (1860-1925). U.S. representative from Nebraska (1891-1895). Unsuccessful Democratic presidential candidate in 1896, 1900, and 1908. Leader of the party until 1912, when his influence helped nominate Woodrow Wilson. Secretary of state (1913-1915). He was prosecuting attorney in the John T. Scopes trial concerning teaching the theory of evolution in Tennessee.

⁶ *The Literary Digest* reprinted one of Rogers' articles, "How to Tell a Butler and other Etiquette" (October 6, 1923, pp. 46, 50).

⁷ Charles Gates Dawes (1865-1951). Vice-president of the United States (1925-1929). Leading financier, lawyer and politician. Originated the Dawes Plan for solving the German reparation payment question and stabilizing the European economy. U. S. ambassador to Great Britian (1929-1932). Held numerous other governmental offices. Rogers refers to Dawes' much publicized outburst against reporters in New York.

Calvin Coolidge (1872-1933). President of the United States (1923-1929); Massachusetts state senator (1912-1915); lieutenant governor (1916-1918); governor of Massachusetts (1919-1920); vice-president of the United States (1921-1923).

HELPING THE GIRLS WITH THEIR INCOME TAX

¹ There were several proposed changes to the Revenue Act of 1921, and Rogers probably became interested because of the possible effect such changes as depreciation revision would have on filing income tax returns.

² Piggly-Wiggly uprising (1923-1924). Clarence Saunders, founder of Piggly Wiggly Stores Inc., was involved in stock manipulation of the corporation. The stock had been the victim of a "bear raid" and Saunders, by buying corporation stock at different brokerage centers in the country, attempted to push prices higher thus maintaining company solvency. Saunders failed, declared bankruptcy, and almost everyone lost.

³ Jessie Reed (Jessie Rogers) (Not related to Will Rogers) (1897-1940); Anastasia Reilly (1903-1961). Rogers evidently used the names of these ex-Ziegfeld Follies girls to make his "corporation." Jessie Reed, the highest paid of the Follies girls, had already married four times when Rogers wrote this article. Anastasia Reilly married Theodore De L. Buhl, a nephew of Florenz Ziegfeld, and was married to him at the time of her death.

⁴ *Mendelssohn's Spring Song*. Jakob Ludwig Felix Mendelssohn (1809-1847). German composer, pianist, organist and conductor. He actually wrote several spring songs.

⁵ OM: *Well, we have had quite a few prominent Visitors in to look us over lately. Mrs. Nicholas Longworth with a Party of Friends were in last night, and were good enough to come back in the dressing room and give me all the latest on Washington.*

She sure is a chip off the old Block. Talk about Pep! And some sense of humor!I told her I had heard her Husband, Nick, might be the next Speaker of the House. She said she didn't know. I told her I would hate to see that as now he had an awful lot of friends. Being Speaker of the House is just like jumping, in a small Town, from Town Marshall to Justice of the Peace. That is as far as you can go politically. So I hate to see Nick get in bad and spoil a promising Career. I can understand him wanting to be Speaker of a House, as I have visited them at home, and it will at least be a Novelty for him.

I asked her who it looked like the Democrats would run. She said she heard more of Ford than any one. Well, that will at least save everybody the trouble of asking who is he, and what has he done?

Among the prominent Movie Visitors last Night was Susse Hayakawa, the Japanese Screen Star and his cunning little Japanese Wife. After introducing them to the audience, I said that they were a Movie couple who were still married to each other, which might not mean so much in their Country, as perhaps it was a Native custom to stay married in Japan, but that in this country it was a Novelty.

We had quite a sensational murder here of Dorothy Keenan, and on account of the prominence of a Mysterious Mr. Marshall they wouldn't tell his real name. They had us all worked up, and when they did tell it nobody knew any more than they did before. He was better known by "Marshall" than by his own name.

After all the fuss the Papers had made over the prominence of this friend of the Girls, I thought it would at least be Bryan or Lodge, or maybe Uncle Joe— at least somebody we had heard of.

Come to find out his only claim to prominence was marrying a rich Man's Daughter. That's a thing you can't hardly keep from doing nowadays and also we find out he was from Philadelphia. Why even the Town ain't prominent. How was the Man going to be well known.

Well, see by the Papers where the Prince of Wales over in England fell off his Horse again today. That's got so it is not News any more. If he stayed on it would be News. England is all worked up over what to do as they are afraid he will be hurt. I should suggest they have men follow along on foot with a Net and catch him each time as he falls.

THE GREATEST DOCUMENT IN AMERICAN LITERATURE

1 *New York Times* (hereafter cited *NYT*): . . . week's . . .

2 *Yes, We Have No Bananas.* A nonsense song of the 1920's made popular by Eddie Cantor. Words and music by Frank Silver and Irving Cohn (1923).

3 Rudolph Valentino (1895-1926). Silent motion picture star whose best known movies were *Blood and Sand, The Four Horsemen of the Apocalypse,* and *The Sheik.* He acquired wide fame as a dashing, daring, and romantic film hero. During this period he experienced contract problems with his studio; thus a beauty clay manufacturing company sent him on a "dance" tour rather than an "acting" tour. His contract did not expressly forbid dancing appearances.

4 Magnus Johnson (1871-1936). U. S. senator from Minnesota who strongly supported agrarian reform (1923-1925); state representative, senator, and unsuccessful candidate for governor (1922, 1926 on the Farmer-Labor party ticket, and 1936 as an independent); U. S. representative (1933-1935).

5 Hiram W. Johnson (1866-1945). Governor of California (1911-1917); U. S. senator until his death (1917-1945). He was reform-minded and his administration as governor of California was one of the most progressive in the country. As a U. S. senator he earned a reputation as an isolationist, for he opposed such measures as United States entry into World War I and the League of Nations.

6 Michelangelo Buonarroti (1475-1564). Italian painter, sculptor, and architect.

Giuseppe Garibaldi (1807-1882). Italian patriot who aided in the unification of Italy.

Luis Firpo (1895-1960). Argentinian boxer known as "The Wild Bull of the Pampas." Fought Jack Dempsey for world heavyweight championship in 1923. He knocked Dempsey out of the ring, but lost the fight.

7 George Michael Cohan (1878-1942). Vaudeville song and dance man who starred in such plays as "Little Johnny Jones," and "George Washington, Jr." He also authored numerous plays and songs.

8 Walt(er) Whitman (1819-1892). American poet who also was associated with various newspapers and magazines. He is probably best known for *Leaves of Grass* (1855).

9 Horace Greeley (1811-1872). Newspaper editor and reformer. Founded the New York *Tribune* (1841). Known for phrase, "Go West, Young Man." Rogers refers more to the timing of remarks, for when Greeley uttered his idea the American West was yet available for settlement.

William G. McAdoo (1863-1941). Married Eleanor Wilson, daughter of President Woodrow Wilson (1914). U. S. secretary of the treasury (1913-1918); unsuccesfully sought Democratic nomination for president (1920, 1924); U. S. senator from California (1933-1939).

10 William T. Sherman (1820-1891). Civil War general who made this famous remark after the war.

PROSPECTUS FOR "THE REMODLED CHEWING GUM CORPORATION"

1 William Wrigley, Jr. (1861-1932). Founded William Wrigley, Jr. Company to manufacture and market chewing gum. He bought Santa Catalina Island in California, improved it greatly, and it became a famous resort area.

2 Henry Cabot Lodge (1850-1924). Massachusetts state representative (1880-1881); U.S. representative (1887-1893); U.S. senator (1893-1924). Wrote several biographies of famous Americans. Taught American history at Harvard. Delegate to the Washington Conference on Arms Limitations (1921). He vigorously opposed the League of Nations.

3 Adolphus Busch (1839-1913). Owner of Anheuser Busch Brewery at St. Louis, Missouri. He developed Budweiser, Faust, and Michelob beer. He was one of the wealthiest Americans of his generation.

4 Rogers refers to John C. Walton, who was elected governor of Oklahoma in 1922 and impeached November 19, 1923.

5 Sid Grauman (1879-1950). Showman and theater owner who built the Egyptian and Chinese Theaters on Hollywood Boulevard as well as several other famous theaters. The first two performers to have their hand prints and footprints recorded in wet cement in front of the Chinese Theater were Mary Pickford and Douglas Fairbanks, Sr.

6 OM: . . . *delicacy served in the shape of Animals or odd shaped Fruits.) We would add some Popular Juice Flavor to . . .*

INSIDE STUFF ON THE TOTAL ECLIPSE

1 A total eclipse occurred on September 10, 1923.

2 Singer Midgets. Vauderville act consisting of thirty-three people, animals and animal trainers, etc. under contract with the Loew Circuit.

3 Jack Dempsey (1895-   ). World's heavyweight boxing champion from 1919 to 1926. Dempsey fought Luis Firpo, an Argentine boxer, for the championship in 1923. Although Firpo knocked Dempsey out of the ring in the first round, Dempsey regained his balance and knocked the Argentine out in the second round.

4 OM: . . . *as I have to go to the Democratic and Republican Conventions, that I would see them from Tia Juana.*

IT'S TIME SOMEBODY SAID A WORD FOR CALIFORNIA

1 Rogers moved to California in 1919 to be near the movie industry. Thereafter California was his official home, although he often was away weeks at a time.

PROMOTING THE OCEANLESS ONE PIECE SUIT

1 Annette Kellerman (1888-   ). Australian swimmer who more than fifty years ago shocked the world by introducing a one piece figure-hugging bathing suit.

216

2 Radium water, a mineral water used in the early twentieth century and popularly regarded as a cure-all for persons suffering from many diseases, was discovered in Claremore in 1903. The city was a favorite health spa for many years.

WARNING TO JOKERS: LAY OFF THE PRINCE

1 OM: . . . this week . . .
2 Edward Albert Christian George Andrew Patrick David (1894-1972). Prince of Wales, became King of England as Edward VIII in January, 1936. He was king only eleven months, for on December 11, 1936, he abdicated the throne to marry an American divorcee, Mrs. Wallis Warfield Simpson. The former king was given the title Duke of Windsor. He was always an avid sportsman, and had played polo with Will Rogers.
3 Mary Pickford (1893-   ) (Gladys Smith). In the heyday of silent films, became known as "the world's sweetheart." Married Douglas Fairbanks, Sr., in 1920, divorced 1935. Their home "Pickfair" is still a major attraction in Beverly Hills.

SPRING IS HERE, WITH POEMS AND BATH TUBS

1 Rogers' mother died in 1890, when he was eleven years old, and this un-doubtedly affected his later attitudes toward many aspects of society.
2 OM: Added: *Why, now they don't even lay out clean Clothes for it. Half the people that bathe every day put on the same Clothes again. That would have been considered almost heathenish years ago. So that only proves that we were cleaner in those days than we are with all our multitude of Tubs today BUT WE SURE HAVE GOT PRETTY BATH ROOMS.*
3 Tutankhamen (ca. 1358 B.C.). An ancient Egyptian king whose tomb was discovered in 1922 in the Valley of the Kings. Rogers evidently read of the dis-covery and the process of preserving the bodies, because stories concerning the episode were in many periodicals.

MR. FORD AND OTHER POLITICAL SELF-STARTERS

1 OM: . . . *of the last week* . . .
2 OM: . . . *And, say, talking about Presidential Candidates, another one of the likely starters in 1924 Handicap for the 75 thousand a year Grubstake made one of the most impressive showings of his entire career during the past week. And that wasn't anybody but the present Skipper of the Mayflower, Mr. Gamaliel Harding. He spoke on Decoration day at Arlington Cemetery, and when I say he spoke, what I mean is, he said something.*
3 Warren Gamaliel Harding (1865-1923). President of the United States (1921-1923); U. S. senator from Ohio (1915-1921). His administration was known for numerous scandals that occurred involving the Teapot Dome and other oil related projects. Often Rogers remarked about the scandals and the sub-sequent Congressional hearings. Harding died while on a train trip through the West. Most of the scandals became known after his death.
4 OM: . . . *Mr. Harding*. . .
5 William Howard Taft (1857-1930). President of the United States (1909-1913); chief justice of the Supreme Court (1921-1930); secretary of war (1904-1908). Held numerous other government appointments during his lifetime. Taft spoke at the unveiling of a monument dedicated to Salmon P. Chase, a former chief justice of the Supreme Court.
6 OM: . . . *last week*. . .

WILSON COULD LAUGH AT A JOKE ON HIMSELF

1   OM: . . . *in the last few days* . . .
2   (Thomas) Woodrow Wilson (1856-1924). President of the United States
(1913-1921). Well-known for his political idealism. Wilson and his diplomacy
often were the subjects of Rogers' humor. Several times Wilson had been in
Rogers' audience, and the humorist had not been certain just how the president
would react to the jokes about the administration and its officials. After the first
time Wilson heard Rogers, he often quoted the humorist and referred to his
acquaintance with him. Wilson had just died, and therefore Rogers paid him tribute in this article.
3   OM: . . . *coming clear over.*
4   OM: . . . *spin a Rope a little and who had learned to* . . .
5   William Collier (1866-1944). Playwright and comedian who was a member of Daly Theatre Company (1883-1888). Appeared in "On the Quiet," "Never
Say Die," and many plays that he co-authored.
   OM: After Collier read: . . . *and Frank Tinney* . . . (Frank Tinney 1887-
1940. Stage comedian whose career was successful until 1924 when a Follies girl
accused him of beating her. He lost his money, family, and his career declined as
a result. Thus the editors of the book chose to omit his name).
6   John Joseph Pershing (1860-1948). Army General who led U.S. troops
into Mexico hoping to capture Pancho Villa, who had led Mexicans in a raid
against Columbus, New Mexico (1916). Pershing was unsuccessful, and was
forced to leave Mexico when President Venustiano Carranza objected to American
troops being on Mexican soil. Pershing later was the commander of the American
Expeditionary Force to Europe during World War I. Army chief of staff (1921-
1924).
7   Francisco (Pancho) Villa (1877-1923). Mexican revolutionary figure who
was later assassinated.
8   OM: . . . *rode* . . .

A JOB WITH THE JAMES FAMILY

1   OM: Original title: WILL ASKS WARREN FOR A JOB
2   George Brinton McClellan Harvey (1864-1928). U. S. Ambassador to
Great Britain (1921-1923). Rumors circulated that he was considering resignation
of this position due to involvement in a controversy with the former British Prime
Minister Balfour regarding allied loans (1923). Owner and editor of *North American Review* (1899-1926); editor of *Harper's Weekly* (1901-1913); president of
Harper and Brothers (1900-1915).
3   Arthur James Balfour (1848-1930). Prime minister of Great Britain
(1902-1905). Held numerous other governmental positions, and was his country's
representative to the Washington Disarmament Conference (1921-1922). Authored
the Balfour Declaration (1917).
4   Josephus Daniels (1862-1948). Editor of the *Raleigh* (North Carolina)
State Chronicle (1885-1894) and *News and Observer* (1894-1933). Secretary of
the Navy (1913-1921); U S. Ambassador to Mexico (1933-1941).
5   Andrew John Volstead (1860-1947). U.S. representative from Minnesota
(1903-1923). Authored the Volstead Act (1919) which defined as intoxicating
liquor any beverage containing more than one-half of one per cent alcohol. The
Eighteenth Amendment ratified 1919 established prohibition as a national policy.

LET'S TREAT OUR PRESIDENTS LIKE HUMAN BEINGS

1   Rogers referred in this article to the death of President Warren G. Harding on August 3, 1923. Harding was touring the western states by train when he
died suddenly and somewhat mysteriously.

2 Joseph G. Cannon (1836-1926). U. S. representative from Illinois (1873-1891, 1893-1913, 1915-1923); speaker of the House (1903-1911). Was often accused of autocratic methods in controlling House procedures.

3 Will Hays (1879-1954). Chairman of the Republican National Committee (1918-1921). President of the Motion Picture Producers and Distributors Association of America (1922-1945). His efforts to improve the medium and create a new image of the industry after the Roscoe "Fatty" Arbuckle scandal and the death of Wallace Reid are detailed in his *Memoirs* (1955).

4 OM: *He didn't come to see our show, that's true, but he went that night to a better one, so he not only had a sense of Humor but he had good Judgement.*

WHAT WITH FRUIT JUICE AND CONSOMME, IT WAS A WILD PARTY

1 OM: In this article Will Rogers used "Exposure" for "Digest" each time it appeared.

2 OM: *. . . couldn't withstand such untruth. Had Mr. Ford gone through and been elected why the Blowout . . .*

3 OM: *. . . this week . . .*

4 OM: *. . . that Will has he had gone completely . . .*

5 OM: *. . . why they . . .*

6 Pauline Frederick (1885-1938). Stage and film actress who starred in many productions beginning in 1902.

7 Cornelius Vanderbilt, Jr. (1898-1974). Founder of Vanderbilt Newspapers, Inc. Rogers refers here to Vanderbilt's first wife, Rachel Littleton, whom Vanderbilt married on April 29, 1920. They were divorced on November 26, 1927.

8 Will Hays was known for his morals. Moreover, this section of the article is a spoof of expose journalism.

9 Harry Ford Sinclair (1876-1956). Oil producer who was involved with the Teapot Dome leases during the administration of W. G. Harding. Sinclair spent three months in federal prison for contempt of the U. S. Senate, but he was acquitted of charges of conspiracy to defraud the government.

10 Albert B. Fall (1861-1944). U.S. senator from New Mexico (1912-1921); U. S. secretary of the interior (1921-1923). Secretly leased naval oil reserves to Harry Sinclair and Edward Doheny. Fall was indicted for bribery and conspiracy; convicted of bribery, he was sentenced to one year in prison and fined $100,000.

11 Paul Whiteman (1891-1967). American bandleader who became famous in the 1920s for pioneering "sweet style" as opposed to the traditional "classical" style jazz.

WHAT WE NEED IS MORE FRED STONES

1 Fred Stone (1873-1959). One of Rogers' closest friends. Rogers' third son, who died in infancy was named Fred Stone Rogers. Stone was an actor who in 1903 created the Scarecrow role in "The Wizard of Oz." Stone was injured in an air crash in 1927, and Rogers replaced him for almost a year in "Three Cheers."

2 OM: *. . . this week . . .*

3 Dorothy Stone (1905-   ). Daughter of Fred Stone who made her New York debut with her father in "Stepping Stones" (1923). Played Princess Sylvia in "Three Cheers" (1928) which was the production Will Rogers starred in after Stone's air crash.

4 OM: *Dorothy, 16, who will be with him in his next show . . . .*

5 Charles Spencer Chaplin (1889-   ). An English comedian who starred in silent films. He made a fantastic success out of creating a tramp character.

6 OM: *. . . during the past week . . .*

7 Edward F. Gallagher and Al Shean. Vaudeville comedians who were sued by Lee Shubert of Shubert Theaters for not fulfilling their contract. Shubert claimed the comedians were unique and extraordinary, and therefore could not be replaced for the theatrical season. Rogers testified for the comedians.

8 James J. Corbett (1866-1933). American boxer. Won heavyweight championship from John L. Sullivan (1892) and lost to Bob Fitzsimmons (1897). He was often called "Gentleman Jim" because of appearance and bearing. Appeared in movies, on stage, and participated in radio programs.

9 Vernon Blythe Castle (1887-1918) (Vernon Blythe). Popular dancer who originated the one-step, turkey trot, and castle walk. He was also an aviator in the Royal Flying Corps and was killed in an aviation accident.

10 Leo Carrillo (1880-1961). Movie actor who played badman in *Viva Villa;* he is best known for his role as Pancho in the Cisco Kid pictures. Started his career in vaudeville. After Rogers moved to California, he and Carrillo went riding together frequently.

OM: Will Rogers used Frank Tinney instead of Leo Carrillo.

11 Phoebe Anne Oakley Mozee (1860-1926). Famous markswoman who traveled with "Buffalo Bill" Cody's Wild West Show.

12 Rex E. Beach (1877-1949). Writer of adventure stories such as *The Goose Woman* (1925) and *Alaskan Adventures* (1933). Will Rogers' first moving picture, *Laughing Bill Hyde,* was based on one of his novels. Rogers visited Beach on his last flight to Alaska. •

ONE OIL LAWYER PER BARREL

1 OM: . . . *Exposure, a weekly Publication,* . . .

2 OM: Rogers used "Exposure," not "Digest" each time the latter word appeared.

3 Edwin Denby (1870-1929). U. S. representative from Virginia (1905-1911); secretary of the Navy (1921-1924). Involved in Teapot Dome scandal by allowing transfer of naval oil reserves from Navy Department to the Department of the Interior. He was not accused of corruption, but resigned in 1924.

4 Edward Laurence Doheny (1856-1935). Oil producer who was involved in Teapot Dome scandal. He was accused of bribing Albert B. Fall in order to get leases on Elk Hills naval oil reserves. Indicted on charges of conspiracy and bribery, he was acquitted.

5 Theodore Roosevelt, Jr. (1887-1944). Assistant secretary of the Navy (1921-1924).

6 OM: *By the way, I hope he stays in there, as I don't think you will find a tinge of Scandal ever rightfully touching a Roosevelt.*

7 OM: . . . *this summer, as I will on the way to the Conventions (If they decide to have any), I* . . .

8 OM: . . . *for the Soldiers Bonus.*

ANOTHER HOT CONFESSION IN THE OIL SCANDAL

1 OM: . . . *various Papers,* . . .

2 Rogers referred to the fact that Sinclair also owned a large racing horse stable which included Zev, the winner of the Kentucky Derby in 1923.

3 Rogers might have referred here to the fact that McAdoo married Woodrow Wilson's daughter, and was also Secretary of the Treasury in Wilson's administration.

THE WHOLE TRUTH AND NOTHING BUT THE TRUTH

1 Thomas J. Walsh (1859-1933). U. S. senator from Montana (1913-1933). A member of the committee that investigated the Teapot Dome scandal.

2 Irvine Luther Lenroot (1869-1949). Wisconsin state representative (1901-1907); U. S. representative (1909-1918); U. S. senator (1918-1927). As a senator he was a member of the special investigating committee looking into the Teapot Dome scandal.

3 John F. Major was a confidant and private secretary of Edward B. McLean, owner and publisher of the *Washington Post*. Allegedly, McLean was involved in the Teapot Dome scandal. Major was called to testify about his employer's involvement in the affair, and when questioned, answered just as Rogers has indicated. Major was in charge of the telegraph line to Palm Springs that Rogers talks about in the comedy.

4 Throughout OM, Will uses "Senator" and "Mr." interchangeably with Walsh.

5 Thaddeus H. Caraway (1871-1931). U. S. representative from Arkansas (1913-1921); U. S. senator (1921-1931). Involved in investigations of the Teapot Dome scandals.

6 It is difficult to ascertain why Rogers mixed both people and places in this line. However, Ohio was a Republican stronghold, and Rogers may have been using his usual satirical approach.

Grover S. Cleveland (1837-1908). President of the United States (1885-1889, 1893-1897).

James A. Reed (1861-1944). U. S. senator from Missouri (1911-1929). Fought President Wilson's efforts to place the United States in the League of Nations.

7 Burton Kendall Wheeler (1882-). Montana state representative (1910-1912); U. S. senator (1923-1947). Nominated as the vice-presidential candidate for the Progressive party in 1924, with Robert M. LaFollette as the nominee for president; the ticket had little chance for success.

8 Harry M. Daugherty (1860-1941). U.S. attorney general (1921-1924), who was tried for conspiracy and acquitted in connection with the Harding scandals. He also wrote a book, *The Inside Story of the Harding Tragedy* (1932).

9 Joseph Taylor Robinson (1872-1937). U. S. senator from Arkansas (1913-1937); U. S. representative (1903-1913).

10 Frank Bartlett Willis (1871-1928). U. S. representative from Ohio (1911-1915); governor of Ohio (1915-1917); U. S. senator (1921-1928).

11 Robert M. LaFollette (1855-1925). U. S. representative from Wisconsin (1885-1891); governor of Wisconsin (1901-1906); U. S. senator (1906-1925). Ran for president in 1924 on the Progressive party ticket. Died in 1925 and was replaced in the Senate by his son, Robert M. LaFollette, Jr.

12 James Thomas Heflin (1869-1951). Alabama state representative (1896-1900); U. S. representative (1904-1920); U. S. senator (1920-1931).

13 OM: . . . *We may retire someday ourselves* . . .

14 James William Zevely (1862-1927). Attorney for the Sinclair Consolidated Oil Corporation and personal counsel for Harry F. Sinclair. Zevely was the man after whom Sinclair named his famous race horse, Zev. Zevely had practiced law in Muskogee, Oklahoma (1902-1917).

15 Edward McLean (1883-1941). Publisher of the *Washington Post*. Involved in Teapot Dome scandal for falsely testifying he had loaned Albert B. Fall $100,-000.

Rogers originally typed the name as McClain. The McNaught editor changed it to McLane. McLean is the correct spelling.

16 William J. Burns (1861-1932). Director of Bureau of Investigation, Department of Justice (1921-1924). Founder of an international detective agency. Questioned about Edward B. McLean's involvement in the Teapot Dome scandal.

17 George H. Moses (1869-1944). U. S. senator from New Hampshire (1918-1933); president pro tempore of the U. S. Senate (1925-1933).

18 Charles Forbes (1878-1952). Director of the Veterans Bureau under President Warren G. Harding. Forbes was sentenced to two years in prison for conspiracy to defraud the government in connection with Bureau hospitals.

19 OM: . . . *every Sunday* . . .

WELL, WHO IS PRUNES?

1   OM: Uses Mr. Walsh throughout rather than Senator Walsh.

2   Ira E. Bennett (1868-1957). Editor of the *Washington Post* (1908-1933). Important witness in the Teapot Dome investigations.

3   Patton B. Harrison (1881-1941). U. S. representative from Mississippi (1911-1919); U. S. senator (1919-1941).

4   Leonard Wood (1860-1927). Army officer who served as governor of Mindanao, chief of staff of the United States Army (1910-1914) and governor general of the Philippines (1921-1927). Prominent candidate for the Republican nomination for president (1916, 1920), but his supporters were too poorly organized to win the nomination for him.

5   Jake Hamon (-1921). Oklahoma oilman who told General Leonard Wood that he would contribute to Wood's campaign for president if Wood would agree to appoint him secretary of the interior. Hamon died before he could be called to testify in the Teapot Dome scandal. Leonard Wood, Jr., the general's son, was called to testify and he was the source of the above story.

6   George Herman Ruth (1895-1948). Baseball star who started his career in 1915 as a pitcher. Successful both as a pitcher and hitter, he joined the New York Yankees in 1920 playing most of his remaining career with that club. He established two records by hitting sixty home runs in 1927, and by establishing a lifetime home run record of 714.

7   Royal Samuel Copeland (1868-1938). Physician and public health official. U. S. senator from New York (1923-1938). Responsible for legislation on pure food and drug laws.

8   Frank Arthur Vanderlip (1864-1937). American financier who was president of New York City National Bank (1909-1919). He was very interested in public affairs and was a frequent public speaker.

9   OM: *(Next Week new Testimony on everything but Oil.)*

POLITICS GETTING READY TO JELL

1   *NYT: Exposure*

2   *NYT: . . . of the week, finds . . .*

3   *NYT: A few weeks ago . . .*

4   *NYT:* Omitted: *And Bankers! Mr. Vanderlip must have felt right at home up there.*

5   *NYT:* Omitted: *I was sorry Ziegfeld wasn't there, as I would have got in a raise in salary if he had heard how my act went.*

6   *NYT: I suppose by the time this reaches an eager Public that Mr. Daugherty will have resigned, as I see where he says he "won't quit under fire." That is the usual remark before leaving. Mr. Coolidge is going to let them all go, as it is a lot easier to get a new Cabinet than it is to get a chance to run for President. I guess this whole thing will end up by all connected with it resigning.*

And say, did you see a few days ago in the Papers where a Burglar sent his Income Tax to the Government? That is not the first time a burglar has sent one in, but it was the first time one ever admitted his calling. The only thing that sounded Amateurish to me was that he apologized for not doing better in his hauls. He said he hadn't done so well last year. Competition is too keen.

He said he wouldn't beat the Government out of a thing. He also sent the Government his address, which he said he knew they would keep secret. Now what the Government ought to do is to erect a Monument to that Bird, and make every man that has all his money in non-Taxable Bonds go by there every day and take his Hat off and bow to him and repeat: "You're a Better Man than I am, Gunga Din."

TWO LONG LOST FRIENDS FOUND AT LAST

1 OM: . . . *this week.*
2 William Ashley "Billy" Sunday (1862-1935). Evangelist who reached the peak of his career between 1910-1920. He strongly supported the passage of the eighteenth amendment providing for national prohibition. He was well known for using considerable slang in his sermons.
3 OM: . . ., *but the last few weeks there seems to be a change of sentiment to shift him up to the No. 1 position.*
4 Gifford Pinchot (1865-1946). Conservationist and governor of Pennsylvania (1923-1927, 1931-1935); chief of the Forest Service in the Department of Agriculture (1898-1910). As governor of Pennsylvania he helped settle a major coal strike and it is to this episode of his career that Rogers refers in this article.
5 Phineas T. Barnum (1810-1891). Known best for developing "The Greatest Show on Earth," a fully diversified circus of three rings under the main top (1871-1891). Combined with a rival (1881), and company changed its name to Barnum and Bailey. Eventually the company became Ringling Bros., Barnum and Bailey, the most famous of circuses.
6 Charles Robert Darwin (1809-1882). British naturalist who suggested evolutionary theory of man. Bryan had been prosecuting attorney in the Scopes trial.
7 Harry Wills (1889-1958). Black boxer who wanted to fight Dempsey. Promoters did not want a racially mixed bout for the championship.

THEY NOMINATED EVERYBODY BUT THE FOUR HORSEMEN

1 OM: Added: *Perhaps by the time you read this they will have nominated a Man for President, but I doubt it very much.*
Rogers attended presidential nominating conventions (1924, 1928, 1932), and he wrote a series of convention articles after each. They will be edited later as a part of *The Writings of Will Rogers.*
2 Alfred Emanuel Smith (1873-1944). Governor of New York (1919-1921) (1923-1929), who sought his party's nomination in 1920, 1924, 1928, and 1932. Although winning the nomination in 1928, he was unsuccessful in his bid for the presidency. The Ku Klux Klan vigorously opposed Smith because he was Catholic.
3 Newton D. Baker (1871-1937). Mayor of Cleveland, Ohio (1912-1916); U. S. secretary of war (1916-1921); member, Permanent Court of Arbitration at the Hague.
Smith W. Brookhart (1869-1944). U. S. senator from Iowa (1922-1926, 1927-1933).
4 Fred H. Brown (1879-1955). Governor of New Hampshire (1923-1924). He was nominated as a favorite son candidate at the Democratic Convention of 1924. He failed to win the nomination. U. S. senator (1933-1939).
5 Charles W. Bryan (1867-1945). Governor of Nebraska (1923-1925, 1931-1935); Democratic candidate for vice-president (1924).
6 James M. Cox (1870-1957). U. S. representative (1909-1913); governor of Ohio (1913-1915, 1917-1921); Democratic nominee for president of the United States (1920).
7 George S. Silzer (1870-1940). Governor of New Jersey (1923-1926). He came very close to winning the nomination for vice-president in the Democratic National Convention of 1924. He had been a dark horse candidate for president before the near nomination for vice-president.
8 Brigham Young (1801-1877). Successor to Joseph Smith, founder of the Church of Jesus Christ of Latter Day Saints (Mormons). Young led the Mormons on their famous trek to the Great Salt Lake in Utah where they established a desert home for their followers.
9 OM: *At the time I am writing this it looks like Smith will be the Lucky one, so I think they will nominate Ralston.*

IN THE MIDST OF A 7 YEAR HITCH

1   The Democratic National Convention of 1924 met for fourteen days in New York City. It took 103 ballots to decide the presidential ticket. John W. Davis was nominated to run for president and Charles W. Bryan for vice-president.

2   Robert L. Owen (1856-1947). U. S. senator from Oklahoma (1907-1925). Helped draft the Federal Reserve Act, known as the Glass-Owen Currency Act, and Farm Loan Act.

3   James Beauchamp Clark (1850-1921). Missouri state representative (1889-1891); U. S. representative from Missouri (1893-1895, 1897-1921). Leading candidate for the presidential nomination at the Democratic National Convention of 1912, but did not maintain his strength in the lengthy balloting that followed.

4   Hoffman House Hotel. Located near Madison Square Park in New York City. The hotel was patronized by aristocrats and the hotel's bar was the most popular on Broadway.

5   OM: . . . *for this weekly letter to you,* . . .

6   Arizona, on the sixty-eighth ballot, did cast one vote for Rogers for president during the Democratic convention of 1924.

7   Jackie Coogan (1914-   ). Child star who began his career at sixteen months. He acted with his father in Annette Kellerman's vaudeville act, and later made films and movies.

8   Baby Peggy (Peggy Jean Montgomery) (1918-   ). Famous child motion picture star who began her career at age two.

"WILL ROGERS JR." REPORTS THE CONVENTION
FOR HIS FATHER WORN OUT BY LONG SERVICE

1   OM: (Except for obvious typing errors, the original manuscript is reproduced as written. *Editor) My papa was not able to come down here today, and as he started in with this to report this Convention, In fact he had always told us children that it was his lifes work, He had devoted the best years of his life to tell of the Democratic National Convention.*

Mama don't know what to do with him he is getting so old and feeble now, But its what he keeps saying that worries us, If we ask him if he wants to go to the Old Folks Home for Veterans of the Democratic Convention why he wont answer he just keeps saying. Alabama 24 and something about for why does the Gentleman arise. He made his will and in it I being the oldest was to carry on this work, and the will says if no nomination has been made by the time I am too old to report, why for my children or either my Brothers or sisters Children keep on with this work.

Now I am not much of a Reporter and I want you Mr. Editor to excuse this as it is my first tril,

I entered the Garden I had on Papas Badge we had it mended so it would stick together. I have been in the Garden lots of times to Circuses, But this was just like a Church everybody was asleep, and one man was reading off of a Geography the name of States that are situated in the Western Hemisphere that dont belong to Canada.

Papa had given me an old Paper that he had saved showing me the names of the places that the Secretary had called out when he first went there. Now I go to school and the teacher had told us what a wonderful Country we lived in and how long it had stuck together, and sure enough, the Places this Secretary read over were almost the same ones that poor old pap had written on his paper. There was a name on his said Wisconsin that we havent got now, and the Phillipine Islands according to Dads old paper it used to belong to us, Why in our School Books Japan has had it for Years. Why Pops old paper was printed before Japan took California. Some of the Candidates had dropped out that was on his list. Only those had had sons to carry on. This Young Ralston and Smith jr. were still on the list, Alabama who on Dad's list only had 24 votes on account

224

of the increase of the Population now has 36. The secretary kept reading the same thing over and over again and a man had a hammer to keep the people awake with. After the man give out reading the numbers they adjourned, I went home to tell Pop what had happened, He said its looking better they are adjourning earlier, and he seemed quite rational. Then I told him that everything would be all right that a man named Brennan and a man named Kramer had said that they would have meeting before tonight at Nine, and pop like to went into Spasms, He said Oh My Lord, Son Those men started holding those same Conferences 20 years ago, Thats whats the matter with this Convention If they never had allowed the Brennan and the tahggart and the Roswell and the Kremer family to have held any Conferences this terrible thing never would have been.

2   Willard Saulsbury (1861-1927). U. S. senator from Delaware (1913-1919); delegate to the Democratic National Convention periodically from 1896-1920. Nominated for the vice-presidential candidacy in 1924.

3   Oscar Wilder Underwood (1862-1929). U. S. representative from Alabama (1895-1896, 1897-1915); U. S. senator (1915-1927). A contender for the Democratic nomination for president in the election of 1924.

4   George E. Brennan (1865-1928). Chairman of the Illinois delegation to the Democratic National Convention of 1924.

J. Bruce Kremer (1878-1940). Chairman of the Montana delegation to the Democratic National Convention of 1924.

5   Thomas Taggart (1856-1929). U. S. senator from Indiana (1916); Democratic National Committeeman (1900-1916). Instrumental in getting Woodrow Wilson nominated in 1912.

David Ladd Rockwell (1877-   ). Ohio banker, member of the Democratic central or executive committees for about 20 years, and active in promoting candidacy of William G. McAdoo for president of United States, 1924.

Norman E. Mack (1858-1932). Delegate from New York to the Democratic National Convention of 1924.

ROPING A CRITIC

1   This article did not appear in the *New York Times*. In fact, as far as can be ascertained only the *Chicago Herald and Examiner,* March 26, 1922, carried this specific article with the following heading:

COWBOY ROPES AND TIES OUR CRITIC

WILL ROGERS AVENGES THE DRAMA FOR ALL
ASHTON STEVENS' INDIGNITIES OF 25 YEARS.

Moreover, no original manuscript exists for this selection.

2   Ashton Stevens (1872-1951). Drama critic for the Hearst newspapers in Chicago. He was also an expert banjo player and Rogers talked about this aspect of the critic's talents.

3   Richard Little (1870-1946). Drama critic for the *Chicago Herald* (1915-1917). Served as war correspondent for the *Chicago Tribune* and wrote column 'Line o' Type or Two' for that paper (1920-1930).

4   Joseph Medill McCormick (1877-1925). U. S. representative from Illinois (1917-1919); U. S. senator (1919-1925). Owner of the *Chicago Daily Tribune,* and stockholder in *Cleveland Leader* and *Cleveland News*.

"THE WORLD TOMORROW," AFTER THE MANNER
OF GREAT JOURNALISTS

1   Original title was "The World Tomorrow."

2   Zev was the famous race horse owned by Harry F. Sinclair and named for Sinclair's lawyer, James William Zevely. Zev won the Kentucky Derby in 1923 and the International Race against the English Derby winner, Papyrus.

3   Mah-Jongg. A Chinese game similar to Dominoes. Very popular in the 1920s in the United States, Australia, and England.
    Epson Downs. A famous horse race track near London.

4   Friedrich Wilhelm Viktor August Ernst (1882-1951). German Crown Prince, eldest son of William II, the German Kaiser. One of Imperial Germany's top military commanders during World War I, he fled to Holland with his father after the Kaiser's abdication. He returned to Germany in 1923, where he remained until his death.

5   Rogers was a strong exponent of air power and could not understand the short-sighted views of Congress.

6   Albert Einstein (1879-1955). A physicist who developed a theory of relativity in 1905. His work was basic to the development of the atomic weapons. He fled his native Germany after Adolph Hitler became chancellor in 1933, and lived in the United States until his death.

SETTLING THE AFFAIRS OF THE WORLD IN MY OWN WAY

1   OM: *Savannah certainly give the Boys a great welcome, but imagine how welcome they are going to feel the first payday over here, "before and after taken"—Home.*

2   OM: *. . . you all last week . . .*

3   Lee Slater Overman (1854-1930). U. S. senator from North Carolina (1903-1930); state representative (1883, 1885, 1887, 1893, 1899).

4   Rogers, as others during the 1920s, might have considered the possibility of a port on the Verdigris providing access to the Gulf. However, he and most others who knew the difficulties involved considered the port as an impossible task. In 1946 Congress authorized the Arkansas River navigation system. The Port of Catoosa, near Tulsa, became a reality when officially opened on February 20, 1971.

A SKINNY DAKOTA KID WHO MADE GOOD

1   OM: *. . . came a little skinny runt kid. He was . . .*

2   Earl Sande (1898-1968). Famous jockey who rode three Kentucky Derby winners including Zev in 1923. Rogers referred to an accident in 1924, when Sande was critically injured in a race. He was not expected to live, but recovered and won the Kentucky Derby again in 1925.

3   John Pierpont Morgan (1837-1913). Aided in the financing of the United States Steel Corporation, International Harvester Company, and many other businesses. Rogers refers to members of his family.

4   Stephen Donoghue (1884-1945). English jockey who won the English Derby six times. He rode Papyrus against Zev and Earl Sande in 1923.

5   Virginia Fair Vanderbilt (Mrs. William K. Vanderbilt, 2nd). Leader of society. Avid supporter of horseracing. Mrs. Vanderbilt helped attend the injured jockeys until physicians could be found. Then she turned her attention to Mrs. Sande who collapsed under the strain.

6   Cary Travers Grayson (1878-1938). Naval physician and personal physician of President Wilson. Became Rear Admiral and U. S. Navy medical director in 1916. He was in his box at Saratoga when Sande was injured, and he hurried to aid the fallen jockey.

7   Joseph Early Widener (1872-1943). Noted turfman who owned stables. Earl Sande often rode for Widener. Wealthy businessman who gave his notable art collection to the National Gallery of Art. He was also an uncle of Harry Elkins Widener, after whom a library at Harvard was named.

8 James I. Russell (1875-1944). Well-known and respected New York surgeon. Director of surgery, Roosevelt Hospital. He attended in 1924 Earl Sande after the jockey broke his leg.

9 Campbell Bascom Slemp (1870-1943). U. S. representative from Virginia (1907-1923). Appointed secretary to President Calvin Coolidge (1923-1925).

10 Fritz Kreisler (1875-1962). American violinist who composed arrangements of classical music for violins and the operetta *Apple Blossoms* (1919).

11 Enrico Caruso (1873-1921). Opera singer who made his American debut in *Rigoletto* at the Metropolitan Opera House in New York City.

INDEX

THE GIRL WITH THE
LOWER BACK TATTOO

AMY SCHUMER

GALLERY BOOKS

New York   London   Toronto   Sydney   New Delhi

G

Gallery Books
An Imprint of Simon & Schuster, Inc.
1230 Avenue of the Americas
New York, NY 10020

Copyright © 2016 by Amy Schumer

NOTE TO READERS: Certain names and characteristics have been changed throughout the work, regardless of whether such changes are specifically identified.

This Gallery Books hardcover edition August 2016

GALLERY BOOKS and colophon are
registered trademarks of Simon & Schuster, Inc.

For information about special discounts for bulk purchases,
please contact Simon & Schuster Special Sales at
1-866-506-1949 or business@simonandschuster.com.

The Simon & Schuster Speakers Bureau can bring authors to your live event.
For more information or to book an event, contact the Simon & Schuster Speakers
Bureau at 1-866-248-3049 or visit our website at www.simonspeakers.com.

Interior design by Jaime Putorti

Manufactured in the United States of America

10 9 8 7 6 5 4 3 2 1

Library of Congress Cataloging-in-Publication Data is available.

ISBN 978-1-5011-5954-1

IMAGE CREDITS
(Interior) Photos by Marcus Russell Price: pgs. 170 and 300; photo taken in an amusement park photo booth: pg. 212; pg. 281: photo of Mayci Breaux by Coco Eros Boutique; photo of Jillian Johnson by Lucius A. Fontenot
(Photo insert) Photo by Ben Hanisch: pg. 7 (bottom); copyright © 2015 Universal Pictures, courtesy of Universal Studios Licensing LLC: pg. 10 (bottom); photos by Marcus Russell Price: pgs. 13 (bottom), 14 (bottom), 15 (both), 16

For Kimby and Jasy

CONTENTS

THE
GIRL
WITH
THE
LOWER
BACK
TATTOO

A NOTE TO MY READERS

Hey, it's me, Amy. I wrote a book! This is something I have wanted to do for a long time because I love making people laugh and feel better. Some of the stories you'll read in here will be funny, like the time I shit myself in Austin, and some will make you feel a little blue, like the time my sister and I were almost sold into sex slavery in Italy. JK. Neither of these stories are in this book, even though both actually happened, unfortunately.

Speaking of, everything in this book really happened. It's all true and nothing but the truth, so help me God. But it isn't the *whole truth*. Believe it or not, I don't tell you guys everything.

This book isn't my autobiography. I will write one of those when I'm ninety. I just turned thirty-five, so I have a long way to go until I am memoir-worthy. But for now I wanted to share these stories from my life as a daughter, sister, friend, comedian, actor, girlfriend, one-night stand, employee, employer, lover, fighter, hater, pasta eater, and wine drinker.

I also want to clarify that this book has NO SELF-HELP INFO

OR ADVICE FOR YOU. Over the last several years, I've been asked to write articles on topics like how to find a man. Or how to keep a man. Or how to rub a man's taint at the right time. I don't know how to do any of that stuff. I'm a flawed fuckup and I haven't figured anything out, so I have no wisdom to offer you. But what I *can* help with is showing you my mistakes and my pain and my laughter. I know what's important to me, and that is my family (not all of them, for Christ's sake, just some of them). And getting to laugh and enjoy life with friends. And to, of course, have an orgasm once in a while. I find at least once a day is best.

So anyway, I hope you enjoy my book, and if you don't, please don't tell anyone.

Wish me luck!

AN OPEN LETTER TO MY VAGINA

First of all, I'm sorry. Second of all, you're welcome.

I know I've put you through a lot. I've had hot wax poured on you and the hair ripped from you by strangers. Some of the strangers have burned you even though I told them you have very sensitive skin. But it's on me for going to a shady-looking place in Astoria, Queens, that you thought may have been a drug front. I've been responsible for getting you yeast infections and UTIs and have worn stockings and Spanx for too long, knowing it could cause you problems. And I want to apologize for Lance on the lacrosse team, who treated you like you owed him money with his finger. That sucked, and I'm totally with you in being pissed. But you've also had a lot of nice visitors, right? Huh? You have to admit we've had a lot of fun together. I even fought to be able to call you "pussy," which I know you prefer, on television.

I've honestly done my best as I've gotten older to only let people visit who will be kind to you, and I feel like I've done my part to keep you healthy. I know that sometimes I let people in you without a condom, but, in my defense, it feels better that way and it was only the people I was dating and trusted. Well, mostly. But we really have lucked out, haven't we?

I'm also sorry for the time I had sex with my new boyfriend and we couldn't find the condom afterward and then three days later I realized it was stuck in me and I had to "bear down," as they say, and fish it out. That must have been a real bummer for you. Or maybe it was fun to have a visitor for so long? Either way, my bad!

So what do you say? Let's grab a beer together. Okay, fine, nothing with yeast. And you're buying.

MY ONLY ONE-NIGHT STAND

I've only had one one-night stand in my life. Yes, one. I know, I'm so sorry to disappoint anyone who thinks I walk around at all times with a margarita in one hand and a dildo in the other. Maybe the misunderstanding comes from the fact that onstage, I group together all my wildest, worst sexual memories—which is a grand total of about five experiences over the course of thirty-five years. When you hear about them all back-to-back it probably sounds like my vagina is a revolving door at Macy's at Christmastime. But I talk about these few misadventures because it's not funny or interesting to hear about someone's healthy, everyday sex life. Imagine me onstage saying, "So last night I got in bed with my boyfriend and we held each other in a supportive, caring embrace, and then he made sweet love to me." The crowd would walk out and I'd walk out with them.

And besides, even *I* sometimes confuse my onstage sexual persona with my reasonable, sensible, real-life self. Sometimes I try to convince myself that I can have emotionless sex, the kind I'm always hearing about from men and Samantha on *Sex and the City*. And I have my moments, but 99.9 percent of the time, I'm not that way. I've never even hooked up with a guy after one of my shows. Isn't that sad? I've been touring for twelve years and not once have I met a guy after I've performed, brought him home, and even made out with him. Nothing. I know some male comics who say they've never gotten laid without the girl seeing them perform first. It's the exact opposite for me. I'm not in this for the dick. I enjoy sex the normal amount, and most of the time it's with someone I'm dating, and I just lie there in Happy Baby pose making it sound like I'm having a good time. When I'm single and one-night stands present themselves, I'm usually still a fairly self-protective chick, and the thought of some mystery cock entering me doesn't get my pulse going. Well, except for this one time . . .

I was on the road doing a tour and traveling between two horrendous cities: Fayetteville, North Carolina, and Tampa, Florida. I'm not scared about writing that and making those people mad, because I know for a fact that no one who lives there has ever read a book. JKJKJKJKJK, but kind of not K. When you go between cities like those two, you get the pleasure of flying on the tiniest short bus in the sky, which for some reason is still called a plane. You have to duck to get on, and you can hear the propellers the whole flight, and also the faintest sound of someone singing "*La la la la la bamba*," but you hope that the latter is just in your head.

It was early morning and I was hungover. As I said, I'd been doing a show in Fayetteville and there is nothing to do there afterward except drink until your eyes close. I got to the airport as I usually do—with zero makeup or bra, wearing sweatpants, a T-shirt, and flats. I'm not someone who looks adorable in the morning. I would argue I look exactly like Beetlejuice—the Michael Keaton character, not the Howard Stern regular. I was enjoying this lovely time in my life when no one took pictures of me unless I photobombed them. I was just a wonderful thirty-one-year-old girl who was opening and closing her mouth, realizing she'd forgotten to brush her teeth—well, less forgot and more I'd left my toothbrush in Charleston and it didn't occur to me to buy one in North Carolina. One way for me to verify that I drank too much the night before is if I wake up with red-wine teeth and enough eyeliner smeared underneath my eyes that I resemble a tight end for the New England Patriots. The point is, on this particular morning, I looked heinous and smelled like curry, and if someone had put a dollar in my coffee cup, thinking I was homeless, I would have thought, *Yep*.

I got to airport security and there he was: a six-foot-two-inch strapping strawberry blond of about thirty-five years. My first kiss was with a redhead so I've always had a weakness for them. He was the most beautiful man I'd ever seen, and I was immediately turned on just looking at him. Quick side note: THAT NEVER FUCKING HAPPENS. Every day, men look at women walk by in skirts and tight jeans and get tiny erections, or at the very least some sort of arousal. But for women it's a rare occurrence to see a dude and think, *Dayummmmm!* I was looking him up and down, trying to find one inch of him that wasn't Gaston from *Beauty and the Beast*, and there was nothing. All he was missing was the ponytail and the bow on said ponytail.

I audibly sighed, and before he walked through the metal detector, he looked at me. All the blood rushed to my vagina, and I smiled at him before immediately remembering I looked like Bruce Vilanch. (For those of you who don't know who he is and are too lazy to Google it, just picture a barn owl wearing a blond wig.) I got through security and walked to my gate—and *boom!* There he was again—looking even hotter than before. He was wearing a crew-neck long-sleeve shirt that was just tight enough around the chest so you knew what was up. It was abundantly clear that underneath his shirt was a place where you would want to rest your cheek and breathe in all his pheromones until he took you like Marlon Brando in *Streetcar* or Ryan Gosling in annnnnyyyyythiiiiinnnnnnggggg.

I ran to the bathroom to try to find makeup in my purse, which is an actual bottomless pit when I need something (and at all other times). I'm not lying when I say my purse has all the contents of an actual ostrich's nest. I'll never do a celebrity magazine "What's in your purse?" story because people would see the array of fun, gross surprises in there and probably think I needed to be hospitalized. I found some blush and ChapStick, and thought, *Perfect. That's all I need to take me from a two to a four.* I looked in the mirror and saw the rosacea I'd created, and laughed at myself. Fuck it. I rolled my sweatpants up to half-calf height, thinking, *Let's highlight my strongest zone.* I brushed my teeth with my finger and splashed water all over myself. I walked out like I was on a runway and floated right past him. He at no time, for even one second, looked at me in the terminal.

I bought some gum and a magazine with Jennifer Aniston on the cover and boarded the plane, defeated. I got to my tiny window seat and started reading about how Jennifer was going to die alone and it wasn't fair, and there he was again, boarding the plane. He walked down the aisle and I watched him, his arms bulging and his huge hands gripping his bag as he navigated his way between the seats. I was thinking, *Maybe when he walks by, I can pretend to sneeze . . . and fall on the floor in front of him . . . and he will trip and fall inside of me.* Then I saw him look right at the seat next to me.

No, I thought. *There is no way he is in the seat next to me.* No, no, no. But YES! *Game, set, fucking match,* I thought, *IT IS ON.*

I never ever talk to people on airplanes. It's a huge gamble that has resulted in such things as James Toback (Google him) telling me, "You don't really know a woman until you've eaten her ass," before we even took off, and a woman showing me pictures of her dead bird for three hours. But on this flight, I turned right to him.

"Hi, I'm Amy."

He smiled, revealing a tiny gap between his front teeth. I love a gap more than anything on a man. "Hi, I'm Sam," he said, in an English accent.

I soon found out that he was in the British version of the marines and was in town for just a few days. I couldn't fucking handle it. It was all too much. I felt possessed and lost all control of my voice, like Sigourney Weaver at the end of *Ghostbusters*. I was in heat, as they say. Who says this? I don't know. Shut up and keep reading about my getting pummeled by this British superhero. We took off and I pretended to be really scared of flying. There was zero turbulence, yet I still found reasons to grab his arm and bury my face in his shoulder, inhaling his scent. I was blatantly throwing myself at him and we both laughed at how aggressive I was being. My clitoris was thumping like the Tell-Tale Heart and I kept thinking of the 98 Degrees song "Give Me Just One Night (Una Noche)." Even though I was slightly famous at the time, he'd never heard of me, which was another major plus. I told him I had a show that night and that maybe I would see him after. We exchanged emails and I prayed to every god that it would happen.

I've been in this kind of situation a couple other times where I could have had a one-night stand and I just couldn't go through with it. Once or twice, my instincts told me no. It didn't feel safe. But mostly I have decided against it just out of pure laziness. I will think of the practical things, like, *When can I leave so I can eat pasta? We are not dating, so I can't do domestic things like brush my teeth and wash my face and put on my eye mask and earplugs. It's supposed to be hot and sexy, but I look like a blond Shrek in the a.m. What will the morning be like? What will we say? Will I order him an Uber? What if he says something hurtful or he tries to have sex with me in the morning when we both know my vagina will smell like a bowl of ramen?* I'm just too pragmatic and lazy for one-night stands. I consider consequences and I don't drink like I did in college.

All that being said, the Sam situation felt different. He was such a turn-on and a fantasy. Even the accent made him seem unreal. It didn't hurt that he'd be returning to his foreign home shortly after the sun rose the next day. After we parted ways in the airport, I went to do my show, and the whole time I couldn't help but hold my breath hoping that I would hear from him. Sure enough, when the show was over, I had an email from him asking me how it had gone. I joked that I had gotten discovered and was going to make it in this business.

He wrote back: "Who discovered you?"

I wrote: "A magician. I'm going to be his assistant." Which I thought was pretty funny.

He wrote: "Is he gonna saw you in half?"

I answered: "I was hoping you would."

BAM! That is the most sexually aggressive yet true thing I've ever written. And it worked.

We made plans to meet up at the dance club in the lobby of my hotel. We had half a beer, we danced to Ice Cube telling us we could do it if we put our back into it, and we left. Walking through the bright lobby and into the low lighting of the elevator was a lot of reality for this sexy affair we were both trying to have. The things that were going through my mind on the elevator were as follows: *Fuck me fuck me fuck me fuck me fuck me.*

I really needed a boost of sexual confidence during that time of my life. I'd recently learned that a guy I'd been in love with and had dated in the past was gay. Even though it had been a while since we had dated, it still broke my heart when he came out to me. And it made me begin to question myself. This person who made me feel beautiful and sexy for so long was attracted to men. I thought, *Am I like a man?* When you get older and wiser, you get your confidence from within, not from the person you are having sex with. But finding out someone I'd dated was gay at that moment in my life was giving me a hard time. I was having trouble feeling like a sexual being and was wondering about my own worth.

Enter Sam—this beautiful, masculine fantasy man who wanted to help Stella get her groove back. The elevator to my room could not travel fast enough.

We got to my very corporate-looking room and wasted no time.

I dropped my bag and we stripped down to our underwear and got into bed. There was no question of what we were doing there. We both had the same goal in mind: to devour each other. *Ewwwwww,* I know, sorry. But it's true. Everything felt right. Kissing him felt right. His body felt right. We went for it. I can't *Fifty Shades* out right now and write a sensual paragraph, so I'll just tell you some facts. We were both very giving (head). We both couldn't believe it was happening (we both came a lot). He was so appreciative and excited (we high-fived at one point). Which felt amazing (the sex, not the high five). Coming off the depressing discovery that a guy I'd had a lot of sex with was attracted to men, it felt incredible to have this heavenly being take me in his arms and make me feel both wanted and beautiful. The sex was perfect. He was perfect. We were both in ecstasy, enjoying and relishing every smell, sound, and touch.

When we were finally finished, I said it was such a pleasure meeting him and wished him good luck in all his endeavors. He couldn't believe I didn't want him to stay. He couldn't believe it so much that he stayed and we had sex at least three more times, with little affectionate breaks in between, telling stories and laughing and holding each other.

I did eventually tell him it was time to go. I was apparently fine having sex with a stranger, but sleeping next to him was just too intimate. He tried to make future plans and I let him know that I wanted this to be a one-time thing. I said it was perfect and that I would never have a one-night stand again because it would pale in comparison. We kissed good-bye, and I went to sleep with the biggest smile on my face, thinking, *Thank you*.

I do realize that one of the best nights of my life was just a one-night stand in Tampa. But I felt like Marlene Dietrich in *Morocco*. Let the record show I am not proposing that everyone limit themselves to just *one* one-night stand. Oh no no no, on the contrary, some of us might be better off if we had *only* one-night stands for the rest of our lives. But for me, this encounter just fell in my lap when I wasn't feeling so attractive to men. Or sexual in general. I was wanting some reassurance, and a night of unexpected sex with a built, British redhead was the Z-Pak I needed to kick the leftover mucus. (Is there an unsexier metaphor? No. Also I feel like that antibiotic never works.)

We all know one-night stands aren't cure-alls for broken hearts and low self-esteem. That shit can backfire hard. We've all tried some form of remedy by way of sex and wound up feeling even more alone and running back to whatever dickface we'd just found the strength to leave. But sometimes one-night stands can fix a specific problem. And even better, sometimes when you're trying to fix a problem with sex, you find that sex is just its own reward. No lessons to be learned. No agenda other than fun. And sometimes tons of well-deserved orgasms from a guy looking at you like you're lunch right when you fucking need it is just what the doctor ordered. Can we make a day National Redhead Day? This man deserves a parade or something.

He reached out to me a couple more times when he was back in the US but I stayed true to wanting to keep sacred what strangely felt like the purest night of my life. And it still is.

I AM AN INTROVERT

I am an introvert. I know—you're thinking, *What the fuck, Amy? You just told us you hooked up with a stranger in Tampa, and now you're claiming to be shy? You're not shy, you're a loud, boozy animal!* Okay, fair enough. Sometimes that's true. But I am, without a doubt, a classic textbook introvert.

In case you don't know what that word means, I will fill you in quickly. If you *do* know what it means, then skip ahead to the chapter about where to find the best gloryholes in Beijing. Just kidding. I don't have that info. Also, just fucking read my description of an introvert. Why are you in such a rush to skip ahead, you pervert?

Being an introvert doesn't mean you're shy. It means you enjoy being alone. Not just enjoy it—you need it. If you're a true introvert, other people are basically energy vampires. You don't hate them; you just have to be strategic about when you expose yourself to them—like the sun. They give you life, sure, but they can also burn you and you will get that wrinkly Long Island cleavage I've always been afraid of getting and that I know I now have. For me, meditation and headphones on the subway have been my sunscreen, protecting me from the hell that is other people.

There's a *National Geographic* photo I love of a young brown bear. He's sitting peacefully against a tree near the border of Finland and Russia. The caption reads something like, "The cubs played feverishly all day, and then one of them left the group for a few minutes to relax on his own and enjoy the quiet." This was very meaningful to me because that's what I do! Except in my case, the bear gets ripped away from his chill spot by the tree, and several people paint his face and curl his fur and put him in a dress so he can be pushed onstage to ride one of those tiny bicycles in the circus. I'm not saying he doesn't enjoy making people laugh, but still, it's hard out there for a fuzzy little introvert.

I know some people who've written books have struggled through it, and you can feel them ripping themselves apart on every page. But for me, writing this book has been one of the great pleasures of my life. Sitting and writing and talking to no one is how I wish I could spend the better part of every day. In fact, it might be surprising for you to learn that most of my days are spent alone, unless I am on set, which is crazy draining for an introvert. As soon as lunchtime arrives, I skip the food service tables and rush to my trailer or a quiet corner and I meditate. I need to completely shut off. This time spent silently is like food to me. I also eat a lot of food. But if I'm not shooting something, I like to be alone all day. Maybe an hour lunch with a friend, but that's it.

When you're a performer—especially a female one—everyone assumes you enjoy being "on" all the time. That couldn't be further from the truth for me or any of the people I am close to. The unintentional training I received when I was little was that because I was a girl *and* an actor, I *must* love being pleasant, and making everyone smile and feel comfortable all the time. I think all little girls are trained this way, even those who aren't entertainers like I was. Women are always expected to be the gracious hostess, quick with an anecdote and a sprinkling of laughter at others' stories. We are always the ones who have to smooth over all the awkward moments in life with soul-crushing pleasantries. We are basically unpaid geishas. But when we do not fulfill this expectation (because we are introverted), people assume we must be either depressed or a cunt. Maybe I'm a cunt anyway, but it's not because I don't want to blink and smile at someone as they tell me they ran cross-country in middle school.

I was living with my boyfriend Rick during the time I started having this realization about myself. But even as a child, I had always known something was up. I didn't like to play for as long as the other kids, and I absolutely always bailed on slumber parties. But as an adult, my mom wasn't around to come pick me up in the middle of the night anymore, and I began to see things more clearly. You could say Rick was the first adult relationship I had, and for the first time, I was playing house with someone, mimicking the way married people dutifully fulfill each other's friend-and-family obligations. I remember going to his family's house for the holidays and realizing I would need to take frequent breaks from the lovely group of people we were hanging out with all day. Every ninety minutes or so, I would retreat to his room or go for a walk. I wasn't made to feel bad about this, but everyone was clearly clocking it. Once, Rick took me to his friend's wedding. After about two hours of small talk and formalities, I went to hide in the bathroom. I had nothing left to give or say, and I felt the unbearable sensation that I was treading water.

It wasn't until I became best friends with some fellow comics and performers that I realized being an introvert wasn't a character flaw. Even when we all go on vacations or on the road together, we take little breaks in our own rooms and then text each other to check in.

This quality is tricky when your job actually requires you to constantly travel and interact with new faces, new towns, and new audiences. You cross paths with lots of people in this line of work, and you feel shitty if you don't give away some of your energy and conversation to every driver, hotel front-desk clerk, promoter, backstage crew member, member of the audience, waiter, and so on. And I do mean "give away." Energy is finite between recharges. That shit runs out. It's not that I don't respect these people working hard at their jobs (which are all jobs I have done, by the way, because I have done every job in the world other than being a doula. More on that later). I know they mean well, and I know there are many people out there who, unlike me, want to tell their cabdrivers all about how their flight was (flights are always fine) and what the weather was like in New York (cold or hot—who gives a fuck?). How many hotel room keys do you want? (A hundred and nine.) I'm just not one of those people, and I don't want to waste their time and energy (or mine) with mindless small talk. Every time a driver picks you up from the airport, they ask why you're in town and what you do for a living. When I was a rookie, I used to tell them the straight answer, but I learned my lesson because this kind of thing would happen every time:

"Oh, you're a comedian?"

"Have I seen you before?"

"Are you on YouTube?"

"Oh, my cousin's a comedian. His name is Rudy Fuckface. Do you know him? Google him."

"Have you ever met Carrotbottom?"

"You know who's funny? Jeff Dunham."

"You should do a show about cabdrivers."

"Oh, I could tell you some funny material for your act."

"Weren't you in that one movie?"

"You weren't? Are you sure?"

"I don't usually like female comics."

That one really gets me. It's not like anyone would so casually say, "I don't usually like black people." Either way, it's offensive to say this to a female comic. And let me guess, you've only ever seen one female comic in your life and it was in the eighties and guess what? You probably fucking loved her.

So to avoid this kind of conversation, for a while I changed my story and told them I was a schoolteacher. But they still had too many follow-up questions for me, and so I started saying, "I tell stories for a living." This was just creepy enough for them to cut the small talk.

I can stand onstage all night talking to thousands of people about my most vulnerable and private feelings—like my thoughts on the last guy who was inside me, or the fact that I eat like the glutton in the movie *Se7en* when I'm drunk. But I really don't do as well at parties or gatherings where I feel like I am obligated to be more "social." Usually I will find a corner to hide in and immediately begin haunting it like the girl from *The Ring*, just hoping no one will want to come talk to me. But in the right time and place, I can be pretty pleasant. For example, I've had several nice exchanges with nude elderly women in gym locker rooms. Even if they are blow-drying their hair with their gray tornadoesque bush out, I will engage.

It is probably no surprise that sometimes I prefer social media to human interaction. This is probably an introvert thing as well. Social media is just more efficient, like online dating. Everything can be quick and painless, and when you find out that someone is crazy or not funny, you can promptly tap out of the conversation. Even the photos a person chooses to post on Instagram can help save you a lot of time. I once ended a potentially romantic relationship because the dude posted a picture of his friend's dog's funeral. Like literally the dog's body being lowered into the ground in a garbage bag. Saying he was honored to be a part of the day. Not even his own dog!

In my opinion, what a person posts on Instagram should be humanizing and accurate. Not that a dog funeral isn't those things. But his post made it clear he thrived on sadness and enjoyed being a part of drama to make him feel alive and important. My favorite pictures to post are of my sister picking up piles of her dog's shit when we go on walks. Why not be real and show all of yourself? One of the first times that I was paparazzied, they caught me stand-up paddleboarding in Hawaii. I didn't even recognize myself. I saw the shots in magazines and thought, *Oh, cool, Alfred Hitchcock is alive and loves water sports*. But nope, it was me. When my friend told me they were online, she broke it to me as if both of my parents had died in a fire. But I proudly posted the worst picture on Instagram right away, because I thought it was hilarious. I will make fun of myself a lot in this book, but understand I feel good, healthy, strong, and fuckable. I'm not the hottest chick in the room. I would be like the third-hottest bartender at a Dave & Buster's in Cincinnati. Another time, when a paparazzo photographed me committing the unspeakable act of eating a sandwich, I immediately posted a correction as to the type of meat it was (they said ham, but it was prosciutto).

On the other hand, there are those men and women we all know (celebrities or regular people) who only post amazing shots of their abs or photos where they look accidentally gorgeous, known as #humblebrags (RIP @twittels, who coined that perfect term). No, and pass to those people. I don't even want to know someone who isn't barely hanging on by a thread. Social media is a great tool for all of us introverts and decent people alike as it speeds up the time between thinking someone is great and realizing they're the worst.

I don't know how introverts survived without the Internet. Or with the Internet. Actually, I don't know how we survive at all. It feels impossible.

Now that I know I'm an introvert, I can better manage this quality and actually start to see it as a positive. For example, it's a known fact that a lot of CEOs are introverts, and being in charge is a comfortable position for me too, whatever I'm working on. I surround myself with smart, talented people, let them do their thing, listen to their ideas, and figure out the strongest ways to collaborate with them to make the best possible final product. I write all my own jokes when it comes to my stand-up, but anything else I've created has been thanks to the collaboration of small groups of funny people working alone together, which is my favorite way to get things done. It should come as no surprise that a lot of writers are introverts, so on my TV show, the writing staff is happy to work together side by side for short stints and then disappear off individually into our productive little introvert pods at home to get shit done. We are mainly a group of cave dwellers who can only socialize for limited amounts of time. On any given day with the writing staff, the schedule usually looks something like this:

Noon: Staff arrives at the office.

12:15: The group orders lunch. We all want soup, but the soup delivery has taken up to two hours, so we get Bareburger. Kyle Dunnigan always takes the longest because he is gluten-and-dairy-free and we all need to hear about it forever. (This year he stopped being G-and-D-free and we are all furious he quit after we had to listen to him talk about it for so long.)

12:16–12:59:	Staff discusses and laments how long it's taking for lunch to arrive.
1:00–1:15:	We consume our lunch and talk about *The Bachelor*.
1:15–1:30:	Bathroom breaks all around. Kurt Metzger tells a story about a weird girl he went down on.
1:30–2:00:	Discuss scene ideas or talk shit about people and watch YouTube videos together.
2:00–3:00:	Discuss what snack we should have. I pee for the hundredth time.
3:00–4:00:	We punch up scripts.
4:00–7:00:	Everyone writes in the safe shelter of their own homes.

It's hard to be in the company of others for very long while being creative, and I don't know how the writers of the late-night shows do it: together all day, churning out jokes and scenes. I feel lucky to have a huge group of people who let each other do their own thing, and the process of writing alone together is the best. My sister, Kim, and I often sit side by side on the couch, writing the same movie together quietly without speaking—not just for hours, but for days. We will say about two sentences to each other and they are always about food.

So in closing, I'd like to pay tribute to the introverts' secret weapon—one of our greatest coping mechanisms for handling social situations. The Irish good-bye is something I've perfected over the years. No offense to the Irish with that term. You guys are geniuses for coming up with this patented method of getting the hell out of Dodge without having to explain why. Even if I'm drunk, I can slip out of any event, very subtle and ninjalike, and with no warning—a classic introvert move I rely upon heavily. I'm like Omar from *The*

Wire. Except no. *"Amy, I didn't see you leave last night . . . you didn't say good-bye!"* You bet your sweet ass I didn't. If I say good-bye to you, it is completely by accident and because you were right in the doorway as I tried to plow through it.

I wish I could Irish-good-bye my way out of this chapter because, true to form, I'm exhausted from writing about myself for this long. But first, before I ghost you like a pro, I want to remind you to stop judging a loud, often tactless, volatile, blond book by its cover. (Except for this book, because the cover is nice and the inside is nice, too.) Just because my job requires me to make fun of myself into a microphone and wear my heart on my sleeve for hire doesn't mean I can't be an introvert as well. Believe it or not, I do have a complex inner life just like you, and I enjoy being alone. I need it. And I've never been happier than I was when I finally figured this out about myself. So if you're an introvert like me, especially a female introvert, or a person who is expected to give away your energy to everyone else on the reg, I want to encourage you to find time to be alone. Don't be afraid to excuse yourself. Recharge for as long as you need. Lean up against a tree and take a break from the other bears. I'll be there too, but I promise not to bother you.

ON BEING NEW MONEY

The term "nouveau riche" is a fancy way of saying you're a rich person who acquired your wealth on your own. You didn't inherit it all from your great-grandfather. You worked for it. Either that or you bought that lottery ticket fair and square. But I actually prefer the term "New Money" because it's a way of saying, "Yes, I am trash and I'm embracing it!"

I am New Money.

I feel lucky to live in America—where people will treat someone like me (trash) as if they come from bloodlines with Benjamins streaming through them. In England, they are not as impressed with people who have made their own dough within their lifetime. New Money is considered gaudy there. But in America New Money is celebrated more than Old, because it was earned in some way or another. We use our new money for stupid shit like spa treatments where eels eat the dead skin off of our toes or baby seal fat is injected into our assholes so we look young again. (A lot of marine life is utilized for some reason.) People applaud us. Go ahead, start a charity and give back a little and no one in the States gives a hot damn how you got it. You were knocked up by a basketball player and took him for all you could? Great, here is your own television show. You made a sex tape with a mediocre rapper? Here is the key to a billion-dollar corporation. Or in my case, hey, you told dick jokes to drunk people in small rooms at places called the Giggle Bone and the Banana Hammock? Would you like a movie deal?!

Looking back, I realize this is technically my second time to fall into the New Money category. My parents were living the textbook New Money lifestyle during my childhood . . . until they slipped into the No Money lifestyle just in time for my delicate preteen years. But I'm getting ahead of myself.

I was born a precious little half Jew in Lenox Hill Hospital on the Upper East Side and sailed the five blocks home to our huge duplex apartment in a limo. Dad's idea. To unbury the lede, my parents were rich. They were rolling in it. I mean, I thought they were. They'd take a private jet to the Bahamas at a moment's notice, and they thought the high life was going to last forever. It didn't.

My dad owned a company called Lewis of London, a baby furniture business that imported cribs and such from Italy. I don't remember why they named it "Lewis of London" but if they were looking for a fancy name that only New Money people would use in order to make something sound high-end and international, they knocked it out of the park. At the time, no one else was selling fine foreign baby furniture, so rich Manhattan parents sought out my father's store, where they could pick up the fanciest tiny infant prisons that money could buy.

I had some extravagant, rich-person things as a little kid. We moved out of the city to a nice suburb on Long Island when I was five, where we would eat lobster once a week and smoked fish for

Sunday breakfast. Or as we called it, Jewing out hard! On lobster nights, Mom would bring the live ones home from the grocery store and put them on the kitchen floor for my brother, sister, and me to play with. At the time, I thought it was just a fun thing we did before boiling the tasty crustaceans, but in retrospect, I realize that we were playing with our future food in a Little-Mermaid-eating-Sebastian way that was very uncool. Couldn't they have just gotten us a pet goldfish? All the other kids were outside riding bikes and we were making our lobsters race each other like gladiators. Sick. Either way, when I remember what it was like to grow up in a wealthy household, the food we ate stands out the most. Come to think of it, that's mostly what I remember about any event or moment in life—the food that was there. A couple years ago, before I had "real" money, I asked Judd Apatow if it was fun being rich, and he explained to me that once you become rich you find out all the good things in life are free. He said you can buy a house, good sushi, and CDs, but that's about it. Still, as someone who waited a lot of tables and ate off people's plates on the way back to the kitchen, fancy sushi sounded pretty good to me.

Anyway, Lewis of London cornered the market—until other stores started selling European baby furniture and my parents lost it all. Which happened, incidentally, during the onset of my father's multiple sclerosis. Cool timing, Universe!!! I don't remember how it felt to lose everything, but I do remember men coming to take my dad's car when I was ten. I watched him standing expressionless in the driveway as it was pulled away. My mom claims she didn't know what was happening financially, but if this were an episode of MTV's *True Life: Squandering That Chedda* they would say, "She blew his millions on furs and homes." And if it were a Lifetime movie, they would say, "She was a victim whose life changed drastically in a split second." I don't know which is true. Probably neither. All I know is that my mom stayed in the house denying reality like it was her job when those men came to take away the black Porsche convertible.

I didn't generally notice the loss, but I did notice a change in the quality of my birthday parties. That's probably where I felt the biggest shift in my family's financial situation. When I turned nine and we still had money, my parents threw me a "farm party" at our beautiful home on Surrey Lane, a quiet street in Rockville Centre. Early that morning, a box with holes in it was placed in the garage. When I removed the lid, a gaggle of baby ducks looked up at me. I thought I'd died and gone to heaven. I remember believing in my heart that I was the little girl in *Charlotte's Web*. I was so in love with those little creatures that I could have sat there and petted them all day, and died happy.

Since we could afford the whole kit and caboodle, real-life farmers carted real-life farm animals to our house in shifts throughout the day. Bring on the donkeys! We had a pony; we had goats; we had chickens. If you're a kid from Iowa and you're reading this, you're like, who cares? A couple of animals in your yard sounds like a Tuesday. But trust me, if you're from New York and you have a cow in your driveway, you're rich—and the most popular kid in school for a year. All of my little friends dressed up in overalls and played in a pile of hay and went fucking crazy. It's gross when you see it for what it really was: a bunch of well-off kids whose idea of a great time was to slum it like poor farm children. I've also been to a food-fight birthday party. Can you imagine starving kids in Syria watching us waste food like that? It makes me shudder.

Don't worry, the irony came back to bite me in the ass soon after. Life got less and less comfortable for us after my parents lost all their money. We began moving into smaller and smaller homes until it felt like we were all sleeping in a pile—and not a fun pile like the monsters in *Where the Wild Things Are*. A sad, poor pile like the grandparents in *Charlie and the Chocolate Factory*. (*Amy, do you ever reference adult books?* No!) By the time I was in college, my mom had moved us into a basement apartment where my sister, Kim, who is four years younger than me, had the one bedroom, and I had to share a bed with my mom. (Quick tip: Do not try to ditch a cab when you are blackout drunk and then get in bed naked with your mother. The cabdriver will follow you home and knock on your door, and then your mother will have to apologize to him and give him cash while you lie giggling and nude under the sheets, where you are experiencing the bed spins . . . I heard from a friend.)

But to be honest, I never felt poor, even when we were. I always had enough money for lunch and to go on field trips with my class. I was always well provided for. We would go to the occasional Broadway show or take a road trip to somewhere with trees and a lake or pond, or a sizable puddle when the going got really tough. We were living above our means, just not *Real Housewives of New Jersey* level. It was more like the staff at Lisa Vanderpump's restaurant. (Yes, I only speak in Bravo metaphors; thank God for Andy Cohen.) Luckily, all of my friends dressed bad and never had any interest in designer clothes or other material things. I've never worn jewelry (or spelled "jewelry" correctly on a first attempt) or name brands. My friends cared a little more than me but it wasn't too noticeable. We would buy shirts from Bebe, but we could only afford the actual T-shirts that read "Bebe." Those shirts were always on sale—and for good reason.

I drove a shitty car, but at least I had a car. Twizzie was a very used station wagon that smelled like a stable but could turn on a dime. I loved doing donuts in that car and would drive as many people home from school as I could fit. I would shout, "Pick 'em up!" (I think it was a *Dumb and Dumber* reference) as I made the parking lot rounds. If Twizzie went above thirty miles per hour everyone in the car felt like they were holding Shake Weights. But, still, it was a car! I didn't feel like a low-income kid. I remember loving my prom dress so much that I wore it to the prom twice—when I went junior year and also for my own prom, senior year. I can't remember ever wishing for something that I couldn't afford. I was very lucky.

It wasn't until college that I began to take note of the fact that I had to work a little harder than the average student to get by. I was living on my meal plan, stealing food from the student union, and scamming drinks off guys when necessary—which wasn't easy because freshman year, I looked like a blond Babadook. I got a job teaching group exercise classes at my college and those classes were my main source of *legal* income. (I sold a little weed and shoplifted from department stores too . . . oops. Shhh. That doesn't leave this book.) Anyway, I was the worst drug dealer ever. I would run out of baggies and have to use entire Hefty garbage bags for the smallest amount of weed. I'd give a gift along with it, like a baked potato or whatever I had lying around the apartment. And every summer when I came home from college, my sister and I would bartend at the only bar in Long Beach, where we served beer and wine and food fried within an inch of its gross life. We would work sixteen-hour days, returning home covered in ten layers of film from the fryer, our feet swelling out of our sensible shoes and aprons filled with dollars. We'd lay our tips out on the bed and count them, some days totaling as much as five hundred bucks, and we thought we were sultans. We'd fall asleep smiling and wake up at eight a.m. to do it again the next day.

When I graduated college I was B to the R to the O to the K to the

E, broke broke. Vanilla Ice broke, before HGTV Ice. I made enough money waiting tables to pay rent and eat nothing but cheap dumplings every day for breakfast, lunch, and dinner. And snack. And brunch. I lived in a closet-sized studio apartment with a Craigslist roommate. One night a bunch of comics were going to get sushi and I couldn't go because I'd spent my last few dollars paying for my five minutes of stage time that night (an investment well worth it, since I bombed in front of all seven disgruntled stand-ups in the audience). Sushi in New York costs more than a blood diamond, so it was out of the question for me. But one of the comics, Lorie S., kindly bought me a California roll. I was so grateful and felt really embarrassed that I needed her to get it for me.

But I worked really hard, and soon enough, instead of buying stage time at open mics and going home hungry, I started making a couple hundred dollars a weekend doing stand-up. And then about four years ago, I started making a couple thousand a weekend. The first very very big check I got was for a college performance where I was paid $800 for one hour. I ran around my apartment screaming for joy.

When I made my first real chunk of change doing the *Last Comic Standing* tour, I took Kim to Europe. Instead of sharing a cot in a filthy youth hostel, we got to stay in real hotel rooms with private bathrooms and everything. They weren't fancy, but we felt like the Rockefellers. Or if you're a millennial, the CEO of Roc-A-Fella Records.

But the thing about Old Money (Rockefellers) vs. New Money (Roc-A-Fellas) is that both still have M-O-N-E-Y. I don't care if the Old Money folks look down on me for being New Money. I will happily clink glasses with them sitting up front on an airplane. What an amazing privilege it is to fly first class! I don't take that for granted. I still recall the first time I stepped foot on a private jet. The first time for anything having to do with money is the best. I was doing a show headlined by Louis CK, Sarah Silverman, and Aziz he-doesn't-need-a-last-name. The show was only in Connecticut so the trip home wasn't far, but when Louis asked if I wanted a lift I said, "Fuck yeah!" People with money feel guilty about having it in front of people who don't, and they don't want to say the words that make others hate them. He didn't say, "Amy, would you like to fly on a private jet I have paid for to travel the mere twenty minutes it takes to get home?" No. He said, "Do you want a lift?" as if we were in an old movie and I was a distressed damsel waiting for a streetcar on a rainy night.

It is awful how wonderful it is to fly private. Just disgusting. I recommend you treat this paragraph like a Choose Your Own Adventure book and skip ahead, so you don't hate me and your life. When you fly private, a car drives you right up to the runway at the exact time your flight takes off. You want to take off at 9:00 p.m., your car drops you there at 8:55 p.m.! No standing in a crowded terminal (which is the right word for that, because it feels like death), no fluorescent-ass airport lighting, no long bathroom lines, no waiting in line for security with frantic people who left too late for their flight. No endlessly long lines to pay ten dollars for a water and gum you don't even like, because they didn't have your favorite. You just get out of your car and walk onto the plane, and you're in the air in about fifteen minutes. There is a car waiting at the other end, right when you get off the plane; they hand you your bag and you go on your merry motherfucking way. I have been on a couple of jets that were fancy hip-hop-video-looking ones and some that were old and dirty. But it doesn't matter. You are alone on there!!!! All of this is to say I feel crazy lucky to be in a position to even set foot on a private jet. I appreciate every second of it. Just like a New Money person should.

I stay in nice hotels, I Uber instead of hailing a taxi . . . even during pricing surges. I can get expensive meals when I want and that's what I do for myself. I'm not going to bullshit you: it feels great to know I could send my niece to any school she wants even though she is already a genius at two and will get a full ride for her grades or a scholarship when she becomes a Division I volleyball player. It's relaxing to know I can pay for my dad to be in a better facility and make sure he sees the best MS specialist in America. I also know how unfair it is that not everyone can do these things. I'm New Money, not an asshole. That's a lie. I haven't lied to you yet in this book, and I don't want to start now. I am an asshole.

The best part about having money is that you get to be an asshole and burn money on stupid shit. If one of my friends is working at a comedy club, I will sometimes pay to have their greenroom filled to the brim with ridiculous bouquets of flowers, like a hip-hop artist's funeral, with wreaths and the whole nine. One of the writers on our TV show made the mistake of telling me he had booked a very small guest role on the TV show *Veep*. Naturally, I had an insane amount of roses delivered to his dressing room to weird out the rest of the cast and embarrass him. I can afford to buy expensive fake astronaut suits in the gift shop at the Museum of Natural History for my sister and me so we can walk around in them all day just to be dickheads and never wear them again (see picture at the end of this chapter, on page 37). I can hire a private chef to cook for me and my family, without needing it to be a special occasion.

My agent is my friend and he is a young guy who is incredibly shy and does not like attention called to him. Unfortunately, I think it's hilarious to humiliate him, so I have, on several occasions, hired a clown to show up at his office while he is in a meeting and make him balloon animals and sing to him. I've rented Ferraris just to drive them for an hour with friends. I've chartered a boat simply because it's sunny outside. I am like a rapper, but a manageable one. I don't buy the Ferrari or the boat; I rent them and purchase all the insurance. I don't load up on Cristal for the ride. I buy a moderately priced sparkling wine and I only drink half a glass because it gives me a headache and I have writing to do. I'm like a conservative, reasonable rookie athlete. Or a lottery winner with a financial adviser and a sick sense of humor. I am NEWWWW Money.

It's weird to be treated differently all of a sudden just because you have been on TV or have some cash. I am not special just because I'm famous right now. I won't be famous forever—not even much longer actually, which is fine with me because it doesn't feel good to have people be nicer to you because of your money. My favorite people in the world still give me shit and treat me like the Long Island trash receptacle that I am. I want to be treated the same way I treat people. One thing I will say for myself is that I am cool about money. Anyone who comes out of the rags-to-riches experience and isn't cool about money is a douchebag. I try to remember where I came from. I remember when a 30 percent tip changed my day, or sometimes even my week. I remember when I had to sell my clothes to secondhand stores so I could do an open mic. I remember when I almost donated my eggs because I didn't know what else to do to make a buck (and besides, I'm Jewish and my eggs go for double the price!). I remember when I went to the Penny Arcade coin-counting machine at TD Bank so I could take my boyfriend out to dinner at TGI Fridays for his birthday.

And now I can take my girlfriends on vacation and buy a California roll for everyone! I've definitely spread the wealth—whether through leaving good tips or helping out worthy causes, friends, and family. This should be standard practice for wealthy people. I get paid a lot for what I do. That is the nature of show business. If you are someone who can sell tickets and get people to see you live, you are overpaid. So there is no excuse not to hook people up. When I left the bartenders a $1,000 tip at the Broadway musical *Hamilton*, I found it odd that it became a viral news story. Doesn't this sort of thing happen fairly often at THE most popular musical in a city where tons of rich people live? If I make a bonus at shows, I pass it on to my openers and to the people who did my hair and makeup. I've given most of my amazing best friends six-figure checks to make their lives a little easier, and I donated the majority of my salary for the fourth season of my TV show to the crew, all of whom have worked with *Inside Amy Schumer* anywhere between two and four years. Every dollar I made shooting the movie *Thank You for Your Service* went to the families of PTSD victims and charities for military families.

It's fun to give money away! I still remember the first time like it was yesterday because it was something I had always dreamed of doing. After getting paid a large sum, I wrote my sister a check for ten thousand dollars and handed it to her in my living room. She looked down at it and said, "Shut the fuck up. No. No. Really? No." She was excited about the money, but mostly she was just so happy for me, knowing how great it must have felt to be able to share. We walked around Chelsea Piers looking at the check and smiling. We ate lobster rolls and cake bites and felt like we were floating. It was one of the best feelings I've ever had in my life. But more than being fun, giving is important! However, my business managers have told me to slow my roll, and my sister has warned me several times not to Giving Tree myself to the point where I am a stump with everyone's names carved onto me. But I'm happier being generous, because even though I know what it feels like to have a surplus of money, I haven't forgotten what it feels like to truly need it. People have had it way worse than me, of course, but I know what it is to depend completely on yourself in life.

———

THE YEAR AFTER my parents lost it all, my birthday party was much different than the barnyard fantasy experience I had during the rich years. The theme was the Lionel Richie song "Dancing on the Ceiling." My dad put a light fixture on the rug in the middle of the living room and the seven kids in attendance danced around it as the song played, over and over again. My dad filmed it with his camera upside down, and then we all watched the recording and ate pizza.

I actually remember it being a great time. It was, and still is, a great song, and the kids didn't care. We didn't need a bounce castle or someone dressed as Rainbow Brite to have a good time—give us some pizza and a disco ball, and there's a party. I didn't even realize we were out of money; I just thought my parents were confused about my level of affection for Lionel Richie.

Today, I'm just as happy as I was when I was waiting tables at a diner or collecting unemployment after getting fired. I don't believe that money changes your level of happiness. But things do get easier, and I feel great in the moments when I can help someone. I still mostly stay home and order Chinese food or sushi. I still get drunk and binge-eat late at night. But now it's just on more expensive wine instead of the boxes of Carlo Rossi that got me through more than half of my life. I'm glad I struggled. I think I'd be an asshole if my money were anything other than the "new" kind. And for the record, when my niece asks me for a car in thirteen years, I will say "Of course" and treat her to a very shiny station wagon that turns on a dime and shakes what its mama gave it any time it goes over thirty miles per hour when she's going to buy her friends forties.

AN INTRODUCTION
TO MY STUFFED ANIMALS

For some reason I've always been drawn to these old, nightmarish stuffed animals. This started early on in my childhood. I never really liked the new, plush, cute animals—the kind with rainbows and hearts that they always market to little girls. You would never see my favorites crowded together in a toy store display. No. I liked these horrifying, broke-down creatures from yesteryear.

I'd like to introduce you to them—in no particular order. (I don't want them to think I have any favorites. Even though, of course, I do.) At some point, I plan to put out a request on Twitter where I ask people to post photos of their childhood stuffed animals that they still have and love. Let me clarify that if you still sleep with these animals, and you are a woman in your midthirties, you are weird. I absolutely do NOT do that every night. I don't. So shut up.

I got Mouser when I was about ten years old at my friend's garage sale on Long Island. I had helped set up the goods they were selling, and I was eyeing him all morning. He just had a good vibe and we clicked. There was debate about whether he is a mouse or a bear, but I always felt he is clearly a mouse. Another confusing fact about his identity is that he is made of felt and velour but he is somehow covered in rust.

Bunny came into my life when I was about seven years old. She was the only one among my stuffed animals who was very new and freshly store-bought when I got her. This particular puppet style of flat rabbit was kind of hot at the time. Despite her being the most corporate of the gang with her mass appeal, I love Bunny, no question. I am calling Bunny a girl but I just now realized that I never actually assigned a gender to any of my stuffed friends.

I got Panda when I was eight years old. She too was kind of on the new side, but because she is so soft, she's gotten the most play out of me. I tattered her up right quick. Again, never thought of Panda as a girl or a guy. Just a panda.

I saw Penny at an antique store when I was seven. We have shared the most forbidden love story of all. I loved her so much, so fast. While my mom shopped around, I held on to this little felt panda puppet with a hard head full of straw and soulful googly eyes. I was heartbroken when my mom refused to buy her for me because she cost forty dollars. But a couple weeks later, we were reunited when my mom surprised me by bringing her home to me. Upon seeing her, I yelled, "Penny!!" My mom was very moved that I'd named a creature who wasn't yet mine. I once lost Penny for a year, only to find out she was at this chick Rachel's house. Rachel said she thought I'd given her Penny, and I explained to her that she was nuts because I would never part with precious little Penny. This second reunion with Penny was especially sweet. I think Penny is a girl but that never defined her. She's a little warrior.

The MVP has gotta be the lady in the photo at the end of this chapter: Pokey. Pokey was my mom's when she was a little girl so I've had her since I was born. She has, without fail, scared the shit out of every single boyfriend I've brought around. When I was a little girl, I was not invited to sleepover parties unless I promised to leave Pokey at home. She's been described as the bride of Chucky and also a nightmare machine. But I don't see her that way. I love her and still put her arm around my neck when I need comfort, just like I did when I was a little girl. Also I'm not sure Pokey is a chick but I do know that I have stained her with enough tears to change her color. She—or he, or it—has gotten me through it all. Pokey is filled with the same hard straw material as Penny's head, and despite my very fluid interpretations of her gender, I did choose to have her recovered in pink fabric and white lace when I took her to the doll doctor (which is a thing). I have never been one to pay much attention to gender identification. We had—well, we *still* have—a cat named Penelope who lives with my mom, but she has both paws in the grave at this point. I named her Penelope before we learned she was actually a boy, but we didn't change her name and we still refer to her as a "her" to this day.

Other stuffed animals have come and gone over the years. I have a two-headed bear that I never named. It was a gift from an ex-boyfriend. It was a pretty perfect gift. Soft and disturbing, which is how I would describe myself. I still have it. It's too perfect, which is also how he would describe himself. I've gotten a lot of stuffed animals from boyfriends over the years. I'm someone who likes to erase all record of an ex as soon as we break up. I try to *Eternal Sunshine* them from my life. I erase all pictures from my cell phone and throw away all gifts. I save printed pictures, but in a box in the closet.

The same ex who gave me the two-headed bear gave me a huge—and I mean huge—stuffed gorilla for Valentine's Day. We named him

Carlos. And don't look into that for some racial undertones. I just liked the name Carlos. We'd joke about how he got me huge gifts even though I had a tiny apartment. He'd buy me giant things that didn't fit in it, sometimes on purpose. Once he got me a huge plant, more like a tree, which made my apartment look like a place Jane Goodall would want to hang out. I had to drag it to the backyard area, which in New York City is really just a frightening alley for rats to frolic in and eat whatever you're storing out there—in my case, boogie boards.

The last stuffed toy I got from a boyfriend is a little stuffed horse. When my two-year-old niece first saw him, she started to call him "Neigh," which is the sound a horse makes, in case you grew up in a city. She now sleeps with Neigh and I have to play the waiting game until she moves on from him, but they've been going strong for a while now. I hope she isn't like that with dudes when she grows up. Or chicks. Or maybe she won't identify as female. Whatever she does will be fine. Or he. Damn, it's hard to write a book and not get yelled at.

I know you just started reading this book so you are still getting to know me, and maybe you are questioning my commitment to these animals. You think I'm writing a fanciful flight about these odd and amusing creatures. But I am 100 percent genuine in my devotion to them. Where does my obsession with them end? Not in a disgusting New York City garbage can where I once made a boyfriend rescue them after we discovered the movers had made a terrible mistake and thrown them all away. (To be fair to the movers, Pokey does look like she belongs in a dark alley in a war-torn village and not in a nice grown-ass woman's bedroom.) You might be thinking of asking me, *Amy, did you commission Tilda Swinton's life partner, Sandro, to paint a portrait of your stuffed animals to commemorate them forever and ever?*

No, that would be taking it too far—oh wait, no, I mean fuck YES I did that.

They're worth it. Each one of them is a ratty, pilled pile of fabric sewn together precariously, but I love them more than most of my family.

DAD

When I was fourteen my dad shit himself at an amusement park.

It all went down one fine summer morning when he took Kim and me to Adventureland, which is exactly what it sounds like: an amusement park filled with adventure, as long as you've never been on an actual adventure or to an actual amusement park. I'd fantasized about the trip the whole week, dreaming about my two favorite rides: the pirate ship and the swings. Granted, they were two of the tamer rides at the park, but for me, they were at the absolute outer limit of my comfort zone. I liked the rides that gave you that feeling of weightlessness that shot from your stomach right down to your vagina when the ride dropped, but I'd never enjoyed a ride that went upside down or spun around until I puked, and I still don't. I guess you could say I have a low tolerance for fear in general.

The movie *Clue* terrified me beyond belief as a child. I slept with a pillow on my back because the chef in that movie was stabbed in the back with a huge kitchen knife. *Not gonna happen to this gal; just try to get a knife through this pillow*, I thought. As if a murderer would enter my bedroom at night intent on stabbing me in the back, see that there was a pillow there, and cancel his plans. I used a similar tactic after hearing about (but not seeing) the movie *Misery*. I slept with pillows covering my legs in case Kathy Bates got a late-night urge to drive out to Long Island, break into my home, and beat my legs with a mallet. Maybe this is why I always slept with (still sleep with) all my scary-looking horror-show stuffed animals. For protection.

Suffice it to say, I was a major scaredy-cat. In fourth grade, I had a talk with the school psychologist about all the things that actively terrified me. I wasn't sent to see him by a concerned teacher, I actually *asked* to see him. I was probably the only nine-year-old in history who requested time with a shrink. After our session, he handed my mom a list of all my fears. This list included earthquakes and tapeworms, which didn't usually come up much where I lived, but my brother was learning about them in school and he couldn't resist the urge to convince me I was nothing more than a sitting duck who was 100 percent going to get eaten alive from the inside by a worm. Highest (and most memorable) on the list, however, was the specific fear that I'd accidentally churn myself into butter. This was inspired by a creepy antique children's book called *Little Black Sambo*, which is one of those stories from the simpler, more racist times of yore when people wrote frightening, insulting tales to help children fall asleep at night. It was highly popular back in the day and has since been rightly banned or taken out of circulation. But my mom had a copy lying around. It's about a boy who goes on an adventure and ends up getting chased by tigers, who circle and circle around a tree so fast that they churn themselves into a pool of butter, which the boy then takes home for his mother to use to make pancakes. Like ya do. Anyway, I was always riddled with fear that I'd somehow be transformed into melted butter, which now doesn't really sound like that much of a bummer. It sounds more like how I'd like to spend my last twenty-four hours on this earth.

Anywhoozle, the morning my dad was going to take us to Adventureland, I woke up and got dressed in denim shorts that stopped just above the knee (crazy flattering) and a long T-shirt with the Tasmanian Devil on it, to let people know what was up. The shirt had to be knotted at the side because it was the early nineties and that's how you rocked out then.

It was not usual for my dad to take us on fun outings, but our parents had recently divorced, so we'd started spending solo time with him. This way, we could sneak in some fun, and he could sneak in feeling like a parent. He picked us up in his little red convertible around ten a.m. (even after he lost everything, he still always drove a convertible). I sat in the front because the back was too windy, and I convinced Kim that she'd like it better. It was about a forty-minute drive from our house, but it felt like four hundred because of the anticipation: the dozen or so rides, the limitless Sour Powers, and the arcade games just inside the park!

My dad always made me feel super loved and did the best he possibly could, but when I was a kid, his identity confused me. He wasn't the golf-playing, beer-drinking family man I saw on TV or in my friends' kitchens. He wasn't so easily labeled—or so easily understood. When he was younger, he'd been a wealthy bachelor living in 1970s New York City—when it was also in its prime. He'd shared a penthouse with his best friend, Josh, who was a well-known actor at the time. He did drugs and slept with girls and enjoyed every moment of his life. When he met my mom, he said good-bye to that lifestyle. Kind of.

Throughout my childhood, he was always in shape—tanned and well-dressed. He was an international businessman, frequently traveling to France, Italy, Prague, and I'd know he'd returned home from a trip before I saw or heard him as his smell was so potent and gorgeous. I thought it was a mixture of expensive European cologne, a faint smell of cigarettes, and something else I didn't yet recognize but later discovered was alcohol.

I never knew my dad to be a big drinker. I never saw him and thought he was even a little buzzed. If you don't know the signs, then they can't be there. I remember coming home from school and see-ing him passed out naked on the floor, but not putting two and two together. I remember that he once apologized to me for missing a volleyball game that he was at, but I just thought, *Oh, forgetful Dad!* I knew he smelled like scotch, but I thought nothing of it. (To this day when a guy I'm with is really hungover or drunk, the smell reminds me of my dad, as I warmly cuddle him closer. When I tell the guy, he laughs, thinking I'm joking.)

I only later found out that my dad was as serious an alcoholic as they came. He needed to go to detox several times when we were children. To his credit, he was clever with his addiction. He only drank when he traveled or when we slept, so . . . all the time and every night. The only thing that slowed down his drinking was mul-tiple sclerosis.

He was diagnosed when I was about ten and was soon in the hos-pital for a while since the disease hit like a tidal wave. It started with a tingle in his feet and fingers and grew to complete numbness and pain in his legs. When he finally got out of the hospital, he kind of went back to normal. I didn't think about his illness and no one brought it up again. I loved my dad, but like any self-obsessed teen, I wasn't worried with his mortality. Even though I saw him lying in the hos-pital bed in pain, I still thought of him as invincible. The morning he picked us up to go to Adventureland, I had pirate ship rides on the brain and can't say I was too concerned about his health.

When we pulled up to the gates of the park, we ran to the high-flying swings and got in line. It was a little chilly, so it wasn't too busy, which meant that we got to go on the ride two or three times in a row before moving on. I loved those swings because I could pretend I was fearless and twist my chair around and around before they shot up in the air to begin the ride, spinning me high in the sky.

I wanted to beeline to the pirate ship, but Kim wanted to go on the big scary roller coaster. We had all day, so I said fine, even though roller coasters brought me zero joy. Being jolted around and the yelling and the possibility of dying didn't—and still doesn't—do it for me. I hated creeping up the hill at a painfully slow pace only to shoot down and hear the screams of all the people filled with regret for coming aboard. But Kim liked them. And I liked Kim. And since I was the big sister, I wanted her to always think I was brave, so I pretended it was no big deal and got in line.

But to be honest, I also wanted to wow my dad. He knew I was a complete chickenshit, and I thought he might notice and say something like "Hey, Amy . . . you going on that ride was very cool and interesting." He loved things like skydiving, which I eventually did when I was older, also to try to impress him, even though I hated every single second of it. So there we stood in a long line that felt like it was moving too fast. I hunched over a bit, hoping I wouldn't meet the height requirement for the ride, but no such luck. I continued to hope that the roller coaster would close down for the day right before we got up to the front, or that there would be a lockdown on the park for a missing kid. There were thousands of kids there. Couldn't just one of them get lost? But alas, no, we were next.

"Do you want to sit in the front car?" the six-year-old-looking kid operating the ride asked us.

"YES!" Kim yelled.

I looked at my dad, who was giving me a most-likely-sarcastic thumbs-up. "Yeah," I added, even though Kim had already hopped in the front.

"I'll be watching you girls!" he said ecstatically.

We waved to my dad as we started creeping up Suicide Mountain, or whatever the roller coaster was called.

I don't remember much of the next two minutes, but finally the car stopped and I opened my eyes. The only silver lining was that I didn't get physically hurt, and it was a great way to practice dissociating—something my siblings and I all perfected by our early teen years. We climbed off, and Kim was thrilled. She'd had the time of her life.

I can't speak for the other maniacs on that ride, but for me, the roller coaster was traumatic. When I walked down that ramp I felt as though the president should have been at the bottom waiting to give me a medal for valor. But there was no medal; just my dad, smiling at us.

"There's no line!" Kim shouted. "Let's go again!"

And so we went, and we went and we went. Each time my dad cheered us on from the bottom. We must have ridden that thing five times when we reached the end of the ride and he wasn't there.

"Where's Dad?" Kim asked.

I told her, "He's probably getting us candy or something."

While we waited for him, we rode the ride again and again and again. After the twelfth go I was feeling real ready to get on that pirate ship, which was the main adventure I wanted to have in this land. Kim was raring to go again, but I had to stop. I thought it might be nice to take a break and maybe have kids someday, and I was sure Dad would meet us when he was done doing . . . *What was he doing?*

At that point in time, I hadn't yet realized how funny my dad is. Most of the things he did or said flew right over my head, and everyone else's for that matter. His sense of humor was so dry that days would pass before people realized he'd insulted them. He threw out perfect one-liners under his breath while talking to waiters or bankers or my mom—and no one heard them but me. Once my grandma was talking to him, and she said, "If I die . . . ," and he corrected her slyly: "*When* . . . " He was even dark with us as children. I remember walking into the kitchen one time and seeing him pretending that I had just caught him in the act of putting our dog, Muffin, in the microwave. He had a way about him that made it seem like nothing could ruffle his feathers or surprise him.

So that day while Kim and I sat on a bench and waited for my father, I saw a new side of him. We waited and waited. I put stupid braids in Kim's hair and made her give me a hand massage until he finally reappeared. When he walked up to us, the first thing I noticed was his expression; he was panicked and defeated at the same time. The second thing I noticed was that he didn't have pants on.

Kim didn't observe any of this because she immediately asked, "Can we get fudge?!"

"Sure," my dad answered.

He and I looked at each other. I was speechless. His T-shirt, which was soaking wet along the bottom half, was long enough to cover his underwear, but his pants were long gone.

"We need to go, Aim," he told me very calmly.

I thought about asking something reasonable, like "Where are your pants, Dad?" But he looked in my eyes and communicated that I shouldn't ask any questions. I went into the country-store-themed shop and got Kim her fudge, and then we all walked briskly to the car. I didn't look to see if anyone was staring. I only watched ten-year-old Kim, who was fully enthralled by every bite of her treat. *Does she really not see that he's pantsless? I know it's called Adventureland but I don't think those adventures involve men over forty dressing like Winnie the Pooh after a wet T-shirt contest.*

We'd just gotten very close to the car when a breeze hit and sent the smell my way. It was shit. Human shit.

It was then I realized, *Oh, my dad shit his pants. Okay.* I quickly leveraged this opportunity to look like a selfless and charitable sister. "You can get shotgun this time, Kimmy!" I was quick on my feet.

"Really?!" she answered. She was so excited to get this privilege that it kind of broke my heart. Amusement park fudge AND shotgun? She couldn't believe her luck. Little did she know she wouldn't be able to enjoy eating that fudge for much longer, or possibly ever again.

We climbed in the car, me in the back, Kim up front with my dad. As he put down the top, I looked in the side mirror and saw Kim's nostrils start to flare. She'd picked up the scent. The most silent car ride of my life began. The fudge sat in Kim's lap for the rest of the ride and her head slowly crept further and further in the direction away from my dad. The entire top was down on the car, but she still felt the need to hang her little head out the side. She looked like a golden retriever by the time my dad pulled up to our house to drop us off.

I was so impressed with her for not saying anything. *What a good girl*, I thought. She kissed my dad on the cheek and thanked him and ran into the house, her face the same exact hue as Kermit the Frog. I hopped out and held my breath to kiss him. I started to walk up our driveway when he called to me.

"Aim!"

I turned and answered, "Yeah?"

He took a breath and said, "Please don't tell your mom." I nodded.

The saddest realization I've had in my life is that my parents are people. Sad, human people. I aged a decade in that moment.

———

THE SECOND TIME my dad shit himself in my presence, I didn't have a roller coaster to keep me from witnessing it. It was right in front of me. Well, more to the side of me.

It was four years later, the summer before I left for college, right before I got on a plane to Montana to stay with my older brother, Jason, for a couple weeks. I worshipped Jason and was always trying to hang out with him. He is almost four years older than me, and as far as I was concerned, he should have won *People* magazine's most intriguing person of the year, every year. He was a basketball prodigy in his early teens but suddenly quit in high school because he didn't want to live up to other people's expectations anymore. He was curious about things like time and space, and genuinely considered living in a cave for months and being nocturnal. He became an accomplished musician without telling anyone. He didn't go to his senior year of high school, choosing instead to earn the credits needed for graduation by driving cross-country and writing about it—somehow convincing the principal of our high school and our mother that this was a great idea. I know this is sounding like that Dos Equis ad that glorifies the eccentric old guy with a beard, but the point is I have been crazy about Jason since I was born and I always wanted to be a part of whatever unusual existence he was living. So I went to hang out with him any chance I had.

At this particular time, my dad was on a kick of wanting to do "dad stuff" for me, so he asked if he could drive me to the airport. When you have MS "dad stuff" becomes playing bingo or giving you rides places. It was midafternoon when he picked me up to head to JFK.

When we got there, I pulled my giant suitcase out of the trunk of his car and navigated the airport entrance without his help. This must have looked strange to other people, seeing this strapping man watch his eighteen-year-old daughter lift and tote her giant suitcase all by herself, but they didn't know he was sick. I didn't really understand the symptoms of the disease, but I did know that it slowed him down, that even if he looked normal he could still be in a lot of pain, unable to do the small physical acts he used to do with ease.

My dad accompanied me as I juggled my bags and checked in, and everything seemed fine. It was pre-9/11 so he could walk me to the gate, and that's exactly what he wanted to do. He kept saying, "I'm going to walk you to the gate." I think it was a big deal for him, because he never did stuff like that for me. That was a mom-type job. But I was glad for his company, because even though my list of fears had definitely gotten smaller by this point in my life, I was still pretty terrified of flying.

We both went through security, shoes on—the good ol' days— and started walking down the long hall to my gate. That particular terminal was under heavy construction at the time, so we had to be careful where we walked. We still had a ways to go when my dad took a sharp right turn and beelined it to the side of the hall. I stopped walking and turned to see what he was doing. He shot me a pained look, pulled his pants down, and peed shit out of his ass for about thirty seconds. Thirty seconds is an eternity, by the way, when you're watching your dad volcanically erupt from his behind. Think about it now. One Mississippi. That's just one.

People quickly walked past, horrified. One woman shielded her child's eyes. They stared. I yelled at one chick passing by, "WHAT?! Keep it moving!"

After he had finished, my dad stood up straight and said, "Aim, do you have any shorts in your bag?"

I opened my suitcase and grabbed a pair of lacrosse shorts. I handed them over, thinking, *Damn, those were my favorite.* He threw his pants in the trash and put the shorts on. I went in for a top-body hug good-bye. I didn't cry, I didn't laugh, I just smiled and said, "I love you, Dad. I won't tell Mom."

I started to walk away from the whole scene when I heard, "I said I'd walk you to the gate!"

I turned around to see if he was joking; he was not. To the gate we walked. I was mouth breathing and shooting dirty looks at anyone who dared to stare at him. Once we got to the very last gate in the goddamn terminal, at the end of a very long hall, he kissed me good-bye and left.

Normally when I would board a plane, the first thing I would do was worry about how scary takeoff would be and try to think of ways to distract myself from the anxiety. But that day, I sat on the plane thinking about nothing. My mind went blank. It was too painful. I didn't think about my fearless father, who was dealing with a mysterious disease. He used to breeze through the airport in a cloud of expensive cologne and flashy watches, and now he'd been transformed into this anonymous, helpless guy who lost control of his bowels in the airport while his teenage daughter watched. He didn't wince or let me see him sweat even once. I mean, he was drenched in sweat. Physically he was being taken over by MS, yet on the inside he was still as brazen as ever. But I didn't think about any of that. I just stared out the window for five hours, fully numb, until I got off the plane in Montana and hugged my brother longer than he would have liked.

I tried to talk about these two shitting incidents onstage. So many parts of these stories are so disturbing that they make me laugh—because it's too much to digest any other way. The image of Kim's head leaning out of the car, the image of me standing next to my pantsless father and the trolley that carted people around Adventureland. I look at the saddest things in life and laugh at how awful they are, because they are hilarious and it's all we can do with moments that are painful. My dad is the same way. He's always laughed at the things that are too dark for other people to laugh at. Even now, when his memory and mental functioning have been severely impaired by his MS, I'll tell him his mind is a pile of scrambled eggs and he will still laugh hysterically and say, "Too true, too true!"

My dad never shows any sign that he pities himself. He never has. He's not afraid to look dead-on at the grim facts of his life. I hope I've inherited this quality of his. I've only seen him cry once about his disease, and that was very recently—when he learned he'd be getting stem cell treatments that would help him feel a lot better, and maybe even help him walk again. That day, he sobbed like a baby. But never before.

I have wonderful early memories of spending time with him at the beach. We were beach bums, and he was a sun worshipper. If it was January and the sun was shining, he'd douse himself in baby oil and sit outside in a lawn chair. He was tan year-round. And if it was summer, we'd get in the ocean early in the morning and get out after the sun went down. We'd body-surf together; that was our thing. All

I wanted to do was take a wave in further than him, but it never happened. I even cheated, standing up and running a little to catch up, but no, he always won.

The most joy I remember feeling as a kid was when a storm was coming and the waves were big. Other people were scared and stayed out of the water, but not us. Not even when the ocean was angry and pulling us sideways. We would have to get out and walk half a football field on the beach before it swept us all the way down the shore again. We swam out against the current and caught the best waves of the day. Nothing kept us out—not rain, not my mom yelling, nothing. I can still picture him looking young and healthy and strong, with his bronzed skin and his black hair soaking. For some reason, I wasn't afraid. Maybe it was because I was with him. Next to him, I was invincible.

EXCERPT FROM MY JOURNAL IN 1994 (AGE THIRTEEN) WITH FOOTNOTES FROM 2016

I've decided to get a journal because some things you just can't say out loud.[1] *I'm 13 years old, and I have several problems. My brother Jason is a senior in high school. He's my half brother, meaning we have the same mother, but his dad died when he was 11. When Jason was two years old our mom married my dad. My dad didn't like my brother, and as a matter of fact, he wished Jason wasn't a part of our family.*[2] *I never noticed, but my Dad actually never went on our "family trips."*[3] *My mom just recently pointed all of this out to me. She said she tried to keep everyone*

---

1   I obviously don't subscribe to this advice anymore, as someone who onstage has gone into great detail about an encounter with an unexpected uncircumcised penis.

2   Yikes, was that true? There is a lot of heavy brainwashing from good ol' mom in this entry. I don't think my dad particularly cared for my brother, but it wasn't personal. He just only liked children that at one point were shot out from his own penis.

3   I don't know why "family trips" is in quotes. They were just family trips; this sounds like my mom was using us to mule drugs. We would go to Florida or Lake George or our farmhouse. I never once held a balloon filled with heroin.

happy by having my dad go in one car and me and my brother and sister go in the other car with her.[4]

Jason's dad was a very big part of his life. My mom informed me that when he died, my dad made no effort to become Jason's stepfather.[5] *They seemed to be acquaintances. This left my mom a single parent, basically, with no help from my father. I'm so glad she pointed this out to me, because I never knew. She allowed Jason to withdraw from our family,*[6] *which is no longer a family.*

My sister Kim is nine years old and in fourth grade. She is very mature for her age. I think she's so mature because I don't permit her to act her age. In her grade there are a few girls who are total &*&*.[7] *They treat her like dirt. It doesn't help that Kim is extremely sensitive. These girls do horrible things to her, like one day they were all sitting at the lunch table, and when Kim sat down, they all got up and left. When my mom told me about it, tears started streaming down my cheeks before she even finished her sentence. My heart broke for Kim. So I hopped on my bike and road straight to those #\$#\$'s*[8] *houses and yelled at them. And told them to leave my sister alone OR ELSE!*[9]

Kim sometimes acts really phony.[10] *She'll act so innocent and fragile,*[11] *and I'll get really mad at her and treat her like crap. My mom tells her to*

---

4   You know that old saying . . . the family that drives separately, crumbles and shatters soon after.

5   This was true, but maybe pointing this out to a tween isn't the best move from a parent.

6   As I previously mentioned, Jason talked his way out of his senior year of high school and got to leave home and roam the country.

7   If I wrote this now I would use the word "cunts."

8   CUNTS!

9   We recently Googled the girl who was the meanest to my sister. We found her on Facebook. She's now a Pilates instructor, of course, and if I had her current address, I'd ride my bike to her house again and tell her she's still a worthless mean girl in my mind.

10   Wow, I was just saying how great she was.

11   Innocent and fragile? Dude, she was nine . . . What did I expect her to act like? Slutty and hardened?

just express herself when someone at school hurts her feelings. I say, "No way. You have to be tough and don't show them they hurt you."[12]

About 8 weeks ago I found out that my parents were getting a divorce.[13] My dad travels a lot, so I wasn't majorly depressed. My sister was, though. After the first five years that my parents were married my mom realized she wasn't in love and never had been.[14] But she stayed with my dad another five years because of me and Jay and Kim, and also because my dad developed a condition with -osis at the end of the word.[15] Anyone who knows my mom will tell you she's the nicest person you'll ever meet.[16] But they're getting a divorce.

I'm going to see a psychologist this Thursday. I don't want to, but I know it's necessary.[17]

I have another problem: my friends. Lauren, Becky, and Kate. I guess you can say we're the athletic, smart, pretty girls of our grade.[18] Becky is sort of slow; she has a moon shaped face with light freckles and pin straight, shoulder length, dirty blonde hair. She's as tall as me but a little slimmer. She thinks she's totally gorgeous and wishes she was Lauren. She's also a snob.[19] Then there's Jen; she's excellent at soccer and totally dedicated, but she's also a ditz and always the last to know what we're talking about. She's 5 foot 3ish and has mousy brown hair and looks very Irish. Everyone does, I guess.[20]

---

12 I stand by this. Never let those cunts see you sweat, which is good advice and a good name for an eighties hip-hop album.

13 Whaaaaat? But Mom kept us all happy by having us drive in separate cars!

14 Again, damn, Mom, lot to lay on a kid who's still in middle school, but okay.

15 It was multiple sclerosis. You couldn't look stuff up on your phone back then, so I just left it at -osis . . . makes sense.

16 "Brainnnnnwasssshhhhh, at the brainwash yeah" (singing this to the tune of "Car Wash" . . .).

17 I still say this exact same thing every single week.

18 Guess I wasn't afraid of feelin' myself.

19 Never too young to talk shit about your friends.

20 Jen is a nurse with three kids now, and we're still close.

I can't believe I haven't mentioned my other best friend, Mark. His hair is chin length and he's always showered and clean. He's a really good soccer player, and he's an excellent drummer. I met him in 5th grade. He started a band this summer, and I was interested in being the lead singer. When it was just me and Mark in the band I was fine, but when it became a real thing I backed away. I strive to be more like Mark.[21] *I think I care too much about how people feel about me. Mark isn't like that at all. If I wasn't friends with him, I wouldn't be half as happy. Now that I think about it, he may be my only real friend.*[22]

Now about boys.[23] *There are several boys I like, but the two I'm concentrated on are Kevin Williams and Joshua Walsch. Kevin is shy, funny, and cool. He has shaggy brown hair and is over six feet tall. He has gorgeous blue cat eyes and a mouth like the joker. I told him that once in biology and he smirked and said he knew. Joshua is a year younger than me, but he's so sweet and adorable. He has black hair and a smaller frame than me, but he's strong and has porcelain skin covered in freckles. He looks like he just hopped off the boat from Ireland.*[24]

Both boys have little speech impediments, I've noticed. Joshua has a speech impediment that makes him sound like the Kennedys. The real ones![25] *And Kevin has a gap in his front teeth and a lisp. Uhhh soo cute.*[26]

I've gotten to first base, which is French Kissing, but I think I'm ready for 2nd.[27]

---

21 I was in love with him.

22 Mark is now the drummer in the band Taking Back Sunday.

23 Sorry, Mark!

24 I was real obsessed with the Irish. Pretty sure I'd either just done a book report on them or watched *Far and Away* at a slumber party.

25 As opposed to those hack, bullshit, fake Kennedys?

26 I have always been turned on by a good impediment, like a baby arm or a stutter.

27 I wasn't.

OFFICIALLY A WOMAN

Everyone says you become a woman when you start your period or lose your virginity. In Judaism, you're deemed a woman when you have your bat mitzvah. I of course saw this ceremony as an opportunity not only to chant my Torah portion but also to make my big stage debut in the temple. I'd been doing musicals since I was five, and I was ready to steal the show. *I'm gonna show these Jews what I'm made of,* I thought in an unracist way. All eyes were on me—just the way I liked it—as I looked out into the crowd from the bimah. My mom was crying tears of joy next to my dad, who was absolutely bursting with pride. I wouldn't have been surprised if they gave me a standing O before I finished. I was nailing it.

I sang those Hebrew words like the little half-Jew angel that I was—without the slightest idea what I was saying. I could have been chanting a call to action to continue apartheid. In Hebrew school they taught us two things: how to read Hebrew and how to read Hebrew. A year before my bat mitzvah I was in class with my teacher, Mr. Fischer, a frightening, expressionless man, the kind who would look the same sleeping or in an earthquake. I was sitting in the first row, and Mr. Fischer called on me to read aloud from the Torah. After about three minutes, I stopped and asked, "What does this mean?" For the first time ever, he showed emotion. He slammed his catcher's-mitt-like hand onto his desk right next to my head and shouted, "Go to the principal's office!" I never asked again.

I'm sure this wasn't the first time I got in trouble for asking a question, and it certainly wasn't the last. In school we were encouraged to ask questions, but sometimes when we did, we were accused of being provocative or rude. Now that I'm out of school and there's no threat of a principal's office looming down the hall, I ask whatever the fuck questions I want. It feels pretty good. Pretty womanly, too.

But none of that mattered on my big day. I didn't care what I was singing; I just wanted to blow everyone's socks off. I belted out the last couple lines of my portion—move over, cast of *Fiddler on the Roof*, your jobs are all in jeopardy—and on my final note, I let loose with all my might. That was when my dream turned into my nightmare. My voice cracked. I William Hunged my last note. My heart started to pound too quickly, and I could feel my face turning into a beet the way it loved to do. Silence filled the room, and I thought I might cry.

Then came the first laugh. Then another. And the rest. I looked out at the people in the seats, and they were all laughing—and looking at me with adoration. I saw Kim nervously giggling, waiting to see how I'd react. I realized that even though it was an accident, I'd made everyone happy, and I wanted to let Kim know that it was okay to laugh, so I joined in. I laughed hard. I was laughing at myself. We were all laughing together—a real laugh that went on for a while.

I'm pretty sure that's why I officially became a woman that day. Not because of the dumb ancient ceremony where children are gifted bonds they can't cash until they're twenty-five (by which time they have lost them). No, I became a woman because I turned a solemn, quiet room into a place filled with unexpected laughter. I became a woman because I did, for the first time, what I was supposed to be doing for the rest of my life. I may not have had that exact thought in the moment, but in retrospect it is so clear to me.

There are lots of "firsts" like this in life, little flashpoints here and there when you're unknowingly becoming a woman. And it's not the clichéd shit, like when you have your first kiss or drive your first car. You become a woman the first time you stand up for yourself when they get your order wrong at a diner, or when you first realize your parents are full of shit. You become a woman the first time you get fitted for a bra and realize you've been wearing a very wrong size your whole fucking life. You become a woman the first time you fart in front of a boyfriend. The first time your heart breaks. The first time you break someone else's heart. The first time someone you love dies. The first time you lie and make yourself look bad so a friend you love can look better. And less dramatic things are meaningful too, like the first time a guy tries to put a finger in your ass. The first time you express the reality that you don't want that finger in your ass. That you really don't want anything in your ass at all. Or to have any creative, adventurous sex for that matter. That you just want to be fucked missionary sometimes and without any nonsense. You will remember all these moments later as the moments that made you the woman you are. Everyone tells you it happens when you get your first period, but really it happens when you insert your first tampon and teach your best friend to do the same.

Speaking of menstrual blood, let's get back to becoming a woman in the temple. After I brought the house down by dropping the ball on my Torah portion, it was time for the rabbi to walk over and speak to me in front of everyone—not unlike a sermon, but tailored to me. I'd been told that most people hated this kind of attention, but I thought, *Bring it on. Let the compliments begin.*

Rabbi Shlomo was a tall man, and he had to reach down to put his hands on both of my shoulders. I gazed up at him and prepared to look humble. He began, "Amy . . . ," and that's the last thing I heard. His breath was so bad, I literally couldn't listen to a word. It took all my strength not to pass out from the stench he was sending my way. I figured out quickly that I needed to gasp for breath while he was inhaling. He was giving me heartfelt words of wisdom and I was doing Lamaze. *What did he eat for breakfast?* I thought. *An adult diaper? A cadaver?*

The speech went on for hours. It was probably only five minutes, but when you're in the panic room of someone's dragon mouth the clock really stops. Just as I was getting dizzy from lack of oxygen, I could tell from his body language that he was wrapping it up. Everyone applauded. I turned away, filled my lungs with fresh air, and smiled out into oblivion. It was official: I was a woman.

Now I could have a short luncheon with smoked fish and bagels and take my closest friends to Medieval Times in New Jersey. Just as God and Golda Meir intended.

CAMP ANCHOR

When I was fourteen, I volunteered at a camp for people with special needs. Camp Anchor is still around today; it's an amazing program that now serves more than seven hundred campers a year. People volunteer there because you can help those in need, it's good for your soul, and it enriches your life. I did it because the boys were doing it, and I wanted to have a soccer player's tongue in my mouth before I died.

I would like to say that I went into it wanting to help others. But let's be real—I was a teenager who only cared about herself. Adolescence is full of awkwardness and insecurity for most people. But in my case it was also full of grand delusions. Besides wanting boys to like me, I also wanted to embody all the impossible combinations: I wanted to be both beautiful and kind, smart and selfless. My mom was a teacher for the deaf, so I'd been around kids with special needs for as long as I could remember. I thought it would be easy, and I knew how to talk to these children like adults. I'd show them love and respect and be giving of myself. I pictured teaching a little girl how to swim and was already patting myself on the back for being such a great person: Saint Amy. People would line up around the block just so I'd smile at them and once in a while give them a hug, like I was a Buddhist street monk, and they'd be eternally blessed. But mostly I was excited to ride the bus and try to fit in with the cute guys.

A lot of the cool older boys from my high school volunteered at Camp Anchor, but I only had eyes for Tyler Cheney. He had soulful brown eyes and a mess of curly hair. He was a great soccer player but also loved Phish and the Grateful Dead. (Wow—could there be any limits to how diverse this guy's interests were?) I loved making Tyler laugh, which wasn't hard to do because he was a complete stoner and his double-digit IQ wasn't what made him attractive. For most of my life I have had the habit of being attracted to hot guys with the intelligence of a jack-o'-lantern and a distended belly. I always loved a belly. Tyler was no different. All I would have to do to make him laugh was quote the movie *Tommy Boy*. I knew it by heart, so he basically thought I was George Carlin. I think he's in finance now and has a hedge fund or something else I can't understand. (How come stupid people can still make money like that? I don't know what a hedge fund is. I want a hedgehog fund. They are so cute and I think I need one. But I would probably kill it by accident. I can't even keep a plant alive. Okay, never mind.)

Tyler sat in front of me in Spanish class and I'd stare at the back of his curly head, trying to will him to turn around and declare his love for me, something that never even came close to happening. But when I heard he was going to volunteer at Camp Anchor, well, guess what, Tyler Cheney? So was I. I'd save the shit out of some kids to be close to him.

On our first day at Camp Anchor, we waited for the bus to pick us up at an elementary school parking lot. I remember I'd laid out my first-day-of-work outfit on my bed the night before. *Wait until Tyler sees me in this*, I thought. A Twitter-blue T-shirt. My flannel plaid blue-and-green boxer shorts that had PENN STATE on them (and not even on the butt; this was a few years before the marketing geniuses decided to put their paws right on the spot where every dude's and most curious women's eyes go right away). I pulled up those shorts, did a half turn in the mirror, and hoped deeply and sadly that this would be the outfit I'd be wearing when Tyler realized I could be good for him. I knew I had a long way to go, because so far I was still just the oily-faced girl whose idea of seduction was to whisper impersonations of America's favorite sweaty three-hundred-pound male comic in his ear. But maybe camp was the place where he would see me in a new light. *If I could just make myself become more his type*, I thought. I tied up my hair in one of those ballerina buns and took a hair dryer to my bangs, but within ten seconds they blew up in the summer humidity so that I bore a striking resemblance to Sammy Hagar.

I sat one row away from Tyler on the bus and was already sweating through my carefully selected outfit, sticking to the green pleather seats, which were torn up and graffitied by badasses whose parents were failing. I listened to Roxette on my Walkman and tried to seem distant and interesting, like Brenda on *Beverly Hills, 90210*, whom I've modeled myself on for most of my life. She was the queen of the impossible combinations. She seemed to have been born with an innocence (me) yet she oozed sex appeal (totally me) and she would fit right in doing something as pure as a sing-along, but only if it ended with her getting railed from behind by Dylan under the bleachers. Sweet, with a dark, dirty edge, just like fourteen-year-old me. Except none of that, and I'd never even been fingered and was deeply heinous looking at the time. But I wanted so badly to make the shoe fit, to be the kind of impossible person Brenda was. Anyway, when the bus pulled up to camp, I took a break from envisioning myself as the center of attention at the Peach Pit, peeled my legs off the seat, and got off the bus. We walked to registration en masse, while I was channeling *We're gonna be a cool, fun group all summer, right, you guys? I'm one of the guys, but you have feelings for me. You will give yourself over to me around the Fourth of July, RIGHT, TYLER?*–type energy.

As I approached the registration desk where we were going to find out what group we were assigned to, I had only two wishes: 1) that Tyler and I would be assigned to the same group, and 2) that I'd get the cutest littlest kids—the five-to-eight-year-old girls, called the "Junior 3s." The groups were divided by sex and age, and I'd seen the Junior 3s listed in the brochure when I was considering volunteering. I wanted to be their cool big sister who'd impact their lives forever. They were adorable, and I pictured us doing the annual talent show and laughing and hugging. I'd give them each a piggyback ride and Tyler would say, "Wow, you must be sore . . . need a massage?" And I'd say, "Sure, maybe later. I just have to make sure everyone gets a turn first." Like a hero. And then I'd give him a massage and slip and fall on his penis and get pregnant and trap him and be on the first season of *Teen Mom*.

"Senior Ten!" announced the elderly woman who I thought was a man until she barked at me.

"Excuse me?" I barked back.

"You will be working with Senior Ten—that is women thirty-five and up. There is your group," she said, pointing to a herd of ladies who looked more *Golden Girls* than little girls.

I was thrown off. "I didn't know there were campers older than me," I demurred.

The woman, who resembled my grandpa when he let his hair grow a little too long, gave me an expressionless nonreply.

"What a fun surprise," I said.

I was a flake, and she could smell it on me. I'd come to Camp Anchor to flirt with boys and put something on my college applications, and she knew it. She saw right through my Chia Pet bangs into my shallow heart and frowned. She handed me my paperwork and sent me on my way.

I slowly approached another volunteer, a beautiful Latina girl from a couple towns over. "Hi, I'm Carli!" she said, beaming goodness. She was here for the right reasons, I thought. She was a beautiful, pure-souled girl, and I was a pug-nosed disaster. She was a Brenda with a twist. Even more gorgeous, sexy without seeming slutty, and charitable on top of it all. That kind of perfection didn't yet make me furious. It just made me want to be exactly like her. Then there was Dave Mack, a gorgeous guy whom I would have immediately fallen in deep West Beverly High love with except for the fact that I could see he'd already set his sights on Carli. *Man, maybe if I had gotten here first I'd have gotten him*, I lied to myself. But he was smart and could see that Carli was a living angel with perfect olive skin and a sweet little tush.

Our group leader, Joanne, was a pretty woman with frizzy blond hair, a pronounced Italian-looking nose, a fanny pack, and a great rack. She was the only one of us who got paid, though I can't imagine it was a lot. She was a kind, strong woman who'd been around the block with these ladies. She was no-nonsense, but she'd still laugh with the rest of us when ridiculousness occurred. Which was often.

Every day, I'd put so much mental energy into wanting to be appealing to Tyler—or wanting to be as flawless as Carli. But the

Senior 10 chicks who I was now spending all my time with had much better strategies. They generally didn't waste energy hiding who they were or faking who they weren't. There was Mona, who was always wearing a baseball hat and a huge muscle T-shirt with Mickey Mouse on it. She was strong and masculine, and her smile would light up a room. Mona had Down syndrome, as did her best friend, Lucy, who had a short, boyish haircut and knock-knock jokes for days. I almost never understood the punch lines, but she was so delighted by reciting them you couldn't help but laugh right along with her.

Another camper, Debbie, was openly flirtatious and boy crazy. She kept her hair braided perfectly so she felt pretty. Plump and youthful, she was like a Juliet looking for her Romeo. She had Down syndrome, too. Blanche had a long, thin, freckled face. She didn't mind being mean and made it clear early on that she didn't like me one bit. I respected that and stayed out of her way. No energy wasted between us faking it.

Enid was schizophrenic and reminded me of Woody Allen in terms of her voice and her physical movements. She had short red hair with tight curls and was very neurotic. She'd often pace around and talk to herself. Once, I nudged her to tell her it was time for lunch, and she replied, "Don't interrupt me, can't you see I'm having a conversation?" Well, damn, she was right. I didn't let it happen again. She couldn't stomach small talk but was kind enough to engage in some good debates with me. She was so bright that I'd forget about her ailments. Much like a stoic big sister, Enid would sometimes refuse to have anything to do with me, but other days we were thick as thieves. By the end of the summer, I was closest with her.

One sunny day it was my job to hang with a camper named Beatrice, a sweet sixty-year-old woman who spoke like Gollum from

The Lord of the Rings and had an even bigger crush on Dave than I did. Dave and Beatrice were sweet on each other. At all the dancing events it was understood that no one danced with Dave but Big B. She was only four feet tall but weighed about two hundred pounds, and though her words were, in general, indeterminable, listening to her speak was a treat. She'd mumble something that sounded like it would only make sense in the Shire, and laugh wildly to herself and slap her knee.

On this particular day we had a huge game of Marco Polo planned for the campers in the pool. Nothing says summer like a game centered around a Venetian merchant sailor who may or may not have traveled through Asia in the 1200s to 1300s. I was fully prepared to win the game: I was younger and faster than my Senior 10s and I knew I could dominate that pool. I was extra motivated knowing that being in bathing suits always made the campers grabby with one another's bodies. Especially mine. They thought it was funny to grab my breasts, and if one of them caught up to me, my boobs would be squeezed like lemons at a lemonade stand. Not that I don't like affection, but they grabbed hard and I bruise like a peach. But before the game started, Joanne asked me to take Beatrice to the bathroom and wait for her while she put on her bathing suit.

I brought her into the muggy bathroom and while she was in the stall changing, I looked at myself in the foggy mirror. I didn't recognize myself. My body was in the adolescent state where I would get frequent growing pains in my legs. Exactly every other day I looked either long and lanky or chubby and potatolike. The only constant at the time was the difference in the size of my breasts. My right one was very much in the lead. The left wouldn't catch up for years and never fully has. The mirror got foggier as I stood and stood and waited and waited.

"Beatrice?!"

She made a Nell-like grumble from within the stall. "*Whloppppr.*"

"Bea, what's goin' on, sister? Let's go, we're gonna miss the game."

After several minutes the door was flung open and out came Beatrice ready for the chlorine in her bathing suit and Teva sandals. There was just one problem: her bathing suit was on backward. Her scoop-back one-piece was facing very much the wrong way, which meant that I was getting a full-frontal view of what used to be Beatrice's breasts. They were long and old; at the time, I'd never seen anything hang on for dear life like this before. They looked like those fake snakes that pop out of trick cans of peanuts. Her cans were attached to her chest and those snakes were loose, skin-colored, and almost to the floor. She looked around the bathroom, anywhere but at me. I looked right at her. I was mesmerized: here I'd been afraid of one of the campers grabbing my breasts, and I was now faced with hers. I could tell that she had absolutely no clue about the wardrobe malfunction and she made a beeline for the door.

"Whoa whoa whoa!" I yelled, trying to block her.

She knew something was off, but she was fired up about the pool. "Poo poo," she said, meaning "pool." I think.

"You need to turn your suit around. It's on backward, honey."

She looked at me with anger in her always-red eyes. I could see that she was ready to go and wasn't going to let me stop her. She was not interested in turning that suit around; it was game time.

I body-blocked the exit, led her gently but forcibly back into the stall, and did what needed to be done. I took those bathing-suit straps in my hands and yanked them down. It was a struggle. The suit was so tight I had to drop down to my knees and use my body weight to get it off her. There we were, Beatrice nude, staring and blinking, and me trying to grip and pull at the spandex swimwear, my face inches away from her vagina and breasts, which at this point were very much in the same general area. Her soft, stretched-out nips rested on my sunburned shoulders while I twisted her suit around and told her to step back into it. She ignored me. She was probably daydreaming about her and Dave summering on Martha's Vineyard next year. Undeterred, I picked up her white and soft-as-porcelain-looking foot and placed it in one leg hole, did the same with the other leg, and then, with all of my might, pulled that tiny suit over her pear-shaped body.

I was dripping with sweat by the time we were finished, and the bathroom could have doubled as a steam room. We walked out hand in hand to the pool. Finally, someone at this camp wanted to hold my hand. I think she knew I needed it. Almost whistling, she led me to the pool, but I was too exhausted and freaked out to join the Marco Polo game. Instead, I sat on a deck chair, staring off into space without moving, as Beatrice splashed around with the other ladies. One of them probably grabbed my breast, but I felt nothing for the next forty-eight hours.

Coming face-to-face with B's unmentionables wasn't even the most memorable moment in the Camp Anchor bathroom. That one is reserved for Sally. She was a Senior 10 who had some sort of aging disorder. Even though she was forty years old, she had the body of a seven-year-old and the face of a much older woman. She had Peter Pan–short black hair with some grays mixed in, tons of freckles, a furrowed brow, and a harsh look in her black eyes. She was very thin, spoke like a child, and always kept to herself. To get her jazzed about any group activity was beyond impossible. I remember approaching her once and, mustering up some false enthusiasm, telling her, "Sally, we're going to the arts-and-crafts tent to make picture frames now!"

She stared into my eyes and looked through my soul. She didn't care. She knew I didn't care. She knew I knew she didn't care. In that moment we nodded and made a silent contract to keep it more real with each other.

One day in the last week of camp, there was a fun hangout planned for all the volunteers at the end of the day. I was wearing cut-off denim shorts with my uniform T-shirt sleeves rolled up. I'd planned a special outfit because I had confirmed that Tyler would definitely be there (I knew because I'd asked him and all his friends three hundred times). I'd noticed earlier that I was the only person not wearing Converse sneakers (like a dolt), so I'd bought a pair that were blue and white and almost identical to Carli's. She'd noticed, and instead of being annoyed, she'd said, "Cool! We have the same shoes!" Did this girl's perfection ever stop? Could you drop the ball just once, Carli? A queef . . . something . . . anything to let me know you're human and not an American Girl doll with perfect titties?

By that point in the summer I was pretty sure she and Dave were an item; they found excuses to touch each other and giggle when they were away from the pack. That night, Dave was whispering something into Carli's ear, and I was left alone with my new sneakers and socks that were too big for them, standing around a piano with the girls in the music tent, failing to learn the words to "We Didn't Start the Fire." I would have done anything to trade places with Carli. The shoes weren't cutting it. She was like Cinderella and I was one of the stepsisters trying to force the glass slipper on my foot so the prince would marry me. Suddenly, out of nowhere, Sally tugged on my sleeve and pointed to the bathroom. She was a woman of few words and she obviously had to go. Members of Senior 10 were always to be accompanied to the bathroom, and on this occasion Sally designated me the lucky escort. Truth be told, I was honored that she chose me to walk her. We headed over to the bathroom together in silence. By that time we were like coworkers. She was about twenty years older than me and had laid it on the line: no pleasantries, bitch. Which I completely appreciated.

We stood in line for the cramped four-stall bathroom where we'd stood dozens of times before, and when she was on deck, she again pulled on my sleeve and I looked down at her (she was no more than three feet tall). She was gazing up at me very intensely, like she was casting a spell of some sort. But you can't yell at one of your campers, "Are you casting a spell on me?!" So instead I asked, "What's up, Sal?" She didn't answer, and she didn't need to. I looked down at the floor and noticed there was liquid shit running down not one but both of her legs and onto her feet, and onto my very new shoes. I resisted the urge to scream my way out of the bathroom and run to the nearest lake. Instead, I kept staring into her black eyes until she was finished. She seemed to want to hold eye contact in this moment and by God, I gave that to her.

After it was over, I focused on mouth breathing while I threw my Converse sneakers in the garbage. The jig was up. I would never be Carli. I put Sally in a stall and told her, "It's okay, Sally, everything is fine." But she wasn't worried. She was kind of looking at me like, *Well, what now, skank?* And my answer to that was . . .

"JOANNE!!!!"

That's how I spent my last memorable moment at Camp Anchor—standing barefoot in human excrement, calling for help. Joanne did come and bail me out, but when camp ended a few days later, I rode home alone in the back of the bus. Word had traveled that I had been knee-deep in doo-doo, and believe it or not, people weren't falling over themselves to hang out with old shoeless Schums. I never got to spend time with the other volunteers that night, and I still didn't know a single line to "We Didn't Start the Fire." I never came anywhere close to making out with Tyler or Dave. Back at school that fall, Tyler dated this unbelievably beautiful blonde named Stacey. They were our school's Brad and Angelina. Had there been a tabloid magazine about them, I would have subscribed. They kind of looked like siblings, which didn't bother me, but in retrospect it is very creepy and also explains why I am drawn to *Game of Thrones*.

Anyway, I got a lot more than I bargained for that summer. I didn't achieve my goal of getting the boy I liked to fall for me. I was running out of Chris Farley jokes for Tyler, and Dave barely even knew I was alive. But I got so much more than knowing that a few teenage stoners I was crushing on could get semihard around me. I got to spend time with the women of Senior 10. I went through war with those chicks. We did it all together, and I would be honored to be in the trenches again with any of those gals. Except for Martha, the oldest one in the group. She dressed like Marilyn Monroe and smelled like a bag of dicks left out in the sun for a year. I would still fight on her side, but I would have to be a sniper stationed far away or something.

Twenty years later, I still keep their faces and names in my heart. They are people and they have feelings—and bodies—like everyone else. And sometimes those bodies produce a ton of poop and you have to stand in it, and sometimes you have to scoop their boobies back into their very backward bathing suits. And they didn't give a fuck about any of that. And it made me feel the same. For a teenager like me, learning to give zero fucks was nothing short of revelatory.

People often romanticize children or adults with special needs, as if they are innocent-yet-wise creatures who can humble us all into becoming better humans. First of all, nobody can be innocent and wise at the same time. That's another one of those impossible combinations. It's as unachievable and improbable as Brenda. Or Carli. And secondly, I'm not suggesting the ladies of Camp Anchor were either one of those things in particular. But they owned their own flaws, and I am grateful I got to meet them when I was only fourteen. I left camp knowing a bunch of women who weren't afraid to claim the guy they wanted to dance with; they didn't change a thing for the men they loved. They weren't ashamed of their bodily functions and they didn't lie to themselves or others. They had no patience for small talk or false pretenses. They would laugh when they wanted to like there was no tomorrow, and cry their eyes out when they felt like it. Basically, I had finally found my people.

HOW I LOST MY VIRGINITY

I always fantasized about losing my virginity the way I think most girls envision their weddings: being surrounded by my friends and family, with a clergyman present. JKJK. But seriously, I've never been a girl who dreamed about her future wedding. Nothing about the white dress or the way I'd walk down the aisle. That was just never in my fantasy Rolodex. I'm not sure why it wasn't. But for many years, I *did* think about the moment I'd lose the big V. I imagined looking the man I loved right in the eyes and kissing him and smiling and intertwining our fingers and then two becoming one and the whole thing being slow and beautiful. Lots of soft whispers of love and its feeling like a levee of good feelings was breaking, orgasms, and happy tears. I thought we'd both be virgins until the moment we took a deep breath and then we . . . weren't, and then we'd cry and hold each other all night. I thought we'd laugh about what a big deal it was that we'd just finally done it, and spend the next day together holding hands and walking around in our own little world experiencing a new kind of calm and bliss until we could hide away again together and repeat our perfect lovemaking, and all would be right in the world. But that is not what happened. I didn't get to have that moment.

About a year before it actually happened, I'd wanted to lose my virginity to a guy named Mike. He wasn't *officially* my boyfriend, but I was crazy about him, and we'd dated off and on since I was thirteen. At age sixteen, I'd felt ready. I went to my mom and my friend Christine and told them: "I think I'm ready and I want to have sex with Mike." Looking back, I realize that going to your mother for a pep talk about losing your virginity in high school is odd. But I was raised with no boundaries, so at the time it felt like the thing to do. I talked to my mom a lot about sex stuff, actually. Whenever I'd have a question, my mom and I would go to Bigelow's clam bar and I'd ask away, all while downing a bowl of New England clam chowder. I'd make her laugh slurping the soup up and asking obscene questions. In retrospect, obviously none of this was okay or appropriate. But it definitely helped make me who I am. During this particular sex talk, however, my mom and Christine both said, "No, don't do it—you need to wait and make it special." My mom pointed out how awful I'd feel if he made out with someone else the next weekend. I thought about it and she was right. I wasn't a hardened groupie following my favorite band on the road. I was a teenager. So I listened to them and held on to my hymen for another year.

Right around that time, I started dating a guy named Jeff. He was a classically handsome, popular guy. But there was something different about him too. He was angrier than most teenage boys, and a little misunderstood. I ignored the signs that he was probably a bit unstable. Signs like when they gave him a fish fillet at McDonald's instead of a Big Mac, he became so furious that he cried. Truly lost it. Real tears of rage. Like the kind of tears guys are only supposed to get when they watch a movie that touches on their dad issues. (So, most movies.) Isn't it funny that they say most girls have daddy issues, when really, every dude does? But this dude had daddy, mommy, doggy, and fish fillet issues. I just thought, *Well, he can't help it. But I understand him. I'm here for him.* Even though we were both generally well liked, when we were together it was us vs. the world.

I've only recently broken my pattern of being drawn to the "you're the only one who gets me" guy. Which is a bad guy to be drawn to, and it's not a coincidence if everyone—including all your friends and family and your dog—dislikes him. But Jeff was charming, and he loved me, and I him. He was the Bieber to my Selena—except that he had no money and neither of us was particularly talented at the time.

We'd somehow gotten into the habit of watching *Monday Night Raw*, which is a televised wrestling show where there is a bad guy in tight shorts who talks smack to a good guy in different tight shorts, and they both get very emotionally invested and show great feats of strength for a few minutes before one guy's arm is lifted in the air by a bald ref with a belly. I didn't enjoy it, because although I'm now friends with some wrestlers and even dated one, it's just not my bag. I appreciate the athleticism and the theater of it all, but . . . it just doesn't do it for me.

I did enjoy that Jeff and I had our own tradition and that we'd sneak forties of beer into my room and make out a little. I lived for these nights. Everything was so new to me. I'd just had my first orgasm a month before—on my own of course. I'd taught myself how to masturbate while watching the movie *Mannequin*. I'm not particularly turned on by that movie (no judgments if you are), but I was watching it alone on the couch one day and I just put my hand down my pants and rubbed the very top of my vagina and finally came. I was so pumped. It was like a new toy. I tried to do it again right away. I soon learned you have to wait about half an hour. I really hope girls are having orgasms. Just in case they're not, you should lick your finger and rub where your vagina comes to a point at the top in a circular motion until you have an orgasm. Show the guy you're with how to do it so you don't resent him for being the only one who is coming. You're welcome, and you deserve it! Also, let him go down on you. Don't be embarrassed. Live your life.

Where was I? Anyway, at this point, I think I'd come close to having an orgasm with Mike, but it turns out I'd been confused by the sensation and thought I had to pee. (Anyone with me here? No? Okay.) I'd excuse myself and go to the bathroom and wipe up all the moisture, which I thought was humiliating. It was later explained to me that that wetness was good. *Thank God*, I thought, since all those trips to the bathroom were getting suspicious.

But at that point I hadn't done a whole lot, sex-wise, with Jeff. We'd gotten to third base, as they say, and I'd tried to jerk him off many times. But it never worked, and it became the cause of major frustration on both our parts. I was getting Michelle Obama arms, but no other good was coming of it. I think he had religious guilt about all sex stuff and couldn't mentally get there. Or maybe I sucked at it. Either way, this seemed to either enrage him or embarrass him. I understand how that could be difficult for a guy, and he was my boyfriend, whom I really loved, so one time I told him to jerk off in front of me so he could get over the embarrassment. I acted supportive of his tugging on himself to completion even though I was kind of grossed out by it. But the plan worked. It helped him loosen up and I was (finally) able to help him reach orgasm. This was important to me because I wanted to have sex with him, but not until we'd rounded third base appropriately. I don't know why I got that in my head. Perhaps because in high school we talk so much about getting to different bases, it seemed everything should go in order. The way it was for me growing up was that the guys were always trying to see what they could "get from us" sexually. We girls were basically conditioned to think we should hold out or we'd be labeled a slut. I wanted to wait to go "all the way" because I just wasn't ready. I wanted a little bit of a lead-up to having sex. Step by step.

After the successful jerk-off *Monday Night Raw* evening, Jeff and I continued to hang out and watch wrestling every week. Mankind and Stone Cold Steve Austin pretended to beat each other up, and we drank beer. One night, as we lay on my bed with the lights off watching wrestling, I was zoning out. The combination of the time of night, the content of the show, and the beer had me in and out of sleep. At one point, I was lying on my back, not paying attention, and suddenly felt Jeff fingering me. We hadn't been fooling around at all, so it seemed strange to go right to that. It started to hurt, which hadn't ever been the case before, so I looked down and realized he had put his penis in me. He was not fingering me. He was penetrating me. Without asking first, without kissing me, without so much as looking me in the eyes—or even confirming if I was awake. When I startled and looked down, he immediately removed himself from me and yelled quickly, "I thought you knew!" This seemed very strange to me, for him to protest so adamantly with such a prepared, defensive line—even though I hadn't yet said a word. I looked down and saw some blood on my bed. I was confused and hurt. He left soon after, and I rolled over and cried.

The next day he apologized. He was very upset, saying how awful he felt and that he wanted to harm himself for what he'd done. I did my best to comfort him, and I was genuinely worried about him. I wanted him to feel better. I was so confused. I was confused as to why he would have done this to me in this way, but the most dominant feeling I felt was that the guy I was in love with was upset and

I wanted to help him. I put my head on his chest and told him it was okay. *I* comforted *him*. Let me repeat: *I comforted him.*

I was still bleeding a little and feeling sore and terribly confused. What had happened was settling in, and I was getting sick to my stomach thinking about it. It made no sense. I was his girlfriend; we'd had conversations about sex and were very open when talking things through like that. I'd just helped *him* figure out how to have an orgasm in front of me. I remember being the more sexual of the two of us. If he'd asked me to have sex that night, I think I would have said yes. I didn't understand why he approached it the way he did. Did he feel like he needed to literally "sneak it in"? He had so much guilt attached to sexual activity, I recall, and lots of fear. Maybe he thought it would be a guiltless, shameless way to do it. Maybe, like the jerking-off sessions, it was easier for him to do it if I wasn't an active participant. I don't know. But he'd made the decision without me. It wasn't about *us*, it was about *him*. I felt sad and betrayed. I thought he really cared about me, but this didn't feel like something someone who cared about you would do. But I still wanted us to be okay.

The strangest part is that even though Jeff apologized and told me how bad it had made *him* feel, I don't remember ever really taking him to task about how it made *me* feel. I did what most girls do and continued on. I didn't know enough about it. I didn't know that it is incredibly common for sex to be nonconsensual. Sexual assault is so widespread, in fact, that we now have big campaigns aimed at teaching boys and young men what it means to get consent.

But I was seventeen years old and I wanted my boyfriend to like me. I still wanted to be with him and I was. We kept right on dating and started having sex regularly a couple months later. The second time we did it, I tried to pretend it was the first time. I even went in my mom's room after and told her I'd lost my virginity. But it was a lie, and I'd also be lying now if I said it didn't feel like my whole experience was ruined. My trust had been shattered—not just my trust in him but, in a lot of ways, my trust in anyone. My fantasy of a beautiful intimate memorable moment between two people had been taken from me in a flash. He took it. I didn't know it then, but I know now that it toughened me up in an irreversible way. For many years, when it came to sex, I didn't get the luxury of just being myself. Half of the time I was too defensive and guarded, assuming the guy wanted to hurt me or take too much. The rest of the time, I was too flippant— almost to the point of being dissociative, as if the act of sex didn't matter much to me. I'd tell myself I could have sex with any guy I wanted, even if I didn't care about him. Neither one of these versions of me was real.

Today, I wish I could say that sex is finally free of this kind of self-consciousness and self-protection for me. But it's not. Until I'm in a committed relationship, I'm on my guard hard. I want to be the one making all the choices. I have to be with someone for a while and truly trust them before sex is fully fun and carefree. And then, I love it. I'm definitely a very sexual chick. But my first experience didn't really set me up for a happy-go-lucky journey to get to where I am today. Women, like men, deserve to enjoy sex and to figure it out on their own terms.

So many girls have nights like my "first time"—or worse. Some girls wake up to a friend or boyfriend having sex with them. Some girls are violently attacked in public or in their own homes. One out of every six women is raped. Of that, 44 percent of those women are under eighteen.

Any time someone comes forward about being sexually assaulted in some way, there are so many opinions about it. People will have opinions about this chapter. Some might say it wasn't a big deal. Or that it was all my fault since I was drinking, he was my boyfriend, and I was lying right there next to him.

Isn't it sad that when a girl says she was sexually assaulted, our first instinct is to think she's probably lying? Statistics and facts tell us the exact opposite. We demand "perfect victims" who better not have been drinking or hanging out at a party in a short skirt or revealing dress or have ever been known to enjoy sex.

The facts in my situation are pretty clear to me still: He was inside of me in a way I hadn't consented to.

Many girls remain silent about their experiences. And that is their choice. I'm opening up about my "first time" because I don't want it to happen to your daughter or sister or friend someday. I want to use my voice to tell people to make sure they have consent before they have sex with someone. I hope all parents talk to their kids about consent, and when you do, please, please don't make the mistake my mother made. Don't do it over a bowl of clam chowder. Because that is just gross and creepy.

I wish I'd have talked to a parent or adult at the time to sort out my feelings of confusion and betrayal. I wish I'd have stood up for myself more and told Jeff that what he did was wrong. It shouldn't have gone this way. I don't want someone reading this to think, *My son isn't rageful and doesn't cry furious tears over a breaded fish sandwich, so he probably understands that he needs to get consent before putting his penis in a girl.* But this happens so frequently that clearly we need to talk about it. Everyone should understand that there are no excuses for nonconsensual sex. People who commit sexual assault should have to pay the consequences for their actions. I used to do some stand-up about this confusing area. I'd call it "grape," as in "gray-area rape." It's not some crackhead who popped out of the bushes in Central

Park and raped me. I wasn't screaming no. He didn't keep forcibly pumping away until he finished. He was only inside me for a short time. But it isn't right that it happened that way. Virginity shouldn't be something you "lose" or "give." Sex is something you share. My first time didn't need to be perfect, but I would have liked to have known it was going to happen. Or have been part of the decision. Instead, he just helped himself to my virginity—and I was never the same.

THINGS YOU DON'T KNOW ABOUT ME

Constructing a list of things you don't know about me is pretty difficult, because I'm an open book. But here's my attempt:

1. I have a bad scar on my left leg from a surfing accident I was in as a teenager. I think it's cool but I know deep down it's gross.

2. I speak sign language. I'm not crazy fluent, but I can communicate pretty well. I've learned the hard way that not all deaf people want to talk to you just because you can sign.

3. I am terrified of spiders, and ferrets make me puke.

4. I am not allergic to any foods, but eggplant hurts my mouth.

5. I have an innie, not an outie (talking about my vagina).

6. The birth control I use is the NuvaRing. (I've never been paid to endorse the NuvaRing, but I believe I should be. Same goes for Rombauer chardonnay.)

7. I have never been pregnant, but I look like I have.

8. I have never had anal sex. (I would be willing, but they say you can't eat for a couple hours beforehand, and I don't see that happening.)

9. No one has ever come on my face (but I think everywhere else has been covered).

10. My favorite food is pasta with Parmesan and I like to eat it as I'm falling asleep.

11. I have been skydiving but I didn't like it because you have to JUMP OUT OF A FUCKING AIRPLANE.

12. I don't go to temple anymore, but I like that I'm Jewish, and I enjoy the grossest Jewish food, like whitefish salad and gefilte fish.

13. I like my feet and my ears. I know my mouth is really small, but I like it, and it has gotten me out of going down on several people.

14. My favorite living actors are Samantha Morton and Mark Rylance.

15. I like smoking pot and I like smoking pot.

16. I have eaten mushrooms a couple times (funnnnnnnnn).

17. I have never done ecstasy, cocaine, or acid. But I feel like I'm already on all of those things.

18. I love Ani DiFranco. You are going to get sick of hearing about this because she comes up a lot in this book. I've been going to her concerts since I was thirteen. I don't want to meet her ever. I'd start crying and ruin her day.

19. I can't stand Rod Stewart's voice.

20. And the seventh thing you don't know about me is that I'm really good with numbers.

21. My sister tested my IQ when she was getting her master's degree in school psychology and I tested as a genius in half the categories and nearly cognitively impaired in the other half.

22. To date, I've slept with twenty-eight people. I can't remember all of their names, but I remember the nicknames I gave them (Third Ball, Pit Bull Guy, Cousin Steve—JKJKJKJK).

23. I faked falling in a dirt pile to get out of running a mile in gym class. I lay in the dirt until someone found me.

24. My favorite poet is Anne Sexton and my favorite poem is "Admonitions to a Special Person."

25. The thing I own the most of is wine, but please send more.

26. I've read the book *Tortilla Flat* ten times for some reason. I've watched *The Royal Tenenbaums* one hundred times.

27. My favorite scene in a movie is when Billy Crudup meets Samantha Morton's character at the daytime house party in *Jesus' Son* and she's dancing to the song "Sweet Pea."

28. At parties, you can usually find me . . . at home. I hate parties.

29. The thing that's on my mind the most is my family.

30. I have a thing for guys with a gap between their teeth.

31. My paternal great-grandmother was a bootlegger in NYC.

32. I'm not sure when I've laughed the hardest in my life, but I am sure that I was with my sister when it happened.

33. The best thing I've ever bought was a comfy bed.

34. The two things I always decline, every single time they are offered to me, are cocaine and ham.

35. I mostly hate being in museums, except for the American Museum of Natural History. I like the dinosaurs and animal tableaus, and they sell astronaut ice cream at the gift shop.

36. My favorite place I've traveled to in the US is New Orleans. The music, food, and people are the best. My favorite place I've been outside the country is Altea, a little fishing village in Spain.

37. I hate horror movies because I get so scared, but I always forget and watch them by accident. I come up with an excuse about why my sister has to sleep in the same room as me. She's nice about it but knows it's because I am a deep loser.

38. I don't know if I want kids. Maybe not.

39. One of my favorite things to do is go dancing with Amber Tamblyn and twerk to the best of my abilities.

40. I've never hooked up with a girl, except on camera for my TV show, but it seems fun. This is unrelated to #39.

41. I meditate twice a day for twenty minutes each time. It helps clear my mind and get rid of stress, and it gives me energy.

42. My sister and I went to Oktoberfest in Munich once and snuck into the tents and had one of the best times of our lives.

43. I am a pathological liar.

44. Just kidding.

CAN'T KNOCK THE HUSTLE

I've been a hustler my whole life. I know you're thinking, *Check your-self, Amy, you are not Jay Z.* But it's true. You can't be a comic and make complete strangers laugh without a strong hustle. Mine has always been solid. Since day one. There is evidence of this as early as my first few months of life. Like most newborn babies, I didn't welcome sleep, and I certainly didn't want to be left alone in a room to sleep by myself. So I figured out how to trick my mother into sleeping on the floor next to me. I cried like hell and didn't let up until she was by my side exactly where I wanted her to be. I'm sure my dad wasn't too keen on this idea, but for months, I kept up this impressive scam, dictating the sleeping arrangements for people who were decades older than me. Suckers!

My hustle has often involved food, because, much like household pets or toddlers, I am food-motivated, which is a handy thing to know about me. I was talking my way into the food I wanted from a very young age. When I was two, I figured out how to break open the kitchen cabinet and eat Cheerios. At six, I lied to my kindhearted grandfather's face, telling him that my mom had given me permission to have another yogurt when she hadn't. I let him take the fall for me, and it was never really the same between us. Even now, I still do this. Just last week, when I was leaving Kim's apartment at one a.m. after a TV night, she caught me sneaking a bag of microwave popcorn from her pantry to take home with me.

When you're a kid, the hustle is oh so necessary. You have so little control over what you get to do: what you eat, what you wear, where you go, who or what you play with. It's a nightmare. So I got started pretty young working on my tactics for negotiating with adults. I came on pretty strong at my friends' houses because their parents weren't used to my methods and strategies. I'd look them in the eyes, serious as a heart attack, and call them by their first names as a negotiation tactic. "Look, Laura, your beautiful daughter and I are going to follow our cake with a bowl of ice cream now. Would you like to scoop it for us, or should I?" Like Laura, most parents were caught off guard, laughed nervously, and said, "Ha ha ha . . . My name is Mrs. Booker, Amy." To which I would reply, "I know your last name, Laura. Now, can you get me a step stool so I can dig around in your freezer for our second dessert?"

Sometimes I'd see that my attempts to close a deal made the adult laugh. And making adults laugh was the most power I could ever have—it made me feel like I was one of them, holding some of the reins they always held, especially with male figures of authority, who always seemed to be throwing the book at me one way or another. Whether it was teachers catching me talking in class or cops catching me with beer in my backpack on the beach, it always felt like my only way to get home free was to make everyone laugh. It always dismantled the power structure within seconds. Being funny was my ultimate hustle! Once when my high school teacher Mr. Simons wouldn't let me leave class to go to the bathroom (okay, it was actually to walk the halls and meet up with my boyfriend, and Mr. Simons was fully onto me), I said very loudly in front of the whole class: "That's cool, Mr. Simons. I'll just stay here, even though I can feel my period blood leaking out of my vagina and about to seep through my pants and onto my chair." Mr. Simons turned red, everyone else laughed, and I strutted right on out of the classroom.

Besides making large audiences laugh at my jokes, I'd say my biggest hustle in life was shoplifting as a teenager. It's not something I'm proud of—in fact it was a spectacular failure in the end. But I probably wouldn't take it back, because even though this is going to sound weird, I learned a lot from executing the old five-finger discount like it was my job. It was all part of my process of honing my instincts, learning how to take what I deserved in life. Don't get me wrong, I do not condone shoplifting. One of the things I learned from the whole experience was NOT TO SHOPLIFT. And I'm aware that when people give you sage advice to grab life by the balls and take what you deserve, they usually mean you should ask for a hard-earned promotion or carve out a little "me time" for yourself, not rob a well-known department store blind. But when I was a teenager, I took that idea literally.

I started out stealing pieces of candy here and there, nothing too serious. When I hear other people talk about their adventures in shoplifting (it's pretty common among teenage girls), they usually recount how they stole something like a cheap pair of dangly earrings or a magazine, and they always attach tons of guilt to it. But I didn't have those feelings because I was targeting the big chain stores. I never took anything from a mom-and-pop shop or an actual person. (To this day, I still hesitate to tell people that I have a record for shoplifting because when something comes up missing I know they'll suspect me. But never have I ever stolen anything from a person. Except food. From Kim's kitchen.)

By high school, my friends and I had graduated to stealing bathing suits from stores in the mall because they didn't have sensors on them and they were easy to take. We'd also steal makeup from drugstores. We didn't take these things because we were in need of them; we didn't wear makeup and we rarely went swimming. We took them because stealing makes a teenager feel cool and powerful. Even white girls in the suburbs want to be badasses. And if that meant robbing J.Crew of a gingham one-piece, so be it. I guess you could say I worked my way into being an angsty teen one stolen shimmery grapefruit-flavored lip gloss at a time.

The first time I got caught was when I was fourteen years old and had traveled to Sacramento with my club volleyball team for a tournament. Being in club volleyball meant that when the regular volleyball season at my high school ended, I'd then compete on teams with kids from other schools. Meaning, I never, ever stopped playing volleyball. It certainly shaped my work ethic (and kept a good thirty pounds off me), but it did mean missing a lot of fun weekend shit so that I could sweat it out in a poorly lit gym, eating pasta salad and catching moments of sleep in between games. Even now, I find myself feeling sleepy and craving pasta salad whenever I'm in a large school gymnasium. Or regular gymnasium. Or library. Or home. Or now.

This is how most of my weekends in high school went:

- Get picked up on Saturday morning at five a.m. and drive two to five hours to a tournament.

- Arrive and suit up to play until you're eliminated.

- Understand that if, God forbid, you make it to the final match, you'll play for up to twelve hours, then take home a little plastic trophy that you will have to pack and move into every new apartment you find yourself in until you throw it away begrudgingly at the age of twenty-four.

Come to think of it, it's not unlike film/TV production, except your parents are with you all day and there are no union rules, so you have to play and play until your little knee pads give out or you bleed through. You consume whatever the parents brought to try to one-up each other. Health wasn't really a thing back then, so we'd eat big chicken-cutlet sandwiches and pasta minutes before having to hurl our bodies back out on the court.

But back to shoplifting in Sacramento. My teammates and I were out exploring the town. We landed in a place called Old Sacramento, which was full of shops selling shitty novelty items for tourists: shot glasses, coffee mugs, T-shirts that said the name of the city and also hilarious phrases like "I'm not gay but my boyfriend is." I'd already been stealing for a couple months, and I'd built up quite the reputation with my regular friends at my school. But since this was the club volleyball league, these girls didn't know me as well and didn't realize what a total badass I was. I couldn't wait to show them.

I wanted to be popular with the three coolest girls on the team, so I called them over and told them how I'd learned to steal. They were really impressed with how easy I made it sound, and we started racking up the most sought-after items in the stores: tie-dye half shirts that said "Co-ed naked lacrosse," snow globes, and of course the coveted "1 tequila, 2 tequila, 3 tequila, FLOOR" shot glasses. (Who writes this stuff? Is it Mark Twain himself?)

About six of us were in on the scam to rob Old Sacramento. After it was over, I walked into my hotel room and emptied my treasures onto the bed. I looked at all of the bounty. In retrospect, not one thing would have cost more than $1.99 to purchase. Not on my watch! 'Cause my watch is free!

It just so happened that my mom was chaperoning this particular tournament, and she arrived at the hotel that night. When she got in, she hugged me and told me she had some disturbing news. She seemed really disgusted that some of my teammates had been caught shoplifting and were taken to the police station. I played innocent, partially because I couldn't bear to disappoint her, but also because I was terrified I'd be caught and my new prize possessions (especially the hat with fake dreads built into it) would have to be returned.

In the morning I saw the three chicks whom I'd gotten into this mess, and I found out they were going to be benched for the tourna- ment. They'd been up all night, crying. They looked at me like, *How could you do this to us, Amy?* I could see the anger on their faces. They hated me. My whole plan to get them to like me had backfired worse than I could've imagined.

In reality, the charge wasn't even going to show up on their per- manent records because they were all minors, but still, they were mad. Honestly, I was a little mad at them, too, for sucking so bad at shoplifting. *These fucking rookies*, I thought. *I should never have taken them under my experienced lawbreaking wing.* Then I thought about it some more and remembered the Sisterhood of the Traveling Volley- ball Spandex, and I decided that the right thing to do, both for these other gals and for myself, would be to admit that I'd stolen, too. Is there such a thing as a hustler with a conscience?

Predictably, I got benched for the tournament. I stood on the sideline with my knee pads around my ankles, fighting off dirty looks from the girls I'd so desperately wanted approval from. I'd flown all the way to Sacramento from New York to play zero volleyball and get some shitty shot glasses that I wouldn't be able to fill with anything other than water for another seven years. I guess I got what I deserved. You can't buy or steal popularity and affection; you have to earn those things the old-fashioned way, not the Old Sacramento way. I think I learned a valuable lesson about teamwork, sisterhood, and friendship that weekend. But unfortunately, I didn't quite learn not to shoplift yet. For that, I would need a felony on my record.

It all went down at a serious department store. Let's call it Schloomingdale's. My stealing had gotten out of hand. This was when my family had slipped from New Money to No Money and we could no longer afford to buy the kinds of nonessential things in life you feel you must have as a teenager. So I employed all my well-honed hustling skills to get what Kim and I "needed." This was a win-win because Kim got to fulfill her quota of teen rebellion and I got to own a white jumpsuit! We started doing it more and more. And it had the side benefit of making us feel invincible and powerful. I don't think my stint with stealing expensive clothing is amusing or sympathetic in any way, but it isn't surprising, either. When you're a teenage girl, especially one with a broken family and no money, you're newly and fully aware of just how mind-blowingly little you matter in the world. And even worse, I was just starting to feel myself creeping closer and closer to that angry edge—that place most women arrive at in college or maybe during their first job—where you realize not only do you matter very little *right now*, but this moment in time is probably the *most* you will *ever* matter. It's all downhill from here. You're eighteen years old, and this is your last chance to TAKE WHAT YOU CAN GET. I know none of this is an excuse for shoplifting. I really don't think it's a cute thing to do, but it's also not shocking that it made us feel as powerful and invincible as it did.

After doing it several times, we felt we were running a great scam. We'd take two of the same item into the dressing room, and then we'd put one in a bag or under our clothes and the other one out on the rack.

"How'd it go in there?" the salesgirl would ask me.

"Not well," I'd reply, trying to display the self-hatred most women feel when leaving a dressing room. But really I'd be celebrating what a genius I was for my incredible "take two, steal one" plan. My genius was brutally halted the day my sister and I were put in the back of a cop car.

We were in the Roosevelt Field mall on Long Island—a typical mall, maybe on the fancier side as far as malls go. Over the years a Gucci had appeared, and a Valentino. But that side of the marble halls always seemed especially empty, so Kim and I chose to hang on to the more lively, shittier side. Give me a Hot Topic and an Auntie Anne's pretzel. That was more our vibe.

So Kim and I were walking past Schloomingdale's when she said, "We should go in. It's sooooo easy to take whatever you want from there. Especially underwear!" I should have thought, *This is a bad idea. You've never scouted this place out, and you don't want to end up in jail.* But instead what I thought was, *Oooooh, I need underwear!*

So we did it. We really did it. We went on a total bat-shit, no-holds-barred spree. We did not stop at underwear. We took jackets, scarves . . . What's this? Dolce & Gabbana has a new perfume? Leopard-print onesies? Don't mind if I do. Cashmere tops? Seven jeans? Well, I think I deserve to own those! Kim had been eyeing a tank top with a bejeweled dollar sign, and why shouldn't she have pajama pants with white doily cuffs to go with it? And if she didn't take that strapless teal bra now, she would never again have a chance to own one. Today was the day! And the pièce de résistance? A leather fedora! We took it all into the dressing room.

I remember squeezing myself into a pair of too-small Guess jeans while I lovingly fondled a Juicy Couture jumpsuit. *I'll save this for special occasions*, I thought. We were high from the adrenaline as we manically, meticulously took the tags off each item. I took the perfume out of the box and stashed it in my coat pocket. *Good thinking, you brilliant girl*, I thought, patting myself on the back. We put all the tags from all the items we were about to be the new proud owners of into the empty perfume box, and we loaded up. We smiled at each other, hugged, took a deep breath, and out the door we went.

We passed a pretty girl with shoulder-length brown hair and dark eyes who'd been lurking in the hallway. *She's cute*, I thought, *but bad energy*. Kim and I walked toward the Bloomingd—whoops, that was a close one—exit that led out into the rest of the mall. We held hands, vibing on the same chemicals in our bloodstreams that are enjoyed by gambling addicts, Formula One racers, and Tom Cruise as we took the plunge past the sensors. They didn't chime. We'd done it. Success. My heart was racing, but I wasn't sweating or doing anything that could be a tell (by this time we were pros). What a perfect excursion. To top it all off we had tickets to see our favorite singer, Ani DiFranco, that night. Which of my new outfits would I wear? *Definitely gonna debut that leather fedora!*

And then . . .

We were swarmed by five people dressed in civilian clothes. It was the girl from the dressing rooms and a guy I'd smiled at while walking around the store. A whole bunch of plants. It was like the scene in *Blow* where the waiters all turn out to be working for the DEA. They circled us, yelling, "Stop right there!" But they didn't touch us. (I later found out that they're not allowed to lay a hand on you; to this day I still regret not running. Had I known they wouldn't have been able to touch us if we ran, I would have Forrest Gumped right the hell out of that mall and not looked back until I reached the ocean or Robin Wright.)

They kept us there in that strange holding pattern until the store detectives came out and got us. They walked us back to a little room in the bowels of the store. Picturing that moment now still gives me the worst pit in my stomach. I went into protective big-sister mode with Kim and was worried about how she would handle this, but more than anything, I was embarrassed. We were caught. We couldn't leave the little room. I couldn't save my sister. I couldn't joke my way out of this. We just had to give in.

The five store detectives crowded into the room. They laughed and celebrated their victory and taunted us a little. It was humiliating. Kim was not looking good. She'd always been my cute little partner in crime, but I knew she'd take this harder than I would. She'd recently acquired the tried-and-true yet mildly disturbing family coping mechanism of dealing with stress and anxiety by dissociating. She was dangerously good at it. She'd basically detach from her immediate surroundings and revert to a kind of catatonic state. I could see she was drifting off, and I was losing her. I had to do something.

That's when my *real* hustle kicked in. I did the one thing I can almost always do to make things better: I made her laugh. As the detectives laid out our clothing on the floor so they could assess the charge, I came alive. I pointed to a pair of flannel plaid pants Kim had stolen. "Where were you gonna wear those, Kim? Did you join a country club I don't know about?" I went into insult comedy. I roasted her choices as a thief. I comforted her with cracks about her taste. She laughed. She stayed present in her body.

"Grand larceny!" the pretty brunette exclaimed, and the detectives high-fived one another. My guess was the bigger the charge, the bigger the bonus. The door flung open and a middle-aged guy with a torso bigger than seemed right for his pit bull face walked in. His hair was graying on the sides but not the top. He was radiating smugness like someone who works at the Apple Genius Bar on the day of a product release.

"So, you thought you'd come in here and steal from my store?"

Kim's eyes were starting to waver, and I could tell she was about to head into a black hole. Before he could get to his next megalomaniacal question I jumped in . . .

"Well, Mr. Bloomingdale" (the cat's out of the little brown bag), "it is such an honor to meet you, first of all. Second of all, do you live in the store?"

Kim blurted out a laugh and then stifled herself.

Needless to say, my jokes didn't save us. I don't blame Mr. Bloomingdale for not appreciating my sense of humor. We got the maximum charge. We were taken to the mall police station, which is a thing, in the back of an unmarked cop car. The cops who drove us were nice; they blasted Pink Floyd's "Comfortably Numb," and I was mostly relieved that Kim wasn't numb anymore, that I could make her laugh even though we were on our way to the clink. We sat there looking at each other and holding hands. It was the end of November, so one of the cops' frozen Thanksgiving turkey was resting between us on the seat. At the station, they took our fingerprints and mug shots, then we sat on a bench while they tried calling our mom. No answer. Thank God.

"Well, sir, actually, our dad is more our caretaker." HUGE LIE. They called our dad and left a message. I explained that he probably wouldn't call back for hours, and that our mother was kind of an absentee figure in our lives. HUGE LIE.

I felt in that moment that it was up to me to be my own guardian. My parents couldn't help me. And I also felt an unmistakable sense of resolve that I had to take care of Kim and get her through this. I blurted out to the cops that I had stolen everything. It was all me. They were all my items. The mall cop told us that because Kim was a minor it wouldn't be a big deal if the charge were on her record. I then took back everything I'd previously stated and tried to pin it all on her.

When it was all said and done, our punishment ended up being community service, but it wasn't too bad. We even made it to see Ani DiFranco at the Beacon Theatre that night, singing at the top of our lungs, celebrating our freedom. What better way to commemorate our last days as rebels than spending an evening screaming out the lyrics of the singer who was basically every eighteen-year-old white girl's Joan of Arc? I remember, during her song "Swan Dive," Kim and I belting out the lyrics *"I don't care if they eat me alive. I've got better things to do than survive!"* and it felt more exhilarating than wearing all the stolen tube tops in the world.

And in the end, getting caught at Bloomingdale's really corrected my game. After all, the hustle I'm honing isn't about shoplifting or lying or winning friends with horrible heists gone wrong. And it's definitely not about grabbing what belongs to someone else just to make myself feel more powerful. It's about being my own best advocate and knowing how to take what I deserve in life without bringing anyone else down. It's about making my sister laugh when we are both in deep shit. Now that I'm all grown up and no longer driving up the price of bad tchotchkes in Old Sacramento, I've graduated on to the next-level hustle—making people laugh. It's something I'm still perfecting: skirting the rules, writing jokes about life's mountains of bullshit—all to make people smile and feel better. There's no sleight of hand or trickery involved. It's hard work—without shortcuts. Making an audience laugh is much more difficult than sneaking out of Bloomingdale's with a fedora under your shirt that only Ving Rhames can pull off, but it's still a hustle I just can't quit.

EXCERPT FROM MY JOURNAL IN 1999 (AGE EIGHTEEN) WITH FOOTNOTES FROM 2016

Dear Journal,

It's a Monday and I'm still home. This break has been a lot of fun. It's been more of a learning experience than anything else. It's time for me to reflect on this past month.[1]

Last Tuesday-Wednesday, some of us went to Gormans.[2] *It was fun. We had good conversations and we danced.*[3] *Thursday we went to Roulettes. It was a lot of fun. We all got to a good level of drunk*[4] *and danced*

---

1 Very deep, Amy. Are you reflecting on a goodwill trip to Guatemala? Or your time volunteering at a shelter? No, you are reflecting on all the bars you went to. What an insightful mind. Proceed.

2 A bar that allowed underage kids to drink.

3 I would imagine the conversations went like this: "I like your shirt, where's it from?" "Armani Exchange." "Oh, that's why it says 'Armani Exchange' on it." "Good catching up with you."

4 Most likely blackout.

like we had never danced before.[5] *We were dancing like lesbians. It was so fun.*[6] *Every guy there would have died for any one of us.*[7] *Right before I left, I ran into Nick.*[8] *I was so glad to see him. He really was exactly what I wanted right then. A guy to be really interested in me and that I would like to mess around with. He was extremely friendly. I told him to call me. He called me the next day and asked me to come to a Long Beach bar. I said maybe, but I would have to see.*[9]

I saw the movie Girl Interrupted with my friends.[10] *It was really good. Saturday night I had over a bunch of girls, three of which go to college with Jess Sap. We got pretty drunk and went to meet up with Nick. He was so happy to see me.*[11] *He bought us drinks all night.*[12] *We didn't pay for a thing.*[13] *I looked amazing.*[14] *I wore this tube shirt from Zara that ties in the back.*[15] *He said the sweetest things to me.*[16] *When the bar closed we*

---

5   I will never be able to express how grateful I am that there is no footage of this.

6   I want to apologize to all lesbians. There is no way lesbians dance the way we were dancing. We must have been incorporating the age-old technique of trying to get the guys to notice us by pretending we were on the precipice of letting the music (most likely "Come On Eileen") take over our souls and make us forget what we knew our sexuality to be and just start licking each other right there on the dance floor of that shitty bar.

7   Inflated sense of self, Amy? I would like to edit together a video of how I saw myself that night and then what was actually happening. I blame MTV's show *The Grind* for making everyone think they were Daisy Fuentes.

8   He was a very hot and strong dude. I remember him looking like Superman or Chris Klein.

9   Yeah fucking right. I'm sure I started getting ready right then for an entire twenty-four hours.

10 It was basically a documentary about all of us, except we were less hot.

11 Red flag.

12 Redder flag.

13 Reddest flag.

14 I am dying laughing knowing what I looked like at this age. The only amazing thing about how I looked was that people were able to identify me as female.

15 I remember this shirt. It was made of wool and thin brown leather straps with three ties in the back. It was insanely itchy and gave me a rash all over my body. It looked like what a poor commoner who gets raped by a soldier on *Game of Thrones* would wear. It was too short, so my belly stuck out, and I had no waist and was shaped very much like an old-timey radio, which I must have wanted to accentuate.

16 Of course he did; I had a target on my head, or my lower back, I should say.

all went back to my house. Everyone else left and Nick and I went into my room. We hooked up for like three hours.[17]

I liked how he kissed but he was very aggressive and rough. He kept trying to "shock" me which is sticking one finger up my ass and one up my vagina.[18] *I had to be on my guard. It felt different, not too bad. I just didn't want him doing that.*[19] *I never let any of my boyfriends do that so why should this guy?*[20] *He kept trying to make me touch myself.*[21] *I was making jokes like "I don't think we're at that stage in our relationship."*[22] *The oddest thing that he did was after he had gone down on me I went down on him for a minute and he was trying to finger me with his toes.*[23] *I was like "no thanks" and he actually asked why.*[24] *He also kept biting my nipples really hard.*[25] *It made me so mad the next day because they were really irritated. So was my vagina from him fingering me so hard.*[26]

He spent the night. I asked if he liked his own space when he slept. He said yes. I jumped up naked and slept in my mom's room.[27] *I woke up*

---

17   This now sounds like a nightmare to me, just an exhausting bacteria exchange. Pass.

18   Thank you, Dr. Schumer, very sexy. I really spared no details, I guess. But what great writing. Don't you feel like you're in the room with me? It's like we are all sitting on his finger as he is trying to put it in my butthole.

19   It's always been my least-favorite way to have my temperature taken.

20   That's good logic, right? No one I loved or trusted got the honor of touching the inside of my butthole. *You must be knighted by the queen before entering a digit into my buttocks* was my philosophy, I guess.

21   Lazy.

22   I think this behavior is probably more typical now with the generation raised on porn, but at the time it was pretty out-there in my eyes.

23   Or as they called it in ancient China, toeing.

24   I would like to present this guy with the medal for brass balls. Why?! You want to know why I don't want your toes in me?! Maybe because that's fucking gross and my pussy is not your own personal moccasin. So until Crocs comes up with a new model called the five-toe vagina shoe, please keep your feet exactly one leg's length away from my lady part!

25   Guys who do this should be the last residents at Guantánamo.

26   If you're trying to make a girl remember you, maybe just write her a poem.

27   Hahahaha. She wasn't home of course. I repeat, she was NOT in the bed. But I love that at eighteen that was already my steeze to skip the snuggling after hooking up.

a couple hours later and drove him home. I had Kim come with me.[28] *He kissed me good-bye on the cheek and told me to call. Later we spoke on the phone and he said that he felt like I just wanted to get him out of my house. He was so right.*[29]

The next night nothing went on. This week I worked at Forever 21 in the mall. They have me at cashier now so it's more entertaining.[30]

---

28 Jesus Christ, Amy, your poor sister! "Hey, want to take a ride across Long Island with this guy who used me as a puppet all night?" She was fourteen!

29 Wow, he was so in touch with what women want.

30 I stand by being excited about this promotion! Little did I know I would be wearing their clothes well into my midthirties.

FAKED IT 'TIL I MAKED IT

There is nothing better than being your own boss. Well, there is, actually: not having to work at all. That is way better. But I've worked so many jobs over the years, and have experienced all of the unique and specific humiliations that came along with each one. And even when I was doing something for hire that involved zero dignity, I still always liked the feeling of doing something useful. Even as a kid, I just wanted to show everyone I could pull my own weight (which was never less than 150 pounds, even in middle school). For as long as I can remember, I was seeking employment. I felt so stifled and useless during childhood. I wanted to contribute. Lemonade stands weren't cutting it. I hated that I was too young to get a job or join a gym. It's amazing these things I was so dead set on having are now two of the worst features of my adult life. But back in the day, I wanted in. I wanted the satisfaction of making my own money and being proactive.

Before I got paid as a performer, most of my paying gigs were pretty unglamorous, regular, shitty, low-paying jobs. I worked in at least a dozen bars or restaurants in Manhattan alone, and when I was in college I worked as a house painter for a while. Every weekend at six a.m., I'd be up on a ladder with a roller and brushes, painting the inside of someone's house, a Chinese restaurant, or a school. But I liked all those jobs. Even at a job I hated, I always loved the feeling I'd get when I was done. The beer at the end of a shift, or the feeling of looking at the clock and seeing it change to the minute you can leave, is so freeing. That moment you're allowed to walk out the door is an experience that cannot be replicated. I honestly feel for people who've never had to work, because they will never know that feeling. The people born rich, with their Gatsby-like days spent lying around fanning themselves, wondering if they should go into town. They'll never know the sheer elation you feel when the manager of a steak-house tells you, "You're cut after you finish your side work!" What a feeling, to furiously roll silverware into napkins and then take that first step outside, breathing the air, knowing that you're now on your own time. Heaven.

My very first job was being a baby model, because I was an exceptionally cute baby. JKJKJKJK. I was a very average-looking infant. By "average," I mean I resembled a pug more than a baby. But my parents needed someone to model the baby furniture they sold. As my parents, they believed I was adorable—that, and they knew I would work for free. I posed in a bunch of the cribs, and I was on the cover of their catalog (it's probably why the company went bankrupt). It was the beginning and end of my print modeling career. I've been meaning to get back into it.

My parents continued to take advantage of my work ethic when they made me model stuff from their second store, Calling All Girls, which sold gifts, clothes, and haunted-looking dolls for girls. It was only a good idea compared to their initial business plan, which was to sell shoes. ("Schumer's Shoes"; this would have ruined my life as a tween.) The slogan my mom devised for Calling All Girls was "No Boys Allowed!" It should have been "No *Customers* Allowed!" because literally no one ever shopped there. Not a smart marketing technique to immediately shun 50 percent of the population. But anyway, "No Boys Allowed" was plastered on buttons and T-shirts that Kim and I constantly wore as little walking billboards for our parents. I guess this slogan was supposed to amp up the marketing to the "fairer sex." But even more than being pro-girl, it was just straight-up anti-boy. Or it could have been read the wrong way, like "No boys allowed, but MEN ARE WELCOME!" There were so many wrong turns to be made with this slogan. And so few ways to go right. I was an eleven-year-old inviting men to approach me. I looked like a walking *To Catch a Predator* ad. Chris Hansen should have paid me, not my parents. Either way, I guess "No Boys Allowed" was supposed to be my mom's not-so-subtle way of telling us that men were bad. I never bought it, but you could say the writing was on the wall, and on the shirt and the button, for that matter.

With the new store, I was not asked to be a print model, I was asked (or rather told) that I'd be spending my weekends at the Javits Center—a huge convention center that held trade shows on the weekends. My parents would showcase their inventory by using Kim and me as display items. We wore "No Boys Allowed" shirts with a picture of a lock and key on them. And the shirts came with a key you would wear around your neck. In retrospect, this was all a little disturbing. I guess my mom thought it was cute for us to be prissy little bitches who "locked" boys out and dangled the key to our goods in front of them. And the unintentional message had a vague anti-rape implication. I mean, there are some countries where little girls are sold into sex slavery and their virginity is purchased, and there I was at the age of eleven, with my seven-year-old sister by my side, literally wearing a key around my neck and a big message that said, "YOU DON'T HAVE ACCESS TO THIS." Anyway, Kim and I would stand there in our booth for hours and hours and help sell—I'm sure—zero more shirts for my parents' store. I don't remember what I was paid, but I liked the idea that I was a model.

Making me her show pony really backfired on my mom, because when I entered my early teen years, I started demanding a weekly blowout for my frizzy, curly hair. Most twelve-year-old girls were not getting blowouts on the reg, but my town hated Jews and I wanted to hide my little fro, so I began to plot how I could get more blowouts. They were not cheap, so I got the idea that I'd sweep up hair at the salon after school if, in return, they'd blow-dry my hair once a week. I don't remember how long I kept up this arrangement, but it seemed very worth it at the time. I guess the salon, much like my parents, wasn't worried about child labor laws. I loved the work too. I was part of a team, and I felt useful, but the shop wasn't that busy. I'd sit anxiously and watch the stylists clipping hair, waiting for any of it to fall on the floor. When it did, I'd rush over to it, like an annoying human Zamboni or Olympic curler. I was too eager, people complained, and I was let go.

It was the first in a long line of completely justifiable firings in my life. I was so eager to work that I'd "fake it 'til I maked it" even if I was completely unqualified to do a job. And then I would end up getting fired when my inexperience was revealed. The second time I got fired was when I lied in an interview at a different salon and got a job as a shampoo girl. I thought I was doing well until I completely blew it with my first bald customer. This man only had hair in a small patch in the center of the front of his head and a thin strip along the bottom in the back, like a clown. No offense to this specific brand of male-pattern baldness, but it's accurate to say that this dude had textbook Bozo hair. I started washing his hair—just his hair, and not the sizable amount of bald scalp. He shouted at me with a lisp, "Wash my whole head pleathe!" I said, "No! Whenever I wash the parts without hair, the water bounces back and sprays me in the face!" He marched right up to the owner, and within minutes I was fired.

I really appreciated the bosses who deliberately overlooked my lack of skills and hired me based on my confidence and bravado alone. I worked at a well-known steakhouse in Grand Central Terminal—a really expensive, white-tablecloth place that catered to fast-talking businesspeople, commuters, and tourists. I was completely unqualified to work there and had no fancy-dining experience, but I lied and said I did. I didn't make it past the first interview, but as I was leaving, I overheard someone who was there for a second interview, which gave me the idea to just show up the next day and repeat what I'd heard. *Fake it 'til you make it!* I thought. The next day, I showed up and confidently said, "Hi, I have a second interview with Frank."

They looked me up and down, confused, but I sat and waited for whoever Frank was. The general manager came out and asked me some questions. The one I remember is, What is the main ingredient in tequila? I answered, "Triple sec?" He told me I was very wrong and that it was agave and hired me anyway. I still don't know why. Maybe my delusional confidence was mesmerizing.

For most of my nine months working there, I was the only woman. It was an all-male staff full of career steak waiters. I had to wear a jacket and tie. The jacket was white, so the dust from Grand Central would settle on me and turn the jacket gray by the end of my shift and make me scratch my face until I looked like I had leprosy. I was too young and blotchy to work there, but I faked it 'til I maked it and eventually got pretty good at it. My sales were among the top there. I'd offer things that weren't on the menu, like a surf and turf, which just meant I'd charge them for a lobster and a filet. I was indeed an asshole.

There were other times I showed up unqualified and ended up doing a great job. Like the time in college when I taught aerobics—or as they called it, "group exercise"—to chicks like me who'd doubled down on the freshman fifteen. I did actually have a certification to teach kickboxing, and I was able to leverage that into a job teaching a lot of other stuff I had never even tried before, like yoga, Pilates, spin, step, and dance. Before you go down the path of thinking I wouldn't be your first pick for a fitness instructor, let me inform you that my classes were very well attended and fun. I'd have the girls yell out the names of their ex-boyfriends or whoever they were mad at while they threw kicks and punches. I gained some fans who'd follow me from class to class. What I lacked in physique and expertise, I completely made up for with my likability and motivational yelling.

There was one job that I couldn't really physically fake. But I tried anyway. I was twenty-one years old, living on the West Coast with Dan, who did not turn out to be the greatest boyfriend (more on that later). Maybe my unhappy home life with him inspired me to make the strange choice to work as a pedicab driver. For those of you who don't know what a pedicab is, it's basically like a horse-drawn carriage, except a person on a bike is acting as the horse. I don't know what got into my head that made me think this was a good idea. All you technically needed to qualify was a bike, and the pedicab company would rent you the cart for twenty bucks a day. They'd help you hook up the cart to your bike, and then it was up to you to pedal around town and find human beings to haul. There was a main street on a huge hill, and I'd ride to the top of the hill and hope people would want to pay me for a ride down it. Of course, that never happened. I'd sit there and wait for about an hour and then ride down to the bottom, where, naturally, people would always flag me for a lift. I wasn't in great shape, so I'd get about halfway up the hill and feel I was about to roll backward—cart, passengers, and all. I'd come to a halt and yell, "Everybody out!" The passengers would have to help me push my cart up the hill. Due to some weird city ordinance, you weren't allowed to quote passengers a fare. You were just supposed to let them pay what they wanted. Can you imagine if prostitutes had to follow this law too? *"That was pretty good, here's a shiny nickel."* Fuck that! I gave them my price like a nice little prostitute.

I did that job for a few months. I lost about three pounds and that was it. More than I lost teaching aerobics, but still, you'd think I would have lost more weight. But I was so hungry at the end of every shift that I'd binge-eat and then drink myself into a blackout so I could forget about having to work the next day. But something I did enjoy about that job was the nice camaraderie among all the pedicab drivers. We'd meet up in one spot in town, park our carts, smoke cigarettes, and talk about how rough our job was.

The ultimate faking-it situation on my résumé was the time I worked at a lesbian bar. All the female bartenders and I would go out and get really drunk before a shift, because despite what I imagined it would be like, bartending for ALL women was a fucking nightmare. The only thing worse than the drunk drama and the indecisive ordering was the fact that no one ever hit on me. All the other bartenders were straight, but I would look over an hour into our shift and they'd be cheating on their boyfriends, making out with female customers. At the end of the night, the bartenders were even drunker than they had been at the beginning of the night, so counting up the money and tips was impossible. Plus, they made us dance on the bar.

It was humiliating. I'm not a good bar dancer. I'd wear a pair of pink underwear that read I LOVE ME and I'd lift my skirt to display this message, and sway around laughing. I ended up getting fired from that job—not for my gross dancing or my raging heterosexuality, but for closing early without permission. One night, I shut the place down at seven p.m. just because I felt like it.

I was always doing whatever I felt like doing at work. Sometimes it's too hard to hide your feelings just because you're on somebody else's dime. Like at one restaurant I worked in, I decided to stop speaking to the clientele because they were so yuppie and rude. I was done with them. But waiting tables kind of requires you to talk to customers, so I got demoted to being the service bartender, standing in one place and only making drinks for servers to carry out to the floor. And now that I'm the boss and can be openly honest about my feelings at work, I try to set a good example for my staff to let them know they are welcome to do the same. Everyone is free to feel their feelings on the set of my TV show. Sometimes when I am extra emotional due to it being that time of the month, I just get on the loudspeaker and announce to all the cast and crew that I have my period. You should be able to be yourself and keep it real at work, no matter what you're feeling.

Once when I worked at a little bodega by the train stop when I was fifteen, I felt my body telling me to eat a lot of the store's hot dogs. So I did. Which doesn't seem that strange except that I was always working a five a.m. shift before school. I was truly ill equipped for that job because even though I was supposed to ring up hot dogs, coffee, snacks, and newspapers, I had no clue how to make change. The coffee would cost $1.85 and they would hand me a five-dollar bill. I'd respond by just staring at the bill, hoping that through black magic the right amount of change would just float out of my hand and into theirs. I'm a great salesman, but numbers hold me back. I consoled myself by eating a lot more hot dogs. They were so good there. My paycheck was a lot lower than I wanted it to be because they were charging me for my enormous hot dog intake.

My bosses were these two late-forties Indian guys who ~~thought~~ knew I was an idiot. They'd make themselves feel good by belittling me. They'd stand next to each other behind the counter and trash me. I didn't blame them, because I was a terrible employee. I quit when summer came around, and shortly after that, the shop closed down for good. Mine was an honest and simple job, and I think if I weren't on this career path, I'd like to go back to eating hot dogs all day. And I'm grateful to those two guys because even though they made fun of me every second I was there, they never fired me.

One of the things I've learned as a boss myself now is to have high expectations of people, but also to keep it realistic. You can't expect someone to work past their potential. If you've hired someone with the mathematical aptitude of a pet rock, and she eats all your hot dogs and doesn't know how to make change, try to figure out how and where she shines, and let her excel in that area instead. I try to be patient and forgiving with the people I hire, just as they are with me. Mutual respect. But when I realize they don't have what it takes, I do the kind thing and let them go. I always think of that goldfish quote often attributed to Einstein: "Everybody is a genius. But if you judge a fish by its ability to climb a tree, it will live its whole life believing that it is stupid." Let that goldfish go someplace where it can join a school—and then hire an actual climber instead.

I still love hot dogs and lesbians as much as the next guy, but it was such a great relief when I could finally quit working for other people and focus on working for myself instead. Nothing feels better than running the show on my own now. I'm guessing almost every person reading this knows how much personal dignity you sign over when you work for someone you don't like or for a company you don't care about. But I still have to give it up to all the horrible bosses I worked for in the service industry, because most of what I know as a boss today has come from those experiences. And from learning NOT to ever be like them. All those mean chefs who belittled the waiters, and the sociopathic restaurant managers who led with fear and intimidation, wielding their minuscule amount of power to scare the shit out of any employee who needed a day off for even the most legit of reasons . . . All those assholes really showed me several specific versions of who I didn't want to become if I was ever in charge. So I guess the nine million waitressing and bartending jobs I had really paid off in the end. But it's also nice to learn by positive example now and then. I got more value from just one day on Tina Fey's set and two days on Lena Dunham's than I got from any other long-term job I've had.

Now that I spend most of my time on sets or onstage, I can finally say I love what I do for a living. But still, most days I can't wait until I am done and allowed to go, which is almost never. And despite my poor track record at restaurants, bars, salons, and mailrooms (yes, I once got fired from a mailroom for throwing away the mail), I'm proud to say I've never been fired from a show business job. Once on a small one-episode TV role I was told I'd be canned if I didn't stop ad-libbing inappropriate jokes, but that's the closest I ever came. And now that I'm a boss and it's part of my job to do the hiring and firing, I get what it feels like to have people's fate in your hands. It's not a sensation I enjoy. Turns out being on the other side can also be full of humiliation and hardship. But it still beats working for someone else. And there's no turning back once you get used to running the show.

———

I GOT MY very first brief taste of being in charge at the age of ten, when I was a basketball referee for a little kids' league. I'd wake up early Saturday mornings and put on my striped shirt and hang the whistle around my neck like a girl boss. Literally. I was still physically a little girl and hadn't even started my period yet. But I was made for that job. It wasn't easy, because the parents were bloodthirsty and insane. The kids were six-year-olds who couldn't even lace up their own shoes, but these parents were calling for technical fouls. I threw my fair share of them out of the game. I'd call traveling on one of the kids and the father would literally get in my face—my ten-year-old, three-foot-eleven face—and yell, "Terrible call!" I'd blow my whistle and point to the door, and the angry adult would leave the room in a huff. It was the most difficult job I've had to date, harder even than hauling three obese men from Green Bay uphill in a pedicab. But somehow I think that job prepared me for everything I do now. It prepared me for being a female boss in an industry that is still mostly run by men. It prepared me for being called fat, ugly, and talentless on the Internet (because, I assure you, every troll online is even more vitriolic and nasty than those adults getting in my face on the basketball court). And it prepared me to get up early, work my ass off, and stand by my calls.

Today I wake up every day, mostly with way too much work on my plate and not enough hours to get it all done. I worry about the people on my payroll, that if I don't do a good job they'll be affected.

I try to treat everyone equally (badly). JK, just equally. I do my best to make decisions that are fair and good for me and everyone else. I'm tired and beaten down a lot of the time. But it still feels so fucking good to know that no matter who or what comes at me, this is my court and I wear the whistle.

EXCERPT FROM MY JOURNAL IN 2001 (AGE TWENTY) WITH FOOTNOTES FROM 2016

I got home around 2:50.[1] *Today I went with my mom and Kim to meet Jay at LaGuardia. We got to meet his good friend from his school, Eileen.*

Throughout the weekend he made his usual fat jokes about me,[2] *and Kim looked so wonderful and thin*[3] *and I felt so heavy and the mixture of all of that has made me decide to try to develop an eating disorder.*[4] *Hopefully it will safely work out.*[5] *I'm sick of feeling confident and then suddenly self-conscious.*[6] *It's too hard. I have become something I never thought I would. I've never had any real issue with my weight but I'm seeing Dan in three weeks and I'm sick of being looked at as the big girl.*

---

1   Wow, very precise. What is this, *Law and Order?*

2   I honestly don't remember my brother making fun of my weight at all. I remember him making sure my ego was in check and that I never got too full of myself.

3   I had no idea that she was battling an eating disorder at the time.

4   Cool idea, Aim! Really smart and not dangerous. What an inspiration. By the way, my swing-and-a-miss at an eating disorder lasted under one day. I think I skipped one meal and then decided, *Nope . . . fuck that noise.*

5   Like they always do.

6   Well, get used to it, bitch. It's for the rest of your life.

I want to feel what it's like to be considered really hot. I hate that that is such a priority to me. But right now it just is.[7]

I can just see myself reading this entry when I'm recovering from the disorder and gaining back the weight, but I have to give it a shot.[8] I've tried everything else.[9] If I don't look much better than now, I will refuse to see Dan. I want to see him and feel thin and beautiful or not see him at all.[10]

This is such a humiliating thing to actually write down, but I'm sort of depressed and I've worked pretty hard and this is just how I feel. So be it. We'll see what happens.

Luv,

Amy

P.S. I guess Dan has too much power over me. I need something else. I've been seriously thinking about the AmeriCorps=Hell yea.[11] I wish it was now. I should be enjoying college not praying for it to end.[12] What the fuck. I want to go to NYU so bad.[13] Towson sucks, Baltimore is bullshit.[14] Get me the fuck out of here.[15]

---

7   I understand what I'm saying here. Feeling this way is a theme in every girl's life, I think, and at that age, you think there's some other version of yourself that is waiting to come out and blow everyone's dick off. I am so glad this is almost fifteen years ago and I know myself and my body now. Sorry, girls this age, but if you can, just skip the self-hatred and the striving to be some other type of girl. Just let that phase pass you by and love yourself how you are. Don't waste any energy on it. If you want to lose a little weight, fine. Make sure you are healthy, but fuck, skip all the rest. You are hot and the person who will love you won't notice ten pounds. I really promise.

8   Not only was I so confident in my ability to develop an efficient eating disorder, but I was also certain I would recover from it. Do you think I get ahead of myself?

9   Except for not drinking like Nic Cage in *Leaving Las Vegas*.

10   This was the boyfriend who made me feel bad about myself and my body so I would have low self-esteem and he wouldn't lose me. More on this prize later.

11   That is like the Peace Corps but in America, which my brother did. Which I never even came close to doing. I am a flake. Also . . . "Hell yea"??? Yikes.

12   That is not true, that is exactly what I should have been doing. People who enjoy high school or college too much are wack in my humble opinion.

13   I don't remember ever thinking that.

14   I disagree with myself here. Baltimore is not bullshit; I grew to really love it.

15   Many people think I have this unshakable confidence, so I hope this look into my most

A few days later:

Dear Journal,

It's been two weeks since my last confession. Haha.[16] *I just read over my previous journal entry. It makes me sick.*[17] *I don't feel that way at all right now about my body. I like my body.*[18] *Before hooking up with Dan I never had a real issue with it.*[19] *If he continues to make me feel self-conscious I really don't want to communicate with him anymore.*[20] *I feel pretty good about myself and my weight right now. Anyway, I'm on a plane on my way to visit Dan haha. Again, with a mere mention of a visit, I'm on a plane to go see this little bastard.*[21] *I hope we have so much fun. I just don't want to take this too seriously.*[22] *He is my friend who I love on a deeper level than other friends. The sex certainly completes it but that's just a factor of our friendship.*[23] *I'm excited to see how this weekend goes. It's Thursday right now and I'm staying til Sunday.*[24]

---

intimate thoughts will support the idea that loving yourself takes time. Like any healthy relationship, it doesn't happen overnight. And sometimes, it can only come to fruition after several failed attempts at eating disorders.

16 What a hack. I seriously thought I was Woody Allen.

17 My emotional swings in my twenties were like those of someone with multiple personality disorder.

18 Oh okayyyyy, boo boo!

19 I was putting the pieces together that this guy was treating me like garbage.

20 Yeah, bitch! I want to jump off the couch and celebrate for this girl—follow this girl, ladies!

21 Turns out I was right. He was a bastard. See chapter titled "The Worst Night of My Life."

22 Hear me now! The "I'm just gonna have fun and not be attached" tactic has never and will never work, sistas. I do not know one girl who wants to get a bunch of different dick. We aren't wired that way, honeys.

23 Damn, you can hear me lying to myself even on the page.

24 Okay, I Googled it and that checks out. It was a Thursday. It was also my brother's birthday. Happy belated, Jay!

BEAUTIFUL AND STRONG

Right before I left for college I was running my high school. I knew where to park, where to get the best chicken cutlet sandwich, and which custodians had pot. People knew me. They liked me. I was an athlete and a good friend and I felt pretty. I felt seen. I had reached my full high school potential. I had an identity. I was looked at as strong, funny, and fair. It was this sweet spot in life when I didn't spend a lot of time questioning my worth. I owned what I had and didn't sweat the rest.

Then I got to college, where the class of freshman girls at my school, Towson University in Maryland, had just been voted *Playboy* magazine's number one hottest in the nation. And not because of me.

All of a sudden being witty and charismatic didn't mean shit. Day after day I could feel the confidence draining from my body. I was *not* what these guys wanted. They wanted thinner, blonder, dumber. My sassy one-liners were only working with the cafeteria employees, whom I was visiting all too frequently, tacking on the freshman thirty, not fifteen, in record-breaking time. No males were noticing me, and, I'm embarrassed to say, it was killing me.

The closest thing to attention I got came from this guy Brett. He was five years older than me and looked like a Hitler Youth. He was also a "super senior," which is a sexy way of saying he should have graduated but needed or wanted another year before entering the real world. He barely ever spoke, which was perfect for all the projecting I had planned for him.

Getting attention from a cute older boy felt like success. I'd get nervous to see him on campus—my heart would race, and I'd smile as he passed and look him in the eyes and feel all the blood rush to my face. I'd spend my time analyzing that interaction and planning my outfit for the next time I saw him. *Should I wear simple clogs or Reef sandals? Will he be at the bar tonight? This calls for a zebra-print mini and a tube top!*

I wanted him to call, but he never called. And then, one day, he called. It was eight a.m. when my dorm room phone rang.

"Amy, sup? It's Brett. Come over."

Holy shit. This is it, I thought. *He woke up thinking about me. He realized we were meant to start a life together—that we should stop all this pretending that we weren't created just to love one another. I wonder where we'll raise our kids? Does he want to raise our family in Baltimore? I'll settle where he's most comfortable. I don't need to raise our kids Jewish, but I certainly won't have them christened.*

I shaved my legs in the sink and splashed some water on my armpits. My roommate stared at me from under her sheets as I rushed around our shitty dorm room, which, in retrospect, was not unlike a prison: neon lighting, randomly assigned roommate, and sealed windows so we didn't have the option to jump to an early graduation.

I ran right over there, ready for our day together. What would we do? It was still early enough to go fishing. Or maybe his mom was in town and they wanted me to join them for breakfast. Knock, knock. I beamed at the door. Knock, knock. *Is he going to carry me over the threshold? I bet he's fixing his hair and telling his mom, "Be cool, this may be the one."* I planned to be very sweet with her but also to assert myself so she didn't think she was completely in charge of all the holiday dinners we'd be spending together. I'd call her by her first name too early so she'd realize she couldn't mess with me. "Rita, *I'm* going to make the green bean casserole this year."

Knock, knock. Knock. Knock. KNOCK! Finally, the door opened. It was Brett, but he wasn't really there. His face was distorted from alcohol consumption and whatever else. His eyes seemed like they'd left his body. They couldn't focus on me. He was standing next to me trying to see me from the side, like a shark.

"Hey!" he yelled, a few notches too loudly, and gave me a painfully hard hug. But I was too busy tilting up my chin, sticking out my boobs, and sucking in my stomach to notice this huge red flag.

He was fucking wasted. I quickly realized that I wasn't the first person he'd thought of that morning. I was the last person he'd thought of the night before, because for Brett, it still *was* the night before. I wondered how many girls didn't answer before he got to fat, freshman me. Was I in his phone as "Schumer"? Probably took him a while to get to "S." But there I was in his room, eighteen years old and wanting to be held and touched and to feel desired. I wanted to be with him, and I imagined us on campus together holding hands, proving that I was lovable and that I couldn't be the troll doll I thought I'd become, because this cool, older guy liked me. I thought, *I'll stay 'til he's sober and we can laugh about the whole thing and realize we really like each other.*

He put on some music and we got into bed. Well, he pushed me on the bed as a sexy maneuver, the move guys so often do to communicate, "Get ready, I'm taking the wheel on this one and I'm going to blow your mind." It's almost never followed up with anything. He smelled like skunked Heineken—well, Heineken, skunk, and Micro-Magic cheeseburgers, which I planned to find and eat in the bathroom once he was asleep. His nine a.m. shadow scratched my face when he came at me (I knew it would look like I had fruit punch mouth for days after this), and his alcohol-swollen kisses made me feel like I was being tongued by someone who'd just been given Novocain.

The music was too loud. I felt faceless and nameless. I was just a warm body, but I felt freezing cold as his fingers poked inside me like he'd lost his keys in there. Then came the sex. I use that word loosely. His penis had all the hardness of an empty banana peel. I knew a few minutes after I walked in that there was no chance of any sort of intercourse. Which was good, because I wasn't ready to actually sleep with him. There was a better chance of a baby climbing Everest than this guy penetrating me.

During this festival of flailing, I looked around the room to try to distract myself, or, God willing, dissociate. The place looked like it had been decorated by an overeager set designer who took the note "temporary and without any substance" too far. I saw a *Scarface* poster, which, of course, was mandatory. Anything else? No. That was it. This Standard White Dude son of an accountant who played more video games and Hacky Sack than I was comfortable with felt the greatest connection with a Cuban refugee drug lord.

He started to go down on me. *That's ambitious*, I thought. Is it still considered getting head if the guy falls asleep after three seconds of moving his tongue like an elderly person eating their last oatmeal? The only wetness coming from between my legs was his drool, because he'd fallen completely asleep and was snoring *into* me. I wanted to scream out for myself: *Get out of here, Amy! You are beautiful, you are smart, and you are worth more than this!* I sighed and heard my own heart break; I was fighting back tears. I could feel I was losing myself to the girl in this bed, almost completely. Then I noticed a change in the music. The song was a bagpipe solo.

"Brett, what is this?" I shook him awake.

"The *Braveheart* soundtrack."

Of course. I should have known. I bet his Mel Gibson poster was in the mail, on its way to hang on the wall proudly next to Al Pacino.

"Can you put something else on please?"

He rose grumpily, fell to the floor, and crawled. I looked at his exposed butt crack, a dark unkempt abyss that I was falling into. I was short of breath. I felt paralyzed. His asshole was a canyon. This was my 127 hours. I needed to chip away at the rock and get out.

Brett stood up and put on a new CD. *"Darling, youuuuu send me."* He climbed back in bed and tried to mash what was at this point his third ball into my vagina. On his fourth thrust he gave up and fell asleep again on my breasts. His head was heavy and his breath so sour I had to turn my head so my eyes didn't water. But they already were watering, because of this album. These songs.

"Who is this?" I asked. The music was so beautiful. The songs were gutting me. *"Cupid, draw back your bowwww."* The score he'd attached to our morning could not have been more off. His sloppy attempt at "lovemaking" was more Mel Gibson than William Wallace. And now the most beautiful love songs I'd ever heard rang out as this man-boy lay in my arms after diminishing me to a last attempt at a booty call. I listened, and I cried.

I looked down on myself from the ceiling fan, as if I were my own fairy godmother. I waited until the last perfect note, then slid out from under him and slipped out the door. I closed it behind me, and I was rescued.

I never heard from Brett again, so I never got to thank him for introducing me to my new self and my new love, Sam Cooke.

———

THIRTEEN YEARS LATER, I still love Sam Cooke, and I still need that fairy godmother from time to time. As a part of my TV show, I have a segment called "Amy Goes Deep" where I interview people who do interesting jobs or have interesting lifestyles. One segment I did that we didn't end up airing was with a professional matchmaker. In addition to letting me ask her questions about her job, she wanted to set me up. Directly after we filmed our conversation, I was going to meet up with the man she'd chosen for me.

It was the most disturbing "Amy Goes Deep" scene I've taped. Keep in mind, I've talked to a climate change denier, a pickup artist, and a diagnosed sociopath. But this woman left the darkest cloud over me. It still makes me feel angry and demoralized. Before we met, she'd sized me up from pictures online and some footage of my performances. She told me very little about the guy she was going to set me up with but emphasized that he was a great catch. She described him as a six-foot-tall, nice-looking guy who worked out. She assured me that he was funny and that he always made people laugh with the insightful things he wrote on Facebook. She went on to instruct me about the benefits of this quality, as if she were speaking to an alien who'd never experienced human emotion before. "When there's great banter, it's really fun and easy—and you feel sexual chemistry happening."

Hearing her "teaching" me—a thirty-four-year-old comic— about sexual attraction and humor in this controlling, prescribed way was making the bile rise in my throat. She asked what icebreaker I'd use to talk to a guy. I asked if she thought I should "push his head down like I was setting off dynamite."

"No," she said, completely humorlessly. "Because the guy is supposed to be the one doing that. You're the woman," she informed me. "You need to be a lady. You need to make it so that he likes you. So that there's a hint of what's to come. I think you just need to sit back and let him take control."

She then informed me that my numerous sex jokes were probably the reason I was still single. How can I say this like a lady? Suck my dick!

If you've seen my show, you know that I expose every part of myself on-screen. I wear unattractive costumes and show my body from all angles. I write about things that I'm truly sensitive about, and I'm often the butt of the joke. But this interview with the matchmaker was, hands down, the most vulnerable I've ever felt. Hearing a dating "expert" inform me why I'm not attractive to men, and then having to put myself out there to meet a man she selected who might actually be interested in me, was very scary.

When the interview finished, I went to a bar to meet the guy, whom I'll call Rex. I'm feeling dizzy even writing this now. I waited at the bar, all of my self-worth leaking out of my sweaty palms, which were gripping a glass of wine like it was the only thing connecting me to the rest of the world. I had a bad feeling. But nothing could have prepared me for who walked in the door.

When I saw Rex, I felt like the *Titanic*, and he was the cluster of icebergs that would finally destroy me. In he walked. He was about fifty-three years old, wearing a denim button-down shirt with a leather vest over it. He was around five foot nine (a solid three inches shorter than the matchmaker's description) and had hair plugs and a significant belly. He was not afraid of exposing his salt-and-pepper chest hair, having left open his top four buttons, which also allowed him to showcase—no joke—a shark-tooth necklace. His own teeth had been freshly whitened and he couldn't wait to flash them as often as possible, which wasn't difficult because he was so excited about his tan that he couldn't stop smiling.

I bought him a drink after we hugged hello. My heart had dropped out of the bottom of my vagina, and the clock was running the second we locked eyes. *I am giving this exactly thirty minutes*, I thought. I focused all my energy on being as kind as possible. He asked me no questions, which I appreciated, because I just wasn't in the sharing mood. There was no time anyway because he needed to tell me about his band that did Bruce or Billy covers. He talked a lot about the kind of guy he was, he stared at my tits, and I witnessed the moment he decided he'd be willing to have sex with me. I was focusing on my breathing and the clock. I was smiling and trying to spread joy, but it was hard because this guy was actually cocky and a dick. I started to wrap things up at about twenty-two minutes in. I said I had so much work to do and how great it was to meet him. He then said exactly this: "You are really cute. The matchmaker told me you were, quote, 'no model,' but I think she's wrong." This made my heart, which had already fallen out of my pussy, proceed to dig a hole through the Earth's crust, mantle, and core. Was this supposed to be the great banter the matchmaker foreshadowed? Was the sexual chemistry right around the corner? I wanted to be sure I'd heard him correctly.

"What exactly did she say?" I asked.

"Well," Rex proceeded to explain, "I wasn't sure I wanted to go on this date and was nervous about it, and she said, 'Don't worry, she's no model.'"

I pointed out to him how rude it was to relay this information to me. I could have done without hearing her assessment of my appearance. He defended himself by saying that he disagreed with the matchmaker. I started to lay out for him why this was still a shitty thing for him to say to me, but then I thought, *Fuck it, why am I engaging with a dude who was born when Eisenhower was president and who loves wearing dead shark parts close to his heart?* I thanked him for his time, hugged him good-bye, and left decimated. Not for myself, but for all the single women out there trying to date. I wanted to run to the top of the Empire State Building and make an announcement to all of them to let them know they are worth so much more than this. That they don't need to wrangle some warm body to sit next to them just so they aren't alone on holidays. That they should never let a magazine or dating site or matchmaker monster tell them they're in a lower bracket of desirability because of their age or weight or face or sense of humor. That they don't deserve to be manipulated into thinking this is something they should strive for—this decaying turkey of a man who'd been encouraged to believe, like so many other men, that he was a great prize for someone like me. Why should I have worked so hard to keep him interested, as the matchmaker suggested women are supposed to do? He wasn't funny, he wasn't particularly nice, and I've been more interested talking to people's pets.

And as for the matchmaker, she makes her living redefining women's dreams, telling them to lower their expectations. She creates and confirms what she thinks you deserve. If you're "no model" I guess she thinks your best hope is to be matched with a man who has a pulse and a bank account, and that you should be grateful if he musters an erection with your name on it. I walked out of there like the building was on fire and I had started it, thinking, *FUCK THAT!*

I'm not going to lie in that freshman dorm bed or sit in that bar with Rex and his vest ever again. And for anyone who has ever looked for love and found nothing more than a denim-on-denim-on-leather-wearing Hair Club for Men dude, I want to say, *Love yourself!* You don't need a man or a boy or a self-proclaimed love expert to tell you what you're worth. Your power comes from who you are and what you do! You don't need all that noise, that constant hum in the background telling you whether or not you're good enough. All you need is you, your friends, and your family. And you will find the right person for you, if that's what you want—the one who respects your strength and beauty.

Most of the time these days, I feel beautiful and strong. I walk proudly down the streets of Manhattan, that same girl I was during my senior year of high school. The people I love love me. I'm a great sister and friend. I make the funniest people in the country laugh. My vagina has had an impressive guest list—truly an inspiring roster of men. I have fought my way through harsh criticism and death threats, and I am alive. I am fearless. Most of the time. But I can still be reduced to that lonely, vulnerable college freshman pretty quickly. It happened that day with the matchmaker and Rex, and I'm sure it will happen again. I'm not bulletproof, and I'm sure I'm not alone in this. As women, we relive our fears all the time, despite our best efforts to build each other up and truly love ourselves. It happens. And when it does, sometimes Sam Cooke isn't enough, and I can't fairy-godmother my way out of it. Sometimes I want to quit—not performing, but being a woman altogether. I want to throw my hands in the air after reading a mean Twitter comment and say, "All right, you got me. You figured me out. I'm not pretty. I'm not thin. I don't deserve love. I have no right to use my voice. I will start wearing a burka and move to a small town upstate and wait tables at a pancake house."

So much has changed about me since I was that confident, happy girl in high school. In the years since then, I've experienced a lot of desperation and self-doubt, but in a way, I've come full circle. I know my worth. I embrace my power. I say if I'm beautiful. I say if I'm strong. You will not determine my story. I will. I'll speak and share and fuck and love, and I will never apologize for it. I am amazing for you, not because of you. I am not who I sleep with. I am not my weight. I am not my mother. I am myself. And I am all of you.

EXCERPT FROM MY JOURNAL IN 2003 (AGE TWENTY-TWO) WITH FOOTNOTES FROM 2016

Dear Journal,

Well it's always a bad sign when I'm not writing. It really means I have something to hide or that I am not living in reality and I don't want to think about it.[1] *This*[2] *past two months have been no exception. I am now in New York on the train on my way to try and get a fabulous waitressing job in the city.*[3]

I have been living in a world mirroring reality but not quite a part

---

1   I like that I believed my journal was this priest I had to confess my sins to. I had this unwritten contract to keep shit real with my journal.

2   It's also a bad sign when a "writer" uses "this" instead of "these" when talking about something plural. Crushing it, Amy!

3   I honestly don't know if I was joking or not with the word "fabulous," but what I learned quickly was that there are no fabulous waitressing jobs, or bartending jobs, or any service industry jobs, except maybe there is a professional head getter. Is that a job? You just lie there and get head? That sounds fabulous.

of it.[4] *I graduated from college blah blah blah. What exactly does that mean?*[5] *I think I know but I've learned that the present truth becomes the future's nonsense.*[6]

The last two months of school were busy but great. The play went pretty well. It could have been 1,000 times better but the director was the worst ever and the cast sucked too.[7]

I am trying to begin my life.[8] *I want everything right now.*[9] *I want to be living in NYC,*[10] *getting paid,*[11] *to act and bartend.*[12] *I've only been home a week and I'm already itching to be raking in cash and going on auditions.*[13] *I want to start a new page.*[14]

---

4   I would love to know what the fuck I am talking about here. I must have been reading a heavy-handed Oprah book club pick.

5   I have a point here. To this day, I maintain that going to college is not essential if you want to be an actor, especially if you truly want to perform. Read some plays and study in an intensive course with the technique that is the most useful for you. I liked the Meisner technique, so I studied that for a couple years after college with William Esper.

6   Slow down, Nietzsche. This is utter garbage. Just babble. I am embarrassed for myself, but that's part of reading from a journal.

7   Pretty harsh, Amy Ford Coppola. What did I expect? It was a state school in Maryland. Did I want Mark Rylance and Meryl Streep to costar with me? We were a bunch of teenagers playing adults. Relax.

8   I remember this feeling so well. Since I was ten I'd wanted to feel like life was really starting and it all wasn't just this prep for it.

9   I did.

10   I do.

11   I do.

12   I like that I was realistic enough to know that I would have to bartend and that I included it in my dream. I upgraded from waitressing to bartending in this one journal entry.

13   Little did I know that auditions are what nightmares are made of. You are judged by a roomful of people who have no respect for you as you read for a role you will not get.

14   I would like for you to believe that I was being poetic and metaphorical here, but I literally meant I wanted to start a new page of the journal entry. There was a whole line left, but I drew an arrow because I was sick of looking at that page.

HOW TO BECOME
A STAND-UP COMEDIAN

Stand-up is my favorite thing to do. Well, that's not true. I love to have an orgasm and I love to watch a good movie or read a good book. I love to eat pasta and drink wine. Those things are probably my favorites. But after those things. Oh, wait, sleep, I love to sleep—and I love to be on a boat. I love to play volleyball with my sister and I love to go see a band or musician's concert right when I am at my peak of loving them. Those are all my favorite things to do. But all joking aside, even though I'm not joking, stand-up is such a huge joy for me. Especially now, because even though you get better and better at it, the experience doesn't change. Or at least that's how I feel.

Standing up there, onstage, under the lights, and expressing something you think is funny or important (or both) and being met with laughter, applause, appreciation, and agreement is a feeling I can't describe. I am a human being and I want to be loved, and some nights I just want to sit around watching movies with my family or my boyfriend. But mostly every night for the last thirteen years, I've wanted to get onstage.

My first official gig was at the age of five. I played Gretl in *The Sound of Music*. But I was performing even before that—for as long as I could speak. In my room as a child, the bed was placed on a platform in a nook that was built into the wall. There were curtains around the nook to create a cozy little place to sleep, but I moved the mattress out so the platform could be my stage instead. I'd gather any family members I could find, emerge from behind the curtain, and perform for them on my little stage. The performances consisted mostly of me telling boring, meandering stories about bunnies or cats or worms. They pretended they were interested even though they must have been dying for a meteor to drop on the house.

I always wanted to perform. My dad filmed everything, which constantly annoyed me—even as a toddler. I'd stop my performance and ask him to put down the camera. We have a video of me throwing a tantrum because he wouldn't obey my demands to stop filming. You'd think I would have enjoyed being filmed, but for me, the experience was all about the audience and the live show. Even when I was three.

My first time going onstage to do stand-up was very last-minute. I was twenty-three years old and had been out of college for two years. A woman in an improv group I was in, a comic of about forty-five, had been doing stand-up for a long time. She was like a female Woody Allen without the marrying someone who was once his daughter. I went to see her perform one night, and like every other asshole who goes to comedy clubs, I thought, *I could do this*.

Not long after that fateful night, I discovered Gotham Comedy Club. It was on Twenty-Second Street at the time and seated about 150 people. I went in and found out that if I brought four people to be in the audience (people who would pay the door price and purchase some drinks), I could perform that night. I can't remember who all four of these lucky souls were. One was definitely my mom, and another was my friend Eileen, a jazz drummer, but I don't remember the others. I had a couple hours before I went onstage, during which I brainstormed the six-minute set I'd perform. The show was at five p.m. on a Tuesday. Still light outside. Great time for comedy. There were about twenty-five people in the audience. I unfortunately have a videotape of the whole thing. My hair is very curly and the only thing worse than my outfit was my jokes. I wore a Mormon-looking short-sleeved white button-down with jeans that would have fit the original version of Jared from Subway, and I ranted about skywriting:

"It's so annoying. It always fades, and you can never really read it. If a guy proposed to me that way, I would say NOoooooooo."

And then I added:

"So do me a favor this summer, keep it at eye level!"

That was my clever little sum-up. *Keep it at eye level. Blech.*

I could vomit thinking about how awful my act was. But I wasn't nervous. I had been doing theater since I was five so I didn't have stage fright. I was pretty confident for a newcomer with zero original thoughts and even less timing. People laughed enough. They laughed because I was young and hopeful and they could feel my energy and enthusiasm. They laughed to be nice. All that mattered was that they laughed. I was *in.* Some of the actual comedians there complimented me. They told me I should work at it and that I could get better. Maybe they were trying to sleep with me. Wait, just remembered my outfit. They weren't.

From then on, I did a couple shows a month. Always "bringers," which means you have to bring between eight and twelve people to sit in the audience and buy drinks in exchange for six minutes of stage time. It's a bit of a racket, but everyone gets what they want. Everyone except the audience. I'd usually rely on my family and friends from Long Island and whomever I was waiting tables with at the time to fulfill my audience quota. It was brutal to need something from people all the time. Later on down the line, as soon as I stopped doing bringers, I deleted about a hundred numbers from my cell phone. I was thrilled I wouldn't ever again have to text, "HEY! WANT TO COME TO MY SHOW?" As I have said before, I'm an introvert, and after shows I'd just want to go home and think about my set, but instead, I'd have to go to a bar with everyone who came to support me. Doing a show already takes a lot out of you, but then to have to kind of "work a room" was too much. It seemed easier to give a lap dance to an angry porcupine than to stand around with my restaurant coworkers hearing what they thought of my punch lines.

My first year of stand-up I'd pace in the parking lot outside Gotham before the show. I'd walk back and forth past the valet attendants and go over the set in my head the way an actor goes over a monologue: over and over again. Then, when I was a few minutes away from being called onstage, I'd get diarrhea. Every time. It was almost a ritual. I'd panic at the thought that they'd call my name while I was still in a cold bathroom wiping myself within an inch of my life, but it always timed out well. Somehow, I consistently managed to empty my bowels, wipe, and flush before my name was called. I even had a few extra seconds to stretch like a long-distance runner before I had to go on. Which I always did, until I saw someone shadowboxing before they went onstage and thought it was so lame that I quit my own ritual of stretching.

Now I can be fully asleep or in the middle of a conversation and walk onstage, but back then it was like sacrificing a lamb with

I was a bundle of joy.

My ride home from being born.

Me and my dad.

Gordon and Sandy Schumer.

Me and Jason looking flyyyyyyyy.

Kim, me, Vinny (my
brother-in-law), and
Abbott, my love interest.

"Hey, I'm workin' over here!"

Happy campers.

At our farmhouse, two and a half.

Rocking out.

Me at age three, always
a flawless accessorizer.

At a magazine
(not-fitting) fitting.

Me as a baby model = nepotism. Also, is there anything creepier to put in a baby's crib than a stuffed sixty-year-old man smoking a pipe?

Panda, Pokey, Penny, Mouser, Bunny, and the two-headed bear.

Cincinnati, thirteen years old.

Dad at the farm.

Dad visiting me at my *Vogue* cover shoot.

Me on a horse, Chicago.

Bahamas, 2016.

Boxing in New York City.
Kim puked shortly after this
photo was taken.

Sisters.

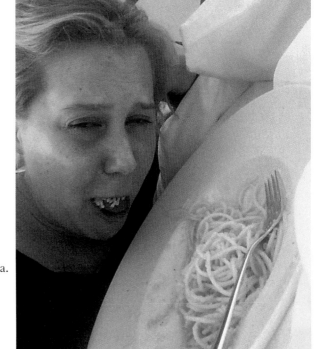

Just a gal eatin' some pasta.

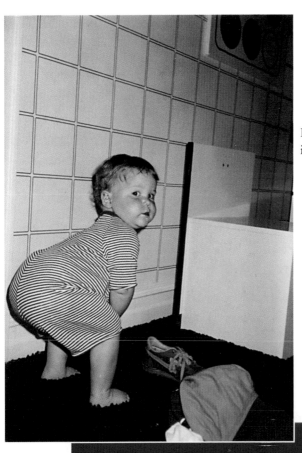

I was twerking before it was hip.

Dancing with my friend Kati in Baltimore, sophomore year of college.

Me and my sister-in-law, Cayce, heading to *Ellen* for the first time. Cayce made this book with me.

Brother and sisters, 2016, Minneapolis.

Siblings on the set of *Trainwreck*.

Rehearsal for the dance
scene in *Trainwreck*.

Me and Kev, my working
partner and brother from
another mother.

Writers of *Inside
Amy Schumer*,
season three.

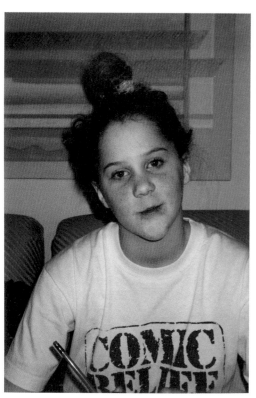

Always had comedy-
writer energy.

Bloomington,
Indiana, 2010.

Age twenty-three.

One of many pyramids with my oldest friends.

Rachel Feinstein, me, Bridget Everett, and Poppy prepare to go onstage.

Heading home from a Boston show with Chris Rock.

A couple hours before filming my special at the Apollo.

Saying we are grateful and that we will do our best is a preshow tradition.

Charleston, South Carolina, 2016.

Minneapolis, 2016.

all the creepy superstitions I had. The strangest one was watching myself. You could buy a VHS tape of your performance from a guy at Gotham for fifteen dollars. I didn't have a VCR at home, so I'd bring the tape to a store that rhymes with West Buy and put it in one of their machines so I could watch my set and take notes. People shopping would walk by so confused as to why a girl had brought a video of herself to a store and was writing about it. Or once someone thought I was on a really low-budget TV show that I'd happened to catch the airing of. But I couldn't afford a VCR with all the money I was spending on stage time and rent.

I didn't graduate to open-mic shows for a while. Open mics are a bigger step because they aren't bringers, and a lot of the time the audience consists only of other comedians. I decided a good place to get my feet wet would be up in Harlem on 106th Street at a place called the Underground. I went up with a lot of confidence. I'd been performing for months in front of real audiences with a couple hundred people in them, so I thought I could handle thirty comedians. (I'm singing these three words:) *Noooo I cooooouldn't!* I bombed. Hard. Not one laugh.

There's nothing quite like your first bomb. You can feel it in your bones. First you think there might be something wrong with the sound. But there isn't. It's you. You're the problem. You and your terrible jokes that are not funny. You realize everyone has been lying to you. There are no friends in the audience laughing so as not to hurt your self-esteem. It's a sea of unfriendly faces, people who do the same thing you do, so they don't think you're cute. They think you are boring and that you're wasting their time. And all they are focused on is their own set and how they should be further along in comedy than they are. I was dizzy when I got offstage. I sat back down with a few other comics who smiled at me in a "sorry for your loss" way.

I hung my head through the rest of the show and realized I had a lot of work to do. I didn't cry but my confidence was in tiny little pieces shattered all over the dirty Harlem floor. Okay, fine, I cried. And I drank several warm beers.

From there, I began doing a couple of shows a week—an open mic here, a bringer there. I'd finish one set and go home to have dinner with my boyfriend, Rick, with whom I lived very happily in Brooklyn. We were both actors who met waiting tables, meaning we were both auditioning for shitty roles in shitty plays and not getting any parts. I remember thinking it was strange that a lot of other comics I knew would do more than one show a night. I could feel their insatiable hunger for stage time and I pitied them. What were they chasing? As if one more five-minute set at a hair salon (yes, they have shows everywhere) in front of ten other drunk open-mic performers would change anything.

And then it happened to me. I thought of my first good joke. The kind that made me feel I had to get onstage to tell it. It happened on the L train on my way home to Williamsburg around one a.m. I was sitting next to an elderly black woman and we were having a nice conversation. Just chitchat. She was Crypt Keeper old, like a California Raisin. That is not racist. If she had been white she would have looked like a yellow California Raisin. Anywhoozle, out of nowhere she asked me, "Have you heard the good news?" At that moment I saw she had one of those cartoony religious pamphlets and I realized she was trying to save my soul. I let her down easily, explaining that I was Jewish and would not be joining her in the kingdom of heaven. That was that. I thought she was just this sweet woman I was connecting with, but she was using me to get salvation points. Little did she know I was a godless, shifty Jew. I walked home from the subway thinking about the interaction and I wrote a joke. A good joke.

I called my sister early the next morning and woke her up. Kim hates being woken up. But she sleeps with her phone on and I know that, so ring ring ring. "Kim, listen, I have a new joke!" She answered me with a supportive, "Good-bye." But I got her to stay on the phone and listen to my joke, which was:

This old woman on the subway asked me, "Have you heard the good news?" She was trying to save me.

I said, "Ma'am, I'm so sorry. My people are Jewish."

She said, "That's okay, your people just haven't found Jesus yet."

I said, "No, we found him. Maybe you haven't heard the bad news."

I listened into my phone for Kim's response. Like I had so many times before. After about three Mississippis she said, "That's funny. Good-bye." And she hung up. But that was all I needed. I loved my new joke. I tried it that night at an open mic, and it went well. But I started working on it. Maybe if I added a couple of wrong guesses of what I thought the good news was, it could be funnier. I went to another open mic, and then another.

A couple weeks later I wrote a new joke:

My boyfriend is always turning the lights on when we have sex, and I shut them off, and he puts them back on.

The other day, he said, "Why are you so shy? You have a beautiful body."

I said, "You are so cute! You think I don't want you to see me."

I loved that joke. I wanted to run it a million times. And I did. I found out there were some clubs where you could "bark"—which meant standing on a corner and giving out flyers, telling people about a comedy show. "Hey, do you like live comedy?" Have you heard those annoying people when you've visited New York? Well, that was me. In ten-degree weather, I'd be out there on a corner trying to get enough people inside so they would let me go onstage. I needed bodies in there, English-speaking or not.

I had caught the bug. I was totally and completely addicted to stand-up, to getting better at it, and it was working. It turns out if you do a ton of open mics and bringers, and if you bark, and if you produce your own shows, and if you have other comics in your shows, and if they have you in their shows, and if you do it every single night several times, and if you are totally obsessed with it, you will get a little better. "Little" is the key word.

Ultimately, anyone who does stand-up is delusional and masochistic. It takes so much work and so much time to be good. To get real laughs requires years and years. I got better little by little. A comic, Pete Dominick, whom I met doing a bringer at Gotham, pushed me hard to get better. He said, "You need to know the name of every club in New York, and you need to get up whenever you can. It has to be an obsession." He was right. Jessica Kirson was the funniest person I'd ever seen. I used to watch her close out the shows at Gotham. She would kill in a way I still haven't seen anyone else do. The audience was physically exhausted from laughing. When she got offstage, your face hurt. She was the first person to let me open for her on the road. I'd go anywhere for nothing. She would give me fifty bucks to be nice, but I was just thrilled she would take me with her.

Then one day—about two and a half years in—I went to a free seminar for new comics at Gotham Comedy Club, the place where I did my first stand-up set. The owner, Chris Mazzilli, had arranged for an agent and a nationally headlining comic to be there to answer the questions of about one hundred comics in attendance. I was furiously taking notes while Chris was talking about the importance of working hard. I'll never forget when he said to the group of hungry comedians, "A good example of a hardworking comic is Amy Schumer. She doesn't know it yet, but I am recommending her to be a new face at the Montreal comedy festival." This was all news to me. I was thrilled he even knew my name. I almost started crying, because he was the first person of authority to make it clear to me that he felt I had something special.

I had an open-mic show right after at a bar. I stepped outside in the rain to head over and it was like that scene in *Fifty Shades of Grey* after Anastasia meets Christian. Yes, I saw it, and so did you. Except I wasn't feeling this way about a hot guy who was going to be dominating me and fucking me in every hole. I was feeling this way about comedy. I don't remember how that open mic went or if any of my jokes worked that night. I just remember feeling like I was flying, knowing that it didn't matter how that show went. All twenty people in the audience could have stonewalled me; I wouldn't have cared. I had major adrenaline running through my veins, and I believed I had a real chance to make it. I didn't know what that meant, but I could feel something was coming.

Soon after, in 2006, I got a college agent. I'd be paid $100 to open for other comedians at universities—sometimes traveling for eight hours to get to one. My first college show was at Bryn Mawr in Pennsylvania, where I opened for a comic named Kyle Dunnigan. Half the crowd walked out during my set, and the other half walked out during his. Kyle is now, ten years later, one of my very best friends and has been a writer on my TV show for four years. He is one of the funniest people I know.

By the end of 2006 I started headlining colleges. The day I found out I was going to be making $800 for one hour, I was running laps in my Brooklyn apartment, thinking to myself, *Would I be this happy if I ever had a baby?* I think the answer was no. After that, I got to do a seven-minute special on a Comedy Central show called *Live at*

Gotham. I killed, and blacked out from excitement. I couldn't believe I was getting to do stand-up on television after only two and a half years.

And then the most unlikely thing of all happened when I auditioned for NBC's program *Last Comic Standing*, an *American Idol*–type reality show for comics that was about to tape its fifth season. I didn't think I had a chance. I thought if I got lucky they might use my audition footage as part of a montage in the first episode, or that maybe I would at least lay the groundwork to make it on the show a few years down the road. That was my real thinking. The audition consisted of doing stand-up in front of three judges. After this first round, about two hundred were cut and some thirty people were invited to perform in the next round, which was an evening show to take place that same night. I called my mom and my boyfriend and they came to the show. At the end of the night, they stood us all in humiliating rows on risers to announce who would receive the "red envelopes," which were tickets to Los Angeles to perform in the semifinals. I stood there, knowing I wouldn't get an envelope and that I would have to stay put while they called all the winners down one by one. My face was turning the color of those envelopes. But then they read my name! My eyes bugged out of my head and I ran forward like a contestant being called down on *The Price Is Right*. They handed me my envelope and I couldn't believe it. I couldn't take my eyes off it. I felt like Charlie with his golden ticket. I looked at my mom and my boyfriend. We were all screaming with shock and excitement.

The two months leading up to the semifinals in LA, I worked out hard every day at the gym and did stand-up every single night. I was out in LA all by myself, staying at a hotel with comedians from all over the country and some from around the world. I was so bright-eyed and bushy-tailed. "The hotel has a pool!" I announced around a lunch table full of comics who had been on the road for as long as I'd been alive. Everyone was very nice to me, despite how annoying I must have been. I was the least experienced of the bunch.

When it came time for the big live taping that would determine which ten comics would compete on the show, I was ready. I wore a V-neck shirt from Express and almost no makeup. Someone told me there would be nine hundred people in the audience. The most I had ever performed for was about two hundred. A producer of the show said, "Amy, eight million people will see this on television." But for some reason that didn't matter to me as much as the nine hundred live people who would be sitting in front of me.

I assumed I would be eliminated, so I just promised myself I'd do the best I could and enjoy every second of it—and I did. At the end, when it came time to announce the top ten people who would be competing, my name was read ninth. "Amy Schumer!" I couldn't fucking believe it! I ran out onstage and waved like I had won a pageant. I cried. All that really happened was I made it onto a reality show, which was pretty much just casting. It's not that I was funnier than the rest of the comics. I was just a good "character" for the show. But I knew none of that at the time and I'm so glad I didn't.

Being on that show was so intense and exciting. Each episode consisted of a different challenge, and strangely, I was the most prepped for these challenges. The other comics were seasoned road dogs who were used to relying on their well-crafted jokes and long stories they told doing sixty to ninety minutes headlining sets on the road. But I only had about fifteen minutes of material, and it all worked in little sound bites—so it was perfect for a reality show. I was up for thinking on my feet, and they weren't.

The final challenge determined the top five comics, who got to go on a national tour together—which would have been great for anyone's career, mine especially. It was explained to all of us that the challenge was going to consist of making models laugh. We would go room to room, one at a time, and do a joke or two for them. I remember saying, "Aren't you guys tired of only being appreciated for your brains?" They laughed. A bell went off to indicate that I was supposed to go to the next room. In that next room sat a clown. There were no more models to entertain. The production had of course tricked us, and the next rooms consisted of a drill sergeant, a transvestite, and a nun. I told my Jesus/bad news joke to the nun and she laughed! I did my best but assumed I was going home.

The people from each room voted on their favorite comic, and when we all lined up for the results I was shocked to hear I had won. Thanks to the clown, the nun, the models, and the transvestite, I was going on the tour! I was thrilled for about ten seconds, until one of the comics who also wound up in the top five leaned over to me and said, "You don't deserve it." I ran into the bathroom and cried, because at the time, I believed him. I was paranoid that I hadn't actually been the funniest, that maybe the producers rigged the results in order to keep me on the show, since I was the young female comic who was good for their ratings. They wanted to film me while I cried, but I wouldn't come out of the stall. I refused to be a girl on reality TV sobbing and being a victim. I wanted to be strong. Later, when I watched the episode air, I saw that without question, I'd performed the best. One of the producers, Page Hurwitz, said, "Amy, it wasn't even close. You won." Nothing bad to say about that comic who told me I didn't deserve it, but FUCK THAT GUY, RIGHT?!

I ended up getting eliminated on the next episode, earning myself fourth place on the show, along with the opportunity to tour the country on a giant rock star tour bus with four men in their forties. We performed in forty-two theaters to crowds of about two to four thousand people—the kind of places I'd never performed in before in my life. I bombed pretty much every single night. Forty-two cities, and I think I ate it in about forty of them. I wasn't ready; I didn't have the road work under my belt. You can fake it for seven minutes—even fifteen if you're charismatic enough—but when you're doing nearly a half hour, people are going to see what you're made of, and at that point I was made of less than three years. Not only was I short on material, I wasn't confident about my jokes yet, because I shouldn't have been. I didn't have the experience to sell it up there.

I'd cry in my bunk on the bus. One of the comics said he thought I was talented but wouldn't ever make it as a stand-up. It hurt. Looking back now, I can see clearly how experienced comics can get bitter. It's a tough business, and often things don't work out the way you think they will. But the rage and jealousy comics can feel for others' success is a highly toxic waste of time. I want to go back to those days knowing what I know now and say to that comic, "Focus on your own goals and how to achieve them. No one took your spot, there's room for all of us."

Anyway, the bus and hotel life on that tour was hard for me. I was lonely and not doing well. One night, after a show, I got on an elevator and a little old woman said, "Which floor?" and I didn't know. I started crying because I couldn't remember where I was. This sad moment is something most road comics, and I'm assuming musicians, can relate to. I had no idea how frequently this would happen to me over the years. It happens all the time.

But even though it was difficult, that tour was also my personal comedy boot camp. I'd logged enough hours bombing and sweating onstage that my molecules were permanently altered. Stand-up recalibrates your fear sensors. It thickens your skin in ways that come in handy all the time. Clocking so many hours under all those lights, while people in the crowd are viewing every expression and hearing every inflection, hanging on every word, just waiting to be moved by you (or to boo you) . . . This experience over and over again can only make you stronger. I think for anyone to become good at something, they have to fail a lot too. And they have to be completely unafraid to fail or they'll never make it to the next level. I did so bad for so long in front of so many people on that tour that I stopped caring. I got desensitized to crowds not liking my jokes. I lost the protective shell that holds so many of us back, and I just started going for it. This, in turn, made me *own* the crowd. Once you own your jokes and stand by them, you can relax. Being tentative sours the crowd. They see your fear and then they can't laugh. They want to have fun, not worry about your next move. If they have to cringe or feel bad for you, their experience is ruined and they are taken completely out of the moment. Like when you fart during sex: sure, you can finish and go through the motions, but something has been lost. Once I figured this all out and wasn't seeking the audience's approval anymore, they were free to have a good time, relax, and enjoy.

After the tour, I started headlining on my own for about a year, which is what doing well on a reality show will buy you. And then I went back to featuring, which is the middle spot after the emcee and before the headliner. I was on the road for years with Jim Norton and Dave Attell, two of my all-time favorite comics. And the answer is no, neither of them ever even tried anything with me. I should be insulted, but I'm not. It's the ultimate compliment to have someone take you on the road with them. They're saying, "I think you're funny, and I also can stand to hang out and travel with you." Jimmy and his bodyguard, Club Soda Kenny, and I had a blast on the road.

They lived to embarrass me, shouting my name across stores and hotel lobbies, inviting stares from everyone around us—something they knew I hated when I was offstage. They loved making me blush, which I actually did a lot more of in those days. I am such a loud little sassafras onstage, but in real life I like to keep a very low profile, and those guys took every opportunity to destroy any hope I had of blending in.

In 2012, I went back to headlining on my own in small clubs with under two hundred seats. I would get paid about $2,000 for seven shows. The weekends would go like this:

- Arrive on a Thursday and have an eight p.m. show.

- Get picked up at five thirty a.m. on Friday to do morning radio. Someone affiliated with the club (sometimes a crackhead) drives you from radio station to radio station. Sometimes there are local news shows to do on camera. If you're lucky it's just two of each. But some clubs fuck you in the ass and you have to do so many. And they say it's to get more tickets sold but it doesn't usually translate to that and is really just promotion for the shitty club.

- Arrive back in your hotel room by eleven a.m. (hopefully, if you're strong enough to refuse going out to breakfast or lunch with the crackhead driver or attention-hungry club owner who snuck on the radio appearance with you).

- Grab an apple and peanut butter from the depressing all-day buffet in the lobby, because you've missed breakfast.

- Desperately try to go back to sleep, but this is impossible because your hotel is in a gross, dangerous neighborhood so the club owner could save $75.

- Use the rusty hotel gym where the chlorine from the neighboring pool burns your eyes.

- Walk to a Red Robin and try to eat healthy even though they have not heard of vegetables in most of the country. So you get a grilled chicken something that comes with garlic bread and ice cream and you realize why Americans are dying.

- Go back to your room and feel utterly alone.

- Text an ex.

- Watch some movie made for TV about a woman who murdered her husband.

- Shower and get ready for your two Friday evening shows. And yes, I know you probably noticed I didn't shower right after the gym but waited 'til evening instead. You do you and I'll do me.

- Do two, sometimes three shows.

- Wake up Saturday morning and repeat a lot of Friday, including working out in the rusty-ass gym again, and hope the red itchy new thing on your knee is a rash from said gym and not from a bedbug.

- Sometimes during the day on Saturday, to pass the time, you go to whatever local attraction there is—a museum, a place where someone famous was shot, or maybe a fort.

- Eat whatever food is local to that city because it is your duty to do so. If you're in Philly, you eat a cheesesteak; if you're in Brooklyn, a cheesecake. If you're in Cincinnati, Skyline Chili; if you're in Tulsa, they don't really have a thing but someone may tell you, "You have to try our pork fried hamburger," or some weird shit. You gotta eat it. Show them some goddamn respect and then tweet them pictures of you on the toilet as a way to say thank you!

- Get ready for your Saturday night shows.

- Do two, sometimes three shows.

- Because you're a girl, you don't hook up after the show. Maybe you have a drink with the staff or maybe you go back to the hotel and get room service if they're still serving it. But usually the hotel you're at doesn't have room service at all.

- Lie awake in bed regretting that you just smoked pot because it's making you think about what you do for a living. *Am I a clown? What do I do? I tell jokes to strangers while they eat nachos.* It weirds you out and you vow not to smoke pot alone on the road anymore.

- The club owner pays you after your last show. It feels like it takes forever for them to total up your share of the money (because it does) and they act like they are doing you a favor. They tell you you didn't make your hundred-dollar bonus even though you could see every seat was filled. Sometimes they hand you a bill and you realize you thought you were eating and drinking for free but you only got 25 percent off the usual tab.

• Fly home early Monday morning and feel good about yourself because you developed fifteen new seconds of your act that weekend.

Even though the road can be brutal, it's the only way to become a stand-up. In order to get good at it, you must get as much stage time as humanly possible. Sure, you can learn how to kill on a shorter set. Maybe you even have a great fifteen minutes. Or maybe you're good at local references in your city and can do really well there. But you have to go out on the road and do every different type of show there is: the one for thirty drunk Harley-Davidson guys at a VFW, the ladies' lunch at the Carlyle, the Christmas party for firemen, the ferry that circles Manhattan, and the comedy festival in Staten Island. You have to do all of it or you will plateau and go nowhere—which is fine if that is what you want to do.

———

I WOULD DO anything for stage time. Actually, let me rephrase that: I have never hooked up with anyone to get ahead in the business. If anything, some people I've dated have set me back. One time my sister overheard one of the bouncers that I've known since I started stand-up say, "Amy's gotten so much work. Wonder how she got it . . ." Then he mimed a dick going into his mouth. I guess I should be angry about this kind of thing, but it couldn't be further from the truth. I've never gotten anything from anyone I've hooked up with, not even a Starbucks gift card—which would have been nice.

During the week between road gigs, when I was home in New

York, I began performing at the Comedy Cellar. That's the club you see on the show *Louie* and in lots of documentaries about comics. I was "passed there" in 2007, which means I got to audition for the booker. I don't know the origin of this terminology, but only in the comedy world would people use such a morbid verb to signify the best thing that could happen to your career. Anyway, if the booker likes you, they then ask you to provide your availability for doing shows. If they don't like you, they say no thanks. I auditioned at the Cellar on my birthday, and Estee, who's been the booker there forever, gave me the phone number to "call in my avails," and I lost my mind I was so excited. I remember celebrating that night and getting so drunk that I got a piggyback ride from the bouncer at the bar and spent most of the night riding around back and forth, laughing and singing.

There is a restaurant upstairs from the Comedy Cellar called the Olive Tree Cafe and there is a booth in the back reserved for comedians. I was hesitant to sit there for years. Once I did, I'd stay quiet. Eventually, over time, I got more and more comfortable, and now it's the place I feel most at home in the whole world—sitting around the table with my best friends. I'm happiest when the table consists of Jimmy Norton, Keith Robinson, Colin Quinn, Rachel Feinstein, and Bobby Kelly. And sometimes we can convince Bridget Everett to stop by. We all trash each other, eat wings, and laugh. When someone dies or gets hurt we cry and laugh again. Doing stand-up and being with comics is home for me. Yes, it was completely thrilling to get my own TV show and to write and star in a movie. But getting onstage to do live comedy will always be what I chase harder than anything else.

Eventually, all my work on the road landed me some specials for TV. I had a half-hour special on Comedy Central in 2010 and then an hour special (*Mostly Sex Stuff*) in 2012. Through all of this, I stayed on the road, always touring, always writing more jokes. This is the only way to get better. I started selling more tickets in the clubs, and then small theaters, and then large theaters that seated about nine hundred people, just like in the semifinals of *Last Comic Standing*.

The skills I developed from doing so much stand-up are the same ones I needed to write a movie and play a lead character who was based on myself. My having been onstage all these years with so many eyes on me as I degrade myself nightly is the reason my pulse doesn't change when Internet trolls try to ruin my day, every other day. One of the things I'm still most proud of is my one-hour HBO special (*Amy Schumer: Live at the Apollo*) and the fact that I got to work with Chris Rock as the director. I never would have been able to work with him if I hadn't been brave enough to ask. We'd been friendly for years, seeing each other at the Comedy Cellar, but I never wanted to bother him—because he is Chris Rock. Then one night we talked after we'd both performed on *Night of Too Many Stars*, an event to raise money for autism. My set had been strong, and Chris stopped by the greenroom and offered to help me if I ever needed it. Which sounds creepy, but it's not. He said exactly what he meant. When you have the disease of being a comic, and you see someone else with some talent and respect for comedy, you want to help. It's in his veins. It's in my veins. A little later, I called his bluff, which was anything but. He started riding around and going to clubs with me to watch my set, give me notes, and help me get better.

One day I just bit the bullet and texted him, "Will you direct my HBO special?" Again, this is the kind of confidence you can only get after years of making a clown of yourself onstage and being met with crickets. When Chris said yes, I couldn't believe it. He came on the road with me and made my set a thousand times better. Getting to work on jokes with him felt like my Make-A-Wish. I know that's not a kind comparison to make. But there is nothing else I can think of that would communicate how significant this time was to me.

One of the greatest moments of my career was hosting *Saturday Night Live*. I'm sure a lot of stand-ups dream of doing that opening *SNL* monologue. I know I have since I was a little girl. You write, rehearse, and perform the show in one week. That's all you get. One surreal, supercharged week to live your dream. One week to rush around the crowded hallways in that historic building. Nothing in my career has felt more exciting. But I won't lie, it was a grueling seven days—one that can definitely be described as athletic. You barely sleep, you constantly eat (well, I did), and you do nothing all week but write, rewrite, rehearse, try on wigs, get sewn into costumes, film promos, pose for photo shoots, rewrite, consider showering, choose sleep over showering, do table reads, rehearse, and repeat. And on the night of the show itself, you are literally running or rushing for the entire hour and a half. Stand-up comedy is live performance, sure, but *SNL* is live performance on meth.

By Saturday night, I was definitely the walking wounded, but I'd never been happier. My very favorite scene was one that Vanessa Bayer and Mikey Day wrote about two overly chipper flight attendants (played by me and Vanessa) who sing the in-flight service announcements before they are suddenly sucked out of the plane—one at a time. Live television doesn't allow for stunt doubles, so Vanessa and I had to actually hurl ourselves out of this plane door in order to make the scene work. I am a clown at heart, and my competitive-volleyball past didn't hurt, so I had no problem going for it. But Vanessa was a little more tentative. I wanted nothing more than to open the entire show with this sketch, so I grabbed her by the shoulders and I said, "Vaness! We are going to have to hurt ourselves, okay?!"

After rehearsing several times, we both felt pretty confident about the stunt. But then on Friday, the set builders moved the airplane onto a platform, which in turn lowered the clearance of the door we were jumping through by a full eight inches. *No problem,* I thought, stupidly confident. Vanessa was up first to try jumping through the new door, and she did, perfectly. But when it was my turn, I bricked my head right into the door. Everyone gasped as I lay on the mat, unmoving. My first thought was, *I will have to do this show with scabs all over my face and a bump on my forehead.* My second thought was, *Let's do this fucking thing again. We have to get it right!* By this point in my career, I had become a pro at falling face-first and getting up stronger. They iced my face and gave me some Advil, and we rehearsed it a dozen more times. I went harder every time I flew through that door and smashed into the mat. And it was worth it. My shoulder hurt for four months after, but that scene is my favorite sketch I've ever put on tape.

After being on one of the most historic stages and having the best night a comic could have in front of a live audience of millions, I woke up the next morning, ready to get back on the road. My episode of *Saturday Night Live* and my HBO special aired within seven days of each other, so getting back on the road was more important than ever. I'd burned all my jokes on those two events—meaning they'd aired on TV to massive audiences, so I couldn't use them anymore because people would know them now. Unlike musicians, comedians are expected to always bring new shit. No one wants to hear the greatest hits, so I was back to square one. This requirement of comedy is exhausting and challenging, but I wouldn't have it any other way. It's exciting and humbling to have to start over—and the payoff is even better. You feel so accomplished when you've accumulated enough material—one joke at a time—for an entire special. And when you're back to zero, it doesn't matter who you are, you're starting the fuck over. It's the scariest, emptiest feeling in the world. Even the greatest, most seasoned comics are afraid they'll never write a great joke again. But you do the work.

And that means hitting the road and getting onstage. I know I'm repeating myself, but it's my number one piece of advice to comics who are just starting out when they ask me how to become successful. Get onstage! If there isn't a comedy room in your town, produce one! Find a place with a stage and a mic and stand in front of people as much as possible. Log as many hours as you can. I still do this. I'm not bullshitting you: the money is good now, but even on my nights off, I am still onstage in shitty little rooms, rock clubs, jazz halls, wherever. Always working hard to get better. I became obsessed a long time ago, and it has never dulled.

No matter how hard you work or how sharp you keep yourself, your popularity and ticket sales will ebb and flow, but I'm very proud to say that right now, as I write this in 2016, I'm touring arenas, doing stand-up for crowds of ten to fifteen thousand people. I'm telling jokes where NBA and NHL games are played. I sold out Madison Square Garden! (I can't believe I just typed that.) For these arena shows, I have the same opening comic, Mark Normand, with whom I've worked with the past seven years. My brother, Jason, also opens the show with his jazz trio, which means I get to hang out on the road with his wife, Cayce, who is one of my best friends and helped edit this book. Their daughter, my niece, hangs out backstage with us. Sometimes my sister, Kim, and her husband, Vinny, are there too. I get to stay in nice hotels and have a tour bus or fly first class or sometimes even travel via private jet. I feel extremely lucky, and I know better than to get too comfortable or think it will last forever.

But I love every minute of it right now. It feels so great to walk out onstage after Mark says my name, to hug him and look at the crowd and give them everything I've got. I vow every night before I go on to do the best show I've ever done. I still bomb, I still kill. Either way, the crowd will let you know the truth. It's masochistic and it's noble. And I never want to stop.

TIMES IT'S OKAY FOR A MAN TO NOT MAKE A WOMAN COME DURING SEX

1. If she's a hooker and the next guy is waiting, but even then, check with her.

2. If she's in a rush and tells you she doesn't have time.

3. If you're on an airplane or anywhere in public. If you get away with having sex in public, get in and get out. But make sure you take care of her when you get home.

4. If you realize that your kids or parents will walk into the room. But again, take care of her later.

5. If she gets a cramp or if she gets hungry.

Note: It is okay to not make a woman come during sex if you made her come before it. I am someone who can't really come from penetration. So I hope you enjoy a nice visit with my clit before the main event!

THE WORST NIGHT OF MY LIFE

Here we go, it's time to tell you about Dan, who has already come up in this book. I thought he was the love of my life for a long time but I allowed him to hurt me in ways that I still don't understand. I met him when I was eighteen years old, and I liked him right away. He'd take his clothes off for no reason and run around without shame. We had a lot in common, especially the shameless-nudity part. I think nudity has the potential to be both beautiful and hilarious, so when given the chance, I pull a Porky Pig on my TV show, which basically means that whenever a scene allows, I'll rock out in a long "boyfriend" shirt with no pants or underwear. Anyway, Dan wasn't interested in a relationship with me, and I pretended I wasn't interested in one with him either.

Dan was fascinating to me. He grew up in Manhattan in an incredible loft and got shipped off to boarding school at thirteen. He was a bad kid—lots of detention and sex. New York City kids don't really drink underage like Long Island kids. Instead they do drugs and bang each other to feel like adults. He effed any girl who would hold still long enough for him to come. Or at least that's how he described it to me. But bad kid or not, I felt he was misunderstood and that I was the *one* person who could really love him. Which, as you know by now, was my cup of tea through most of my twenties.

The first night I slept with him was at his mom's place in NYC. The apartment was incredible—huge, with high ceilings, and decorated impeccably. There was so much about him and his home that was "cool" to me. It was "cool" that, at night, when he came downstairs to let me in the building, he was barefoot and in his underwear. Barefoot on the pavement in Manhattan. It was "cool" he had a Dexter Gordon poster in his room. And it was "cool" that he knew about art. His family friends were famous, culturally elite people. This was thrilling to me. I wanted no part of my suburban upbringing anymore, and I was smitten with him and the life he was projecting. I knew we were meant to be together, but he wasn't convinced that I was the girl for him. Maybe it was because the only poster I had in my room was of Ani DiFranco, and if you asked me who our family friends were, I would have said the Muppets. Or maybe it was just that Dan was a real don't-want-to-join-any-club-that-would-have-me-as-a-member type of guy. But I was playing the long game, and I took my time winning him over. I even drove him cross-country when he moved to the West Coast. We were twenty years old driving a U-Haul across America, and by the time we got to Vegas, he was mine. I could feel the shift in him when I'd finally worn him down. He could see the look in my eyes, which said: you. are. mine. bro.

We were together, and we were running low on money, but he still decided to buy a pair of Gucci sunglasses from an outlet store. Red flag? I chose not to notice those sorts of fun little quirks. I thought that because his parents were rich, he was rich. This was a puzzle I didn't fully solve until a year later when I was living with him and had to peddle that horrible pedicab around town so we had grocery money, which he proceeded to spend on alcohol.

And yes, when we were still in Vegas, he screamed at me at the top of his lungs and shook me so hard that I had to run and hide until he calmed down. It was the first time I saw this behavior from him. I'd never seen him even a little upset before. And how did I reward that behavior?

I moved in with him a year later. We lived together for one summer on the West Coast when I was just twenty-one. We had an apartment up on a hill and very close to the beach. Every day, I'd wake up early and teach a kickboxing class at the Y, then go play in a female beach volleyball doubles league, then meet up with him and drink and fight and fuck. It was everything you could want, if what you want is Penélope Cruz and Javier Bardem's relationship in *Vicky Cristina Barcelona*. And if you didn't see that movie, I was the Whitney to his Bobby. (Quick shout-out: I loved Whitney so much and still can't believe she's gone.)

Anyway, Dan and I would go to happy hours with friends and get drunk, and then he'd get mad at me and shove me a little. Sometimes, from the shove, I'd trip over something and fall, and get hurt. But of course it was an accident. I got hurt by accident a lot that year. He'd get jealous about something I did and would squeeze my arm too hard and I'd get a horrible bruise. But of course it was an *accident*, and he always felt terrible afterward. I'd comfort him and we'd move on until the next time it happened. But it's not like I was in an abusive relationship, right? I mean, I wasn't a passive girl. I've been easily standing up for myself for as long as I could talk. I'm the girl who would bully the bullies in middle school—defend the kids who got made fun of. I'd always prided myself on being strong, assertive, and independent. It couldn't happen to me, right?

On a regular basis, Dan would say things to me I didn't let any-one else say—passively hurtful things to let me know I wasn't as pretty as the other women he'd dated. He'd point out areas of my legs and arms and stomach he thought I needed to work on. He'd pull the shower curtain open and laugh at my naked body. Once he even pissed on my legs and feet while laughing. I'd cry and go for a walk and we'd start over. But come on, I was smart and funny and a loudmouth who spoke her mind. I definitely wasn't in an abusive relationship, right? That only happens to girls who don't believe in themselves. Right?

It proceeded to get worse and worse, and I started escaping the apartment whenever I could. I'd go to Starbucks, lock myself in the bathroom, and sit on the floor and cry. I knew I should go back to the East Coast, but I thought no one would ever love me as much as he did. I believed he was just as passionate about me as I was about him, and that if I did a better job of not making him mad, we'd be fine. I really felt he loved me. And I really loved him. I think some-where in the course of our relationship, I started to confuse his anger and aggression for passion and love. I actually started to think that real love was supposed to look like that. The more you yelled at each other, the more you loved each other. The more physical and demeaning it got, the more you were really *getting through* to each other. And the more I was willing to stand by him, the more he'd understand I truly loved him and that we should be together forever. And he always felt so bad about what he'd done after he shouted or bruised me. Surely he wouldn't beat himself up so much if he didn't love me so much. It's not abusive if they feel really bad afterward and promise to love you the rest of your life, right? Right?

Wrong. Knowing what I know now, it's clear as day. Of course. And being frightened and hurt and abused isn't reserved for insecure women who are easily intimidated, or women who come from unstable environments, or women who have never seen a positive male role model. I learned from a TED talk about domestic violence by Leslie Morgan Steiner (these are mostly her words) that women of all income and education levels are affected. I also learned that I was a typical domestic violence victim because of my age. In the United States, women ages sixteen to twenty-four are three times more likely to be domestic violence victims than women of any other age. Also, every year in the United States, five hundred women in this age bracket are killed by their domestic abuser. A domestic abuser doesn't just have to be someone you live with. It means anyone you are in an intimate relationship with. I was a statistic.

What made things so confusing with Dan was that we usually had the best time. We were manic together. He was obsessed with me in a way that made me feel high. We had sex several times a day. I thought it was because I turned him on so much, but I now believe it was because it was a way for him to have my undivided attention. We'd laugh until we were in tears, fuck, pledge our undying love, and then the next moment we'd be in shouting turmoil and he'd be screaming at me and squeezing me too hard.

One humid summer night we went out with our friends to a new bar. We were all dressed up and excited to get into the new hot spot. I love dancing—always have, always will. Am I good at it? Nope! But that has never stopped me. I grabbed my girlfriend and we hit the floor. Sometimes Dan would dance, but on this evening, I think because I'd talked all day about how excited I was, he wanted to sour it a little. I dance like all other white girls: in a sexually suggestive way that says, "This is what it would be like to mount me." It's completely false advertising. Also, I don't do it well, and over the years several black people have pointed this out to me—to my face.

Anyway, my girlfriend and I were gyrating and body-rolling on the dance floor when out of nowhere Dan came up and grabbed my arm. He didn't like how the guys in the bar were looking at me, and he thought I was flirting with them. I left the dance floor and we drank and drank, and kissed in a booth, and then the song "Real Love" by Mary J. Blige came on, and you know I had to dance to that. It's like a law that all women turn into the Manchurian Candidate when that song comes on.

A guy came up to me on the dance floor who I would have bet my life was gay. We sang the song and danced together. We were giggling and half grinding but made no actual contact. It was totally innocent. Dan walked past me on the dance floor on his way to the bathroom and whispered in my ear, "You're disgusting." I was furious. I thought, *I'll show you disgusting*, and began to dance very sexually with another guy on the floor. When Dan came out of the bathroom he again dragged me to the booth. And that was when I did something that I'd never done before and never, ever, will do again: I spit right in his face. I don't know if I thought I was a character in *West Side Story* or if it was just the booze that gave me major balls, but I did it. And this maneuver awakened the beast in Dan and fired off my fear signal in one instant. He got a look in his eyes that scared the shit out of me, and I ran. I ran right out the door of the bar and I kept running.

I ran to our friend's house down the street, but he caught up to me. I tried to calm him down and I told him that it was probably better if we spent the night apart to cool off. That was the smart thing to do, and he was smart, so I was sure he'd agree, maybe call me a bitch, then storm away. Right? No, the smart thing did not happen. Instead, when I got out my phone to call my friend, he grabbed it out of my hand and whipped it at a nearby tree, where it shattered. He put his hands on my cheeks and squeezed my face hard. My head was throbbing, and I could tell this night was different. I wasn't safe. And I knew it.

I told him I was going to walk to my friend's house and asked him to leave me alone. He wouldn't. He followed me. My heart was pounding while I listened to his footsteps behind me on the quiet side streets. I kept walking and walking, and then for a second I didn't hear his footsteps. But it was too late when I realized he was right behind me. I tried to pick up the pace, and this pissed him off, and he pushed me onto the hood of a parked car. I banged my head and my elbow hard. This was more than he'd done before. This was an actual violent outburst. I didn't get hurt "by accident" this time. He saw the car right there and pushed me onto it intentionally. I burst into tears, kicked my shoes off, and ran down the street as fast as I could, listening to my own breath, trying to slow down my heart rate like my volleyball coach had taught me. I think Dan had surprised himself.

I heard voices coming from a nearby backyard and I ran into the open front door of this random house, sobbing, with no shoes on, makeup running down my face and a welt on my head that was already becoming a bruise. I staggered into the living room, and there sat about eight *Breaking Bad*–looking huge Hispanic gang members. They had bandanas and tattoos, they were not fucking around, and they definitely did not want me there. I begged them to let me use the phone to call my friend and promised I'd then leave. Naturally, they made me promise not to call the cops.

I heard Dan screaming for me through the screen door, and at that moment I realized that being with the gang felt infinitely more safe than being with Dan did. But I quickly understood that my presence threatened to get them caught doing whatever it was they were doing. Some of the guys went outside to try to get Dan to leave, but he was causing a real commotion and standing his ground. I ran outside to get him to quiet down, and he got into a fistfight with one of the gang members until his eye and lip were bleeding. As the guy was pounding Dan with his fist, I instantly switched teams and began to defend Dan. When you are an abuse victim, your logic and instinct can become warped like this. It was similar to the night in high school when I realized Jeff was helping himself to my virginity, and I ended up comforting him for hurting me, even though it should have been the other way around. Here I was defending another guy who was actively betraying me. "Get off of him!" I yelled, running toward Dan, who was taking a serious beating. The gang members kicked us both off their property, fearing the cops would come.

We walked to his car in silence. Dan had seemingly calmed down. He was even laughing a little, talking about how crazy the night had been, and so I did too. I wanted to comfort him and make him feel like we were in this together. We got into the car, and I drove the fifteen minutes home. The events had sobered me right up. I tried to keep him calm. That was my only goal. He mentioned ordering food when we got home, and I let him know in a very collected, kind way that I wasn't going to stay at our apartment that night.

And there it was again. The beast reawakened right before my eyes, the same beast I'd seen earlier that night, but this time, it was much angrier. He started banging his head against the window and screaming. He took my hand and used it to punch himself in the face. He broke the side mirror with his own hand, and I was scream-crying, begging, pleading with him to stop. I agreed to sleep at home if he'd stop hurting himself. It was a bad idea to negotiate with him like that, because what came after I agreed to sleep at home was so much worse.

When we got home, I went inside and got right into bed. I was exhausted and just wanted the night to be over. I had nothing left. I begged him to leave me alone so I could sleep. But he kept tormenting me, sitting and staring at me. He shook the bed to scare me, saying, "I don't want you to go to sleep." I told him we'd talk in the morning but I really needed to rest. I told him that if he wouldn't let me sleep I was going to leave. He was quiet for a couple minutes. I closed my eyes, and then opened them again to see him standing over me, staring. I told him that was it and got up to leave. He ran to the kitchen and broke a mug—not a glass, a *mug*—over his head, and then started banging his head on a light fixture attached to the ceiling. It wouldn't break. I was screaming for him to stop, when he grabbed a huge butcher knife from a drawer. And that's when I was sure he was going to kill me. It may sound clichéd, but I saw my life flash before my eyes. I thought, *This is how I die? I can't believe it.* I thought about my sister and my mom finding out that this was how I'd checked out. This thought awoke the beast in *me*. This was my moment of clarity. I had to get away from him. Fast.

I threw a glass against the wall as a diversion and raced out the door, running through our apartment complex, banging on all the doors, begging for someone to let me in. It was just like *American Psycho*, him chasing me and gaining on me at every turn. I knocked on five different unanswered doors before one opened up, and I flung myself inside, locking the door behind me. Dan immediately started pounding on the door. I looked up at the elderly man who'd let me in and said, "Thank you so much, I need to call the police." I'd seen this guy around the complex for months, mostly shuffling to the Dumpster and back, and we'd wave once in a while. He had a bushy mustache and eyebrows that were salt-and-pepper colored, like his hair. He looked like a cartoon. It was the second stranger's house I'd entered that night. I remember thinking to myself, *How much worse can it get than the Latin Kings' headquarters?*

It was worse. I breathed the air in the apartment and it was stale and vaguely smelled like sewage. I noticed that his wife, whom I'd never seen before, was in a hospital bed near the window. Her arms and legs had been amputated and her mouth was cocked open, head to the side. I still don't know if she was alive or not, but I think so. It was a terrifying and disorienting scene. I went to the bathroom, which was full of furniture and filth, and locked myself inside with their phone. I called a cab and stayed in there until it arrived.

I walked outside, numb, when the cab pulled up. Dan was still out there, but he'd calmed down too. I could have called the cops on him. I could have pressed charges. But I didn't want to. I felt bad for him, seeing him standing there alone. I worried about how he'd feel the next day. Even after all Dan had put me through, I couldn't dream of having him arrested. But I did finally see my situation for what it was—a case of domestic abuse. I was finally able to empathize with the millions of other women who'd been in this same situation. I was them and they were me.

I took the cab to the house of a couple that I knew. They let me sleep upstairs, and the guy of the couple slept next to their front door with a bat, which I'm still very grateful for. I flew back to New York the next day, still worried about Dan and how he might be feeling. I knew he'd feel awful and lonely and would be in a lot of pain, but I was choosing to live. I thought a lot about my sister and how I wanted be the kind of person who made her proud. I couldn't face her if I stayed another day with a man I believed would eventually kill me.

The next awful chapter of this story—and something that it pains me to tell you—is that we got back together one more time after that, during the New York City blackout of 2003. (In that heat, I would have fucked a salamander.) It wasn't for very long, but the loneliness of New York City and my feelings for him weakened me. I think I reunited with him because I still longed to be close to him. And I wanted to punish him for hurting me so much in the past. I thought I could do more damage from the inside. I was his girlfriend, which meant I had free rein to criticize him and point out why he was the worst. I'm not proud of that. But there was a part of me that wanted to be with him again so I could hurt him back.

We finally broke up a few months later and said good-bye to each other one morning when I was fully able to see him for who he really was. I could see that he presented to the world the facade of a certain kind of man who wasn't really there. He had the poster, but he couldn't name one Dexter Gordon album. He said he loved me, but every step of the way he'd hurt and sabotage me. I realized later that he put me down so much because he was probably terrified that I'd realize he was nothing and leave him. Which is exactly what I did.

I'm telling this story because I'm a strong-ass woman, not someone most people picture when they think "abused woman." But it can happen to anyone. When you're in love with a man who hurts you, it's a special kind of hell, yet one that so many women have experienced. You're not alone if it's happening to you, and you're not exempt if it hasn't happened to you yet. I found my way out and will never be back there again. I got out. Get out.

THINGS THAT MAKE ME INSANELY FURIOUS

1. People who run down mountains. Have you ever been hiking and had someone run past you downhill? I secretly root for them to tumble to their—as far as I'm concerned—timely death.

2. Girls with their hair down at the gym. Unless you're covering horrible burn marks like that girl from *The Craft*, pull that shit up in a ponytail.

3. Couples working out together are vile. You can't spend one hour apart? Also, the guy showing the submissive girl how to do everything makes me retch.

4. People who act like the mayor of the fucking gym. I don't even smile at people I know at the gym because all I want to do is leave the whole time. If I make eye contact with someone I know and they look away immediately, I know they are a great person and I feel very close to them.

5. Apparently the gym and all forms of exercise, based on the first four items on this list.

6. Also, people named Jim. Because it sounds like the word "gym."

7. People who misspell the word "you're" when telling me I'm fat ("your fat").

8. People who stand too close to you while you're in line for something. Make like Onyx and bacdafucup. I wish everyone was a football field away at all times, but I understand this isn't possible, so please, just give me six inches. But twelve would be great. (No penis puns here.)

9. Clear-cut mail-order-bride situations where the guy is disgusting and the woman is beautiful and seems trapped. I pray that these women find a way to steal the man's money and run off with it.

10. Radio commercials. Every single one ever.

11. People who say "I eat to live. I don't live to eat." I wish all ten plagues upon your house.

12. Guys who don't make sure the girl comes.

13. Really drunk people. You may be thinking, *Amy, you fucking hypocrite*. But I'm not. I love drinking, but I almost never get fucking hammered anymore. Not much anyway, since college. Even when I would black out in college, no one ever knew. My speech was just a little slurred.

14. Okay, you were right; number 13 was fucked up for me to say. I do get drunk. But still, you shouldn't.

15. Watercress.

16. People who look up, like at the ceiling, when they talk. Unless a pigeon has flown onto a chandelier above my head, look down here.

17. Also, birds inside. Any bird in an airport or mall or anything makes me out of my mind, crazy furious.

18. Selective outrage.

19. Drivers who floor it when a light turns green and then brake hard at a red light. I lie to a lot of Uber drivers and tell them I'm pregnant so they will drive safer. They don't know I'm not and really neither do I. I guess I could be.

20. *The Big Bang Theory.* (The TV show, not the theory.)

21. People who judge me as a sinner. Fuck you.

22. Hotel-room deodorizers. They plug in these huge machines that make all the rooms smell the same and it's all like baby powder and funerals. It makes your eyes water and your skin itch.

23. People who talk too loud in public. I have yelled at strangers. I will say "shhhhh" and no one is exempt. I once shushed Vin Diesel.

24. People with egos that don't let them acknowledge the truth.

25. Black jelly beans. Also, black licorice makes me mad but not furious.

26. House music. It is the worst. I love going out and dancing to hip-hop but it's almost impossible to find a place that plays it anymore because they have all been replaced by this horrible excuse for music.

27. Celebrity DJs and bad-boy chefs. Questlove doesn't count. He is a drummer and an amazing DJ.

28. Grown women wearing jean shorts that are small enough to be a diaper, because I can't come close to being able to rock them. I need a denim burka at this point.

29. Talking to anyone I don't know on an elevator. (I guess this counts as small talk, which I've mentioned several times as something I detest, but it's even more unbearable in an elevator because you're trapped!)

30. People who go to Starbucks to write. Yuck.

31. People who bring a book to a bar deserve to be stoned. Don't try to look mysterious and interesting. You are reading in a bar.

32. People who eat impeccably healthy. Fuck you!!!!

33. Most kids who aren't my niece. Some kids are cute, but most need to tone it right on down.

34. Guys who try to flirt with you even though you give clear motherfucking indicators that you are not interested. JUST STOP!!!!

35. Girls who act like prudes. We've all had to clean cum off our skin while making eye contact with ourselves in the mirror.

36. Guys who don't like to have sex a lot. At least twice a week or get out of here. (I know I should be sympathetic, but I have no patience for that.)

ATHLETES AND MUSICIANS

I recently came into contact with the hugest dick you can imagine. And when I say "hugest dick," I mean largest penis. I don't mean he was a dick. But I'm getting ahead of myself. So, let me back up and properly introduce this as the chapter where I will tell you in major detail about hooking up with a few athletes and a musician. I am telling you because I think you may find it interesting. And also because even though we all know there is no holy grail of a person who will finally be the key to our everlasting confidence, because we are all just damaged little children, we still hope that someone who is killer with a guitar or puck will hold the key to eternal self-love at the tip of their tip. No? Just me? Well, read along anyway.

I will not name names. Right now, maybe you're thinking: *Fuck you, Amy!! I bought this stupid book and I want to know who these dudes are!* I hear you. I want to tell you so bad. It makes it a lot funnier having a face and name to go along with these terribly disappointing tales. But I can't do that. It's not a legal matter. It's just that I would personally like to have more sex in my life, and what guy in his right mind would get down with me if he knew he and his penis might end up in my next book?

Also, if we ever meet in person I'll probably tell you the actual names of these athletes and musicians. But in the meantime, let's start with the first athlete I hooked up with, who was a lacrosse player, of all sports. I'd been going through a particularly lonely time. As I write that, I realize every single one of the hookups mentioned in this chapter was a direct response to a breakup. I've learned the lesson that the grieving process after a breakup will not be sped up by hooking up with someone else. The way I usually advise my friends is by saying, "It's gonna take time. Let's just watch movies and go on long walks." But I don't tend to follow my own advice. I also sometimes tell a good girlfriend, "You need to have sex with someone." Are you noticing a pattern, that I am a hypocrite and a flake?

Anyway, about this lacrosse player . . . We were both newly single and he was better looking than me and from a wealthy family, but he could apparently stomach fucking me, which is literally how it felt when we had sex. I was funnier and smarter than him, but that didn't matter to me at the time. What mattered in that moment was that he was cute and he had a working penis. We went on a couple dates, which had all the excitement of watching toenail polish dry on a cadaver.

During dinner, I felt the way you always hear men supposedly feel when women are talking. I was enduring it, pretending to laugh at his jokes, letting him ask me a lot of lame questions you'd expect to hear during a job interview, such as "Where do you see yourself in five years?" He asked, if I could have lunch with anyone living or dead, who would it be? I answered, Mark Twain. To which he said, "No, it has to be someone real." And still, without even thinking twice, I went home with him. When we kissed, there was absolutely no chemistry, which confirmed our mutual lack of interest in one another. And yet from sheer muscle memory our bodies were still able to have inter-course. I think we hooked up a few times before our different levels of attractiveness and senses of humor caught up to us, and he called to tell me that he'd started seeing someone else. I was shocked that he felt our few unappealing hookups obligated him to notify me he was off the market. I said, "I understand," in as serious a tone as I could muster. We truly did a great job of wasting each other's time.

The next athlete was in the NFL. Which means he played foot-ball. This time I went to the city he lived in, and he came to my hotel. We'd been out three or four times but hadn't hooked up yet, and this was going to be *the* night. He got to my room and we had a drink and I could already feel I didn't want this. I said I was exhausted and needed to go to sleep, and when he kissed me, I just wasn't feeling it. Our chemicals didn't mesh well together. That has happened a couple times in my life, where the kiss just doesn't taste right. It's nothing personal, just science. He grabbed my ass and kissed me and I stopped him and said good night. I made up some excuses about why I couldn't hang out with him until he stopped asking.

Another athlete I dated was the famous professional wrestler I met on Twitter. I know you're probably thinking this would be a good moment to trash wrestling, but I have no interest in doing that. This guy was a true athlete. He was healthier, stronger, and more disciplined than most people who play a sport involving a ball or uni-form. When I met him, I had no interest in wrestling, though I had spent time pretending to like it for guys in the past (see chapter titled "How I Lost My Virginity"). But once I saw professional wrestling behind the scenes, I was amazed by the athleticism and theater of it. Anyway, we met when I was doing a show in Phoenix, Arizona. I was alone in my nice hotel and decided to order some crab cakes. I know what you're thinking: landlocked Arizona is world-famous for its killer seafood and surfing. But I convinced myself it was a low-carb option even though we know that outside Baltimore, Maryland, crab cakes are 99 percent bread. Turns out there was enough *actual* crab in these cakes for me to get the most violent food poisoning you can imagine. I quickly went from being completely healthy and fine to being a convulsing vessel of foul bodily fluids spouting from every orifice of my body. A couple times I had to decide between sitting on the toilet and bending over it to puke. It was a real Sophie's Choice of human waste. (Spoiler alert: there is no happy ending.)

Despite my predicament, I was still convinced I was going to perform that night. I was especially excited because the cute wrestler was going to be in the audience, and so was the comedian David Spade. I wound up lying on the floor of the bathroom in my own puke with the club owner and his kind mother standing over me. I was hallucinating from dehydration and an ambulance was called. Luckily, David Spade is a hero and he did the show for me that night. It's the only show I've ever had to cancel from illness. I once lost my voice in the middle of a set at Governor's Comedy Club on Long Island, but I still didn't leave the stage. Since my mom and I both know sign language, I signed my set to her so she could deliver it to the crowd.

So that night in Phoenix, I ended up having an overnight stay at the hospital. My very kind friend Jackie, who was working with me that weekend, spent the night sitting in a chair next to my hospital bed. When I woke up, I learned that I'd been inundated with countless messages on Twitter that mentioned the wrestler. Turns out the wrestler had led a campaign among his followers to get me to follow him. He had about a million followers, and it felt like I got a tweet from each and every one of them. He had been at the show I missed, so he knew I'd been hospitalized. As I sat there waiting to be released from the hospital, I clicked "follow" on his page and wrote him a direct message: "Okay, I'm following you. What do you want?" He wrote back, "Hi, how are you feeling?" He was really sweet and offered to pick me up from the hospital.

In addition to this very kind gesture, the wrestler was really easy on the eyes—and I figured probably hands—so we started talking and made plans to meet up. We met in Denver, had a nice weekend together, and actually began seeing each other a few weeks later. We did our best to date, despite the fact that we were both on the road all the time and I was still in love with my ex. I once even asked him if I could take a short dating hiatus from him to go to Mexico with my ex and then resume our dating when I returned. He rightfully told me no. I realize that was an insane request but I sometimes forget that a man may actually have real feelings for me.

He was so physically perfect, smart, funny, and kind. But I remember being in some hotel with him, seeing his knee pads drying on the radiator, and thinking I was in the wrong story. Naturally, I got back together with my ex. (Always a great idea.) The wrestler and I are still good friends, and I'll be very happy for whatever lucky lady ends up with him, even though he's a recent ex and I usually wish rare Amazonian skin diseases on their new girlfriends. Which brings me to the musician.

The musician was probably the saddest experience of all. He's famous and I'm a fan. I would never have ever ever ever thought he'd be interested in me. Any of these guys actually—these are dudes who have access to tiny models. But what I've learned is that guys are guys, no matter how famous or hot, and they all basically want to hook up with anyone they're even moderately attracted to who will hold still long enough for them to rub against them. Does that sound like an insult? Because it's actually something that I love about men so much. I love the simplicity of the drive they have to fuck. Their biology is beautiful to me. We ladies work so hard to be attractive for them and we really don't need to. Their driving force is to put their penises in our buttholes. Meanwhile I'm worried if he can see the roots of my highlights. I have thoughts like, *Should I get a French manicure?* HE DOESN'T CARE. HE WANTS TO JAM HIS WIENER IN YOUR POOPER!

Anyway, I met this musician for lunch. I thought we were just friends but he hugged me in a masterful way I will never forget. He slid his hand along my lower back, starting at my hip inside my leather jacket. When he hugged me I realized, *Oh, this is a date.* We were both going through breakups, so we complained about our exes and ate ramen. We were having such a good time that we made plans to meet up later that same evening. I was very much not out of the woods with my feelings for my ex, but revenge-dating a rock star seemed like a pretty good plan.

We met up at the Bowery Hotel and had some drinks. Showing up to this second location for the second date in one day with this guy totally freaked me out. He was now going to be evaluating me as a woman he might want to hook up with, or date, so I of course lost all my self-esteem while I was getting dressed to meet him. I got nervous and I put too much into it. The early hangout was lunch with a friend, but this was a fucking date with a fucking rock star! He commented, "You're like a different person than you were earlier today," immediately detecting my plummeting confidence. We walked around and watched some stand-up comedy at a nearby club. I told him I'd had a great time and tried to say good night, but he talked me into one more drink at the hotel. The bar was closed by then so he suggested we order drinks from room service and went up to his hotel room.

By this point, I'd accepted as fact that there was no way he was attracted to me, and I figured he must have just liked hanging out with me. This is how it's been my whole life. I've always assumed that men see me as just one of the guys, so when someone is interested in me as a girl I am floored. This hang-up has gotten better over time, but it's not completely gone. Anyway, we had a drink in his room and when I got up to hug him good-bye, he kissed me. We didn't have good chemistry but I was flattered, and this was the first person I'd kissed who wasn't my boyfriend in the last four years, so I went with it. We got in bed, we got naked, and I couldn't have been less present. It was like what I would imagine Pat Sajak feels like at this point on *Wheel of Fortune*. If you look deep into his eyes, he is a full-blown zombie.

I could see the two of us like I was out of my body and I felt so sad for us: a rock star and a whatever I am. But no matter who you are, you still feel all the same shit as everyone else. We both missed our exes. We didn't do much of anything. We touched each other and tears started rolling down my cheeks. I wasn't crying but they were just coming out. He noticed and held me. We lay there in the dark, eyes open, listening to each other breathe. I was in so much pain at the time and I could feel his pain too. We didn't judge or want anything from each other. After he fell asleep, I slipped out of the room. I'm grateful he was so sweet and as sad as I was too. I felt less alone for a couple moments, and I'm sure I was the most disappointing hookup of his life. Which I am actually a little proud to say. It's good to stand out, even in that way. He will never forget me!

I'm now seeing a real pattern in these stories: I have been a huge disappointment to hook up with. I've always thought of myself in these hookups as the one who was shortchanged by a bummer guy, but upon further reflection, it seems like it really was me who was the bummer. Interesting. Oh well. No time to unpack that. On to the huge cock.

I want to preface this story by saying I have no interest in hockey. I have gone to a couple games and had fun—but that's mostly because

I went with my sister, and we gave ourselves fake bruises. We only went to Rangers games at Madison Square Garden, and I'd wear a neck brace and two black eyes, and put Band-Aids all over Kim. I don't know why we used to do that, but we liked to look like we had gotten all bloodied. Most people would ignore us and look away as quickly as possible, but some people would ask what happened and we would say we got into a thing with each other.

Kim and her husband love hockey, and they always talk about one of their favorite players. They love how he plays and are always mentioning that he's funny and cool off the ice, too. They bring up this dude all the time with me. He followed me on Twitter, so I followed him back, and when I told my sister he was following me, she flipped out. She was like, "You have to message him! You would love each other!" So I did. I told him he was my favorite player, and I think I said if he ever wanted to come see a stand-up show to let me know. He showed me enough respect not to pretend to be interested in seeing a comedy show and instead asked me if I wanted to get a drink. I said yes and was very excited that Kim would think I was the shit. She never does.

On the day of our date, I went to the location we'd agreed on and waited for nearly forty minutes. He was texting me saying, "Sorry, leaving soon!" I left the place angry but got a text shortly after telling me that he was very sorry and that he would meet me anywhere I wanted. I made him go to Fat Cat, a basement bar in the village that has jazz music and Ping-Pong. When I arrived and saw him from across the room, I realized he was with all of his friends.

So I was now on a group date with a bunch of rowdy guys. I was yelling over the music and trying to communicate with him, but we had all the rapport of the Pope and Rick Ross. We didn't know what to talk about, couldn't hear each other, and didn't understand each other's sarcasm. I finally gave up and started talking to his friends. They were treating me like some whore that their famous athlete friend was gonna bang—which, in their defense, was what I was. Except I didn't have the patience to stick it out. So when he told me that they were going to another bar, I said I wasn't and started to say farewell to my sister's favorite athlete. He said, "Well, no, I'll just go with you then." I was shocked. He didn't even say good-bye to his friends. We went to one more bar on the way home, and I watched him play a dumb golf arcade game and listened to him discuss his dreams and his family. I couldn't believe I was going to hook up with this beautiful, tall, talented guy whom I could barely understand or connect with. He was using hockey terms, thinking I was a huge fan, but I'd only been to a few games in my life and understood nothing. He asked me exactly zero questions about myself, and that was the perfect amount. I wasn't interested in building a future with this guy, I was just sticking around to see if he'd be willing to hook up with *me*. Even though in my eyes we were a physical mismatch on the level of Miss Piggy and Charles Grodin in *The Great Muppet Caper*. Or Kate Hudson and anyone I've ever seen her paired up with. I often feel this way with men who have been willing to be physical with me. Fortunately, most men are driven toward a wet hole more than a perfect face—especially late at night.

We went to his apartment, and he put on the TV show *Workaholics* and went down on me right away. I thought he was such a sweetheart for doing that. I came, thinking he was a prince. But then I saw the reason for his chivalry. He took his dick out and I became a cartoon. My jaw hit the floor. Which, coincidentally, was the only way his dick was going to fit in there. I have a small mouth, and the size of this hog was like nothing I'd ever seen. No way was that going near my vagina. I felt like a musician performing on the deck of the

Titanic, knowing there was nothing I could do but go down. I felt like I was trying to fit an entire Thanksgiving turkey in a toilet paper roll: not happening. He tried to act like his dick wasn't that big, as if it were a normal size and I was just being skittish and weird, but after several attempts, I determined I could not fellate this fellow. Feeling badly, I tried to be a team player and said we could give sex a go. I lay back and tried to think of a more relaxing environment, like Guantá-namo Bay or the shoe display at the Holocaust museum, but it wasn't going to happen. He encouraged me to try to make it fit, to which I said, "I'm not going to try to force it in and deform my pussy just so I can have sex with you once. Sorry, bro. I'd rather not have to pick up my NuvaRing off the subway platform because it keeps falling out of my new gaping vag, courtesy of your endless BFG of a cock." I was making him laugh and this was clearly not his first rodeo with a girl chanting, "Hell no, water buffalo!"

So we did the only classy thing we could do. We made out while I jerked him off in my general direction. When he came, it landed mostly on my stomach. I got up to clean myself off and he said, "Where are you going? You got a mess on you!" and he went to get me a warm washcloth and a dry one. I then watched this member of the NHL clean me very carefully. Maybe he was afraid I'd try to steal his DNA like a hip-hop wife, but it was the sweetest thing to witness. He looked like a little boy working on a science project. I got dressed, and he seemed legitimately confused and sad that I was leaving. He asked if I would stay and watch a movie and when we would see each other again. I felt like we were starring in two different movies. I explained that I had had a great time with him and that we would never see each other again. I did the walk of shame at four thirty a.m. You may be recalling an earlier chapter where I told you I'd only had one one-night stand in my life and thinking this counts as number two. But I don't consider it a one-night stand unless sex occurred. Sex where a penis enters your vagina or butthole. (Why don't I write romance novels? My prose is so arousing!)

I called my sister in the morning from a Starbucks and told her what had happened and we both laughed so hard we were crying. I'd only gone out with him so she'd think I was cool, and that is definitely not what happened. She thought it was the saddest thing she'd ever heard. We still laugh to tears whenever he takes the ice. Does that sound mean? Did you have a moment reading this story when you felt bad for him? Please don't. Please don't shed any tears for this rich, famous, and perfect-looking athlete with a huge cock. He's just fine. He has no doubt had many wonderful sexual experiences aside from with me. He's now married to a gorgeous, tiny woman, and whenever I see pictures of them I think, *Good luck with that, sweetheart!*

LETTER TO THE EDITOR

I've always been a sucker for magazines—even the ones that tell me I am doing everything wrong as a woman. I grew up covering my bedroom walls with magazine photos of Jason Priestley and Luke Perry. I'd steal *Redbook* from my mom and *Mademoiselle* from my dad. Hahaha, just kidding; my dad didn't read *Mademoiselle* but I thought writing that would create a good funny rhythm. *Amy, stop explaining your jokes and get on with it.* I buy and flip through tabloids, which I believe causes cancer. I'll also buy a *Time* magazine if I feel like looking like a genius, and I put it on top of the stack so if anyone sees me, they think, *Hmmm, what a smart, important girl. I wonder what's under that*—Newsweek? The Economist? I can't think of any other smart magazines, which lets you know I'm Long Island trash who came close to not graduating high school.

Anyway, I like magazines on a flight or when I'm laying out on the beach hungover. I've never thought too hard about them, and I definitely never, ever imagined that I'd actually be in them, much less see my face slapped on the cover. My first few appearances in magazines were as a writer. After I'd been doing stand-up for a few years, I started receiving offers to write funny articles for women's magazines. I wrote for *Cosmo* a couple times, and it was really fun. I wrote about things similar to what I'm covering in this book. So when I was asked to write an article for *Men's Health* magazine, I was fired up. I pride myself on being a comic who appeals to both men and women, so I was excited to get exposure in a dudes' periodical as well.

I met with Ryan, an editor of sorts for the magazine. He was forty-five minutes late to our meeting—never a good sign—but he was really apologetic and complimentary of my stand-up, so of course, all was forgiven. We got down to business and brainstormed what I'd write about: sex! My cup of tea. All good in the hood.

Ryan and I started discussing the photo to go along with my article. I had some concepts I thought were pretty funny: me holding a copy of the magazine with a front cover that read "The Daddy Issue," or me dressed as a sad stripper next to a "No Jokes in the Champagne Room" sign. Ryan laughed at my sick ideas and said he'd pass them along to the art department.

Over the next month and a half we settled on the finished piece. A few weeks later I was backstage getting ready to film the stand-up portion of my pilot for Comedy Central when I got an email from Ryan putting me in touch with the fact-checker about one last sidebar. And that's when I saw the layout of the article. It was accompanied by three huge pictures—and I couldn't help but notice that *not one of them was me*. Each one featured a very slender, heavy-titted model, whose ages ranged from old enough for military service to too young to rent a car.

Minutes later I had to go onstage in front of cameras under bright-ass lights and tell jokes that were supposed to be funny and empowering, but all I wanted to do was throw in the towel and switch to the path that *Men's Health* obviously saw for me. This path probably involved writing in a broom closet for the rest of my life or standing at the bottom of a hole putting lotion on my skin that they dropped down in a bucket for me. Or at least that's how they made me feel. I could just hear them saying, "Schumer's a very fun girl. Bright, with a face for podcasting."

I emailed Ryan and asked about the pictures, and his reply was something along the lines of, "Sorry, it wasn't my call! Now's the time we really need you to sign off on that sidebar."

I was brushed off. And even though I can imagine everyone at *Men's Health* shaking their heads and saying, "Ugghh, just another crazy homely woman creating problems because she's not hot enough," I told him I wouldn't do any more work until I got some answers. So Ryan—who was really a nice guy, just doing his job, probably—put me in touch with the editor, a man I'll call Jake. And here is the reply I got.

Hey Amy—

Just read your note to Ryan, and I apologize if there's been any confusion over the art treatment for your story. In fact, we very rarely run author images with any story, and that applies equally to Amy Schumer and Jonathan Safran Foer and Jesse Eisenberg and Augusten Burroughs and Garrison Keillor. All well-known names, all people we turned to for wit, intelligence, and nicely turned phrases, but not for photo shoots. So you're in very good company among the non-photographed.

When I heard your complaint, though, I winced a little. I hate for any of our contributors to be smarting over a detail of their piece. So we've hunted down a good photo of you—you're right, there are plenty—and have incorporated it into the spread, so everybody knows who wrote this, and can congratulate you when they see you on the street (or marquee).

Please, accept my apologies.

Now, you want to write a funny essay about double standards in male beauty and female beauty? Game on.

Many thanks for the sweet piece, in any case. Our guys are going to love it.

Best,

Jake

• • •

Jake,

I appreciate your response. That's certainly an impressive list of authors. But I feel the need to point out that not one person on that list is a woman. I know you are aware that there is a difference. Were the nature of their essays sexual and did you run a picture of younger thinner dudes above their words? I'm having trouble finding the humor in the double standard at the moment.

Thank you for including a photo of me. [*The photo they ran was pinky-nail-sized, smaller than one of the models' nipples.*] I would like some more details about that. Is it very small next to the giant model shots? I think that may just highlight the situation. What is the picture? I would like to see it. I know it's too late to pull the whole story, but I would prefer that to feeling swept under the rug.

I do not accept your challenge for a follow-up story. Pardon me if my trust and faith in your publication has been shaken.

I'm sure you are a great guy who is fun to get a beer with and has a good relationship with his exes, so know that this is not personal to you or your team. But I will not take this lying down. (You can have your comedic experts on staff add a joke after this line.)

Amy

• • •

Amy,

Damn. I was doing much better after your first note.

Truly, I'm sorry you're angry. We simply sought the best person to write the piece. And you were that, which you showed on the page.

Design/photo/artwork is an entirely separate realm, in my mind, so it never occurred to me that you'd be the photo subject for your own piece. You already did your part with the writing.

Think of a financial story: the writer expresses her expertise on money, and the artwork depicts cash. Writer does one part, photographer does the other, supporting the same idea. Then magazine people mesh words and images together on the page.

That's what we do all the time, and in this case, too.

Not sure I can ever convince you, so I'll stop trying. But it's exactly what happened with this story.

Jake

• • •

Jake,

Thank you for your financial advisor comparison. We are totally on the same page now. Want to get a drink sometime? I'm on a diet. I'll give you a heads up when I'm under 110.

Amy

Amy,

Ha. Phew!

Yes, let's grab a drink. I'll have beer, you can have water, and all will be good.

Happy to send you a copy of *The Women's Health Diet* to speed you on your way to 110.

Cheers,

Jake

• • •

Jake,

I hope you are blessed with daughters. All joking aside, is it too late to pull the article? I honestly don't want it to run.

I think the picture is distracting and has nothing to do with the piece. You look at the design, image, and photo as 3 separate things, but I believe the reader experiences it all together.

Amy

• • •

Amy,

Presses rolling. I hope you win an award for it.

I have two sons. Maybe they'll marry somebody's daughters.

Jake

And that was that. I don't know if Jake could tell I was being the biggest wiseass on earth, but interestingly enough, some time later, after that issue of the magazine was published, he added a large photo of me to the online version of the article, along with his defense for having initially chosen the model pics over a picture of me. Needless to say, my opinion of magazines shifted a lot after this experience. What was once just a glossy, mindless form of entertainment became something that seemed a little darker.

I know I don't look like the models they use in *Men's Health*. Their aesthetic is pretty consistent: a Svedka vodka–style fembot chick who just got out of the shower, with huge breasts on an otherwise young-boy body and an expression that says, "I'm sexy and powerful unless that's not what you want, master." Bless those gals; they work hard. So do the Photoshop editors, but I'm not going to buy into what the editors and their advertisers want. I'm not going to accept that that's the way it should be just because that's the way it is. People like women with more to their bodies too. Some people like a thick ass they can grab on to and a back they can touch without being met with a row of ribs. Nothing wrong if you enjoy the ribs. Just saying. I'm beautiful too. I am worthy of being in front of the camera. I can hear them around a conference table in their soulless office now: "She's just mad that she's busted; she should get over it!" But it's not that simple.

I'm mad because girls as young as eight years old are being shamed about their bodies. Fifth graders go on diets and admire Instagram pics of celebs in waist trainers. Some of the people I'm closest to have struggled with eating disorders. I'm mad at an industry that suggests that painfully thin is the only acceptable way to be. Please don't get on me for skinny shaming. If that's how you are shaped, God bless, but we gotta mix it up, because it's upsetting and confusing to women with other body types. When I'm onstage performing for over ten thousand people, I look out at the crowd and about half of the women in the audience have their arms folded to cover their stomachs. We're endlessly shown that being dangerously thin is the only way to be valuable—or even acceptable.

Why can't girls above a size 4 walk a runway? What are they afraid of? Will the whole runway tip over? Do they think models size 6 and above can't make it to the end of the runway without stopping midway for a burrito? Enough, enough with these waifish elves walking your impossible clothing down an ugly runway with ugly lighting and noisy music. Life doesn't look like that runway. Let's see some ass up there. And not just during the specially themed "plus-size show." We girls over size 6, 8, 10, 12, 14, 16 . . . we don't want a special day, we want every day, and we want you to get out of our fucking way because we are already here! You are living in the past, all you dated, strange magazines representing the weird fashion world that presents bizarre clothing that no one I have ever met wears.

Now that I've been on some of these magazine covers, I can tell you that even the chick on the cover doesn't love this situation. When you pose for a cover, a lot of magazines don't allow you to choose how you look or what you wear, and they generally Photoshop you until you look like everyone else. Google "magazine covers women," then click "Images," and you will get a screen full of dozens of magazine covers. Now squint just a little bit, and you'll see: everyone looks like the same person. It's sick. Why are we taught that we all need to look like one girl? Some of us want to look like ourselves. How we were born, a little goofy with some rough angles and some beautiful ones. I have been lucky to be part of some photo shoots that gave me license to look and feel like myself, thanks to photographers like Annie Leibovitz and Mark Seliger. Underappreciated fact: photographers are *artists* who enjoy mixing it up and presenting creative and varied images to delight and surprise people. Can you imagine photographing women in the same cover-shot pose all the time? There is nothing wrong with celebrating beauty, but beauty comes in many forms!

And how about we all agree that we don't need to slap a warning label on the page any time we show some form of "alternative" beauty? The "plus-size" label sends an us-vs.-them message: *These are the special magical plus-size ladies who are still lovable and beautiful—despite their size.* Why create categories for women's bodies? "Plus-size" is a pointless term that implies anything above a certain size is different and wrong. When *Glamour* put my name on the cover of their "Chic at Any Size" issue without asking me, I was frustrated, because I don't want to be a part of that message.

A few days after I got Jake's last email in that fun pen-pal exchange, I got out of the shower and stopped to look at myself in the mirror. I looked blotchy and messy and not at all like the girls in those magazines. But I was still fucking beautiful. I'm a real woman who digests her meals and breaks out and has sweet little pockets of cellulite on her upper thighs that she's not apologizing for. Because guess what? We all have that shit. We're all human beings.

I'm mad at myself for wasting any time caring about a magazine that runs articles with titles like "How to Tell If She's Good in Bed" and "Nine Ways to a Stronger Erection." What the fuck do I care? I want no part of that noise. I want something else. Women's magazines, I'm looking at you! Maybe run some fun photos, make some waves, and add more than one article per issue about women who are smart, creative, or interesting. I know there are bigger problems in the world. But this is something I care about deeply. This is my thing. I want to shout it from the fucking rooftops: You can't shame us or label us anymore. Join us instead—and EVOLVE FASTER so we can all work together!

I don't think magazines are the enemy. But I think they can do better. I want to be a part of that. If more magazines will have me, I will continue to scrunch up my nose and laugh on their covers; I will continue to pose pantsless with fire Photoshopped on my crotch; I will keep running fearlessly through Chinatown in shapeless silk pajamas and a blizzard of confetti. Beauty doesn't have to be so strict, stringent, and serious. Some of these magazines have sold us short. They have asked us to believe in their labels and their sameness. For a minute, I subscribed. But that minute is up. And I hope it's up for all of you.

Photo taken in an amusement park photo booth.

SECRET BAD HABITS

Kim and I got really fat one summer. I'm not fat-shaming us. It was worth it. We both like to expand and contract like accordions depending on the season. If it's hot, we drink white wine and tequila; if it's cold, we drink red wine and scotch and tequila. So, basically, we always weigh around the same. I usually weigh anywhere between one hundred forty-five pounds and six million pounds. That summer we were not wanting for anything.

I was told by someone somewhere at some point that I should listen to my body. If my body wanted ice cream, it got ice cream. Cinnabon? Okay! Cinnabon ice cream is a thing? Pick it up and put some pretzels in it—and oh, they must have forgotten to add peanut butter. Not a problem. I'm on top of it. Amy, you had a bottle and a half of wine tonight on your own because you felt your "body needed to relax." What is a good way to go to sleep? Good question, Amy. How about ordering a gluten-free pizza and also pasta from Seamless and putting the pasta on top of the pizza and eating it? Good call. But a word of advice: if you're gonna get pastitzza (which is not a thing, except for with me), only order it if you're already falling asleep and you'll be woken up by the buzzer when the delivery guy gets there. Cool idea!

I was blessed with a mother who made junk food completely contraband in our house. This means it was bad and is not another word for "condom," as I suspected before my editor explained it to me. If you're thinking my mom did me a favor, *ehhhhnnn* (buzzer sound). Her restrictions did not have the desired effect. Instead of giving me a healthy in-moderation-only attitude toward shitty-for-you food, I acted like an Amish kid on Rumspringa any time I was near it. I'm talking any time I was around soda or pizza at a birthday party, I would wile out. I went full-metal-jacket crazy eating it all. Especially as a little kid.

Once when I was nine years old, I went to the circus with my friend Lauren. Her mom innocently offered to grab me something from the concession stand, and I was like, "What do you mean? I can have whatever I want?" She said—get this—"Yes." In that moment, the whole world stopped around me. My vision blurred, and I blinked maniacally, unable to respond. She must have thought I was waiting for her to read me the menu of options—which is what she did.

"Well, honey, they have peanuts, popcorn, cotton candy, pretzels, giant chocolate chip cookies, lollipops, soda, and hot chocolate."

To which I answered, "Yes." Then, I ate so much, it's a miracle my little stomach—which had now become a piñata containing everything in Willy Wonka's factory—didn't explode all over a dancing elephant.

Every time I went to a birthday party where junk food was made available to me, I'd return home to my mom at the end of the day very, very ill—my chin sticky with dried soda and Cheetos dust under my fingernails. All my friends who were allowed to eat that stuff in moderation were so confused as to why I would eat myself sick. Just like Italian kids who are allowed to sip a little wine with their dinners and never end up binge-drinking as teens, most kids can handle moderate exposure to this food. But I had to be secretive about it so my mom wouldn't find out. I had friendships based on who lived near bodegas and candy shops. There was one girl I didn't care for even the slightest bit, but I knew if I went to her house, I could get enough Sour Patch Kids to kill a large giraffe, which I did. RIP, Smokey.

In college, my roommate Denise couldn't leave her food lying around because I'd come home from class or the bar and find a box of Twinkies and eat the whole thing. She'd make a tray of lasagna, and I'd slowly, square by square, eat the entire dish. I'd wake up like Garfield to her screaming my name. I had to tell her to start hiding it from me. I couldn't even know it was in the house. She started running out of places to hide her snacks because I would always find them. I would ransack my own apartment like the Gestapo. One night she brought a guy home, and he found a box of Devil Dogs under her pillow. He was really weirded out. She was totally embarrassed and blamed me, but I of course acted like I didn't know what she was talking about.

Even as a full-grown adult woman, I still have this habit. I curb it within reason. But there is no other way to describe that particular summer: Kim and I got fat. I was just about to start filming the second season of my TV show, so I panicked and asked her to lose some weight with me. There is no reason she should have said yes. She's very married and is not on camera very much. Kim is one of those girls with a natural *Playboy*-model type of body—the kind that, if it were mine, I would have had so much fun with by now. I'd be carrying every disease known to man and monkey. Instead, I'm shaped like a cactus, and when I don't shave for four hours I feel like one, too.

But Kim agreed to work out and eat well with me because she is kind and knows my favorite thing to do is eat and drink with her. She was all too aware that I'd throw away our health plan the second she agreed to booze or a cookie, so she had to join me in the diet if she wanted to ensure I stuck with it. She keeps me from eating and drinking myself to death most of the time, but when she is having a moment of weakness I can sniff it out, and I strike like an MMA fighter avenging his closetedness.

So we signed up for this CrossFit-type insane workout and actually went most days. It's one of those programs that puts you through Navy SEAL–style guerrilla warfare training that is completely over-the-top and unnecessary unless you're a runway model or about to compete in the Hunger Games. But we went. Every day we were on the verge of death. Sweating and wheezing. Walking out shaking and dizzy. It was horrible doing these workouts that were originally developed for people who needed them TO SURVIVE. Pilates was developed by Joseph Pilates, who worked with soldiers during World War II. He created his method to help very wounded soldiers get back into shape. Now it's mostly used by housewives who want child-soldier abs and who refuse to let their asses go where gravity is inevitably dragging them. All these boot camps and diets where they teach you to survive on minimal amounts of food like a prisoner of war are just not right. But Kim and I were committed to getting healthier, so we went.

The instructors were all gorgeous—girls in tiny spandex shorts and sports bras, with perfect hair and flawless faces without makeup. I think it has now been established that without makeup I look like Charlize Theron in *Monster*. The guys were also in ridiculous shape and were super hot. But there was one who was so beautiful and charismatic that it was confusing. I don't know if it's because we were so light-headed or because he was actually funny, but he kept us laughing and having fun while we sweated and sucked wind like George Burns on an elliptical.

This particular instructor, whom I'll call Neal, looked like a fake Greek sculpture of a man; he was so handsome you couldn't look at him for very long. He was toned and tanned to perfection—beyond what you are imagining now. He spread his attention evenly in the class, walking around and winking and squatting next to us as we did wall-sits and crunches. He'd literally take a knee and encourage you with a hand on your lower back. I think every girl left the class with a stupid grin, giggling, "Bye, Neal!" Kim and I are smarter than those girls, right? We're annoyed by physically perfect people, because *fuck you*. They can't also be funny. YOU AREN'T ALLOWED TO HAVE IT ALL! But even we were not immune to his charm. We would roll our eyes and look at each other like *What the fuck?!* because we couldn't believe how hot he was and how he could reduce us to smirking schoolgirls. He always made it very clear in class that he was available via the Internet to provide extra personal training outside of the usual class sessions. He'd say it over and over during workouts, and while I felt stupid even mentioning it to my sister, one day I said, "I kind of feel like he was saying that specifically to me . . . not just because he thinks I need help, but because he kind of likes me."

I was fully ready for her to tell me I was an idiot and needed to slow my roll and remember that my current Mrs. Potato Head shape was what got us into this mess in the first place. Kim has often messed with me when I have a crush on a guy and he has zero feelings for me. There was a guy who worked on season one of my TV show whom I was crazy about. So cute—this little bike-riding hipster who wouldn't give me the time of day, even though I was literally paying for his time of day. One afternoon while shooting, Kim said, "Oh my God, Aim, don't turn around, he is looking at you!" "Really?!!!" I shrieked. I slowly turned around and he was sleeping on a pile of equipment. What I'm saying is that not only does Kim *not* lie to me about guys having no interest in me, she enjoys it. But after I asked her about Neal, she said, "Dude, me too, I felt like he was saying it to you!" This was all I needed.

I've talked onstage and in these pages about how I can have low self-esteem at times. But I'm also always completely ready to accept and believe the fact that I am prettier than I ever realized. On the evolution chart, this guy and I were at opposite ends. I was dragging my knuckles, sniffing around for bananas, throwing my own feces at tourists, and he was a Disney prince but with more sex appeal. I reached out and was all, "Can you help me with my diet?" and he was all, "Sure, let's meet up at this healthy-eating place," and I was all, "*Here comes the bride.*" So we met up and we hung out a couple fitness-based times before I texted him while a little buzzed one night saying I wanted to make out.

On our next few dates, he'd let me know he was interested but also stomp on my ego, saying things like "Looks aren't the most important thing to me." *Wow, thank you*, I thought. *I really lucked out—I am so busted looking, but I still have some qualities for which you can muster an erection.* We wound up hooking up a couple times, and I could tell that he hoped I was going to just blow him. But he didn't realize how lazy homegirl is. I've given maybe eight blow jobs to completion in my life. I have to really love the person and feel they deserve it, or just be in a dirty mood. But they still need to deserve it. So, yeah, eight total. No joke. We had sex a couple times, always at my place.

To be honest, I never really enjoyed making out with him because the whole time I was thinking, *Why would he do this with me? It makes no sense. What does he have to gain from this?* It's not that I was down on myself, but it just didn't add up. I saw all the girls who were actual real-life, young-as-fuck supermodels in class swooning over him. But there he was with me, eating my dumb-ass pussy. Not ass pussy, but my vagina. Anywho, the point is he was hot and I am me, and we never went to his apartment. Always mine. Until one night. And that's when I found out about his secret bad habit.

We all have habits we don't want people to know about. Most are fairly harmless, but we still keep them a secret because we feel like we should. Some people only eat fast food in secret, and some people, like my sister-in-law, watch reality TV that is so trashy it should be illegal. How do I know that? Because I watch it right there with her and make her watch even worse TV. Some people like to eat the inside stuffing of their couch. Only God can judge you, brotha!

Anyway, the night I found out about Neal's secret, I had taken him to an event with me. We were progressing—he was hot enough and had enough confidence to actually confuse me into thinking he was cool and that we might even start dating for real. (Typing that just made me short of breath.) So we went to a fund-raiser for a disease, Lyme or alcoholism or something, and it was embarrassing to be there with him, because everyone was looking at me like, *Give me a break, bitch.* And they were right. Not that I don't deserve someone hot like that, or whatever I'm supposed to tell myself, but there *is* a line. You can be with someone kinda a li'l bit hotter or less hot than you, but if the levels are too off, people are furious. It's sick and sad. But I wasn't surprised. His hotness was just in the ridiculous range. I felt like we were in that scene from *The Little Mermaid* where Ursula sings the song about stealing Ariel's voice and I was one of the weeds on the floor and Neal was Ariel. (Hmm? Don't worry about it. All my metaphors aren't gonna hit.)

I got myself nice and drunk to deal with the humiliation—I don't care what anyone says, it's a great technique. We left hand in hand, excited about continuing the evening together. Walking to the car, I thought, *Maybe we will have something more. Is this my next boyfriend?* In the car, I was feeling good about "us" and I said, "Let's go to your place." "Okay," he said, "but it's kind of a mess." I let him know I wasn't the type of girl who would ever care, and off we went.

That night, we walked past his nice doorman to the nice elevator and walked down his nice hall and he opened his nice door— and there it was. What had probably once been a beautiful studio apartment had become an overstuffed locker. It looked like a garage door had opened on *Storage Wars*. The mess was bad—the kitchen and bathroom were black with mold, all porcelain surfaces coated in hair and grime, and there were unwashed dishes and towels covering every inch of the counters. I'd seen messes in men's apartments. It's not that uncommon for a guy to have a disgusting apartment, especially if he's single. I actually think it's endearing. I love a guy with a shitty apartment with nothing hanging on the walls. I like for guys to dress basic and be hanging on by a thread with their style. I don't trust a guy with taste. It seems unnatural to me.

But Neal's apartment went far beyond endearingly dirty. It was more than dirty. It was like *Jumanji*. Filled to the brim with unnatural things that didn't belong in an apartment. I mean, there were piles upon piles of just stuff. Piles everywhere. Piles of books and clothes and sneakers and furniture sitting on top of other furniture. There were magazines and papers stacked in tall symmetrical towers, but there were also messy mountains of stuff. Like big, haphazard pyramids made of boxes of merchandise and exercise contraptions and unopened packages. There were bottles of things, protein powders and health-food products. Junk mail and paperwork, CDs, rolled-up posters, jump ropes, empty grocery bags, knee pads (knee pads? WTF) . . . It was a nightmare to look at. A filthy, stacked-to-the-ceiling nightmare. There was barely room to walk around. You had to walk sideways through the narrow pathways he'd cleared. This boy was not a collector. He was a hoarder.

I instantly sobered up. Now I had to act. *I'm an actor*, I told myself. *I can do this.*

"I told you it was messy," he said. "Is it bad?"

"No!" I shrieked too loud and fast. "It's a really nice apartment."

I shut myself in the bathroom and noticed a bra and girls' things hanging on the door. I'd previously been suspicious he had a girlfriend—some little model walking in Paris at Fashion Week, I had guessed. Even though I've never been to Paris and I don't know when Fashion Week is. (It seems like it's every fucking week though. Does anyone else feel that way?) Anyway, I don't think this bra could have belonged to a recent girlfriend. Based on the expired time stamp of everything else in that apartment, that bra could have been hanging there for years. It could have been Amelia Earhart's bra. I stalled in the bathroom, marveling for a moment at the fact that a man so perfectly waxed, so expertly coiffed and immaculately molded, could emerge from this bottom-of-an-orangutan-cage bathroom every morning.

After I pulled myself away from deep breathing in the bathroom, he continued leading me around the apartment through the pathways he'd cleared. It felt like being led through a maze. It smelled dusty and like his dog, a sweet pit bull who followed us single file through the pathways. He offered me a drink and I said no. That's how bad it was. I never turn down a drink when I'm with a new guy. I typically use dating a new guy as an excuse to go on a Keith Richards–type bender. But I just couldn't see myself touching my mouth to a wineglass that lived in his apartment. He led me to the only clear area— the love seat in front of the TV, which he obviously sat in frequently since it wasn't covered with stuff. He made room for me on the love seat and we watched TV. Rather, I *pretended* to watch TV, unsure of how to leave. *Does he know how bad it is? If he does, he could be planning on killing me.* I looked at him to see if he was on edge. Nope, he was laughing hard at whatever MTV nightmare we were watching.

So what did I do? *Well, Amy, you obviously left. You thanked him for a lovely evening.* No, no, good friend, that is what a normal person would do. What I did was let him lead me to his mattress that had no sheets on it, and he went down on me. It was an out-of-body experience. I was looking around the room at the stacks of things he had accumulated over the years. Gifts from Nike and Adidas. Dog toys and a broken lamp stacked on top of a broken desk, covered in even more magazines and CDs. The dog and I made eye contact. I felt like we were sending each other the same message: "HELP!" I got dressed. I specifically remember putting my boots on and making myself pause to feel what it felt like to be in my thirties and having a sexual encounter like this. *Never again*, I thought. I said good night and walked back out to the city street full of steaming trash where things were nice.

It was three a.m. and the garbagemen were pulling up right as I entered the clean night air. I was clearly beginning my walk of deep shame and they knew it. They howled at me and I laughed at myself. There was no denying the state I was in. I went home and showered for eight years. The next day Neal said to me, "You inspired me to get my place together." I didn't know what I had said to make him do that but I thought this sounded like pretty good news.

"Oh, cool, you're gonna get rid of some stuff?" I asked.

"No, I'm going to get some new furniture."

I couldn't think of anything to say. I don't know what caused his condition. My only guess is that maybe he grew up without a lot and struggled—and maybe material things and name brands and just having stuff makes him feel successful. He could measure his place in the world by how much he had accumulated. This analysis is based on watching about three episodes of *Hoarders* and asking no one. I have no information is what I'm saying. But like every other girl I'm friends with, I like to diagnose people without any research.

He called me a few days later and I hung out with him one more time, just as friends, at my place with my sister. I didn't want to suspiciously disappear after seeing his apartment, but I couldn't go back there. And since Kim and I had already declared victory in our weight-loss journey, given our impressive combined loss of six pounds, I had no reason to attend his fitness class anymore either.

He wasn't a bad guy at all—he was quite the opposite. I've seen him in passing since then, and he's doing very well for himself. I wonder if he knows he has this affliction. I mean, this guy very clearly grooms himself within an inch of his life. His body is an absolutely immaculate temple. But his actual temple, on the other hand, is macu-late. I don't know what that means. But it is.

Sometimes I think I have the opposite problem. Most of the time I throw away shit I need. I can never find anything I need. I even lose my NuvaRing a few times a year, and that is supposed to be inside me. All human beings have secret compulsions and habits. Including me. But now any time I see someone who is so physically beautiful they almost don't look human, I remember there's definitely something totally fucked about them that will bring them right back down to earth. I'm kind of grateful to the guy because he made my pastitzza-as-I'm-falling-asleep habit seem a lot more forgivable.

MOM

I have trouble with people who maintain that their mothers are perfect. Are you dating a guy who can't make a decision without running it by his mom first? Break up with him. (Unless his mother is Caroline Manzo from *The Real Housewives of New Jersey*, but she is the only exception.) Definitely end it with this guy if he and his mother have one of those dynamics where you can tell the mom always kind of thought she would end up with her own son. Trust me—leave. Do you think your mother always has the answer to everything, including great suggestions about your hair, clothing, and relationships? I recommend you examine your view of her. I want to be patient and let you discover it in your own time. That's a lie. Actually, I just want to pull the entire rug out from under you and rush you to see the light.

Everyone's parents have fucked them up in one way or another. This is part of the natural order. It's the circle of life. Mothers are people—not angels from heaven or *Ex Machina* error-free service bots. Just because they pushed you out of their vaginal canals does not mean they have all (or any) of the answers. Before they had you, they were flailing around like idiots, just like you are right now. My point is, they are just people. Most likely extraordinarily flawed people.

Which brings me to my mother. Yes, yes, just like your mother, she did her best. But I was one of those kids who grew up thinking my mom was a saint. An actual goddess walking the earth. I worshipped her. But one day, I learned my mom wasn't perfect. The day I learned this also happened to be the day my childhood best friend, Mia, and I fell out forever. It wasn't a wacky coincidence. My mother was having an affair with Mia's father.

I met Mia on the first day of fourth grade when I was nine years old. I was the new kid at school and no one would talk to me, except her. She was the only one who didn't mind my bossiness and incessant lying. I'd just finished telling everyone at my new school that I was a bikini model from California, along with several other fabrications that didn't exactly win them over. I remember thinking she looked like Tinker Bell, so lovely and scrappy, when she approached me at the lunch table to say hi. She had dirty-blond unbrushed hair and was beautiful, tiny, and fragile. We became instantly inseparable. We had a few other friends who came in and out of our world, but I only saw them as a hindrance. I thought she was fascinating, brave, and confident.

I became a part of Mia's family and she became a part of mine. She had an older brother my brother's age and a younger sister my sister's age, so our families were perfect matches. We had sleepovers as often as our parents would allow us, and we spent our time choreographing captivating dances that we showcased for anyone we could get to hold still for five minutes. Our choreography secret was to match up the dance moves to the words in the song. For example, for Paula Abdul's song "Cold Hearted," we would shiver and act cold when Paula sang the word "cold." We'd point to our hearts for the word "hearted," and when that future *American Idol* judge sang the word "snake," we would—guess what?—each make a snake motion with one of our arms, slithering it up our fingers, wrist, and elbow. Calling all *America's Best Dance Crew* choreographers, we got you if you need help!

I had no doubt in my mind that we'd one day marry twin brothers and all live in a house together. It seemed like nothing could ever possibly come between us.

Our parents met at temple and became close friends. For those of you who aren't Chosen Ones, temple is a very regular part of life for Jews. We'd go to Shabbat service Friday night and the kids would go to Hebrew school Sunday mornings. Every summer my family would join Mia's at their lake house in upstate New York. It was five hours away by car, and her parents would drive in their station wagon that always smelled like cats and stale Fritos, but I didn't mind as long as I could sit in the seat in the back that faced the cars behind us. We'd wave to the drivers of those cars, then give them the finger and disappear—greatest gag in the book. My deathly carsickness, which I've always been prone to, was worth having just to see the change in the faces of the people who were just trying to get from point A to point B and really didn't need to deal with some stupid-ass kids telling them with their small fingers to fuck off. But we'd laugh our heads off for the whole ride.

Mia's mom, Ruth, was similar in stature to my mom—kind of short, blond, with a killer bod. Given my blind spot for seeing my mother as nothing but perfection, I remember thinking that Ruth wasn't as funny or bright as my mom. But she was kind and didn't take any shit from Mia or me. When we were thirteen, she caught us smoking Virginia Slims and drinking Boone's Farm on her roof (like a couple bosses) and she was not having it. She was a good mother and always took care of me like I was her own, like when she yelled at me when I snuck a *Redbook* magazine over to her house to share the sex articles with the other kids. I remember reading aloud that it entices a man if you dress up in his tie and nothing else. We were probably nine at the time, and she chewed me out, like a real parent. I recall feeling sorry for her, merely because she wasn't my mother. In fact, I always felt bad for any woman who had to be near my mom because they weren't her. She was, in my eyes, a queen.

This is a lot, right? I know.

As for Mia's dad, Lou, he was a smart, overweight businessman who wore huge, thick-framed glasses. There was nothing flashy about him. He adored his family and they adored him back. He worked long hours so he could provide them with the best life possible. They were the standard nice, Catskills-going Jewish family on Long Island.

The summer I turned thirteen was a great time for Mia and me. We were becoming teenagers and we got to hang out constantly up at the lake house. After our parents would go to bed, we'd come alive, sneaking out and meeting up with local boys on the beach to drink and get felt up. When school started in the fall, we were never apart. She was so unself-conscious and strong. Not physically—she was basically a string bean—but she knew what she stood for, and I wanted to stand for it right next to her. She was whip smart but could be totally silly and without any ego, and she always made me feel like she wanted me around. I felt I'd met my soul mate. I had.

And then one day after school I came home and saw my mother slumped on the couch. She'd clearly been crying hard. Her eyes were almost sealed shut and her nose was really red. She was usually composed, deliberate, and happy, and I'd never seen her cry like this. It felt like the ground was shifting beneath my feet when she reached out for me with both arms.

"What is it? What happened?" I asked her. She opened her mouth to explain the tragedy to me but the tears started again and she couldn't catch her breath long enough to tell me. Because she couldn't communicate vocally, she had to sign it to me. Since she is a teacher of the deaf, we all know a good amount of sign language in my family. Slowly, her hands trembling, she rose and signed to me, "I am leaving your father. Lou and I have fallen in love with each other." I signed the word "again" because I needed her to repeat herself. Again she signed, "I am leaving your father. Lou and I have fallen in love with each other."

I was not shocked that she was leaving my dad. I wasn't ever under the impression that she was too fond of him. I'd never seen them hold hands or kiss, and she'd always expressed an air of vague annoyance toward him. Even though my dad was funny and handsome, it was hard for me to believe my perfect mother had stayed with my imperfect father for so long. I thought of her as Mother Teresa for staying with a man who never deserved her. Looking back now, I of course realize how unhealthy it was that as a teen, I had such a strong sense of alignment with one parent against the other. My father was no angel. He drank in secret and I know he did dirtbag things behind my mom's back (in their earlier days, I'm pretty sure she once walked in on him getting head from a hooker), but he never pretended to be perfect.

When she told me that she and Lou were in love, it didn't register who she was talking about because it seemed so unlikely. My first thought was, *That's funny, Mia's dad's name is Lou too.* But then I put two and two together. Flashes of dinners and trips and moments at the temple with our families shot through my brain. Even though I'd always found him to be plain, he must have been special somehow, because my mother was in love with him—and I never questioned anything my mother said or did.

She sat there on the couch looking so helpless and sad, seeming so alone and without hope. I decided in that moment that I'd be her savior. I threw my arms around her and said, "Well it's about time. I always knew you were too good for Dad. I'm happy you're in love." When my mom heard these words, the wave of hugs and kisses and praise that came my way was overwhelming. I believe no one has ever been as grateful as my mom was in that moment. Looking back now, I'm horrified that she let me play that role. To allow your thirteen-year-old to be your support system while you are simultaneously ripping her world apart is not a kind thing to do. I was a child, new to my teens, and she was treating me like a seasoned psychiatrist. And because I was the kid who always followed her lead, who outright *worshipped* her, I thought this must have been completely appropriate. I actually felt *honored*.

After she stopped crying, I bravely sat next to her in silence. And then, as I had always been trained to do, I felt fine. I believed everything was going to be OKAY. When we were kids and would fall or get upset, she'd never ask if we were all right. Instead, she'd say, "You're okay," in an upbeat tone and trick us into believing it. This is how we were raised: we were always oppressively OKAY.

I went to bed that night feeling OKAY, if a bit uneasy. I woke up in the middle of the night and couldn't fall back asleep. I had a headache. I lay there, staring at the ceiling, hoping it had all been a nightmare. I was thinking about Mia and her family when I heard the back door being unlocked. I moved my curtains aside to look down at the driveway and saw that my dad was home. I took a step toward my bedroom door and paused. What would I say to him? Did he know? A sudden, sharp pain in my temple stopped me in my tracks. I winced and lay back down. I'd never experienced a headache like this before. A faint, almost inaudible knock on my door was followed by a whisper: "*Aim?*"

The door opened and my father was standing there. "Hey, Dad."

He sat down next to me. "Hey, baby, I heard you moving around in here. Why are you awake?" I told him about my headache, and I looked in his eyes and could see that he had been briefed on his new shattered life. He seemed calm though—collected on the outside, but still broken behind his eyes. He used his thumb to rub my temple. I breathed in his smell deeply as he softly sang a sleepy rendition of "It Was a Very Good Year" by Sinatra. My dad sang this song often. His nightly standards also included "You've Got to Hide Your Love Away" and "They Call the Wind Maria." To review, these are songs about lost youth, stuffing down your feelings, and a hurricane. Not really a ray of sunshine for a kid. It hit me that this was probably the last time he would sing them to me. I felt a heaviness in my chest that stung and pulled me back into a deep sleep.

I woke up to pancakes, eggs, and orange juice on the table. My mom was bright-eyed and cheery and had an "It's gonna be a great day" way about her. She talked to me as if everything were normal. She made no mention of the previous day's events and neither did I. Then she asked if I wanted Mia to come over after school.

I thought, *Is this a joke?*

But I said, "Okay." And my mom explained, "I don't want all of this to harm your friendship." Hearing her say this made me believe it was actually possible. I thought, *I learned everything I know from this adult, and I trust her completely. If she's acting like this is all OKAY, then sure, there's nothing complicated about remaining best friends with Mia when our parents are having an affair. Nope. Nothing at all.*

In retrospect, I wish my mother had been visibly affected by what was going on. How could she get up so early and smile so brightly? But that was always her MO—to decide on a new reality that made sense to her in the moment and force us to live in it with her. I know there is a lot that she hid from me and plenty I don't know about what happened with her and Lou. But I wish she'd considered the ripple effects of her actions and then fought her desire to have this affair. At the very least, I wish she could have just been honest that she was weak and lost—that she pursued Lou because of the bad place she was in. I can't speak for her, but I don't believe she tried hard enough to think about everyone who would be affected by the relationship. Even worse, she got me on board. She made me my favorite breakfast and recruited me to be the cheerleader of her mistake. There was no *"How are you feeling today, Aim? This must be a lot for you to deal with."* So I acted like there wasn't. In the meantime, the stress and agony that was suddenly bubbling to the surface had nowhere to go, so it was promptly internalized.

I had a blinding pressure cooker of a headache for years to come.

As Mom cleared the dishes, I asked her where Dad was. "He's moving his things into the office," she answered with a frightening Stepford quality. *Bam*, pain—right at the front of my head. I went off to school anyway, feeling that I needed to be as sunshiney and strong as my mother. Nothing was a big deal as long as we didn't act like it was. When I sat down in my chair for math class, I immediately saw that Mia's desk was empty. I stared at it. Headache. Shooting, searing pain. Then just as the second bell rang, the classroom door flung open and Mia ran to her seat without looking at me. My eyes were fixed on her all forty-two minutes of class. She didn't even glance in my direction. She looked cool and relaxed like always. *She must not know*, I thought. *What am I going to say to her? "Hey, Mia, your family is ruined because our parents are two sad and lonely people who chose some fleeting moments of joy over keeping their families happy and safe. Do you want to go get some Sour Patch Kids after school?"*

The bell rang and class was over. I packed up my books, breathed through my headache, and approached her. "Hi," I said.

"Hey," she said, and handed me a folded letter, while smiling like everything was fine. "Please give this to your mom, and promise me you won't read it." I nodded my head and I meant it. She skipped away and I immediately stepped into the bathroom and furiously opened the envelope. I was too curious. You definitely would have, too.

It was an utterly hateful letter to my mother—written by Mia. Each word more hurtful than the last. It was filled with angry questions and accusations, like *"I thought you were an angel but you are the most evil thing I've ever seen. I hope you go to hell . . . You've ruined my family. How could you do this?"*

Three spite-filled pages. I couldn't believe that someone—Mia especially—could write something like this to my mom. In my mind, my mom was innocent. She'd painted herself as a precious victim, and she had successfully brainwashed me into believing in the romantic forbidden-love story she was living out with my best friend's father. As far as I was concerned, my mother was Hester Prynne in this situation, and I wasn't going to let these people burn an innocent woman at the stake for following her heart.

I marched down the empty hallway and stopped in front of the door to the biology class I knew Mia was in. Without thinking I barged in. "I need to talk to Mia," I told the teacher. He must have heard the "don't fuck with me" tone in my voice because he let her walk right out. She came into the hallway and shut the door behind her, at which point *we were off.* "I told you not to read it!" "Fuck you!" "How could you?" "I hate you!" Back and forth—both of us screaming and crying until two teachers had to break it up. While being guided away from each other we locked eyes. We both looked surprised. I was taken to the nurse's office to calm down, where I lay on a cot and breathed heavily. By the time my mom came to drive me home, my head was throbbing, my temples beating like a heart.

In the weeks that followed, I got used to the headaches. I had to witness Mia's mother sitting on our doorstep, begging my mom not to do this to her family. My mom did it anyway. I had to see Mia in the hallways at school while I was aching to talk to her. Hold her. Be with her as I had been every day for the last five years. It was devastating to go through such a confusing and stressful experience without my best friend. We stopped going to the temple where I'd just had my bat mitzvah. It was too uncomfortable to show our faces there after my mom had wrecked a home in the community. Thus ended an important chapter in my relationship with Judaism, the religion in which I had been raised, spending every weekend of my whole life studying and celebrating. My friends and my religion were gone. The whole town knew, and instead of being angry with my mother, I stood by her with a vengeance. I looked them all dead in the eye, daring them to just try to fuck with either of us.

I had to watch my father move from the office into a sad, sterile bachelor's apartment on Long Island with a roommate. My mother rewarded my loyalty—or perhaps paid for her guilt—by giving me the master bedroom she used to share with him. Mia and I avoided each other for the rest of middle school and high school. I felt the familiar shooting pain in my head any time I would pass her in the hall or on the street. I missed her all the time. I still do. She reached out on Facebook a couple of years ago to congratulate me on my success, and I immediately gushed about how I missed her, how sorry I was, and how wrong my mom was. She never responded.

As for my mom and Lou, their relationship lasted all of a couple months. It was a very strange experience for me and my siblings. One year earlier we'd been on family vacations with Lou's family, and now he was coming along on *our* family vacation to San Diego—as my mom's boyfriend. He'd moved out of his family's house and gotten a place of his own. It turned my stomach to watch them hold hands. I remember ordering clams and sucking them out of the shell the way we always did with my dad. But Lou insisted we use our forks. Watching him with my mom at the hotel pool, I could tell she was already over him. My brother, sister, and I all felt the same heaviness in the salty San Diego air, but she did her usual act of pretending everything was fine. She expected us to do the same, but this time we did not oblige. Something about that trip finally lifted the veil for me. I was beginning to see her for the flawed, confused, lonely human being that she was. No worse than the rest of us. But my imaginary image of her shattered and has never returned.

She broke up with Lou on the flight home.

In the years that followed, she dated several other men, swearing that each was "the one." And through it all, I remained intensely close to her—all the way up through my twenties. I used to bring her to comedy clubs with me and we were very much a part of each other's daily lives. We were enmeshed, with not a single healthy boundary between us. And I was always defending the questionable choices she made in relationships. We have had a different journey than most mothers and daughters. Maybe it helped my mom cope with life to manage and guard our relationship so closely. She couldn't control or deal with reality, but she could control me.

Now, in our thirties, my siblings and I have begun to become more vocal with each other about the hardships of growing up with our mom. We've each had our own specific struggles, but they're rooted in the experiences we shared of being emotionally suppressed or manipulated by her. As it turns out, being OKAY ALL THE TIME as a child makes for a difficult entry into adulthood.

When I was about to turn thirty, I was beginning to think about writing a book about my life (which eventually became *this* book). I went back through the journals I've kept from the age of thirteen and started reading what I'd written about Mia and Lou. As an adult reading the words of a child who was telling this awful story, I was able for the first time to separate my mother's actions from my adoration of her. It became very clear that she manipulated me in unhealthy ways, and that the remnants of that manipulation were still a part of our present-day relationship.

With all this pain refreshed in my memory from reading my old journals, my mother happened to call to discuss my upcoming birthday. I remember her cheerful tone—the same one she'd had that morning so long ago when she made me pancakes right after turning my world upside down. "I know what we are doing for your thirtieth," she said. "We are going on a helicopter ride around Manhattan and then we'll get hibachi and massages!" I was suddenly flooded with anger. I told her, "I don't want to go on a *Millionaire Matchmaker* date with you for my birthday!" *This is not OKAY. Those are all things SHE would want to do on HER birthday*, I thought. And then I was fully furious. I wasn't just mad at her for having a short, destructive affair with my best friend's father when I was thirteen. I wasn't just mad at her for the string of other men who came into our lives after Lou. I was mad at her for manipulating me into supporting her through all this. And for making me believe the lie she was selling— the lie of her projected flawlessness and innocence.

So at the age of twenty-nine, I began to forge a new relationship with her—one with Fort Knox–level boundaries. Redirecting a relationship between two people who've been abnormally close for thirty years is not an easy thing to do. We had a period of my expressing my feelings about the past, followed by a period of our not speaking. I tried again and again to lay it all out for her, to explain my grievances and pain. And sometimes she did try to listen to where I was coming from. She stopped just defending herself and started to hear me, but ultimately I think it was too much for her to accept the gravity of what she had done—and the effect it had had on me and my siblings. We finally landed in a place where we have remained for several years. We are kind to one another but I keep my boundaries clear. We speak regularly and keep each other up to date, but far less frequently.

Now, after some years of reflection, I understand her a little better. Like all of us, she's a product of her own fucked-up childhood. She was damaged by her own mother, who was an emotionally neglectful narcissist. I have no idea what it must have been like to be in her situation when she started the affair with Lou—to have three kids and a husband who didn't make her feel loved. But I still wish she could have just been honest with us. And with herself. We're all trying our best, making mistakes, and hanging on by a thread. I wish she could have showed us an authentic emotion or two, allowed us to accept weakness and vulnerability as a part of life. Life is full of pain and disappointment. I've made a whole career out of pointing this out and reliving it in ridiculous ways so everyone can laugh and cry along with me. I wish my mother understood this too.

It's relaxing sometimes, just being human.

I still have to work hard not to internalize my feelings so they don't manifest themselves in the form of headaches and other physical problems. And I'm still at my core a girl who longs for her mother. We all are. When I think of the moments in my life that I've felt the most comforted and loved, I think of her. Being tucked in at night, or walking into the house starving from volleyball practice to find dinner already waiting on the table for me. Feeling her arms around me as she carried me through the swimming pool. The safety of wrapping my arms around her as she slowly moved through the water, guiding me, loving me. She is still the person I want to talk to when I wake up from a nightmare. When I call her in the middle of the night after a bad dream, which happens a couple times a year, she always picks up the phone. *Always.* When she tells me, "It will be okay," I believe her and go back to sleep. I love her.

But make no mistake, if I knew I was going to eventually *become* her . . . ? If it were like *World War Z* and I had five seconds until I transitioned into fully *being* my mother? I would hara-kiri myself without a second thought. If you're a parent reading this, chances are you're not as tricky as my mom. I know she is a rare flower. But don't go patting yourself on the back too quickly. No matter what, you're still going to mess up your kids too. And they're going to hate you for a minute (or two or three) while they pick up the pieces of their childhood. Anyone who claims to skirt this system is just lying. And that's a far worse offense in my book.

No matter what my mother put me through, I'm still grateful to her for raising me to believe I'm talented, smart, and beautiful. She made me who I am—someone who, ironically, places the highest value on being vulnerable, honest, and real. I wish we could have a normal mother-daughter relationship. If such a thing exists. I don't know if that's possible for us, but I believe family is a constant negotiation. I have never given up on her. I can't, and I never will.

NYC APARTMENTS

Last year, I bought my first apartment in New York City—an absolute dream come true. I've lived here pretty much all of my adult life, but always as a renter, and I've always wanted to *own* a place here. I was born in Manhattan, and after spending the first several years of my life here, I had to admire it from the far reaches of suburban Long Island for the rest of my childhood and teen years. As soon as I could make my way back after college, I did, and I've lived here ever since—in almost every corner of this island, I might add. Even after my career picked up, I stayed in New York instead of moving to Los Angeles, like most people in this business end up doing. I will never leave. It's home, the place where I can absolutely be myself—even if being myself means I have to nest with cockroach carcasses, rat droppings, and even worse, boyfriends.

I fucking love New York. It just makes sense to me in a way no other place does. Growing up in the suburbs wasn't for me: big houses separated by big yards and fences on wide streets. Big parking lots outside of huge stores. When you're in the city, everyone is so unquestionably close to everyone else, physically, that there's no choice but to bump into other humans at all times. It always seemed so *cozy* in comparison to Long Island. Like in the movie *Beaches* when they share a shitty apartment in New York and sing Christmas carols. That's what I longed for when I was a kid, imagining myself as a grown-up with my own place.

There's more than one benefit to being on top of each other all the time. Everyone has to walk the same streets, smell the same gross hot-garbage stink, and no one gets to be better than or different from anyone else. The painful humanity is everywhere. The fucking queen of England could knock into you on the subway and you'd be like, WATCH IT, CUNT. Hahahahaha. I've never called anyone a cunt on the subway. But that image really made me laugh. Someone please make a cartoon of that.

I've lived in nearly every neighborhood in all the boroughs of New York City, with the exception of the Bronx and—*of course*—Staten Island. No offense to the Wu-Tang Clan—I'm on a strict no-Shaolin (Staten Island) policy. So many of the important life lessons I've learned are written all over this city—the streets, subways, bars, restaurants, theaters, parks, and comedy clubs. Fortunately, those lessons have all been completely obscured by a fine mist of urine and spray paint, with a confetti of bedbugs and survival sprinkled into the mix. This is the magic of NYC: you're always starting over and moving fast. That could actually describe a lot of things in life: my relationship with my mom, my career, my digestive tract. I have, in essence, learned nothing, other than to *keep moving*.

I'm used to moving. I've been a comic on the road for over a decade. And before I went away to college, our family changed residences just under ten times. But it's nice to be in one place now. I love my apartment. It's full of all the things that make a home homey.

In the bedroom, a great bed with soft jersey T-shirt sheets, and of course, my disgusting stuffed animals. In the kitchen, a good frying pan for eggs every morning, and a bunch of fancy teas that I never drink. Also a bunch of wine that I *do* drink (enough to outlast the apocalypse). And in the living room, there must be a good-size TV. It can't be humiliatingly small, but can't be too large either—I don't need to watch *The Bachelor* on IMAX. I just need to DVR *SNL* every week and be able to see the whites of the Bachelor's eyes. It's a one-bedroom on the top of a four-story walk-up, and the lobby and hallway are kind of gross and no one wants to visit me because there are a lot of stairs to climb to get here, but I don't care. It is MINE and it took me thirty-four years to get! For the last ten, I was always renting something, living with a new roommate, constantly moving around and storing stuff at my mom's place. It's exhausting to think about how many times I moved and how many landlords I paid more than 50 percent of my monthly income.

I never wanted to compromise and put down stakes in any other city. It always had to be New York for me. I know I can be a flake, but this is one goal from which I never deviated. Even if it meant I had to live in a shoe box, I never cared, as long as it was a New York shoe box. My first New York apartment was on Orchard and Hester on the Lower East Side of Manhattan. It was a studio that cost $800 a month—and it was *tiny*. A tiny apartment in New York is unlike any other in the country. I've gone and stayed with friends who worked as production assistants in Portland, Oregon, who'd describe their apartments as small, and then I would walk into a large one-bedroom with a balcony and think, *Fuck you. You have no idea.* Small in New York is small for real. Like you can reach over and flush your toilet while standing at your front door, which thankfully has nine locks. And you don't even have the spare real estate in the corner that is your kitchen to stock some box wine, because the container is literally too big for your fridge. I was twenty-two years old at the time and couldn't afford the rent on my own, so I put an ad on Craigslist for a roommate. Yes, a roommate—in a studio apartment. Hey, I said I wanted cozy, right? This was it. This is a reality that many New Yorkers have lived. The apartment was maybe about thirty feet by twenty feet, and it was filthy when I moved in. My mom and I scrubbed it clean and decorated it cute. I made the bed with my favorite sheets, and I was in heaven that it was mine.

I got a response to my Craigslist ad from a girl named Brittney who was from the South and coming to the city for art school. We spoke on the phone once and she moved in. I know this sounds like the setup to a shitty horror movie, but she was sweet and clean and we got along great. We never fought. We couldn't afford cable but we had a little TV, so we watched DVDs of *Sex and the City* and *Will & Grace*. Now that I think of it, it may have been the best time of my life.

After paying rent, I could barely afford to eat. Fortunately, we lived in Chinatown, where food can be very cheap. There was a dumpling factory right around the corner from us, and for five dollars you could get a huge bag of them—enough to eat for a week. I ate a record-breaking number of dumplings that year. No nutrition, but delicious. My face would swell and lips would blister from the salt. Because the only way to consume them is by drowning them in high-sodium soy sauce.

The price of real estate—or just the price of rent—in this city can really warp your judgment. Rent is so high and good places are so scarce that sometimes you talk yourself into very bad ideas. Case in point: When I moved back in with Dan after the blackout of 2003, I told myself that my instinct to make it work with an abusive ex had nothing to do with his nice two-bedroom apartment. But of course it did. Not that I wasn't enjoying folding my Murphy bed into the wall every night. It was a great way to kill the bugs in there and have space to lie on the floor and cry.

Dan was living with his friend Rob at the time, in Murray Hill. Both he and his roommate were children of privilege who could always rely on some rich relative to give them dough when the going got tough, but they had no jobs and no money of their own. The neighborhood was vile, home to young corporate America, shitty bars playing shitty classic rock, and shitty white kids drinking their parents' money away. I'd take the subway to work and sling rib eyes all day at the steakhouse in Grand Central Terminal while Dan would do God-knows-what. He tried his best to be reliably sane for a while, but he eventually started acting nuts again and was scaring me. Remember: this was the same boyfriend who pulled a knife on me. I knew it was dangerously stupid to continue living with him, but instead of moving out myself, I convinced him to move home with his mom. Which wasn't a tough sell because she happened to be a kind person with a dope-ass apartment. Right at the same time, Rob had been invited to travel around Europe with a cousin, but he didn't want to go and leave his girlfriend, Mary, behind. But Mary was sick of him and was eyeing the apartment, so she convinced him to go. After both boys left, Mary and I lived there alone. I remember the day Dan and Rob were both officially out of the house. Mary and I jumped on our beds like little girls to celebrate our healthy relationship decisions and getting them out of our lives. But mostly I think we were delighted at how funny it was that we'd evicted our boyfriends from their own apartment. The bottom line to this sad story is that I would have done anything to be able to live in the city I loved. And even though "anything" included making a regrettable choice with a dude, I still take it as a good sign that I was persistent enough to fight my way from one gross overpriced domicile to the next.

I was always pushing and struggling for the easiest setup and the cheapest rent. I once shared an apartment with a married couple in Brooklyn who needed a roommate to make rent. Or so they said. They'd give me lots of attention and make me feel really wanted, but I soon figured out it was because they didn't want to be alone together anymore. I see now that my presence was meant to distract them from their impending divorce. Some couples have a kid to try to save their marriage—these two had a twentysomething waiter/ stand-up/actress who ate more than her fair share of pantry items she didn't purchase. Their tactic didn't work and they eventually split up, but they helped me get by for a while—so shout-out to that couple who prevented me from having to move back in with my mom or eject myself to the suburbs.

I'd also like to give a shout-out to the single-lady roommate who'd descend the stairs completely naked from the waist down, sometimes to get attention from my boyfriend. Here's to the old guy who was still living in my new apartment on the day I moved in. My roommate and I had to pack all of his clothing and box up his huge collection of vintage nudie magazines. One of them featured a girl wearing a varsity sweater, and she looked so much like me. The magazine was called *Babyface*. I was flattered there was a market for girls like me, who resemble that eighties doll Kid Sister or one of the Garbage Pail Kids. Oh, and one more very special shout-out goes to the roommate who invited exactly one-third of Manhattan to our place for a Halloween party, which ended when I found an aggressive dude ass-fucking a woman in a cowgirl costume in my unlocked bathroom.

All in all, the common thread in my sad string of NYC apartments is that I put up with a lot of vermin and weirdness and "coziness" so

I could be where I wanted to be. I believe you should fight for what you want. I'm proud of almost every housing decision I made in the sense that they kept me in the city where I needed to be. I wouldn't have made it this far as a comedian or human if I hadn't stayed here.

I guess I only strayed from this pattern when I would get distracted by a guy and moving became a dating tactic—a not very sly but surprisingly effective dating tactic. Besides the aforementioned time I moved back in with Dan, I set up a real nice home life with my boyfriend Rick when I was twenty-five. He wasn't at all ready for us to live together but that didn't stop me from pressuring him to let me move in with him. I've lived with four boyfriends in my life and I've tricked each of them into it. It always ended poorly. I don't think I even wanted to live with Rick, but I wanted him to want to live with me. Being a woman is so fun!

Anyway, Rick and I lived together in Brooklyn in a small but not completely horrible one-bedroom apartment. We'd work hard all day at our respective restaurant and office temp jobs, and then I'd do a stand-up show at night, which I was just starting at the time. Around ten p.m. one of us would make dinner, then we'd watch a movie we'd gotten in the mail from Netflix. We'd drink wine, smoke pot, and eat ice cream. The fridge was big enough to house all of these things! It was heaven. What more is there to life than being stoned and full and having sex, unless of course you're too full? Anyway, after living together for a while, Rick and I were in love and really excited about each other. We would make each other laugh and gaze into each other's eyes—and it felt like life was going to be all right. But I was with him during a big turning point in my life—when I got the full-blown comedy disease (which I told you about in "How to Become a Stand-up Comedian"). I had it bad, and the only cure was to get on the road and do more comedy. I couldn't imagine putting anything else first in my life. Not even a guy I loved. I was also learning that I was an introvert (one of the first things I told you about myself in this book) who worked best when she had large spans of time to herself. So even though the fake-married life was nice for a while, I realized it wasn't for me. At least not in that moment in time. After we broke up (when I was on *Last Comic Standing*), I basically lived on the road for a while.

You'd think I would have learned my lesson about living with a guy, but not too long after, I became infatuated with this hot dude from my acting class, Devin, and eventually ended up moving to Astoria just to trap him into dating me. Which worked. But the joke was on me. Not only did I move into the worst part of Queens, but I also got bedbugs, the 9/11 of bugs, which provide both a logistical and existential nightmare when they come into your life. They are nearly impossible to get rid of—so I had to subject my poor elderly stuffed animals to a scary ride in a high-heat dryer. And everyone I knew was quietly reevaluating their friendship with me. This is not an exaggeration and it's another classic New York story—some people will straight-up take you out of their phone when they learn you have been hit with this plague. But bedbugs aside, there are many beautiful places in Astoria—just not where I lived!

I went to the grossest carpeted gym of all time there. It was billed as being "just for women"—which almost always is code for "subpar." The whole thing was built on a slant, so when you'd run on the treadmill, one leg would take all the weight. There were a lot of Muslim women in the neighborhood, and they would be on the ellipticals in their burkas while their husbands sat in the lobby area, waiting for them to finish their workouts, staring at the rest of us while they waited. I've been more comfortable getting a pelvic exam from a gynecologist with Parkinson's. *Amy, that is unsympathetic to people with that horrible disease and now we are mad and writing about it on message boards.* Okay, you're right, I'm sorry. But relax: my first-ever gyno actually had Parkinson's and it was awful. He was a million years old, and I found out that he'd died when I went in for one of my annual checkups. The new guy told me the news while his fingers were inside me and my ovaries were being squished. The previous sentence is also the title of my next book.

In defense of the Rick and Devin situations, I think there is a lot to be said for just picking up your things and moving to the neighborhood of the guy you like. When you're a child, you're friends with people based on proximity—and I've found it's the same for men. That's why so many of them sleep with their nannies, because THEY'RE THERE! And besides, I'm still great friends with both of these guys. They're both amazing actors, and Devin Dane (hahaha, his real name is Kevin Kane) has become my working partner in everything I do.

I feel like I could write a whole book on all the gross, weird places I've lived and all the bizarre or wonderful roommates I've had. Each place was just a temporary stop on the road to getting me where I wanted to be. I never quit moving and I didn't bother getting too comfortable because I wanted to be ready for whatever came next.

Now that I finally own a place, maybe I will stay for a while. I have everything I need. I even live near a small body of water, where I like to do my preferred form of exercise—a long geriatric walk while nibbling on a scone. And, guys, I got a wine refrigerator for my kitchen! (Is that not relatable? Have I sold out from my days of drinking single-serving box wine with a straw? No, because I still drink those too. It's just that I recently learned that I drink my chardonnay too cold, and I didn't even know that was possible, but now I am dedicating my life to correcting that error!) Anyway, as long as I'm in this city, not too far from my second home (the Comedy Cellar), I'm happy.

I suspect I will never stop moving. Literally. I might live in a few (hundred) more apartments, but they will always be on the same island of Manhattan and I will continue to circle this same pond over and over again, until I am an elderly woman. I know there are probably bigger, better bodies of water in LA, but I'm pretty sure it's illegal to transport a baked good from one location to another there. Can you imagine walking into a Beverly Hills SoulCycle with a fistful of quiche? I have to do that sometime. But even if they were cool with it, LA would never feel like home to me.

BLACKOUTS AND STEM CELLS

I pay my taxes. I vote—for my favorite reality show contestants, but also in elections. I call my friends on their birthdays. I use a bath towel no longer than a week before washing it. I drink the recommended amount of water daily. And I can hold my liquor. All of this makes me a grown-up. Actually, as I write this, my twenty-four-year-old assistant just brought me a snack of crackers and hummus, so maybe I still have some work to do.

But when I was in college, I was a far cry from adulthood. I did none of the things listed above. By junior year of college this is how I drank: I'd have two beers in my dorm room, then go to the bar, where I'd enjoy about four martinis. Four *real* martinis—I'm talking Ketel One up and dirty, and I would always go back to the bartender and complain that they'd made it too dirty so I could get more vodka added for free. Everyone else ordered normal college stuff, like vodka cranberries or Jack and Cokes, but it was always beer and martinis for me. And then sometimes I'd end the night with some wine or champagne, even though I had nothing to celebrate.

As it turns out, I also won the genetic lottery and am one of those chicks who is prone to blackouts. For those of you who haven't been to high school or college parties, blacking out is when your mind goes to sleep but your body keeps right on doing whatever your drunk-ass self thinks is a good idea. Blacking out is NOT passing out asleep in a drunken stupor. It's quite the opposite. Your brain is sleeping like an innocent little baby, but your body is at a rave and it keeps making decisions. Decisions such as, *Let's eat something called a "walking taco" from a place in Chicago where you eat a taco mixed in a Fritos bag and jam handfuls of it in your mouth.* This is why blacking out is incredibly dangerous. You might look like a regular drunk girl, but you're actually a zombie who won't remember shit later. A really thrilling part of blacking out is the fact that sometimes you wake up while you're *still doing* whatever horrible thing you chose to do when you fell into it. You suddenly reemerge in your body like a time traveler and have no idea how long you've been out.

My most memorable (technically my *least* memorable) college blackout happened this way: My brain was completely checked out and then all of a sudden I was back in my body and aware of everything. I looked southward and there was a stranger going down on me in my bed. Huh? What? Hello?!! I'll say that again. Someone I had never in my life met or seen before was tonguing my vagina like he was digging for gold. I had a boyfriend at the time and this was not him. I didn't know this dude, but he was obviously getting to know me. I lightly tapped him on the shoulder because I didn't want to startle him, and also because what do I know about this guy at this point? Obviously, I know he's a true gentleman—he's going down on me, and that is a move worthy of knighthood. On my vagina's very best day—when I know I may have a visitor soon so I've just showered and really tended to it with care—it still smells like a small barnyard animal. A freshly washed goat or something of that size and potency. A cute one that you'd want to buy little pellets for and feed at a zoo. That's on its best day. On its worst day? After a night of drinking? It's probably like an unwashed shark tank. I imagine going down on me after a night on the town must be like Indiana Jones entering some sort of a cobwebbed room where he'll need to choose a cup wisely.

This saintlike man looked up at me after I tapped him. He was hot, so I patted myself on the back and thought, *Nice job, Schumes*. He looked up but stayed down there, and for a minute it looked like I was giving birth to him. I said, "Hi, I'm Amy, I don't believe we've had the pleasure." He was very confused. As gently as I could, I explained what had happened. He left prrrrrretty quick. I stormed into my roommate Denise's room and asked, "Why did you let me bring some random guy home? You know I have a boyfriend!" She was in shock and immediately defended herself. Apparently I hadn't even seemed very drunk and had walked around the bar with this guy all night, our arms around each other like we were a couple. Denise assumed I had consciously made the choice to be with this guy and ditch my boyfriend. I literally didn't remember meeting him. I saw him a few years later in a bar and apologized profusely. He seemed a bit unnerved but tried to pretend like he didn't mind. Knowing what he'd encountered between my legs that night, I'm guessing he was probably thrilled to have received such an easy get-out-of-jail-free card from me. He probably shuddered at the sight of me and started having sudden memory flashes of deep-sea fishing and an old sunken ship covered in plankton and kelp. I'm not ashamed of this, either. Vaginas are supposed to look and smell like vaginas. Keep your strange scented washes away from me, women's magazines. I'll allow my vag to keep its natural aroma of chicken noodle soup, thank you very much.

There were other notable blackouts during college, like the time I ate an entire Papa John's pizza, or when I ditched a cab and skinned my hands running from it. I also once went home with some dude who owned more than two pit bulls, which is the reddest flag there is, and my sister still loves to remind me about the time I put her in a car with strangers so I could stay out longer. My blackouts have usually involved eating like it's my last meal, but the time my brain went night-night while I let a stranger wake up my unwashed vagina definitely still gets the top prize. I want to encourage any young lady reading this to avoid drinking to the point where you're unsafe, especially if you have this cool genetic quirk and are prone to blacking out. It's crazy unsafe, and I lucked out with a nice dude who treated my vaginal area like a Golden Corral.

But let's get back to the part about how I'm a seasoned, smart adult now. I drink wine and scotch fairly regularly—sometimes a martini or tequila, just to mix it up—but not excessively, and I definitely don't drink to the point of blackout. Not only did College Amy teach me a lesson, I truly don't enjoy being drunk anymore. I'm not recommending dead sobriety here. I mean, don't be cray. But I don't like to get anything more than a little tipsy now. I'm in a really good place and have gotten my behavior under major control.

Guys, I blacked out a few months ago.

I'm not proud of this. I don't think it's cute or even funny. But sometimes when a sad and complicated set of circumstances lands you in the emotional and physical gutter, all you can do is laugh. After you cry. And drink.

It all started when a woman named Meg went to see *Trainwreck* with her friend. Meg has multiple sclerosis and didn't know MS would be such a large part of the movie but ended up really liking the fact that it was included in the story. She reached out to me because she said she wanted to hook my dad up with an incredible doctor in New York who had helped her.

Dr. Sadiq is the only doctor in the US who is FDA approved to treat MS patients with stem cells. To me, the idea that my dad could feel better wasn't even in the realm of possibility. I was grateful to Meg and excited for my dad to meet Dr. Sadiq, but I also didn't want to get my hopes up too high. Over the years, I'd noticed a change in my dad's willingness to take his meds and follow doctors' recommendations. He's offered physical therapy several times a week in the facility where he lives, but he was going infrequently or sometimes not at all. I sent an acupuncturist to him for a few months, and without telling me, he told her to stop coming. One day a couple of years ago, we got into an argument about it, which ended with his shouting that he just didn't want to try anymore.

This crushed me. Realizing that he'd thrown in the towel and wanted to passively allow the disease to do what it would broke my heart. People with MS deal with a lot: difficulty with eating, walking, and controlling their bowels (as has been well documented in this book)—not to mention the toll it takes on cognitive abilities and emotional stability. My dad was never the kind of guy to have a hopeful outlook on life. He was always dark. Even in his heyday, when he was young, rich, and handsome, he could make Tim Burton seem like Richard Simmons. But this was different. He was telling me to back off and let him decay. I don't blame my dad for wanting to give up, but it still destroyed me to hear him say it.

Since then, I've been mourning my dad while he's still alive. One certainty of his MS is that his physical abilities will decline more and more until they're entirely gone. This has led us to experience a lot of "lasts" together. The most heartbreaking one was the last time we went bodysurfing. We'd always loved riding the ocean waves together, so when it became clear that he wasn't going to be able to walk much longer, he asked me to go to the beach with him one last time. It was a pretty cloudy day, and there was a chill in the air. There were only one or two other people on the beach. I put on a brave face as we walked into the ocean. The waves were rough enough that you had to use your leg strength to make it in past the break. He struggled. It was crushing me to see him getting knocked down. I led us in and turned my face out to the ocean horizon so my dad wouldn't notice my heart falling out of my chest and into the sea. Seeing your parent physically incapable like that is something I wish on no one.

We waited for a good wave. The last wave we would ever ride together. When we saw it rolling in, we made eye contact and nodded to each other like musicians agreeing to play the bridge. We bent our knees, leaned toward the shore with our arms over our heads, and dove. It was a long, hard wave, and we rode it all the way in. We could feel the power of the ocean carrying us. When we stopped, I picked up my head to see where my father was. He was right next to me, squinting through the salt water and wiping the hair out of his eyes. He looked over at me and we smiled big at each other, bugging our eyes out to keep each other from bawling. I took his hand and helped him walk back until the wet sand turned dry. We caught our breath and tried not to take in the gravity of the moment.

I never wanted to give up hope that we could someday go out there again. But none of the MS studies I'd ever read made this seem possible, so I decided that instead of trying to heal him, I'd do whatever I could to make his time on this earth as pleasurable and comfortable as possible. If he asked me to bring him five hundred Werther's Original hard candies to suck on incessantly, I would. If he wanted booze (even though he never asked me), I'd get it for him. If he asked me for pot cookies (which he did), I'd bring them. I'd do anything for my dad. Buy him a lap dance, a lapdog, whatever it took.

So when I received Meg's email about Dr. Sadiq, I thought about the promise I'd made to my dad to let him be, and I thought, *FUCK HIM! He's going to see this doctor!* I didn't care if he had to be brought in on a stretcher kicking and screaming. Well, he can't kick, so just screaming.

I didn't even ask him. I just told him he was going to see this special doctor, and made it sound exciting and magical and as if it were something to look forward to. And he bit.

The next day, he traveled the two hours from Long Island to meet Kim and me at Dr. Sadiq's office in Manhattan. It's always a gamble what version of my father I will get. The medication can often make him out of it and kind of mean, but when he got off the elevator at the doctor's office that day he was smiling and didn't say anything hostile to the staff. My dad can be a huge wiseass who lashes out in a funny way at people, but sometimes it's altogether unfunny and just unkind. I've seen him scream at very gentle, nice orderlies who are just trying to help him back into his chair. He is rude to nurses—dismissive and cold if they're lucky, and flirty and aggressive if they aren't. But that day, he didn't make inappropriate eye or ass contact with the nursing staff. At one point when the nurse asked who was older, Kim or me, he answered, "The big one," as he pointed at me. But other than that fun insult, things were looking up.

My dad and I held hands as Dr. Sadiq explained what the stem cell treatments would entail over the next six months. Less than halfway through the conversation, my dad interrupted Dr. Sadiq, who was midsentence.

"I have to pee."

His attendant wheeled him to the bathroom, where he stayed for a very long time. Longer than normal by five times. The doctor continued while my dad was in the restroom, explaining that the stem cell treatment could at the very least improve him significantly, even potentially making it possible for him to walk again. This was amazing news, of course, but Kim and I must have seemed like we weren't sold, because Dr. Sadiq started offering up references who could testify to the quality of his treatments.

"No, doctor, we aren't worried about you," I said. I came right out and admitted that I was afraid my dad would either completely resist the treatment or become so difficult that the doctor would eventually refuse to treat him. Dr. Sadiq—a man so determined and dedicated to his work that he often sleeps in his office—jokingly explained, "Oh, no, I am treating him whether he likes it or not. He can punch me in the face and call me names, and I will not let him get out of this." And then the doctor, in his matter-of-fact way, said something that should have been obvious to me.

"Your father doesn't want to get his hopes up."

A pang shot through my entire body. Of course. Why didn't I see this myself? It's a huge theme in my own life and even in my movie. *Trainwreck* is in many ways a love letter to my father. It's my way of saying, *Even though you have wronged people and made mistakes, I love you, and your life hasn't gone unwitnessed.* I wanted him to see himself as I see him, as a human who is sick and flawed but who I think is pretty wonderful, most of the time. I guess the need to protect yourself to the point of being an asshole runs in the family. My dad and I have both been burned so many times that we use humor and darkness to keep potential pain at bay. I'd been giving my dad such a hard time for his unwillingness to fight his MS, but he was being resistant for good reason. He'd already been beaten to the ground countless times. Literally.

Kim and I teared up a little and nodded as our dad was rolled back into the room. I squeezed his hand and could tell his mood had soured a little.

I held my breath and could not bear to look at my dad. Dr. Sadiq explained every detail of the next six months of his life, and while he didn't make it sound easy, he did focus on the results.

Throughout the discussion, my dad kept looking at the floor and Dr. Sadiq would gently reprimand him, "Look at me, Gordon." When he finished his explanation, my dad was looking down again. There was a long silence. We all sat there very still.

And then my father looked up and said: "Okay, I will put my hope and faith in you."

Kim and I couldn't fucking believe it. Never had I ever heard my dad say the words "hope" or "faith." I think my dad could be at the Wailing Wall or sitting with the Dalai Lama on a mountain in Tibet and he'd be annoyed that someone next to him was humming too loudly or complaining that he was hungry. What I'm saying is he's not a spiritual guy.

I threw my arms around him and then sat back down before the tears started falling uncontrollably down my face. I leaned over and said, "I'm so proud of you! I love you!" It wasn't just that he'd accepted treatment. It was that he still had some hope left in there.

We set up our next appointment with Dr. Sadiq and said our good-byes, and went home to spend the evening with my very kind boyfriend, Ben. I was feeling emotional, but I held it together. We got cozy in the living room and I exclaimed, "I had a tough day. I want to have some wine tonight!" I opened a bottle and had a glass. We started watching the latest episode of *Girls*, and it was coincidentally about Hannah's father, who was struggling with living his life as a gay man, having just come out of the closet to Hannah. The parent/ child roles were reversed, with Hannah coming to his rescue when her father was sad and disoriented. The episode ended with their walking through Times Square together, him sadly saying, "I don't know what to do," and Hannah saying, "That's okay, I'm here . . . and I'll always be here."

Any tears I'd held back in my entire life came out right then and there. The floodgates opened and I bawled hard. Thank God I'm a very very pretty crier. Ben was sweet and watched a lot of mucus drain from my nose onto the couch, and hugged me after I finally caught my breath. When I was done crying, I drank another glass of wine and took a hit of weed. I wanted the day to end because it was hard enough having all of those realizations about my dad, but it was also new to have a boyfriend with me, witnessing the whole thing. Being the child of an alcoholic father and *whatever my mom is* has made me almost incapable of believing that the people I love won't leave me or hurt me in a way I didn't think they were capable of. I have to fight against all of my impulses and warped instincts to accept any sort of love. This night was no exception.

It was time to call it a day. And fast. So I took five milligrams of Ambien, which is on the higher end of the normal nightly dosage for me, and I started to get ready for bed. My limbs were a little sore from the eleven-mile bike ride Ben and I had gone on that morning. (Ew, we're an annoying white couple.) I was physically and mentally drained—and a little drunk. Throwing Ambien into the mix was not wise, since, as I learned the hard way, it enhances the effects of alcohol and vice fucking versa. If the details of what happened next were left to me, I'd tell you that I had one more glass of wine and then woke up the next morning.

But according to my loving, patient boyfriend (who was staring forlornly at the ceiling when I opened my eyes the next morning), a LOT happened after that last glass of wine.

According to Ben, shortly after I prayed to the holy trinity of Ambien, wine, and weed, I began dipping crackers into butter as if it were guacamole. While he watched me in this feeding frenzy, I kept accusing him of judging me. He said I was chasing him around the living room saying, "You're judging me!" with a lot of sass and he was responding with "You're getting butter all over the apartment!"

Then I sat down on the couch to watch television and continue eating my buttermole. I turned on *Keeping Up with the Kardashians* (his least-favorite show) and wouldn't shut up about Khloé and how much she's changed. At least that's what Ben thinks I said, because he could only understand about 30 percent of my yammering. I ended up heating up two frozen pizzas, one of which I burned, before he finally convinced me to go to sleep. In bed, I aggressively stacked all the pillows on my side instead of the usual division of two and two. Then I laid my head on top like the princess and the pea. He said, "Amy, we each get two pillows," to which I elegantly responded, "Not tonight, motherfucker!" Cue the Stevie Wonder song "Isn't She Lovely."

Anyway, the lesson here is don't combine alcohol, Ambien, and weed on the same day that you take a marathon bike ride, find out your dad's will to live has been restored, and watch a heartbreaking episode of *Girls* that hits way too close to home. If you learn one thing from this book, let it be that.

This blackout at age thirty-four was a far cry from some of the dangerous situations I got myself into during college, but I still wouldn't recommend that anyone engage in this kind of activity— not even grown-ups who are in loving, supportive relationships and safely drinking under their own roofs. Ben was pretty generous about the whole thing. He wasn't judgmental or critical, but he was concerned. He didn't like that I decided to "check out" on him. With good reason. It's not fair, and I haven't done it since.

It was a hard couple of years, seeing my dad check out on life like that, knowing that he really meant it when he said he was done trying to improve his condition. A part of me gets it. Things are grim for him most of the time. I'm strong and healthy, and I still have to fight the urge to give up about twice a day. Three times a day during awards-show season. In his younger, healthier days, my dad traveled, partied, philandered, and drank. I know he must miss those times. I feel fortunate I'm still able-bodied enough to make poor choices.

Sometimes when I visit him and he's looking particularly dead-eyed or sad, I try to amp up his spirits. Roll him outside for a walk, get him involved, force him to mix it up. He's still in there when he wants to be—and it's nice to see. Knowing there's a possibility he will walk again has made everything brighter, and it feels like he's coming back. I push his wheelchair into the fresh air, and make him look up at the sky. I watch the sun hit his face and he comes alive, every cell of his body lighting up to cause trouble, just like he was meant to do.

AN EXCITING TIME
FOR WOMEN IN HOLLYWOOD

Imagine you just wrote and starred in your own movie for the first time. The movie premieres, it does well, and you feel like you're on top of the world. And you are exhausted because making a movie is a lot of work, and also because you had to lose (and keep off) ten pounds you usually like carrying around with you. (Because no woman is believably lovable unless you can see her clavicles from all angles.) Then, before you're even done celebrating the premiere of your movie, which you poured your guts into, it's explained to you that actors aren't really paid to act. What they're paid for is to do press.

What a gross discovery.

I get it. Movies are really expensive to produce so the studios have to make sure people actually go see them. I apologize if you saw way too much of my face in ads and billboards and commercials in the summer of 2015. If this is how you're feeling, you can thank the marketing people. And trust me, no one was sicker of hearing my voice than I was.

I'd never starred in a movie before *Trainwreck*, so I was virtually unknown in other countries. This meant I had to sign up for an intense international press tour to promote the movie. Press tours consist of visits to multiple cities where you sit in rooms with journalists (usually while on camera) who ask you to talk about your movie so they can go away and write hopefully positive stuff so people will go see your movie. On that press tour, I was interviewed by what felt like every journalist in the world—from the most well-known news stations to dudes who were taping the first episode of their podcast. I had to say yes to everything, because the studio was taking a chance on me. I was a new employee, and that is when you have to act excited for the opportunity and be a good little worker bee.

When you first hear that you're going to Australia, Germany, London, Amsterdam, Dublin, and on and on, you think, *FUCK YEAH! Free trip! I've never been to Berlin!* And then you realize that you will spend every second of every day being asked the same questions by every single interviewer, and you will be expected to perform the answers for them as if they are freshly coming out of your mouth for the first time, every single time. Without fail, every last one of them asked, "How autobiographical is your movie?" I started to feel like a soulless show pony. Talking about yourself all day long like that leaves you with a kind of emptiness that's hard to describe. And it's a lot to take on for someone like me who is so unfortunately prone to honesty.

On top of feeling like it was up to me to convince people to buy tickets, there was the added burden of being a woman. Because every time there is a female lead in a movie, everyone bugs out and says, "Will this be a turning point for women?" or "What does this MEAN for women in comedy?"

So the pressure is on. Because the movie doesn't just have to do well so that I can feel proud of it or so the studio can make money—it has to do well for the 50 percent of the population I am now apparently representing. *What will this mean for our gender for years to come!??* That line of questioning is pretty loaded. Especially since this was my first movie, and I don't even pretend to speak for all women. I write about my life and how I see and experience the world, without assuming that my views are universal.

So anyway, I went on a huge press tour, not just for the movie but for all of female-kind. And just like everywhere else, since the dawn of man, every interviewer's favorite question was, "Is this an exciting time for women in entertainment?" or "What does this mean for women in Hollywood?"

"Isn't this an exciting time?!"

And I wanted to scream, "NO!"

First of all, I don't consider myself a "woman in Hollywood." I'm not even totally sure what that term means. But if I were to play free association with myself and I heard that term, I guess I would think of someone who either has her own abbreviated celeb name, like J. Law/Lo, or someone who has looked very hot in a few movies who also, I don't know . . . has her own lifestyle blog or her own product line? Like an Alba or a Paltrow. I have none of those things. "A. Schu" never really caught on like we were all hoping it would.

Also I am literally not a "woman in Hollywood." As you know, I have always lived in New York, and no, it doesn't feel like an exciting time. The exciting time will come when nobody has to answer that stupid question. Everyone, on the count of three: Stop asking that. Forever. Just stop. One. Two. Three! And besides, Hollywood is not at all exciting for women. I'm sure no one is too shocked to hear that it's an industry of people who judge most women almost solely on their appearance, and where every day women feel themselves barreling toward death and decay while smaller, hotter actresses like Selena keep appearing like Russian nesting dolls. It's an industry where you go from playing a lead love interest to a turtleneck-and-knit-vest-sporting grandmother who, despite missing her husband, still has a lot of love to give to pets, in half the time a leading man turns into a grandpa.

I'm of the belief that in most industries, women have to work twice as hard to get half the credit. After putting in so much effort to make a good movie, it felt pretty demeaning when they called it a "female comedy." This meaningless label painted me into a corner and forced me to speak for all females, because I am the actual FEMALE who wrote the FEMALE comedy and then starred as the lead FEMALE in that FEMALE comedy. They don't ask Seth Rogen to be ALL MEN! They don't make "men's comedies." They don't ask Ben Stiller, "Hey, Ben, what was your message for all male-kind when you pretended to have diarrhea and chased that ferret in *Along Came Polly*?"

On the press tour, many interviewers actually acknowledged this issue and came right out and asked, "Is there a lot of pressure on you to speak for all women?" I appreciated that they got right to it. Maybe it's a good question. I understand that I have enough eyes and ears on me that what I say and do matters. This is a responsibility that I'm honored to have—because it's an opportunity to do my best to help empower women in the only way I know how: by writing a story about a woman from the woman's point of view.

Trainwreck was about equal opportunity. Equal opportunity to be a commitment-phobe—even if you're a girl. But some of the interviewers were thrown off by this. Many of them asked me why I chose to write a role reversal for the guy and the girl. Meaning, why did I make the girl the one who had trouble being vulnerable and the guy the one who wanted more of a commitment? Why was the girl the one who had a bachelor pad and a string of one-night stands, and the guy was the one with a highly respected career and a sober lifestyle? Interviewers were always shocked when I explained that I hadn't done this intentionally, but that I wrote something true to my experience. Women get a reputation for being the crazy, overly sensitive ones in relationships, but in my experience, it's the dudes who do that. Not that I and most of my friends aren't sensitive flowers. We just don't invest as much or as quickly in relationships, and we don't get our egos as involved. I'll admit to exaggerating LeBron James's character. We made him overly concerned about his friend's love life, the way girls are often characterized—and this is something I haven't actually witnessed from my male friends. But that is where the gender role reversal begins and ends in *Trainwreck*. I was writing what felt honest, real, and compelling, coming from my perspective and my real life. And even though I'm not gonna cop to representing all women, I'm also pretty sure I'm not the only chick with these experiences.

Nonetheless, the slut-shaming was off the charts. Maybe it was just a cultural thing that made the foreign journalists seem out of line. Some interviewers brought this vibe: *Well, you talk about sexual subject matter in your movie, so I can say anything I want to you.* Which made me want to shower for the rest of my life. One of the interviews I did in Australia went viral when the journalist asked me the question "So your character is a skank, do you have a word for skank in America?" I told him that it was a rude question and we went back and forth a little bit, and of course, if you do anything other than just smile and nod and thank them for their time, if you actually have an unfavorable or emotional response to a rude question, the shit hits the fan. People react as if you obviously can't take the heat and need to get out of the kitchen. But I've never been a smile-and-nod type of girl, nor have I ever been one to get out of the kitchen.

The worst experience was in Berlin—surprise, surprise—when I sat with the same interviewer twice. He was a man in his late fifties or early sixties, wearing jeans and a button-down. He was balding up top and was letting it grow a little long in the back, half pageboy, half Robert Plant. He wore glasses and didn't let social norms pressure him into smiling, ever. I first sat with him and Bill Hader. He asked Bill if he liked playing a doctor, and then he asked me what I was like to have sex with. Bill didn't like this question and stood up for me, but I said it was fine and explained that it was like being with one of those performers who stand on boxes on street corners spray-painted entirely silver. You can't tell if they're statues or not but every couple minutes they move slightly. The only difference, I said, is that no one ever gave me a dollar. (I need to amend this at this time and say that since then, my boyfriend did, very generously, slip a dollar under my door once after sex. I sat on the toilet and watched it make its way into the bathroom as I waited until my body agreed to pee so I wouldn't get a UTI. I stared at that dollar feeling loved.)

That same Berlin interviewer was, for some reason, allowed to come back later and interview me again, this time with Vanessa Bayer, who plays my friend and coworker in *Trainwreck*. He was immediately abrasive and started asking me things that seemed to express not only his dislike for the movie but also for every breath I had ever taken. He said these exact words: "Why do you think it's okay to make people uncomfortable?" As he said this I caught sight of a large hole in the crotch of his pants and realized that not one but both of his testicles were exposed. I looked him in the eye and said, "I don't want to embarrass you, but I would like you to cover your lap." Vanessa looked down and saw and nodded while her face turned bright red.

She concurred that his balls were like the answer, my friend, blowin' in the wind. He looked down, crossed his legs, regained his composure, and said, "Where was I?" I said, "You were asking me why I thought it was okay to make people uncomfortable."

After the three hundredth interview talking about how many people I'd slept with and then awkwardly transitioning to my dad's illness, I thought, *Fuck this, I'm never doing a movie again.* Just kidding! I am going to make more movies. But I'll never do that much press again. And I'll never lose weight again. Well, not that much anyway. I look stupid skinny. My large, Cabbage Patch head stays the same size and the rest of me shrinks to a different proportion. And what's the reward? To be a "woman in Hollywood"? No thank you!

Then again, maybe what it means to be a "woman in Hollywood" is to be one of the many angry, bemused, and ravenous women who just wanted to be actors or artists, and who were made to believe this option would actually be available to them after they jumped through five thousand hoops in high school and college and in the gross offices of agents and managers and the quiet church basements where they performed one-act plays and musicals within an inch of their lives. Maybe a "woman in Hollywood" is just a person who was going about her business and trying to live her dreams—the same as all her male counterparts—but along the way she got held up, hungry and exhausted, by fending off insane double standards and stupid-ass questions from journalists.

If that's a "woman in Hollywood," then fine, maybe I am one. Guilty as charged.

But even though the foreign press couldn't be more wrong about the "exciting time" all us women in Hollywood are having, not all journalists misunderstood me and my movie. I was so grateful I got nominated for a Golden Globe, which is determined by the Hollywood Foreign Press Association. The night of the Golden Globes was a dream. My whole family came with me, and even though I didn't win, I was lucky enough to lose to a friend whose work blows my mind. Some of the journalists from the Hollywood Foreign Press Association who were there that night were amazing. I spoke with many of them and left the interviews feeling nourished, grateful, and understood. Maybe I wasn't just a trainwreck of a girl after all! I started to feel better and comforted myself by trying to see myself through their eyes, remembering some of the kind things they'd said to me. But I was promptly brought right back down to earth when I saw how *Trainwreck* had been renamed in some of the foreign markets:

Italy: *A Disaster Girl*
Bulgaria: *Total Damage*
Czech Republic: *Derailment*
Russia: *A Girl Without Complexes*
Germany: *Dating Queen*
Finland: *Just the Night*
Portugal and Poland: *Derailed*
Hungary: *Disaster*
France: *Crazy Amy*
French Canada: *Hopeless Case*
Argentina: *This Girl Is a Mess*

So since I didn't win the Globe that night and get to stand at the podium to make a speech, I want to take this opportunity to thank all the journalists in all the different countries I visited. First, I'd like to thank all the people who pointed out that I was a woman. Your compliments were phrased very precisely so that I was never just described as "funny," but rather, a "funny *woman*." You made sure

I didn't lose sight of my ovaries. Thank you. Without your constant reminders, I may have just forgotten my uterus on a crosstown bus, but you guys made me perpetually aware that I bleed once a month *and* I can tell a joke! I also want to thank the guy who called me a skank. I could see how unhappy you were in your own life, and I deeply felt for you. If you're out there, I want you to know that I am very happy and experiencing a good time in my life. And lastly I want to especially thank the balls of that journalist in Berlin. If it weren't for you guys I would probably be able to sleep at night, and who the hell wants that. *Auf Wiedersehen.*

MAYCI AND JILLIAN

It was July 23, 2015, and *Trainwreck* had been out for about a week. I was so happy to be home, having just landed in Los Angeles after spending the aforementioned week doing very tiring press for the movie, this time in Australia. It was especially sweet to be home since that trip had not been too uplifting. I was supposed to go out to dinner with my friend Allan that night. He's one of my very good friends, though I don't know if his name is spelled Alan or Allan. I also have major questions about how to spell his last name.

I was jet-lagged and having some hard-core back pain from all the travel, so I booked a massage. I walked out of the hotel spa feeling great—generally excited about life, fortunate, and rejuvenated. I looked at my cell phone and had a lot of missed calls from my publicist, Carrie, who'd also sent me many texts telling me to call her right away. I started giggling. If she was trying to contact me that urgently, I was certain that a naked photo or a sex tape of me must have gotten out. I had sex with my boyfriend on a computer camera once when I was twenty and it was totally awful. We were in no way focused on each other. We were looking at ourselves on the monitor. I'd bought black lacy lingerie with a garter belt. I didn't understand that you have to be a Victoria's Secret model to not look insane in a getup like that. A still of Rupert Murdoch in a rocking chair would have looked sexier than I did in that outfit. All in all, it was a horrible sight and I apologize in advance for that sex tape in case it ever does get out. I have major, major sympathy for anyone whose phone or computer has ever been hacked, and I really hope it never happens to me. But nude photos don't scare me. I'm sure they will leak someday, and I don't know how I'll feel then—but on this particular day at this particular moment in my life, I think I'd laugh if it happened. And apologize to all who had to see the footage or shots.

So on July 23, 2015, I was preparing myself for news of my sex tape leaking and was gearing up to calm down my publicist and let her know I didn't care. I dialed Carrie and I was already smiling. My giggling had become a full laugh by the time she answered.

Then she said, "There was a shooting in a theater in Lafayette, Louisiana, at a showing of *Trainwreck*."

My heart broke right then and there. I mean it. The only other times I felt sadness that heavy in my life were after a surfing accident when I was sure I was losing my leg, and upon hearing of the deaths of a couple of close friends. The news crushed me. I went to my hotel room, turned on CNN, and became almost catatonic. I didn't yet know that two beautiful, smart, strong women would die that night. I didn't know about Mayci Breaux, who was just twenty-one years old and a sweet, kind, gorgeous churchgoing girl who was set to marry her high school sweetheart. And I didn't know about Jillian Johnson. She was just thirty-three years old and an active member in her community. A great wife and stepmother, she was a smart and creative business owner, a musician, and a beautiful artist. I needed to know every detail, and I wanted to fly straight to Louisiana to be with the families who were affected by this tragedy.

My friend Allen came over to my hotel room and let me put my head on his lap while I cried. He called the necessary people and took care of me. I was pretty out of it for a couple weeks. I had more press to do for *Trainwreck* and a vacation planned with friends, but I wanted to cancel everything.

I read about the disturbed man who killed Mayci and Jillian and injured nine other people. I don't believe in giving mass shooters their moment in the sun. I don't want to write his name. I never have and never will say it. But I do want to outline some facts about him. He loved the Tea Party. He publicly hated women and praised Hitler. This man purposefully selected my movie as a place to shoot and kill women.

Here are a few other facts: In 2006, he was arrested for arson (and was denied a concealed weapons permit in Russell County, Alabama, as a result), though the arson charges were eventually dropped. In 2008, his family members asked a court to involuntarily commit him for mental health treatment because he was a danger to himself and others, but he was only committed on an emergency basis and never reached the stage of having a judge rule on his mental competence. Also in 2008, his former intimate partner filed a protective order against him—but no final order was issued by the court. Despite all that, in February 2014 he was able to legally buy a gun in a Phenix City, Alabama, pawn shop—the gun that would become his murder weapon.

He was not prohibited from having guns, but he was precisely the type of person who should be barred—a person with a dangerous criminal history who abused and threatened family members, and who had contacts with the mental health system. Several states have passed laws often referred to as "gun violence restraining orders," which allow family members of these types of dangerous people to ask a court to temporarily prohibit the person from having guns. If granted, not only do these orders prohibit the person from buying a gun, but they also require the person to turn in the guns they already own. Had this tool been available to this man's family members when he threatened them, maybe everything would have turned out differently for Mayci and Jillian.

Knowing this is unbearable. Knowing this is enough to make me want to do something.

And yet, gun-violence restraining orders are just the tip of the iceberg. Because even if every single state had more laws like this in place to keep guns out of dangerous hands, there's still a gaping loophole that makes it easy for *anyone* to buy guns through unlicensed sellers, perhaps at gun shows or online—because for those sales, there are no background checks and no questions asked. Surveys conducted over three decades consistently show that 30 to 40 percent of US gun transfers take place without a background check. In many states getting a gun is easier than getting birth control. Read on. It gets even better (worse). In several states in this country, it's legal to buy a gun if you're completely blind, and in most states it's legal to buy a gun if you're on one of the terror watch lists. I'm going to tell you that again. If you can't see *anything at all*, you can buy a gun. If you're on not just the "no fly" list but literally the list of people our government suspects are terrorists, you can Legally. Buy. A. Gun.

Don't get it twisted. I'm great friends with plenty of gun owners. I believe law-abiding Americans have every right to own a gun. But I think there is room for improvement. Don't you? Haven't enough shootings happened? You know who says no? The people who profit the most from gun sales. But 92 percent of Americans—including

82 percent of gun owners and 74 percent of NRA members—support criminal background checks for all gun sales. Yet the gun lobby opposes this most commonsense of policies. And their lapdogs in Congress—whom they've bought and paid for—fall in lockstep behind them. As you may have noticed by now, there are a lot of lists in this book. I've included another one at the end of the book on pages 322–323—it's a list of congresspeople who've taken money from and been influenced by the gun lobby. Enjoy!

It was especially striking to me to learn that gun violence is specifically a women's issue: women in America are eleven times more likely to be murdered with guns than women in other developed nations. In the eighteen states that require background checks for all handgun sales, 46 percent fewer women are shot and killed by intimate partners than in the states that do not.

Do you know much about all of this? Before the Lafayette shooting, I didn't. You owe it to yourself and your family to be educated about it, because it's a problem we can chip away at, together. For more details on how to get involved, see page 321.

As I've documented in this book, I've mostly been able to find the humor in the absolute darkest moments. It's hard to do that with this, though. I know that for many of you, this might not be a chapter you signed up for and you may be thinking, *Get back to telling your vagina jokes! Make us laugh, clown!* I hear you. When I've written sketches about gun safety on my TV show, people have responded by saying they wish I'd just be funny. They tell me to stick to comedy because that's what they come to me for. I'll tell you what I tell them: No! I love making people laugh and am grateful that I'm equipped to do that. But when an injustice affects me deeply, I will speak about it—and I suggest you do the same. I wish I could muster the energy to put a clever and sarcastic spin on some of the grave statistics about gun violence in America, but I have to tell you, I just fucking can't. I was able to write a funny scene about gun safety on my TV show this year, and if you want to laugh along, please watch, but for this chapter in my book . . . I'm not laughing. I think about Mayci and Jillian every day. I carry pictures of them on the road with me, and when I see that yet another American or several Americans were killed senselessly and avoidably by guns, all I can think is enough is e-fucking-nough. Period.

I began working with Senator Chuck Schumer, a distant cousin of my father's, to advocate for sensible ways to stop gun violence. I sit on a committee for Everytown—a movement of Americans working together to end gun violence and build safer communities. As I was drafting this chapter, no lie, I got an invitation to the White House to meet President Obama and was there when he announced a set of new executive actions to address this national crisis.

The White House allowed me to bring a few guests, so I brought my sister, my brother, and Ben. There are few people I'd drop everything and fly across the country for on such little notice. President Obama is one of them. Common and Tatiana Maslany from *Orphan Black* are two others. What I'm saying is, it was thrilling to get to be there. We were joined by the rapper Wale and two guys from the Washington Wizards basketball team who are advocates to end gun violence. I was hanging out with them for most of the visit.

When it was time for the president to come into the room to meet us, we formed a receiving line. I straightened the Wizards' ties and belts and then saw that I had some dirt on my leg, so I quickly licked my finger and rubbed it off because I'm as elegant as I am hygienic. We were all transformed into little kids helping each other on picture day. As we neared the president, we were asked to write our name and occupation on a fancy little card and hand it to a stoic naval officer so he could announce us to the president before we shook his hand. When it was my turn, the officer looked at what I'd written on my card and, without missing a beat, announced with military precision, "Amy Schumer. She is a model!"

I stepped forward, and President Barack Obama smiled at me. We shook hands, and he spoke first:

"You're very funny, Amy Schumer." He sounded just like he sounds on TV.

"So are you."

"We really enjoyed *Trainwreck*," he said.

I said, "You saw *Trainwreck*?!!!"

He nodded and said, "Of course."

I couldn't believe it. He was so cool. He was keeping the conversation going with me and I didn't want to take any more of his time so I rushed our picture together. I was losing my mind in the picture, so moved and thrilled. He thanked me for my work trying to end gun violence, and I thanked him back and walked into the room where the press conference would take place.

A bit later, the president faced the cameras, standing in front of the parents of children whose lives were taken by gun violence—many from the shootings at Sandy Hook Elementary School in Newtown, Connecticut. He delivered the most eloquent, honest speech I will ever hear. He talked about the first graders who were killed. He repeated the words—"*first* graders"—and shed a few tears. I could see them. He wiped away the ones on his left side but not the right. After a few beats, he wiped both eyes. He spoke about how it was all too easy to get firearms on the Internet or at gun shows without a background check. Then he outlined the plan to fix that and much more.

When the press conference was over, I stood in the room for a while and was approached by people wearing buttons with the pictures of their slain children on them. Parents, wearing their dead children on their lapels. They just wanted to tell me about their kids. Some had lost their kids in Columbine. A nice couple whose daughter was killed in the Aurora movie theater shooting told me she had been a fan of mine. I listened and hugged them and promised I would keep fighting with them.

During the entire day at the White House, I was thinking of Mayci and Jillian. I'd been holding back tears for hours but when the president mentioned the shooting in Lafayette at the press conference, I couldn't stop myself from crying. Those women will always be in my thoughts. I will not forget them. I'll work hard every day to honor their memory and live in a way I hope would make them proud.

In the months since the White House, I've said many things about guns onstage or aired those gun-related scenes on my TV show. I'm always immediately hit with criticism from people on the Internet. That's putting it very lightly. Many of them feel incensed about the idea of the government wanting to "take away [their] guns," which is not at all what I'm advocating for. What most people in this movement care about is ending gun violence and making our communities safer. People rage at me on Twitter (and this is actually one of the nicest, most sanitized kinds of insults I get): "You're out of your league, Schumer! Stick to what you know!" Of course most of them call me a fat cunt, which I have grown to love.

But they are wrong (not about my being a fat cunt; that's subjective). They are wrong to say that I'm out of my league. Because I *do* know this issue. And you do too. Anyone who lives and breathes and has an opinion about whether or not first graders should get shot at school is qualified to speak on this issue. I'm not a politician nor an

NRA-hating shifty Jew, as some people see me in certain parts of the country. Most members of the NRA are great people. But their leaders are the cuckoo birds. I'm just an American who thinks we can have more common sense about keeping our families, children, and friends from being shot to death by an unstable person who never should have been able to get his hands on a gun in the first place.

Mayci Breaux   *Jillian Johnson*

I want to thank Jason Rzepka and Noelle Howey at Everytown for helping educate me about gun violence statistics and gun laws. I also want to thank the families of Mayci Breaux and Jillian Johnson for providing these photos and allowing me to honor the memories of Mayci and Jillian.

THINGS THAT MAKE ME HAPPY

1. My toddler niece laughing or doing pretty much anything. I love how she pronounces my name and yells,
   "Mimi!" when she sees me. Also her hair, which for a
   while looked like Benjamin Franklin's.

2. Scones. And not the store-bought ones that come six to
   a plastic container. I'm talking Alice's-Tea-Cup-in-NYC
   scones, either the vegan one (not because I'm vegan but
   because the texture is dope) or one with some form of
   chocolate (not white chocolate, real chocolate). Also,
   fine, the store-bought ones.

3. Seeing the people I love happy.

4. Riding a horse. We had a little farmhouse upstate when
   I was a kid, and I learned to ride at a local stable where
   I would go around in circles on the smallest horse. Since
   then, I'll get on a horse any chance I get. Zero questions
   asked. One day a few years back, I was lying on the couch

watching *Game of Thrones* at my sister's house, and she came into the room and said, "Babe, do you wanna ride a horse?" She lives in a normal neighborhood in Chicago where there should never have been a horse nearby, but I silently got up and followed her outside and there was a horse across the street. His name was Norman. We are now friends.

5. Telling a new joke that I'm excited about onstage, even if it doesn't do well. Telling a new joke never gets old.

6. Hearing my brother, Jason, play his horn. We both love Miles Davis, John Coltrane, and Thelonious Monk, but Jason plays really loose, crazy stuff called "free jazz." It's the kind of jazz you hear in the background when Claire Danes is very stressed out on *Homeland*. But I just love hearing him play it. Doesn't have to be onstage either. Sometimes at his house, I will all of a sudden hear his horn from another room, and the beautiful sound instantly makes me feel at peace.

7. Watching British or Irish sexual-assault-based crime shows at my sister and brother-in-law's house. The thicker the accent, the thicker the reason I need to change my underwear by the end. (Ewwwww.) I mean it. I have to watch these shows with subtitles.

8. Sitting with my friends at the Comedy Cellar and making fun of each other. Particularly Keith Robinson, who is never, ever right about anything but still commits to his arguments as if his life depends on it.

9. Coming.

10. Being on a boat or Jet Ski that is going way too fast and screaming my head off.

11. Snuggling on the couch with my sister's three-legged dog, Abbott. We have this really cool relationship where I don't give him treats, so I know his love for me is entirely non-food motivated.

12. Making people laugh to the point of wiping tears away.

13. Waking up next to the person I am in love with and immediately rolling away from him to hide my busted-ass morning face and baby-diaper breath. But he pulls me toward him, cuddling my butt into him, not caring at all.

14. My sister. Playing volleyball with her, watching *Orphan Black* and eating pasta with her. Drinking with her. Smoking pot with her. Traveling the world with her and making TV shows and movies we are proud of together. Making her laugh on camera. I will sometimes force her to be in a sketch for my TV show and one of my favorite things is making her laugh during the scene, ruining as many takes as possible. I know she panics and is worried that she's wasting everybody's time by laughing, but I can't help myself.

15. I like when a small animal rides on the back of a larger animal (think Sir Didymus and Ambrosius in *Labyrinth*). Or a video of a lion and a seal becoming friends or something like that.

16. When someone in a motorized wheelchair passes, I like holding my hand up to cover the person's body, so it just looks like a head whizzing by.

17. When the dog bites. When the bee stings. Sorry.

18. Laughing and yelling at my girlfriends from high school when they try to smoke pot in the bathroom of wherever I am performing, no matter how classy. They tried to smoke pot at both *SNL* and Carnegie Hall.

19. Hearing my sister on the phone with a delivery place after they bring the wrong food or don't include enough sauce. She starts out very calm and rational but then spins the fuck out after thirty seconds.

20. Sitting on the couch with a girlfriend, facing each other, and having long conversations about what's going on with the guys or girls in our lives. Yes, with wine. I didn't think I needed to add that, but if you're gonna make a big deal about it, yes, of course, with wine, unless scotch is needed.

21. Making a new friend. When you're over your twenties it's hard, but once in a while someone comes along that you really want to invest time in and it's so special.

22. Smoked salmon.

23. Watching Dave Attell onstage. No one makes me laugh harder.

24. Sex. I know I already said coming, but sex is pretty great and should be mentioned.

25. Falling in love.

THE SUN WILL COME
OUT TOMORROW

I'd been single for about three years when I met Ben. Well, that's not totally true. There are three dudes who might read this and say, "WHAT THE FUCK, SCHUMER?!" And I'd be like, "Don't call me 'Schumer,' that is part of the reason why we broke up!" I'm kidding, but there are three guys who were my boyfriends over the course of those years. Whoops! I mean four. I just remembered another one. But each was over after a couple months, and I never got to the point of feeling like a real couple with any of them. We played at it. We tried it on like jeans to see what it would feel like. After a month or two, one of us would call the other one "baby," or meet the other's friends, or make hypothetical future plans, but we never got there. I never made it there with anyone during the last few years before Ben.

I found myself feeling very satisfied in my work during that time. I know that sentence may sound like a cry for help. "I'm just happy really throwing myself into my work right now" (*as she chases a bottle of pills with a liter of Jack Daniel's*). But I mean it. This kind of unlikely satisfaction can actually happen. It was almost unsettling to be so okay with being single. I was almost certain that I'd start needing some sort of romantic stimulation or sexual activity to feel totally good about myself, but the need never came. I was feeling great, working my ass off doing stuff I was really proud of. (Such as a scene on my TV show depicting a girl who uncontrollably farts when she's scared, which ultimately leads to her being murdered.) It helps that my work is actually fun.

I'd already been through the panic that sets in when all your friends get married in their twenties and start having kids. This was then followed by the even worse panic when you turn thirty and you're still single. During that phase, I was terrified, and I started making pacts with male friends that if we were still alone in our forties, we'd get married and allow each other to see other people but keep our commitment to grow old together. Compared to the marriages I witnessed growing up, a prearranged, late-in-life marriage with a friend (or two) actually didn't seem that crazy. It was, however, probably a little nuts that I started making so many pacts for marriage. I was setting it up so that my forties could be a sort of reverse *Big Love* situation—a bunch of real live brother-husbands. How does that not exist?!

My parents have both been married. A lot. Three times each, to be exact, which teaches you never to invest too much in loving someone because he may be replaced within a couple months. I've had UTIs that lasted longer than some of my parents' marriages. And these marriages have led to a constant revolving door of siblings. The first time your parent is dating someone long enough and seriously enough for you to meet his or her kids, you invest. You think, *Wow! This person may become my new sister or brother. Maybe we'll share clothes and get tea together on Tuesdays at Alice's Tea Cup!* You show interest in them as human beings. You ask them questions like "When is your birthday? Do you like beets? Ever used a vibrator?" Okay, not the last one. But by the time marriage number three and stepsibling number whatever come around, you just kind of learn their name and maybe, if you're up to it, you get a feel for their general vibe.

By the time my father met his second wife, Melissa, I'd already learned this strategy. Dad's marriage to Melissa happened, in no small part, so he could benefit from her health insurance. What could be sexier and more romantic than that? Meet-cute alert! If I had to make a three-second movie to illustrate this relationship, it would open with a very unlucky woman dropping her wallet. Her Blue Cross Blue Shield card dramatically falls out, and my dad slowly picks it up without making eye contact with her. When things became official between them, Melissa introduced us to her daughter at a dinner at Ruth's Chris Steak House.

My father has been to most of the restaurants in this chain all over the country, a point of pride for him, and he'll tell you—if you'll listen—how many and which cities he has yet to visit. It became a tradition that our dad would take me and Kim there, and we would start with the calamari (I like the ones with the legs because I'm gruesome; I'll also eat cow tongue sandwiches and gefilte fish. I don't give a fuck!), then have potatoes au gratin, creamed spinach, and filets, still loudly crackling from all the scalding-hot butter they are drenched in. So when my dad introduced us to the person who was to be our new(est) stepsister, he naturally chose Ruth's Chris. Kim and I were already wise to the fact that this insta-sibling wouldn't be in the picture for long, so when she started talking about how excited she was because she had always wanted sisters, it kind of broke our hearts. We drank underage and choked down our steaks as fast as we could to get through the meal.

The marriage with Melissa lasted a few months and out went that sibling. I still think of her every time we . . . NEVER. I never think of her.

But back to my parents and their parade of marriages. My mom was already one divorce deep when she met my dad. Her first husband's name was David and they had one son together—my brother, Jason. When Jason was a few years old, they divorced, and my mom married my father soon after that. I was born a year later, and then Kim somehow snuck into this world. We're all four years apart. When Jason was eleven years old, he lost his dad, who died suddenly of a heart attack at the age of thirty-nine. After my parents divorced, my mom dated several dudes.

There was, of course, the first man she dated after the divorce, named Lou, whom I told you about in the chapter "Mom" and who also happened to be the father of my best friend, Mia; and then John, who wound up being at the very least a cokehead, but my siblings and I think more likely a crackhead. My mom thought it was time to move this guy in with her children after knowing him a few months. One weekend when my mom went to a volleyball tournament with my sister, she left me alone with John and he took off to indulge in a weeklong drug bender, leaving me at home. I was a teenager at the time, so I was psyched. But still, it's probably better not to live with a crackhead. To give my mom the benefit of the doubt, I suppose there are worse things than moving a crackhead into your house with your children, like maybe . . . no, a crackhead is the worst thing. After he left me alone, my mother ended their engagement briefly, until they got back together and he did the same thing again a few months later.

Then there was Andrew, who was very, very slow. I mean, I Am Sam would have schooled this guy in a game of Heads Up. There was

Doug, my mother's childhood sweetheart who resurfaced for a brief time, and Hank, whom we nearly moved in with.

There were a few more, none of whom I liked, and in fact I'd try to scare the suitors away. As soon as my mom would introduce me I'd call them "Daddy" and do anything I could to weird them out. I'd look them in the eyes and say, "My mom makes men fall in love with her and then gets tired of them. She will dispose of you like Kleenex in a week." They would giggle, thinking it was cute. Until they hit the bottom of the bin.

Our mother's third marriage was to her boyfriend Moshe, a Persian Jew from Israel who owned an auto mechanic shop in Queens. Moshe was stubborn, loud, embarrassing, and full of strong convictions. He and my mom were a real couple and genuinely loved each other. I found out they had gotten married by looking through photos she left on the counter one weekend when I was home from college. One photo showed them with two witnesses standing in front of a justice of the peace. I yelled into the other room, "Did you and Moshe get married?!" She shouted back, "Yeah!" They did it so that he could stay in the country, but then 9/11 happened and no one was too keen on granting citizenship status to an Iranian Jew. After a handful of years they divorced, and shortly thereafter Moshe had to go back to Israel to take care of his parents and was never allowed back in the US. I still miss him to this day. He was kind, and he loved us and our mom so much.

Since Moshe left the picture, my mom dates from time to time, and I hope she finds someone to grow old with, if that's what she wants. Sometimes it seems like she may just want to be alone, and I understand that instinct, too. As someone who is on the road all the time, I know very well how difficult it can be to share your life with a person once you've become so used to being on your own. You have to ask questions like "What do you want for dinner?" or "Can I have more of the blanket?" or "Can I have more of your dinner?" or "Can dinner be pigs in a blanket?" And that can be harder than you think. But it can also be really nice. I'm getting distracted. What is better than pigs in a blanket? Read my next book for the answer; my next book's title is *NOTHING*.

Then one day, out of nowhere, the fear I had of growing old unmarried just faded. My life was feeling full. Despite my parents' various attempts at marriage, I'd hear stories of happy second marriages, or tales of people not meeting until they were in their fifties or sixties, and feel calm about the whole thing. I was settling nicely into my thirties. I was dating a little but was not at all as consumed with it as I had been in my teens and twenties. The days of *He didn't call me today and it's three p.m.—what does that mean?!* were truly behind me. I realized that nothing was missing. I felt pretty and strong in my own skin. From the inside. Not from the reflection I saw while staring into some dude's pupils. I was feeling like I had it all.

I had a pretty big year. You've already heard all this earlier in the book . . . My movie came out, I hosted *Saturday Night Live*, and I filmed a one-hour special for HBO directed by one of my idols, Chris Rock. So many of my dreams were coming true all at once, and a lot of people were paying attention to me, including Barbara Walters. She'd just labeled me one of the "most fascinating people" of the year. Sure, why not? I didn't feel particularly fascinating, but if Babs thought so, it must have been true. I taped an interview with her during which she asked me one of those questions about where I saw myself in five or ten years. I answered that I would want to be writing, producing, directing, and creating. She was surprised. She said, "You didn't say married and with children." I was surprised too, because the thought hadn't even occurred to me. I laughed to myself and said to her, "Yeah, I guess you're right. I would love to have those things but I don't know how realistic that is for me."

And maybe I gravitated toward that answer because my job isn't exactly compatible with married life, and mostly because I was beginning to think that my parents were, at their core, both loners. Maybe I was like them. What's wrong with being alone anyway? Being alone is sometimes a great place to be, but people are always trying to correct this "problem" for you, even if you yourself don't have any kind of problem with it.

Seeing my parents as "a unit" these days is even more of an argument for remaining alone. Sometimes my mom will help me out by bringing supplies to the hospital where my dad lives, and watching them interact is strange. They were married for fourteen years and had two kids together, but now they talk with all the warmth and recognition of two people who maybe attended the same high school for a year but at different times. Their distance from each other probably started on day one of their marriage, something I really don't need all the details of but I'm sure one day I'll hear, because my dad likes to share. One day he told me about this woman, Lana, who went on to become his third wife. They had dated in the seventies back when my dad was hot shit. Tan and athletic, funny, and rich to boot. (I don't know what "to boot" means. But you already bought this book and you can't take it back—it's too late.)

Lana was crazy about my dad. Back in the seventies she'd bring her pots and pans over to his bachelor pad and cook for him. She was head over heels, and she hung around long enough and forced herself into being my dad's girlfriend. I have no judgments about that, by the way. As you know by now, I have moved to Astoria, Queens, to trap a man into a relationship and cooked him skirt steak with creamed spinach and a baked potato, because that is the one meal I know how to make. (And if you come over and notice out loud that I have never used my stove I will cut you with a never-used kitchen knife.) Anyway, one day, Lana's parents came to Manhattan to visit. Lana and Dad had been up in his penthouse apartment hanging out and smoking "grass," as my dad calls it. "And, Aim," he said, "this was really good grass." They were all heading downstairs in the elevator to go out to dinner, and when they got down to the lobby, a beautiful woman walked into the building. My dad said he stepped away from Lana and her parents, and walked right up to her and said, "Excuse me. Have you ever seen the penthouse in this building?" She said no. He asked, "Would you like to?" She said yes. The next thing my dad said to me was, "And that was the only time I've ever been tied up."

So to reiterate the facts here: My father left his girlfriend and her parents in the lobby of his building in order to go upstairs and have sex with a complete stranger, who apparently loved bondage. And he felt the need to tell his daughter all about it, thirty-plus years later. Lana's father was pounding on the door and calling my dad nonstop, so he locked himself in the apartment with the stranger for hours. And yet somehow, thirty years later, Lana still wanted to reunite with him and became my stepmother number two.

———

ABOUT A WEEK after the Barbara Walters interview, I was hanging out with my friend Vanessa Bayer, and we were talking about the latest with dudes. We both always had a guy or two we were juggling but not excited about. Which, by the way, means just texting and not actually meeting up. I realize it may have sounded like I was trying to say, "Vanessa and I were dealing with a bunch of different dick," but we weren't. We were always texting people. Not that there's anything wrong with juggling dicks. Which is the title of my third book—*Juggling Dicks*. So Vanessa said she'd heard of a dating app for your phone specifically aimed at creative people that attracted a lot of celebrity members. We decided to sign up. You pick some pictures of yourself to post and a song that will play if people click on your profile. I chose the song "Dirty Work" by Steely Dan thinking this was pretty funny to put on a dating site. In my main profile picture, I was wearing sunglasses and a baseball cap with no makeup. It was a selfie and I made a gross face, looking as though I were dying, because I was hiking, so I was. I also put up a picture of Sophia from *The Golden Girls*, Claire Danes making her cry face on *Homeland*, and one more normal photo where I was smiling and wearing a sweatshirt. Vanessa and I posted our profiles at the same time and scream-giggled like little girls.

We clicked on the profiles of a couple guys who looked cute, and it seemed like every dude was either a model or a photographer. They all posted the same two Rolling Stones songs and the same photos of themselves riding a motorcycle, chilling with a bulldog, holding an old-timey camera in Europe, or doing a cannonball off cliffs somewhere tropical. They were attractive—too attractive—and clearly a bunch of full-time pussy magnets. It was very discouraging. Vanessa and I had only been on this app about four hours and already I was feeling ready to throw in the towel, loofah, and disposable razor.

But I decided to hang in there. I made myself click the "like" button on maybe four guys' profiles, and within forty minutes, I got my first match. The guy was Ben. He was dancing with his grandmother in his profile picture at what looked like a wedding. His song was "LSD" by A$AP Rocky, my favorite song on that album. He wasn't an actor or photographer by trade like all the other guys—and he didn't live in LA or New York. He was a Chicago guy. We sent each other very simple hellos and short, funny messages.

A few hours passed and we were still messaging each other. He was funny, kind of odd, and interesting, and that made me paranoid. *This must be a trick. I'm a celebrity, and I will be reading this whole conversation on some trashy website tomorrow.* I had slowly worked myself into a full frenzy. I told him that I wanted to FaceTime to make sure I wasn't being catfished by a basement-dweller with a comedy podcast. He said, "Sure, no problem." We tried, but the Wi-Fi in my ancient apartment building wasn't working, so he called me instead and we spoke on the phone the old-fashioned way for a few minutes. He sounded like Christian Slater and was just as funny on the phone. He had heard my name but had never seen my movie, stand-up, or TV show. I liked talking to him. We hung up, and I thought he seemed cool and that I'd like to meet him at some point, but I didn't think much more about it.

I messaged with a couple other guys on the app and even made some loose plans to meet a few of them, but I never followed up. I took my profile down in under forty-eight hours. The experience was too intense, and if I saw one more guy looking off into the distance on a boat, I was gonna open my wrists and get into a warm bath. A few weeks later, I reached out to Ben because I was going to Chicago to visit my brother. He told me that he was actually driving to New York City. He is a furniture designer and was bringing something he'd constructed to a client. We made plans to meet for a drink at my place the next night. My sister immediately vetoed this dangerous idea and made me suggest a small, quiet restaurant to meet at instead.

I know it was a bold move to invite a guy I'd never met in person up to my place for a drink, but it does not really compare to my dad acting out *Fifty Shades of Grey* in his penthouse. Speaking of which, I'm sure you're dying to know if Lana forgave my dad after he ditched her to be hog-tied by a total stranger. The answer is yes, and she is N to the U to the T to the S. She had an adopted Vietnamese daughter, who was about seven years old. Her name was May, and when we all found out our parents were getting married, May was very much under the impression that Kim and I were to be her sisters for life. She clung to us in a heartbreaking way, and we played along even though you didn't have to be a psychic to guess the fate of this union. I'd have loved to have kept in touch with May, but her mom made sure this didn't happen.

My dad was in his late fifties and already in a wheelchair and very sick by their wedding day. We went to a place on Long Island that was part chapel, part someone's living room, and mostly haunted house. The person who married them seemed like he would be a waiter at the Jekyll and Hyde Club—very creepy looking and overweight, like the guy in *Beetlejuice* in the dinner-table scene where they all sing "Day-O." Lana, our shiny new stepmom, wore a white dress, a veil, and dramatic makeup, including a drawn-on mole.

The reception was at a Chinese restaurant, and there were about forty people there who were 98 percent Lana's guests. Lana's friends were all very strange with a hint of disturbing, and they were mostly people from her community theater. After her thespian friends gave toasts, Lana got up and read a—no exaggeration—twenty-five-minute speech, which was meandering and pointless. Nonetheless, I thought my dad should at least look in Lana's general direction while she read to him, her new *husband*. He never even glanced at her. Not once during the whole damn rant. He just ate moo shu pork and shrimp fried rice, and never acknowledged her presence during the whole speech. She didn't seem to mind too much. It was clear that she was just giving a performance, and she was thrilled to have so many eyes on her, even if none of them were my father's.

It was a rough day, and it turned into a rougher night. It seemed like things couldn't get much worse. Kim was nearly catatonic by the time the evening wound down. We'd both drunk as much boxed white wine as we could get our hands on, and that's when events hit rock bottom. I felt a tiny hand on my shoulder and a sweet voice ask, "Amy, will you sing 'The Sun Will Come Out Tomorrow' with me?" It was my new sister, May. She was such an innocent, beautiful little angel. I could not fucking believe I was about to sing a song that I loathe in a Chinese restaurant on Long Island with my temporary Vietnamese stepsister. I wanted to turn to her and say, "I can't! That song is a lie! You have such a hard road ahead of you! Your mom is cray-cray, and I'm going to take you out of here and raise you myself so you have a shot at happiness in this awful world!" But instead I said, "Yep." She stood up on a chair and held hands with Kim and me, and we all sang, "When I'm stuck with a day that's gray and lonely, I just stick out my chin and grin and say, *OHHHHHHHHH!*"

In the end the sun didn't come out tomorrow on this relationship. Six months after Lana moved my disabled dad all the way to New Orleans, she decided she'd had enough of him and kicked him out. He ended up on the curb. Literally. She up and left him alone in his wheelchair and he wheeled his way to the side of the road. After that, he moved to a hospital on Long Island, and I haven't heard from Lana or May since.

And I wouldn't say the sun came out when I met Ben either. Not because things weren't awesome, but because I try not to talk in metaphors about my relationships anymore. After everything I've witnessed with my parents, I like to keep things super basic—no solar analogies or rose-colored filters of any kind. Just the Valencia one on Instagram, because I look super good in that one. But the night I first met Ben in person, there was no literal sun to speak of; it was raining. I'd just had acupuncture, so there was oil in my hair and there were deep red lines on my cheeks from being facedown on the table, but I put on jeans instead of sweatpants and walked downstairs to meet him outside. I got out into the rain, and Ben was standing there, no umbrella or hood, with a soggy paper bag with a bottle of wine in it. We smiled at each other and in that moment, everything felt right.

I didn't lie to Barbara, but my thoughts on love and marriage are always evolving. I'm sure in the past I've said marriage is stupid. Marriage makes someone sign a contract promising something they really can't deliver. I'm sure I will again say marriage is dumb. But I can also imagine why it could be lovely. There's something beautiful about truly being there for another person. In the movie *Moonlight Mile*, Susan Sarandon and Dustin Hoffman play a married couple who fight a lot but still really love each other. They talk about how they're there to "witness each other's lives." I love that description of commitment. I don't think my parents ever signed up for that. They didn't show me what a good marriage looks like or how to stick it out to the end. When you have a sick parent, you can't help but think of the end. Like literally, the final moments of life come to mind when I begin to love someone. I think, *Will this dude push my wheelchair?* And even scarier, *Would I be willing to push his?* These are not light thoughts, and they're not easy to sort out when you're in the early stages with a person you care about.

I don't know what will happen with Ben of course. Maybe we'll grow old together, or maybe we'll be apart before this book is on shelves next to Godiva chocolates and gift cards. I would like to think that good things can happen for me in relationships with men, but maybe I think too much about the wheelchairs. I might just be a product of my parents. But it still seems worthwhile to suspend my disbelief for as long as I can—to keep myself open to accepting love—and to give mine every day.

WHAT I WANT PEOPLE TO SAY AT MY FUNERAL

Amy is dead, and we can all sleep a little easier. She was honest and fair, and she demanded the same from all of us. But it was exhausting. Even though she made everything more fun and exciting, it's a relief in some ways that she's no longer with us. We all get lazy with our lives and stuck in what we think we deserve. We all accept too easily that life has to be hard and forget to make sure we have the most fun we can. Amy made sure we laughed and didn't take any shit. If she was your friend, she'd do anything for you. She'd defend you and die for you, even sometimes when you didn't want her to. She went above and beyond, at times even making things harder. She once wrote a Facebook post congratulating her friend on getting a role in the new Woody Allen movie even though her friend was not going to be in that movie. She did it because her friend was in pain from a recent breakup and Amy knew her friend's ex would read the post and be jealous. That is an inappropriate thing to do. That is one of the reasons we will be able to continue on without her.

Amy would give you the shirt off her back, even if you didn't ask for it, and never mention it again. She was generous. She was also pushy and would talk shit to anyone in her way. She was fun to drink and smoke pot with. She was fun to eat mushrooms with. She was not fun to watch television with because the whole time she'd say, "Wait, who is that? What did he just say?" She was not a good listener. She was so easily distracted that you had to say, "Amy, I need you to really listen," to get her attention, and even then there was only a 40 percent chance she'd hear you.

She made us feel better. She demanded that we feel better. It could be exhausting. But we will miss it. We will miss her. But she'll always be with us. But not really, because as I mentioned up top, she's dead. Does anyone know if they're validating parking? Oh, it's New York, and you guys don't do that here. Well aren't you so lucky. You guys are smarter for living here and not LA.

RIDER FOR THE FUNERAL OF AMY SCHUMER

First and foremost, no one should call this a "celebration of life" or a "memorial." It may only be referred to as THE FUNERAL OF AMY SCHUMER. No bells or whistles.

There is a zero-tolerance policy on flowers. No wreaths, bouquets, corsages, single carnations, greenery, or flora of any kind is allowed. Everyone should bring some sort of a pasta dish and pour it into the casket. Not a pasta salad. Don't be an asshole.

The actual body of AMY SCHUMER should be propped up on a chair in the northwest corner of the room, wearing aviator sunglasses and her trusted snow hat that reads, "No Coffee, No Workee," a motto in life that she will continue to stand by in the afterlife.

WARDROBE

All guests should be comfortably dressed. Think sweatpants, velour, and comfy socks. Absolutely no high-heeled shoes are permitted. No guest shall be permitted entry if they are wearing a waist trainer, unless they are AMBER ROSE. She can wear whatever the F she wants.

CATERING/HOSPITALITY

Please provide at least two (2) sandwiches per guest. Sandwiches must be from Defonte's in Greenpoint, Brooklyn, and should be either the prosciutto or the mozzarella.

The signature cocktail of the night should be a Moscow mule.

Amazing appetizers should be abundant. For example, those puff things where you're not sure if you are eating bread, cheese, cream, or all of the above. Do not be sparing with things that you dip in crème fraîche or anything truffle-based. Absolutely no French macarons are permitted, but the Jew kind are okay. None of these foodstuffs should require the use of utensils. Pigs in a blanket as far as the human eye can see. I repeat, pigs in a blanket as far as the human and pig eye can see.

Please provide:

- Twenty-two (22) cases of Rombauer chardonnay. Oaky as shit!!!!
- Fifteen (15) cases of Opus One cabernet, the kind John Cena introduced to the deceased.

FACILITIES

There shall be no bathroom attendants permitted in the bathrooms. Please make two (2) fun side rooms available, with one (1) room providing trivia and the other providing hair-braiding stations. HARPISTS should play background music, but only in the bathrooms, which should be small—such that the presence of the HARPISTS prevents everyone from washing their hands.

TALENT

The following people should speak at the funeral:

- Keith Robinson
- Rachel Feinstein (because she will trash Keith)
- Jimmy Norton
- Colin Quinn (because he will trash Norton)
- Vincent Caramele
- Cayce Dumont
- My niece
- Lena Dunham

- Mark Normand
- Allan Haldeman
- Kevin Kane to close it out

MUSIC REQUIREMENTS
During the ceremony, BRIDGET EVERETT will sing "That's All." Intro, outro, and other interstitial music to be provided by a great bluegrass band—STEVE MARTIN AND THE STEEP CANYON RANGERS if they're up for it.

SECURITY
The following people (who never did anything to the deceased, but she just doesn't want them there) are not permitted at the funeral, nor may they attend any after-party-type event:
- Donald Trump
- Mario Lopez, unless he brings Elizabeth Berkley
- The boyfriends and girlfriends of AMY SCHUMER's friends are only permitted to attend if she liked them. In order to qualify for this status, they must be very kind and loving to said friends exactly all the time. If they are ever not nice to said friends, they must stay five (5) football fields away from the funeral
- Anyone who has ever gotten laid because they teach improv, with one exception being Neil Casey

MISCELLANEOUS REQUIREMENTS
Please post signs around the room(s) stating, "No small talk, no inside jokes." Please provide a large glass bowl at the entrance for those who wish to participate in an optional key party.

AFTER-PARTY AND BURIAL

After the funeral, guests will participate in an Edward Forty Hands party. All guests should have forties of Olde English duct-taped to their hands and are not to be untaped until said bottles are completely empty. This party should be DJ'd by Questlove and there needs to be ample room for everyone to dance. First song should be "Put It in Your Mouth."

Immediately following the Edward Forty Hands party, guests should proceed to the ocean in Long Beach, New York, for a Viking funeral. The body of AMY SCHUMER will be transported to the beach by horse-drawn carriage, because she was "worth it," and will be laid to rest in a tiny boat. The boat should be set on fire with a flaming arrow and gently pushed out to sea.

FORGIVING MY LOWER BACK TATTOO

When I was on the Comedy Central roast of Charlie Sheen, I told Mike Tyson that he had a slutty lower back tattoo on his face. I said, "Men don't know whether to be scared of it or finish on it." He heckled me for a minute, shouting high-pitched insults I couldn't understand, before I improvised a way to stop his interruptions, asking, "Is his interpreter here?" Now, that is just not a smart thing to say when you're twenty feet away from an ear-biting ex-con who was described as making a "comeback" after serving six years in prison for rape. But I did what any desperate comic would do. I committed to the moment, put myself in immediate danger, and went for it—which is exactly how I wound up with my own slutty tattoo, right where the good lord intended: on my lower back. Yes, I have one. What a hypocrite I am. I roasted Tyson while sporting my very own shitty, humiliating, not-even-on-straight, slightly-raised-because-the-guy-sucked-and-went-too-deep-and-it-got-infected tattoo of my own.

I'd wanted one for years. I saw so many tribal varieties while I played beach volleyball with my sister on Long Island, and I thought they looked badass. I wanted to get a tattoo that communicated "Don't fuck with me, because I don't give a shit about anything and I've been through it all," even though I was only eighteen and all I'd been through was the cereal aisle at Key Food. I was not a badass. I didn't feel strong or confident or particularly tribal. I thought I could literally stamp myself with those qualities, and if I could fake it long enough, they'd become real. And, unlike with an orgasm, I think that tactic works sometimes. The point is, my heart was in the right place seeking those things. Too bad my lower back got in the way.

The summer I was eighteen, Kim and I were on a road trip passing through Myrtle Beach. We decided to get some tattoos after careful consideration that consisted of seeing the shop; saying to each other, "Should we get tattoos?"; nodding; and going in. We browsed around, looking in different books and examining the designs on the wall, before we picked out the "art" we wanted on our bodies for the rest of our lives. I thought the guys who worked in the shop were just being cool allowing us to look around, because at fourteen, Kim was so clearly too young. I figured once they knew we were serious about getting all tatted up, they'd tell Kim she couldn't get one since she was a minor. We walked up to the counter and with confidence that can be described as wavering at best, I told the sun-damaged muscle-bound surfers that we'd like them to deface our young bodies with the two worthless designs we had so painstakingly chosen. "Cool," one of them said. "Let's go."

What the fuck? Was this a game of chicken to see who would break first? I tried to hide my confusion and appear bold and skeptical by asking: "How long will it take to get them put on?" The reddest-faced one pointed at me and said, "Yours will take ten because it's bigger, but hers will take about seven." "Ten hours?!" I shouted.

"Minutes," red-faced-emoji man replied. Kim had picked out a little fairy that she wanted on her hip, but mine was a big tribal mother-fucker, the size of a small possum. Ten minutes seemed like a very short amount of time, but what did I know about tattooing? "And how much will they cost?" I asked, projecting a lot of authority, amping up my New York accent so they wouldn't overcharge us. He said mine would be twenty dollars and Kim's would be ten. WHAT?!!?

I was beyond confused. Kim and I looked at each other and had the same thought, but as the big sister, I spoke up. I proclaimed, "We're not gonna do anything with you guys. We'll pay the full price!" The whole shop stood still. It was like a record had scratched. I looked around and noticed we were by far the least attractive girls in there, and if they were going to try to get sexual favors it wouldn't be from the two busted-ass Long Island teenagers. Then the man whose tank top exposed his nipples said, "You know this is a *temporary* tattoo shop, right? Tattoos are illegal in South Carolina." At that moment, I became the one with the reddest face. We slowly backed out of there like cats. Kim and I didn't speak on the walk back to our bedbugged hotel. It was too embarrassing.

When we finally got our real tattoos one year later (when we were ready to make great permanent decisions), we actually went to our mother for permission. I told her we'd wanted them for a really long time and had selected exactly the right designs and placement. You'd think a year would have matured our aesthetic, but I was still set on a big tribal configuration and Kim still wanted that dumb fairy. Upon hearing this request our mother responded like any parent and told her teenage daughters, "No fucking way. You smell like pot! Go to your room, you're grounded, you no-good skanks!" Oh, wait, nope, not our mom. Our mom responded with, "Well, what are we doing just sitting here talking about it? Let's get in the car!" She drove us to the East Village, where we went into the back room of the shadiest shithouse and got our "ink," as the douchebags call it.

I went first. When I say it killed, no, it fucking KILLED. It was like being stung by a thousand bees every second, or dozens of tracker jackers for all you young adult–fiction fans. The guy doing it wasn't very skillful, so he went way too deep, which caused the tattoo to keloid and scar. *Hawt, Aim, tell us more!* Okay, he was also very drunk, so the tattoo came out crooked. The guy's name was Kurt and he looked like an overweight asthmatic Son of Anarchy. I was dying from the pain, but I wanted to be brave for Kim so that she wouldn't be scared. So while tears ran down my face I smiled, saying that it wasn't that bad. The whole time my mom was beaming at both of us, so happy to be a part of this wonderful event we'd live to regret immediately. Naturally, my tattoo got infected and hundreds of tiny bumps formed around it, and it healed horribly. This display of rash and inflammation is exactly what every sexy young lady wants float-ing just above her ass. To this day, it's still raised like a *Mad Max* war boy's head scar.

So now, fifteen years later, I'm thirty-five, and any time I'm in a bathing suit people immediately know in their hearts that I'm trash. Any time I take my clothes off for the first time in front of a man and he sees it, he also knows in his heart that I'm trash and that I make poor, poor decisions. And now that the paparazzi think it's interest-ing to take photos of me doing absolutely nothing noteworthy on a beach somewhere, the whole world has been treated to photos of my lower back tattoo hovering crookedly over my bikini bottoms. But I promise you from the bottom of my heart I don't care. I wear my mistakes like badges of honor, and I celebrate them. They make me human. Now that all of my work, my relationships, my tweets, my body parts, and my sandwiches are publicly analyzed, I'm proud that I labeled myself a flawed, normal human before anyone else did. I beat all the critics and Internet trolls to the punch. I've been called everything in the book, but I already branded myself a tramp, so the haters are going to have to come up with something fresh.

The summer before eighth grade, in my pre-tattoo days (or, as I call them, my PTDs), I landed the nickname "Pancakes." A large group of my friends and I—and the boys we liked—were walking around the neighborhood on a warm night with beer in our book bags, ready and willing to run from the cops when they found us, as they often did. On this particular night, we'd just enjoyed Dr Pepper shots and Irish car bombs at my friend Caroline's house. For those who grew up Amish, a Dr Pepper shot entails dropping a shot glass full of amaretto into a pint of beer just moments before chugging the whole thing. Somehow it tastes like Dr Pepper. Add Bacardi 151 and a lit match to make it a Flaming Dr Pepper shot. Also say good-bye to all your loved ones. The Irish car bomb is a shot of Bailey's dropped into a pint of Guinness—and is also highly, highly offensive to any Irish person who has lost a friend that way. Once a year I'm provoked to drink one of these terrible combination drinks with little to no convincing needed.

We walked up the block to an elementary school on Caroline's corner, sloppy and excited by the drinks and the freedom. While we were hanging on the playground, the ten guys somehow convinced the six girls to lift up their shirts and show them their boobs. They'd presented the very good argument of "Why not?" We had no counterargument for that, so we lined up and, on the count of three, lifted our shirts.

I wrapped my fourteen-year-old fingers around the bottom of my Gap tee and yanked it over my pimpled, plump face with abandon. I was nervous and excited, and probably buzzed. I peeked at the boys over the top of my sensibly priced T-shirt and realized they were all looking only at me. Not at Denise, who had the biggest boobs, or at Krystal, who had the greatest abs, or at Caroline, whom they were all fighting over at the time. I was in the solid-medium range, boobwise, so I was shocked by how much attention mine were getting. I can remember the boys' faces: they looked as if someone had just done a sick move in a basketball dunking contest, like "Ohhhh!!!!" They covered their mouths and high-fived one another. I then looked down the line and realized that all the other girls had just shown their bras. In a perfect metaphor for my life, I had revealed too much. I'd pulled up my entire bra too. I was the only skins player on the team. That was also the moment I learned the unforgettably fun lesson that I had larger-than-average nipples.

The nickname "Pancakes" (and also sometimes "Silver Dollars") stuck around long enough that its life span and evolution could have been slowly, carefully chronicled in a Ken Burns–length documentary. At least that's how it felt. But really it was just the remainder of the summer. I was HUMILIATED and didn't think I'd ever live it down. Of course, by now I've been around a lot of different women and watched a lot of porn, and I know that our body parts come in all shapes and sizes. (Men's too! Did you know their body parts *also* come in a wide variety of shapes and sizes, but strangely, the media almost never discusses it?) At the time, I was stunned to learn that my silver dollars were not the norm.

Anyway, that day on the playground turned out to be prophetic for me. I displayed everything to everyone and learned that there would be a price to pay for doing so. This was my very first experience of the stripped-down, cold, unprotected space where vulnerability meets either confidence or shame. It was my choice, and I had to learn (I'm still learning) how to choose to be proud of who I am rather than ashamed. Lucky for me, I'm a woman, so I've had the opportunity to practice this lesson over and over and over and over and over and over and over and over and over and over again. Ultimately, I just decided, fuck it, yeah, that's my body, so what? There was more power in that position than I realized at the time.

As women, most interactions from around age eight on teach us to keep things cool so no one is inspired to, God forbid, call us the U or F words: "ugly" or "fat." I'm not the first to point out how women are taught that our value comes from how we look, and that it takes a lifetime (or at least until menopause) for most women to undo this awful lie. As someone who is crazy impulsive and incapable of taking any shit from other people, I've been criticized from so many angles and laughed at for all the wrong reasons. But, as many comics have realized, there is a gift in being laughed at, or heckled, or even booed off the stage. When your fears come true, you realize they weren't as bad as you thought. As it turns out, the fear is more painful than the insult. I boxed for a few years, and when I started sparring, I was so afraid of being hit, of experiencing that physical pain. But I learned that trying to avoid the pain didn't protect me from it. Oddly enough, getting punched in the side of the head or taking a shot to the gut *did* protect me. I got hit and it hurt for a second, but then I realized I was okay, that I could take it. And then the pain passed. After having all my fears realized and being insulted to no end, I got stronger. Being scrutinized for the ten years since I was first on a reality show has made me feel invincible. There's nothing left. So what if someone says you're fat or you're ugly? SO WHAT? Most women I know are far less afraid of being physically hurt than they are of being called ugly or fat.

I have a tramp stamp and I'm on the cover of *Vogue*. The puffy blue-green tendrils of ink underneath my skin weave together in a meaningless formation, but I've found the meaning in it. I fully accept myself as the girl with the lower back tattoo. This is not to say that I don't have regrets. Fuck yes, I regret getting this ugly tattoo that I thought signified toughness when it really just symbolized how lost and powerless I was when I was an eighteen-year-old girl. But I forgive that girl. I pity that girl, and I love that girl.

Ironically, the tattoo represents the opposite for me today. It reminds me that it's important to let yourself be vulnerable, to lose control and make a mistake. It reminds me that, as Whitman would say, I contain multitudes and I always will. I'm a level-one introvert who headlined Madison Square Garden—and was the first woman comic to do so. I'm the "overnight success" who's worked her ass off every single waking moment for more than a decade. I used to shoplift the kind of clothing that people now request I wear to give them free publicity. I'm the SLUT or SKANK who's only had one one-night stand. I'm a "plus-size" 6 on a good day, and a medium-size 10 on an even better day. I've suffered the identical indignities of slinging rib eyes for a living and hustling laughs for cash. I'm a strong, grown-ass woman who's been physically, sexually, and emotionally abused by men and women I trusted and cared about. I've broken hearts and had mine broken, too.

Beautiful, ugly, funny, boring, smart or not, my vulnerability is my ultimate strength. There's nothing anyone can say about me that's more permanent, damaging, or hideous than the statement I have forever tattooed upon myself. I'm proud of this ability to laugh at myself—even if everyone can see my tears, just like they can see my dumb, senseless, wack, lame lower back tattoo.

ACKNOWLEDGMENTS

I would like to express my most sincere thanks to the following people:

Mayci Breaux and Jillian Johnson, you are always with me and will forever be at the top of every list I make for the rest of my life.

Everyone at Everytown, especially Jason Rzepka and Noelle Howey. Also, Chuck Schumer and all the other people in America who fight every day for more sensible gun laws.

Howard Stern, who opened up my world to these opportunities.

Estee and Noam at the Comedy Cellar.

All the comics who make me a better and worse person: Jim Norton, Dave Attell, Bobby Kelly, Keith Robinson, Colin Quinn, Jess Kirson, Kurt Metzger, Pete Dominick, and Judy Gold.

Opie and Anthony and Chris Mazzilli.

Mark Normand, love you, brother.

Chris Rock, you are just the best guy.

Judd Apatow, you changed my life. Thank you for seeing something in me.

Eddie Vedder, I want to thank you for being the kindest human being I have ever met; for being the reason my dad, sister, and I used to sing together in the car at the top of our lungs; for taking the time to call my dad—a person you'd never met who is stuck in a hospital and can no longer drive around with his girls—just to make him smile.

Carrie Byalick, how did we get here? Thank you.

Allan Haldeman, Josh Katz, Guy O, and Berkowitz, I can't believe it but I love you guys. Thank you.

Everyone at Comedy Central, especially Kent Alterman, Doug Herzog, and Michelle Gainless—but even more than them, Anne Harris and JoAnn Grigioni.

Everyone at Universal, especially Donna Langley, Ron Meyer, and Erik Baiers.

Everyone at Fox, especially Stacey Snider.

Alison Callahan, for editing this book and seeing a higher order in the chaos of content I created. Making sense of my life is a gift you didn't know you were giving me. Thank you also for laughing in all the right places and encouraging me when I needed it.

Everyone else at Simon & Schuster and Gallery Books, including Jennifer Bergstrom, who is the best and most beautiful cheerleader anyone could ever want for their book; Nina Cordes; Jennifer Robinson; Carolyn Reidy; and Louise Burke. You Gallery Gals are funny and creative, and were very supportive of my writing the book I wanted to write. Thank you.

To Elisa Shokoff, Jules Washington, and Chris McClain—the team who recorded the audio version of this book—thank you for allowing me to sob openly, and for providing tea and hugs when I needed it.

David Kuhn, who believed in me and this book from the very start.

Kate White, thank you for giving me my first writing job and supporting me through the years.

Mark Seliger.

Marcus Russell Price.

My parents.

My high school volleyball coach, Cheryl Scalice, who taught me so much about working hard and getting better.

Cydney, thank you for supporting me through my life for the last seventeen years. You are a great mother and friend.

Vickie Lee, I love you.

Kimmy Cupcakes, Dre Money, and Kyra for elevating me and listening to me all the time.

Leesa Evans, thank you for always making me look good, but more importantly thank you for always making me feel good.

Lena Dunham, thank you, my love. You get me through.

To my hoes Rachel Feinstein, Bridget Everett, Nikki Glaser, Jenny T., Angie Martinez, Sappy, Feiny, Ca, D., Kati, Kate, Jessi Klein, Jennifer Lawrence, Jessica Seinfeld, Amber Tamblyn, Natasha Lyonne, Chelsea Peretti, Natasha Leggero, America Ferrera, Vanessa Bayer, Kyle Dunnigan, and Dan Powell. Yes, Kyle and Dan, you are my hoes.

To the people who influenced me the most: Lucille Ball, Gilda Radner, Carol Burnett, Miss Piggy, Gloria Steinem, Whoopi Goldberg, Goldie Hawn, Shari Lewis, Ani DiFranco, Joan Rivers, and Janeane Garofolo.

To the people I admire, some of whom gave me chances early on, and all of whom inspired me to do better: Ellen DeGeneres, David Letterman, Jimmy Kimmel, Stephen Colbert, Jon Stewart, Jay Leno, Seth Meyers, Tina Fey, Julia Louis-Dreyfus, Jerry Seinfeld, Anne

Sexton, Sarah Silverman, Margaret Cho, Parker Posey, Wu-Tang Clan, Steve Martin, Chris Farley, and all the Muppets.

Kevin Kane, my life partner, you make me better in every way.

Vin, thank you for talking sense into all the crazies around you.

Cayce Dumont, thank you for making this book possible with all your hard work and for getting me through this. You made this happen and I love drinking with you and talking shit and watching bad TV. You are the smartest person I know and I love you. Also, thank you for giving birth to my favorite person.

Ida, we can't wait to see what you do.

Jasy, you are the coolest, greatest brother in the world and I can't believe I get to hang out with you.

Kimby, thank you for keeping me laughing and happy and alive. You are half of me.

And Jesus. JK.

ENDING GUN VIOLENCE ISN'T EASY, BUT A MOVEMENT HAS SPRUNG UP OVER THE LAST FEW YEARS THAT IS ACHIEVING REAL VICTORIES AND MAKING US SAFER. IF YOU WANT TO GET INVOLVED, THE THREE MOST IMPORTANT THINGS YOU CAN DO RIGHT NOW ARE:

1/ JOIN THE MOVEMENT. Millions of people are getting organized and demanding that our elected leaders do more to address the gun violence crisis that claims ninety-one American lives every day. The largest organization fighting for this change is Everytown for Gun Safety—which I work with. Most of the key gun safety battles play out at the state level, and if you want to get involved in your area, text JOIN to 64433. Everytown will keep you updated on what you can do now and in the future.

2/ BE HEARD. You may not realize it, but oftentimes the difference between a law passing or not is a few hundred phone calls. The average congressperson represents fewer than 750,000 people. The NRA is great at getting their supporters to reach out and help stop or pass gun legislation. But gun safety advocates need to be just as vocal. You can dial 1-888-885-4011 to be connected with your senator. Tell them you want them to vote for a criminal background check on every gun sale now!

3/ VOTE FOR GUN SAFETY. If our current elected leaders won't address this crisis, then we need to elect new leaders. It's generally wise to vote against the congresspeople who have taken the most money from the gun lobby and for those who have voted in favor of universal background checks. Senators who voted for universal background checks in the strongest background check bill to date (in 2013) can be found here: http://politics.nytimes.com/congress/votes/113/senate/1/97.

And finally, here is a list of people in Congress who have taken money from and been influenced by the gun lobby:

Kelly Ayotte	Ted Cruz
John Barrasso	Steve Daines
Dan Benishek	Sean Duffy
Sanford Bishop	Michael Enzi
Roy Blunt	Joni Ernst
John Boozman	Deb Fischer
Ken Buck	Jeff Flake
Richard Burr	Cory Gardner
Ken Calvert	Lindsey Graham
Shelley Moore Capito	Chuck Grassley
Bill Cassidy	Heidi Heitkamp
Thad Cochran	Dean Heller
Mike Coffman	Jody Hice
John Cornyn	John Hoeven
Tom Cotton	James M. Inhofe

Johnny Isakson

Ron Johnson

John Kline

James Lankford

Mike Lee

Mia Love

Thomas Massie

Kevin McCarthy

Mitch McConnell

Martha McSally

Alex X. Mooney

Jerry Moran

Markwayne Mullin

Rand Paul

Stevan Pearce

David Perdue

Rob Portman

James E. Risch

Pat Roberts

Mike Rounds

Edward Royce

Marco Rubio

Paul Ryan

Ben Sasse

Tim Scott

Richard Shelby

Michael Simpson

Daniel Sullivan

John Thune

Thom Tillis

Scott Tipton

David G. Valadao

David Vitter

Tim Walberg

Roger Wicker